JOHN WILLIS

SCREEN WORLD

1986

Volume 37

CROWN PUBLISHERS, INC.

NEW YORK

Lily Claudette Chauchoin
at 3

with Norman Foster (her first husband)
in "Young Man of Manhattan" (1930)

with Maurice Chevalier
in "The Big Pond" (1930)

with Henry Wilcoxon
in "Cleopatra" (1934)

"Sign of the Cross"
(1932)

with Clark Gable
in "It Happened One Night"
(1934)

with Fred MacMurray
in "The Gilded Lily"
(1935)

with Bonita Granville
in "Maid of Salem"
(1937)

with Charles Boyer
in "Tovarich" (1937)

with John Payne
in "Remember the D
(1941)

with James Stewart
in "It's a Wonderful World"
(1939)

with Shirley Temple
in "Since You Went Away"
(1944)

with Walter Pidgeon
in "The Secret Heart"
(1946)

1935   1941   1951   1961   1979

TO

CLAUDETTE COLBERT

whose versatile talents, and seemingly ageless beauty
for over 60 years, have made her one of the world's
most admired and beloved actresses.

with Orson Welles
in "Tomorrow Is Forever"
(1946)

with Don Ameche
in "Sleep, My Love"
(1948)

with Sessue Hayakawa
in "Three Came Home"
(1950)

3

DANNY GLOVER, WHOOPI GOLDBERG
in "THE COLOR PURPLE"
© Warner Bros.

CONTENTS

EDITOR: JOHN WILLIS

Assistant Editors: Stanley Reeves, Walter Willison

Staff: Joe Baltake, Marco Starr Boyajian, Mark Cohen, Mark Gladstone, Miles Kreuger, John Sala, Tiko Vargas, Van Williams
Designer: Peggy Goddard

Acknowledgments: This volume would not be possible without the cooperation of Ian Abrams, Gary Aldeman, Lisa Agay, Tom Allen, Jane Alsobrook, Audie Back, Dorothy Baker, Fred Baker, Joe Baltake, Amanda Barber, Nina Baron, Cindy Berkowitz, Mike Berman, Jim Bertges, Rose Blasi, Joseph Brenner, Susan Brockman, Donette Brown, Dian Burkett, Ken Burns, John Calhoun, Ben Cammack, Fabiano Canosa, Eileen Nad Castaldi, Philip Castanza, Helen Cavanaugh, Lloyd Cohen, Robert Conkling, Bill Connelly, Gary Croudus, Lynne Dahlgren, Alberta D'Angelo, Zelie Daniels, James Darbinian, Ira Deutchman, Donna Dickman, Michael Donnelly, Anne Dillon, Robert Dorfman, Dennis Dorph, Betty Einbinder, Catherine Ericson, Suzanne Fedak, Dore Freeman, Renee Furst, Ted Goldberg, Joseph Green, Lorita Green, Christina Haller, Lisa Halliday, Allison Hanau, Richard Hassanein, Amy Heller, Gary Hertz, Sam Irvin, Jefrey Jacobs, Michael Jeck, John Jordan, Andy Kaplan, Helen Kavanaugh, Ken Kenyon, Susan Kleiner, Allison Kossow, Don Krim, Jack Kurnes, Ann Lander, Maryanne Lataif, Wynn Lowenthal, Peter Lowry, Arlene Ludwig, Jeff Mackler, Howard Mahler, Craig Marks, Virginia McClure, Pricilla McDonald, Jeff McKay, John Miller, John Moss, Robert Newcombe, Bill O'Connell, Kevan Olesen, Janet Perlberg, Jim Poling, Gerald Rappoport, Jackie Rayanal, Ruth Robbins, Reid Rosefelt, Melisa Rosen, Richard Rosenberg, Kelly Ross, Ed Russell, Cindy Ryfle, Suzanne Salter, Nicole Satescu, Karen Schafer, Les Schecter, George Schrul, Barbara Schwei, Mike Scrimenti, Eve Segal, Ron Sherwin, Jacqueline Sigmund, Marcia Silen, John Skouras, Stephen Soba, Barbara Sperry, David Springle, Alicia Springer, John Springer, Laurence Steinfeld, Moira Stokes, Stuart Strutin, Ken Stutz, John Tilley, Maureen Tolsdorf, Bruce Trinz, Ron Wanless, Christopher Wood, Stuart Zakim, Michael Zuker

1. Sylvester Stallone

2. Eddie Murphy

3. Clint Eastwood

4. Michael J. Fox

5. Chevy Chase

6. Arnold Schwarzenegger

7. Chuck Norris

8. Harrison Ford

9. Michael Douglas

10. Meryl Streep

11. Robert Redford

12. Sally Field

13. Kathleen Turner

14. Dan Aykroyd

15. Bill Murray

16. Jack Nicholson

1985 TOP 25 BOX OFFICE STARS

(tabulated by Quigley Publications)

17. Jessica Lange

18. Goldie Hawn

19. Charles Bronson

20. Cher

1985 RELEASES

January 1, through December 31, 1985

21. Mel Gibson

22. Pee-Wee Herman

23. Burt Reynolds

24. Roger Moore

25. Sissy Spacek

Tom Cruise

Molly Ringwald

Robert De Niro

7

THE AMBASSADOR

(CANNON GROUP) Producers, Menahem Golan and Yoram Globus; Director, J. Lee Thompson; Written by Max Jack; Associate Producer, Isaac Kol; Editors, Mark Goldblatt, Thierry J. Couturier, Peter Lee-Thompson; Photography, Adam Greenberg; Music, Dov Seltzer; Production Manager, Avi Kleinberger; Assistant Directors, Gidi Amir, Tal Ron, Ronit Ravitz; Lighting, Avram Leibman; Sound, Eli Yarkoni; Art Director, Yoram Barzilai; Costumes, Tami Mor; Special Effects, Yoram Pollack; Color by TVC; Rated R; 97 minutes; January release

CAST

Hacker	Robert Mitchum
Alex	Ellen Burstyn
Stevenson	Rock Hudson
Hashimi	Fabio Testi
Eretz	Donald Pleasence
Rachel	Heli Goldenberg
Tova	Michal Bat-Adam
Abe	Ori Levy
Assad	Uri Gavriel
Ze'ev	Zachi Noy
Shimon	Joseph Shiloah
Stone	Shuulik Kraus
Asher	Yossi Virginsky
Lenny	Iftah Katzur
Gadi	Shai Shwartz
Rafi	Ran Vered
Reuven	Assi Abaiov
Abba	Avi Kleinberger
Cafe Owner	Haim Banai
Laboratory Manager	Peter Freistadt
Laboratory Technicians	Dani Noiman
	Rahel Steiner
Helen	Dana Ben-Yehuda
Dvora	Zehava Keilos
Marilyn	Ester Zebco
Hilton Doorman	Yoni Lucas
Doctor	Avi Pnini
CBS Correspondent	Yosef Bee
Journalist	Ross Shepher
Mike	Bob Stevens

and Harmati Talmon, Dan Toren, Haim Giraffi, Shimon Ben-Ari, Shmueli Ben-Ami, Yorman Zargari, Itzhak Neeman, David Yafet, Avi Korman, Gil Ben David, Ygal Even-Or, Shuli Cohen, Sasson Gabai, Albert Iluz, Moshe Ivgy, Shalom Yemini, Albert Amar, Moti Shirin

Right: Ellen Burstyn, Fabio Testi
Top: Robert Mitchum, Ellen Burstyn, Donald Pleasence
© *Cannon Films*

Rock Hudson

Rock Hudson, Robert Mitchum

MARIA'S LOVERS

(̶ANNON GROUP) Producers, Bosko Djorjevic, Lawrence Taylor-
̶ortorff; Director, Andrei Konchalovsky; Screenplay, Gerard Brach,
̶ndrei Konchalovsky, Paul Zindel, Marjorie David; Executive Produc-
̶, Menahem Golan, Yoram Globus; Photography, Juan Ruiz Anchia;
̶ore, Gary S. Remal; Editor, Humphrey Dixon; Costumes, Durinda
̶ood; Designer, Jeannine Oppewall; Choreography, Loyd William-
̶n; Production Manager-Assistant Director, Joseph Winogradoff;
̶sociate Producer, Rony Yacov; Special Effects, Bonnie Taylor;
̶GM Color; 103 minutes; Rated R; January release

CAST

̶aria Bosic	Nastassja Kinski
̶n Bibic	John Savage
̶n's Father	Robert Mitchum
̶arence Butts	Keith Carradine
̶. Wynic	Anita Morris
̶rvey	Bud Cort
̶sie	Karen Young
̶nie	Tracy Nelson
̶nk	John Goodman
̶e	Danton Stone
̶ Griselli	Vincent Spano
̶na	Lela Ivey
̶ra	Elena Koreneva
̶er	Anton Sipos
̶reman	Larry John Meyers
̶thy	Anna Levine
̶lvia	Tania Harvey
̶rtender	Bill Smitrovich
̶sie's Mother	Nardi Novak
̶ndelson, the Photographer	Eddie Steinfeld
̶da Jerk	Norman St. Pierre
̶est	Father Raphael Rozdilski
̶my Psychiatrist	Vladimir Bibic
̶rry	Gary Hileman
̶uck Driver	"Porky" Albert Kaiser
̶n Whose Car Was Hit	Clayton D. Hill
̶uisa	Ann Caulfield
̶bushka	Mary Hogan
̶ve, the Wonder Dog	Frankie

Right: Robert Mitchum, Nastassja Kinski
Top: Nastassja Kinski, John Savage
Below: Vincent Spano, Nastassja Kinski, John Savage
© *Cannon Films*

Robert Mitchum

Nastassja Kinski, Keith Carradine

THAT'S DANCING!

(MGM) Producer, David Niven, Jr. and Jack Haley, Jr.; Executi▪ Producer, Gene Kelly; Written and Directed by Jack Haley, Jr.; Ad▪ tional Photography, Andrew Laslo, Paul Lohmann; Editors, B▪ Friedgen, Michael J. Sheridan; Music, Henry Mancini; Associate P▪ ducer, Bud Friedgen; Costume Designer, Ron Talsky; Assistant Dir▪ tors, Ira Halberstadt, Richard Hinds, Joel Tuber; Production Associa▪ Jan Walchko; Music Supervision, Harry V. Lojewski; Sound Edite▪ Paul Hochman; In Metrocolor and Dolby Stereo; Rated G; 105 minut▪ January release

CAST

Special Appearances by .... Mikhail Baryshnik▪ Ray Bolger, Sammy Davis, Jr., Gene Kelly, Liza Minnelli

The Dancers .... Fred Astaire, Mikhail Baryshnik▪ Ray Bolger, James Cagney, Cyd Charisse, Dan Dailey, Jacques D'A▪ boise, Sammy Davis, Jr., Isadora Duncan, Dame Margot Fonteyn, B▪ Fosse, Carol Haney, Robert Helpmann, Michael Jackson, Mari▪ Jahan, Ruby Keeler, Gene Kelly, Paula Kelly, Michael Kidd, Char▪ Laskey, Bambi Lynn, Shirley MacLaine, Leonide Massine, Ann M▪ ler, James Mitchell, The Nicholas Brothers, Rudolf Nureyev, Don▪ O'Connor, Anna Pavlova, Eleanor Powell, Jane Powell, Tommy Ra▪ Debbie Reynolds, Chita Rivera, Bill "Bojangles" Robinson, Gin▪ Rogers, Moira Shearer, Shirley Temple, Tamara Toumanova, J▪ Travolta, Bobby Van, Vera-Ellen, Vera Zorina

The West Side Story Dancers (The Jets and Their Girls) Tucker Smi▪ Tony Mordente, David Winters, Eliot Feld, Bert Michaels, Da▪ Bean, Robert Banas, Scooter Teague, Harvey Hohnecker, Tom▪ Abbott, Susan Oakes, Gina Trikonis, Carole D'Andrea, Frances▪ Bellini, and The Busby Berkeley Dancers

Cameo Appearances by .... June Allyson, Ann-Margr▪ Lucille Ball, Jennifer Beals, Busby Berkeley, Eric Blore, Monte Bl▪ John Brascia, Lucille Bremer, Irene Cara, Leslie Caron, Betty Ca▪ Marge & Gower Champion, Joan Crawford, LeRoy Daniels, D▪ Day, Gloria De Haven, Norma Doggett, Buddy Ebsen, Taina E▪ Louie Fuller, Clark Gable, Judy Garland, Virginia Gibson, Be▪ Grable, Cary Grant, Jack Haley, June Haver, Judy Holliday, J▪ Iturbi, Van Johnson, Nancy Kilgas, King, King & King, Ruta L▪ Vivian Leigh, Peter Lorre, Susan Luckey, Ray MacDonald, De▪ Martin, Matt Mattox, Joan McCracken, Liza Minnelli, Ricardo M▪ talban, George Murphy, Gene Nelson, Julie Newmar, Marc Platt, D▪ Powell, Jeff Richards, Mickey Rooney, Rosario & Antonio, W▪ Shaw, Frank Sinatra, Red Skelton, James Stewart, Lyle Talbot, R▪ Tamblyn, Tarita, Lilyan Tashman, Robert Taylor, Lana Turner, Et▪ Waters, Bobby Watson, Annabella Whitford Moore, Esther Willia▪

Left: Paula Kelly, Shirley MacLaine, Chita Rivera in "Sweet Charity" Above: Donald O'Connor, Gene Kelly in "Singin' in the Rain" Top: Shirley Temple, Bill "Bojangles" Robinson in "The Littlest Rebel" Below: James Cagney in "Yankee Doodle Dandy" © MGM/UA

Judy Garland, Ray Bolger in "The Wizard of Oz"

Ginger Rogers, Fred Astaire in "Swing Time"

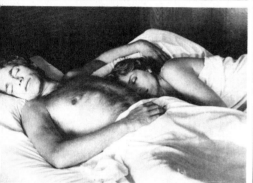

John Getz, Frances McDormand
Top: Frances McDormand, Dan Hedaya

BLOOD SIMPLE

(CIRCLE FILMS) Producer, Ethan Coen; Director, Joel Coen; Screenplay, Joel Coen & Ethan Coen; Executive Producer, Daniel F. Bauer; Associate Producer, Mark Silverman; Photography, Barry Sonnenfeld; Designer, Jane Musky; Music, Carter Burwell; Editor, Roderick Jaynes, Don Wiegmann; Color by DuArt; No rating; 97 minutes; January release.

CAST

Ray	John Getz
Abby	Frances McDormand
Julian Marty	Dan Hedaya
Private Detective	M. Emmet Walsh
Maurice	Samm-Art Williams
Debra	Deborah Neumann
Landlady	Racquel Gavia
Man from Lubbock	Van Brooks
Mr. Garcia	Senor Marco
Cracker	William Creamer
Strip Bar Extorter	Loren Bivens
Stripper	Shannon Sedwick
Girl on Overlook	Nancy Finger
Radio Evangelist	Rev. William Preston Robertson

Right Center: John Getz, Frances McDormand
© Circle Films

M. Emmet Walsh

THE FALCON AND THE SNOWMAN

(ORION) Producers, Gabriel Katzka, John Schlesinger; Director, John Schlesinger; Screenplay, Steven Zaillian; Based on the book by Robert Lindsey; Photography, Allen Daviau; Co-Producer, Edward Teets; Executive Producer, John Daly; Editor, Richard Marden; Costumes, Albert Wolsky; Designer, James D. Bissell; Music, Pat Metheny, Lyle Mays; Associate Producer, Michael Childers; Assistant Directors, Patrick Crowley, Hans Beimler; Sound, Rene Borisewitz; Dolby Stereo; Color by DeLuxe; Rated R; 131 minutes; January release

CAST

Christopher Boyce	Timothy Hutton
Daulton Lee	Sean Penn
Mr. Boyce	Pat Hingle
Mrs. Boyce	Joyce Van Patten
Boyce Children	Rob Reed, Rob Newell,
	Karen West, Arturo Comacho, Annie Kozuch
Dr. Lee	Richard Dysart
Mrs. Lee	Priscilla Pointer
David Lee	Chris Makepeace
Gene	Dorian Harewood
Laurie	Mady Kaplan
Larry Rogers	Macon McCalman
Tony Owens	Jerry Hardin
Eddie	Nicholas Pryor
Debra	Betty Lou Henson
NSA Inspector	Stanley Grover
Guard	Bob Arbogast
Alex	David Suchet
Mikhael	Boris Leskin
Karpov	George C. Grant
Guard	Anatoly Davidov
Lana	Lori Singer
Carole	Jennifer Runyon
Clay	Dan McDonald
Ike	Marvin McIntyre
Kenny Kahn	Dan Ingraffia
U.S. Embassy Official	Valerie Wildman

and Tom Nolan, James Hardie, Burke Byrnes, Vic Polizos, Drew Snyder, Michael Ironside, Bob Nelson, Arthur Taxier, Philip Corey, Martha Campos, Herbie Wallace, Steven Miller, Jeff Seyfried, Steve Duffy, Carlos Romano, Valerie Wildman, George Belanger, Leopoldo Frances, Abel Franco, Raul Martinez, Guillermo Rios, Jaime Garza, Gilbert Combs, Greg Brickman, Justin DeRosa, Fred Hice, Laura Harris

Right: Lori Singer, Timothy Hutton, Sean Penn
Top: Anatoly Davydov, Sean Penn, David Suchet,
Boris Leskin
© ORION

Lori Singer, Timothy Hutton

Sean Penn, Timothy Hutton

12

THE BREAKFAST CLUB

(UNIVERSAL) Producers, Ned Tanen, John Hughes; Director-Screenplay, John Hughes; Co-producer, Michelle Manning; Photography, Thomas Del Ruth; Design, John W. Corso; Editor, Dede Allen; Music, Keith Forsey; Executive Producers, Gil Friesen, Andrew Meyer; Costumes, Marilyn Vance; Production Managers, Richard Hashimoto, John C. Chulay; Assistant Directors, Robert P. Cohen, James R. Giovannetti, Jr.; Additional Music, Gary Chang; Choreographer, Dorain Grusman; Special Effects, Bill Schirmer; Songs by Various Artists; A & M Films/Channel Production; Technicolor; 97 minutes; Rated R; February release

CAST

Andrew Clark	Emilio Estevez
Richard Vernon	Paul Gleason
Brian Johnson	Anthony Michael Hall
Carl	John Kapelos
John Bender	Judd Nelson
Claire Standish	Molly Ringwald
Allison Reynolds	Ally Sheedy
Allison's Father	Perry Crawford
Brian's Sister	Mary Christian
Andy's Father	Ron Dean
Claire's Father	Tim Gamble
Allison's Mom	Fran Gargano
Brian's Mom	Mercedes Hall

Molly Ringwald, Anthony Michael Hall, Emilio Estevez
© *Universal*

CERTAIN FURY

W WORLD) Producer, Gilbert Adler; Director, Stephen Gyl-aal; Photography, Kees Van Oostrum; Editor, Todd Ramsey; Exec-e Producer, Lawrence Vanger; Music, Bill Payne, Russ Kunkel, rge Massenburg; A Prize Films Production presented by Entertain-t Events, Inc., Tambarle; Production Manager, Fran Rosati; Assis-Directors, Marin Walters, Bill Mizel, Jonathan Vanger; Costumes, da Kemp; Special Effects, Thomas Fisher, Bill Purcell, Dean kwood; Color; 89 minutes; Rated R; February release

CAST

let	Tatum O'Neal
y	Irene Cara
er	Nicholas Campbell
pier	George Murdock
Freeman	Moses Gunn
ey	Peter Fonda
rman	Rodney Gage
er	Jonathon Pallone
tdog	David Longworth
tal	Dawnlea Tait
a Gibbs	Alana Shields
la	Sharon Schaffer
ius	Gene Hartline
er	Peter Anderson
on Guard	Catherine Mead
ic Defender	Dean Regan
e	Ted Stidder
k	Shirley Barclay
ff	Joe Golland
don	Bill Murdock
d	Stuart Kent
tri	Frank Turner
e	Paul Batten

Cam Lane, Paddy White, Stephen E. Miller, Bruce McLeod, ny Kusian, Gil Adler, T. J. Jimmy McLean, Angie Tavahan, y Kalinski, Bill Buck, Gary Chalf, Daryl Hayes, Tom McBeath, Scott, Frank Serio, Howard Storey, William Taylor, Stephen ne, Dale Wilson, Debby Lynn Ross, Sharon Schaffer, Jacob , Bruce Barbour, Bill Ferguson, Alex Green, Gene Hartline, ge Josef, Ken Kersinger, J. J. Makaro, Tony Morelli, Bill Stewart, ii Janzen, Sandra Hall

Right Top: Irene Cara, Tatum O'Neal
Below: Tatum O'Neal, Nicholas Campbell
© *New World*

Tatum O'Neal, Peter Fonda

MARTIN'S DAY

(MGM/UA) Producers, Richard Dalton, Roy Krost; Director, Alan Gibson; Screenplay, Allan Scott, Chris Bryant; Photography, Frank Watts; Editor, David de Wilde; Music, Wilfred Josephs; Designer, Trevor Williams; Costumes, Lynne MacKay; Sound, David Lee; Production Manager, Marilyn Stonehouse; Assistant Directors, Bill Corcoran, Donald Brough; Special Effects, Neil Trifunovich; A World Film Service Production; Presented by United Artists; In color; 98 minutes; Rated PG; February release

CAST

Martin Steckert	Richard Harris
Dr. Mennen	Lindsay Wagner
Lt. Lardner	James Coburn
Martin	Justin Henry
Karen	Karen Black
Brewer	John Ireland
Hitchhiker	Saul Rubinek
Youngman	Dwayne McLean
Garby	Frank Adamson
Gas Station Attendant	Hugh Webster
Train Driver	J. W. Carrol
Train Engineer	Bob Windsor
Berglas	Jeff Braunstein
Newscaster	Dini Petty
Young Steckert	Martin Buckert
Malvern Cop	Bob Aarrons
Truck Driver	Bob Collins
Teenage Girl	Roberta Weiss
Prison Van Guard	Robin McCullogh
Donovan	Wesley Murphy
Mike	Ralph Small
Marksman	Richard Blackburn
Senior Policeman	Richard Donat
Waiter	Eric Fink
Malvern Wife	Pat Hamilton
Cops	Philip Akin, Michael Millar
Prison Guards	George Buza
Radio Operator	Cathy McClenahan
Jim	Simon Reynolds
Karen's Daughter	Jaclyn Stevens
Hydro Repairman	Eugene Clark
Driver	David Rigby

Richard Harris, Justin Henry
Top: Lindsay Wagner, James Coburn
© *MGM/UA Entertainment*

14

HEAVEN HELP US

(TRI-STAR) formerly "Catholic Boys"; Producers, Dan Wigutow,
...k Carliner; Director, Michael Dinner; Screenplay, Charles Purpura;
...tography, Miroslav Ondricek; Designer, Michael Molly; Editor,
...hen A. Rotter; Music, James Horner; Associate Producer-
...duction Manager, Kenneth Utt; Assistant Directors, Peter Giuliano,
...orah L. Marrs; Costumes, Joseph G. Aulisi; Costumers, Alfred C.
...ne, Beverly Cycon; Songs by various artists; HBO Pictures/Silver
...en Partners; Color; 104 minutes; Rated R; February release

CAST

...ther Thadeus	Donald Sutherland
...ther Timothy	John Heard
...hael Dunn	Andrew McCarthy
...ni	Mary Stuart Masterson
...ney	Kevin Sillon
...sar	Malcolm Danare
...	Jennie Dundas
...ndma	Kate Reid
...er Abruzzi	Wallace Shawn
...ther Constance	Jay Patterson

...George Anders, Dana Barron, John Bentley, Imogene Bliss, Philip
...co, Donahl Breitman, Nolan Carley, Al Cerullo, Jr., Calvert Defor-
...Patrick Dempsey, Christopher Durang, William Eustace, Henry
...ren, Janice Fuller, Pamela Galvin, Stephen Geoffreys, Richard
...ilton, Jody Jensen, Mary Koch, Paul Marchand, Kachina Myers,
...Polizos, Douglas Seale, Yeardley Smith, Sherry Steiner, Jimmy
...Weeks, Mel Winkler, Ed Zang

**Right: Patrick Dempsey, Kevin Dillon, Andrew McCarthy,
Malcolm Danare, Stephen Geoffreys**
© *Tri Star*

**Kevin Dillon, Dana Barron, Yeardley Smith,
Malcolm Danare
Above: (L.) Donald Sutherland, (R.) John Heard**

**Jennie Dundas, Andrew McCarthy
Above: Mary Stuart Masterson, Stephen Geoffreys,
Patrick Dempsey** 15

Kurt Russell, Mariel Hemingway
© Orion

THE MEAN SEASON

(ORION) Producers, David Foster, Lawrence Turman; Director, Phillip Borsos; Screenplay, Leon Piedmont; Based on the novel "In The Heat of the Summer" by John Katzenback; Photography, Frank Ti; Editor, Duwayne Dunham; Music, Lalo Schifrin; Color; 106 minutes; Rated R; February release

CAST

Malcolm Anderson	Kurt Russell
Christine Connelly	Mariel Hemingway
Alan Delous	Richard Jordan
Bill Nolan	Richard Masur
Andy Porter	Joe Pantoliano
Phil Wilson	Richard Bradford
Ray Martinez	Andy Garcia
Kathy Vasquez	Rose Portillo
Albert O'Shaughnessy	William Smith
John Palmer	As himself

Top: Andy Garcia, Richard Bradford, Kurt Russell
Below: Kurt Russell, Mariel Hemingway
Top Left: Richard Bradford, Kurt Russell
Below: Richard Jordan

TUFF TURF

(NEW WORLD) Producer, Donald P. Borchers; Director, Fritz [Ki]rsch; Screenplay, Jette Rinck; Story, Greg Collins O'Neill, Murray [Mi]chaels; Photography, Willy Kurant; Designer, Craig Stearns; Music, [Jon]athan Elias; Co-Producer, Pat Kehoe; Associate Producer, Bob [Ma]nning; Editor, Marc Grossman; Assistant Directors, James R. Mur[phy], Jesse Wayne, Stuart Hagen; Choreographer, Bob Banas; Cos[tum]es, Kathie Clark; Special Effects, Reel Efx. Inc., John Hartigan; [Son]gs by various artists; CFI Color; 112 minutes; Rated R; February [rel]ease

CAST

[Mo]rgan Hiller	James Spader
[Fra]nkie Croyden	Kim Richards
[Nic]k Hauser	Paul Mones
[Stu]art Hiller	Matt Clark
[Pag]e Hiller	Claudette Nevins
[Jim]my Parker	Robert Downey
[Ro]nnie	Olivia Barash
[Spi]ckey	Panchito Gomez
[Ed]die	Michael Wyle
[Fe]ather	Catya Sasson
[Ma]n at Bus Stop	Frank McCarthy
[Sec]urity Guard	Art Evans
[Mr.] Russell	Herb Mitchell
[Sec]retary	Ceil Cabot
[Ho]ward	Donald Fullilove
[His]tory Teacher	Vivian Brown
[Bri]an Hiller	Bill Beyers
[Re]ynolds	Jered Barclay
[Mr.] Croyden	Lou Fant
[Ro]nnie Parker	Gene Pietragallo
[Nu]rse	Donna Fuller
[Du]ffy	Evonne Kezios
[Be]tsy	Cheryl Ann Clark
[Bre]n	Matt Gavin
[Bo]y	Chad McCann
[Ban]d Leader	Dale Gonyea

[and] William J. Bergman, John Berry, Jr., Rick Braun, Mark Campbell, [Ja]mes R. Coile, Peter Freiberger, Andrew Kastner, Jack Mack, John [Man]uolo, Greg Smith, Randy Dreyfuss, John Ewen, Tom McShane, [Ru]s Moczulski, Ray Zimmerman, Jim Carrol, Eric Kiertzner, Mike [Sim]a, Tom Sims, Fiona Morris, Cecilie A. Stuart, Robert Alvarez, Edye [Ri]ca, Gerie Berling, Kerry Brennan, Sheri Cecil, Gary Christopher, [Pa]t Cranston, Marco De La Cruz, Amy Greenberg, Tamara Hensick, [Ke]n Highbie, Roger Kachel, Randy Lang, Laura McCoy, Cathy Mil-[ler], Lysa Nalin, Jeanne O'Connell, Kelly O'Fallon, Fred Quihuis, [Da]vid Rogers, Anita Russell, William Walentowski, Ric Watson, [Mi]chelle Whitney-Morrison, April Underwood, Tony Young

Right: James Spader, Robert Downey
Top Right: James Spader, Kim Richards
© *New World*

Kim Richards

James Spader, Kim Richards

TURK 182!

(20th CENTURY-FOX) Producers, Ted Field, Rene Dupont; Director, Bob Clark; Screenplay, James Gregory Kingston, Denis Hamil, John Hamill; Story, James Gregory Kingston, Richard C. Sarafian, Anna Rush Lehmann; Photography, Reginald H. Morris; Designe, Harry Pottle; Editor, Stan Cole; Music, Paul Zaza; Costumes, Lin, Wayne; Associate Producer, Gary Goch; Executive Producers, Pe, Samuelson, Robert Cort; Production Manager, Tony Ray; Assista, Directors, Ken Goch, Henry Bronchtein; Sound, James Sabat; Spec, Effects, Connie Brink; Video Effects, Tom Hanlon; DeLuxe Colo, Panavision/Widescreen; Dolby Stereo; 98 minutes; Rated R; Februa, release

CAST

Jimmy Lynch	Timothy Hutt
Terry Lynch	Robert Uri
Danny Boudreau	Kim Cattr
Mayor Tyler	Robert Cu
Detective Kowalski	Darren McGav
Jockamo	Steven Kea
Himself	Paul Sorvi
Detective Ryan	Peter Boy
Hanley	James S. Tolk
Hooley	Thomas Qui
Dr. Salco	Norman Park
Power House Chief	Dick O'Ne
Man in wheelchair	Maury Chayk
Patient in ward	Vasili Bogazian
TV Interviewer	Richard Zol
TV Producer	David Wo
Himself	Roger Grims
Himself	Bill Beu
Herself	Sara Lee Kessl
Himself	Tom Du
Herself	Donna Hano
Herself	Roseanne Scamarde
Governor Marconi	Lou Criscue
Reporter	Tucker Smallwo
Sergeant	Joseph Tot
Mayor's Secretary	Adrienne Hampt
Security Guard	J. R. Ho
Hard Hat	E. Brian De

and Jimmy Ortiz, Niccole Bruno, Al Mancini, Natalie Gentry, Ste, Stahl, Robert Trebor, Kaitlin Hopkins, Stephen Nemeth, Daniel G, man, Mike Hagerty, Robert E. Weil, Bob O'Connell, Leonard Term, Francine Joyce, Bob Moresco, Jim Manley, Jeanette Larson, Jose, Jamrog, Harold Baines, Damon Evans, Anthony Errante, Rob, Walsh, Jack McGee, Michael LaGuardia, John A. Murray, Lee Stee, Dick Martinsen, Barry Kivel, Robert Hodge

Left: Timothy Hutton
Top: Robert Urich, Timothy Hutton
© 20th Century Fox

Peter Boyle, Robert Culp

Darren McGavin, Robert Urich, Kim Cattrall

WITNESS

(PARAMOUNT) Producer, Edward S. Feldman; Director, Peter Weir; Screenplay, Earl W. Wallace, William Kelley; Story, William Kelley, Pamela Wallace, Earl W. Wallace; Co-Producer, David Bombyx; Photography, John Seale, A.C.S.; Designer, Stan Jolley; Editor, Thom Noble; Music, Maurice Jarre; Associate Producer, Wendy Weir; Production Manager, Ted Swanson; Assistant Directors, David McGiffert, Pamela Eilerson; Costumes, Shari Feldman, Dallas D. Dornan; Sound, Barry D. Thomas; Costumes, Paula Cain, Michael W. Hoffman; Special Effects, John R. Elliott; Songs by various artists; Technicolor; Dolby Stereo; 112 minutes; Rated R; February release

CAST

John Book	Harrison Ford
Rachel	Kelly McGillis
Schaeffer	Josef Sommer
Samuel	Lukas Haas
Eli Lapp	Jan Rubes
Daniel Hochleitner	Alexander Godunov
McFee	Danny Glover
Carter	Brent Jennings
Elaine	Patti LuPone
Fergie	Angus MacInnes
Stoltzfus	Frederick Rolf
Moses Hochleitner	Viggo Mortensen
Bishop Tchantz	John Garson
Mrs. Yoder	Beverly May
Sheriff	Ed Crowley
Zenovich	Timothy Carhart
Tourist Lady	Sylvia Kauders
Mrs. Schaeffer	Marian Swan
Schaeffer's Daughter	Maria Bradley
Angel Food	Rozwill Young

and Paul S. Nuss, Emily Mary Haas, Fred Steinharter, John D. King, Paul Goss, Annemarie Vallerio, Bruce E. Camburn (Amish), William Francis (Town Man), Tom W. Kennedy (Ticket Seller), Ardyth Kaiser, Thomas Quinn (Couple in Garage), Eugene Dooley, Victoria Scott D'Angelo, Richard Chaves, Tim Moyer, Nino Del Buono, James Clark, Joseph Kelly, Norman Carter, Craig Clement (Detectives), Robert Earl Jones (Custodian), Michael Levering, Cara Giallanza, Anthony Dean Rubes (Hoodlums), Bernie Styles (Counterman), Blossom Terry (Mother in station), Jennifer Mancuso (Little Girl), Gary Epper, Bob Minor, Anderson Martin (Stunts)

1985 Academy Awards for Best Original Screenplay, Best Film Editing

Left: Harrison Ford, Lukas Haas
Top: Lukas Haas, Kelly McGillis, Brent Jennings, Harrison Ford
Below: Michael Levering, Alexander Godunov
© *Paramount*

Kelly McGillis, Harrison Ford

Kelly McGillis, Lukas Haas, Harrison Ford

19

ALAMO BAY

(TRI-STAR) Producers, Louis Malle, Vincent Malle; Director, Louis Malle; Screenplay, Alice Arlen; Designer, Trevor Williams; Photography, Curtis Clark, Editor, James Bruce; Executive Producer, Ross Milloy; Associate Producer, Ken Golden; Music, Ry Cooder; Assistant Directors, Fred Berner, Mark McGann; Costumes, Deirdre Williams; Sound, Danny Michael; Special Effects, Gene Griggs; Metrocolor; 98 minutes; Rated R; March release

CAST

Glory	Amy Madigan
Shang	Ed Harris
Dinh	Ho Nguyen
Wally	Donald Moffat
Ben	Truyen V. Tran
Skinner	Rudy Young
Honey	Cynthia Carle
Luis	Martino Lasalle
Mac	William Frankfather
Ab Crankshaw	Lucky Mosley
Sheriff	Bill Thurman
Wendell	Michael Ballard
Leon	Gary Basaraba
Buddy	Jerry Biggs
Brandon	Mark Hanks
Father Ky	Khoa Van Le
Leroy	Tony Frank
Diane	Caroline Williams
Pete	Max Evers
Reverend Disney	Buddy Killen
Mrs. Ranney	Doris Hargrave
Tex	Harvey Lewis
Cal	Ed Opstad
Quick Finance	Christopher Blum
Woman Shopper	Xuan Thi Le
Bao	Lan Ti Do
Mai	Le Nguyen
Ho	Tuan Tran
Marge	Carolyn Farnsworth
Rita Venable	Jeannette Hudson Gray
Tim Hurt	David Ivanowski
Kandy	Mary Carroll Kinnett

and Barbara Opstad, Norman Spells, Ken West, Ray Benson Seiffert, Johnny Gimble, Tony Anastasio, Richard Hormachea, Wally Murphy, Reese Wynans, Donna Callaway Nugent, Laura Casterline, Reathel Bean, Jay Patterson, Sally Sockwell, Jimmy Ray Weeks, Stan Wilson

**Right: Amy Madigan, Ed Harris
Top: Ed Harris, Amy Madigan**
© *Tri Star*

Ed Harris

Amy Madigan, Ho Nguyen

ALWAYS

(SAMUEL GOLDWYN) Producer, Jagtown Films; Director-
Screenplay, Henry Jaglom; Photography, Hanania Baer; Lighting, Jim
Rosenthal; Sound, Ike Magal; Associate Producer, Judith Wolinsky;
Assistant Editor, Francesca Riviere; from International Rainbow Pic-
tures; Color; 105 minutes; Rated R; March release

CAST

David	Henry Jaglom
Judy	Patrice Townsend
Notary	Amnon Meskin
Judy's Father	Bud Townsend
Lucy	Joanna Frank
Eddie	Alan Rachins
Peggy	Melissa Leo
Maxwell	Jonathan Kaufer
David's Neighbor	Bob Rafelson
David's Brother	Michael Emil

and Richard Michael Kaye, Martina Finch (Young Couple at party),
Peter Rafelson, Thatcher Keats (Young Men at party) Andre Gregory
(party Philosopher), Sheila Ochs, Arlene Lorre

**Right, Below Right, and Below: Patrice Townsend,
Henry Jaglom**
© *Samuel Goldwyn Co.*

Ruben Blades
© *Crossover Films*

CROSSOVER DREAMS

(CROSSOVER FILMS) Producer, Manuel Arce; Director, Leon
Ichaso; Screenplay, Leon Ichaso, Manuel Arce, Ruben Blades; Story,
Manuel Arce, Leon Ichaso, Kenny Vance; Photography, Claudio Chea;
Editor, Gary Karr; Music, Mauricio Smith, Ruben Blades, Conjunto
Libre, Andy Gonzales, Jerry Gonzales, Yomo Toro, Virgilio Marti,
Marco Rizo, The Ballistic Kisses; Designers, Octavio Soler, Richard
Karnback; Associate Producers, Carl Haber, Octavio Soler, Claudio
Chea; Executive Producer, Susan Rollins; In association with Max
Mambru Films; Color; 86 minutes; Not rated; March release

CAST

Rudy Veloz	Ruben Blades
Orlando	Shawn Elliot
Lou Rose	Tom Signorelli
Liz Garcia	Elizabeth Pena
Ray Soto	Frank Robles
Neil Silver	Joel Diamond

KING DAVID

(PARAMOUNT) Producer, Martin Elfand; Director, Bruce Beresfor; Screenplay, Andrew Birkin, James Costigan; Story, James Costiga; Based on "The Books of Samuel I and II," "Chronicles I," and "Th Psalms of David"; Photography, Donald McAlpine; Music, Carl Davi Designer, Ken Adam; Costumes, John Mollo; Editor, William A; derson; Sound, Brian Marshall; Special Effects, Kit West; Associa Producer, Charles Orme; Production Managers, Clive Challis, Luc Trentini; Assistant Directors, David Tomblin, Roy Button, Steve Har ing, Victor Tourjansky; In Color; Panavision Widescreen; Dolby St reo; 114 minutes; Rated PG-13; March release

CAST

David	Richard Ge
Young David	Ian Sea
Jesse	Arthur Whybro
Joab	Tim Woodwa
Eliab	Simon Dutto
Abinadab	Michael Muell
Shammah	Valentine Pell
Saul	Edward Woodwa
Ahinoab	Aliche Nar
Ishbosheth	Marc Drew
Malichishua	Ned Vukov
Jonathan	Jack Kla
Michal	Cherie Lung
Abner	John Cast
Doeg	Christopher Malcol
Zabad	Roberto Renr
Runner	Anton Alexand
Samuel	Denis Quille
Nathan	Niall Bugg
Ahimelech	Hurd Hatfie
Guardian	Lorenzo Pia
Agag	Valentino Venanti
Goliath	Luigi Montefic
Armor Bearer	John Halla
Achish	Tom Milia
Palastu	Massimo Sarchie
Abigail	Jenny Lipma
Ahinoam	Genevieve Allenbu
Maacah	Ishia Benniso
Amnon	James Coomb
Absalom	Jean-Marc Ba
Young Absalom	Shimon Avida
Tamar	Gina Bellma
Bathsheba	Alice Kri
Solomon	Jason Cart
Young Solomon	Nicky Van Der Wep
Ahitophel	David De Keys
Jehosaphat	John Gabri
Uriah	James List
Messenger	David Geor

Left: Richard Gere, Edward Woodward, Cherie Lunghi, Jack Klaff, Aliche Nana Top: Jack Klaff, Ian Sears Below: Richard Gere, Alice Krige © *Paramount*

James Coombes, Gina Bellman

David De Keyser, Richard Gere, Jean-Marc Barr

DESPERATELY SEEKING SUSAN

(ORION) Producers, Sarah Pillsbury, Midge Sanford; Director, Susan Seidelman; Screenplay, Leora Barish; Photography, Edward Lachman; Designer-Costumes, Santo Loquasto; Editor, Andrew Mondshein; Music, Thomas Newman; Executive Producer-Production Manager, Michael Peyser; Assistant Directors, Joel Tuber, David Dreyfuss; Songs by various artists; Color; 104 minutes; Rated PG-13

CAST

Roberta	Rosanna Arquette
Susan	Madonna
...ez	Aidan Quinn
...ary	Mark Blum
...m	Robert Joy
...eslie	Laurie Metcalf
...rystal	Anna Levine
...olan	Will Patton
...n	Peter Maloney
...arry	Steven Wright
...ay	John Turturro
...ictoria	Anne Carlisle

and Jose Santana, Giancarlo Esposito, Richard Hell, Rockets Red Glare, Steve Bosh, Daisy Bradford, Annie Golden, Richard Edson, Ann Magnusson, John Lurie, Mary Joy, Rosemary Hochschild, Iris Bacon, Victor Argo, Shirley Stoler, J. B. Waters, Arto Lindsay, Henry Adler, Marty Gold, Alvy West, Michael R. Chin, John Patrick Hurley, Timothy Carhart, Curt Dempster, Shirley Kaplan, Lazaro Perez, John Hoyt, Gary Ray, Gary Binkow, Michael Bramon, Joyce Griffen, Paul Austin, Richard S. Lowy, Donna Ritchie, Kim Chan, Michael Badalucco, Elie J. Boubli, Harsh Nayyar, Keita Whitten, Adele Bertei, Peter Castellotti, Wende Dasteel, Steve Eidel, Michael Kaufman, Ilene Kristen, Carol Leifer, Richard Portnow

Top: Madonna Right: Rosanna Arquette
Right Center: Rosanna Arquette, Aidan Quinn
© Orion

Madonna, Rosanna Arquette

MASK

(UNIVERSAL) Producer, Martin Starger; Director, Peter Bogdanovich; Screenplay, Anna Hamilton Phelan; Based on the true story of Rocky Dennis; Photography, Laszlo Kovacs; Designer, Norman Newberry; Editors, Eva Gardos, Barbara Ford; Co-producer, Howard Alston; Associate Producers, George Morfogen, Peggy Robertson; Production Manager, William Watkins; Assistant Directors, Katy Emde, Lisa Marmon, Robert Q. Engelman; Rocky Makeup, Michael Westmore, Zoltan; Costumes, Tony Scarano, Robert Chase, Marla Denise Schlom, Sandra Culotta, April Ferry; Sound, Keity Wester, Crew Chamberlain; Special Effects, Dan Lester; Songs by various artists; Technicolor; 120 minutes; Rated PG-13; March release

CAST

Rusty Dennis	Cher
Gar	Sam Elliott
Rocky Dennis	Eric Stoltz
Evelyn	Estelle Getty
Abe	Richard Dysart
Diana	Laura Dern
Babe	Micole Mercurio
Red	Harry Carey Jr.
Dozer	Dennis Burkley
Ben	Lawrence Monoson
Mr. Simms	Ben Piazza
Lisa	Alexandra Powers
Eric	L. Craig King
Lorrie	Kelly Minter

and Joe Unger, Todd Allen, Howard Hirdler, Jeannie Dimter Barton, Steven James, Cathy Arden, Andrew Robinson, Ivan J. Rado, Anna Hamilton Phelan, Wayne Grace, Nick Cassavetes, Les Dudek, Jo-El Sonnier, Rebecca Sharkey, Paige Matthews, Patricia Pelham, Gale Ricketts, Stan Ross, Scott Willardsen, Marsha Warfield, Allison Roth, David Scott Milton, Creed Bratton, L. Charles Taylor, Rummel Mor, Barry Tubb, Norman Kaplan, Marilyn Hamilton, Anna Thea, Louis Waldon, Toni Sawyer, Lou Felder, Christopher Rydell, Beth McKinley, Jill Whitlow

Winner of 1985 Academy Award for Best Makeup

Right: Cher, Sam Elliott, Eric Stoltz
(Back to Camera) Top: Cher, Sam Elliott
© *Universal*

Soon-Teck Oh, Chuck Norris
© *Cannon Group*

MISSING IN ACTION 2
THE BEGINNING

(CANNON GROUP) Producers, Menahem Golan, Yoram Globu Director, Lance Hool; Screenplay, Arthur Silver, Larry Levinso Steve Bing; Photography, Jorge Stahl; Music, Brian May; Designe Michael Baugh; Editors, Mark Conte, Marcus Manton; Associate Pr ducer, Christopher Pearce; Production Manager, Conrad Hool; Ass tant Directors, Joe Ochoa, Terry Buchinski, Steven Kossover; Co tumes, Poppy Cannon; Special Effects, Dick Parker, Joseph Quinliva TVC Color; Panavision; 96 minutes; Rated R; March release

CAST

Colonel Braddock	Chuck Nor
Colonel Yin	Soon-Teck C
Nester	Steven Willia
Colonel Ho	Bennett Oh
Mazilli	Cosie Cos
Opelka	Joe Michael Ter
Franklin	John Wesl
Dou Chou	David Chu
Lao	Professor Toru Tana
Soldier	John Otr
Emerson	Christopher Ca
Guard	Joseph Hi
Kittle	Dean Ferrandi
Francois	Pierre Iss
Kelly	Mischa Hausserm

and Randon Lo, Michiyo Tanaka, Andrea Lowe, Nancy Martin

POLICE ACADEMY 2: THEIR FIRST ASSIGNMENT

(WARNER BROS.) Producer, Paul Maslansky; Director, Jerry Paris; screenplay, Barry Blaustein, David Sheffield; Based on characters created by Neal Israel, Pat Proft; Photography, James Crabe; Editor, Bob Wyman; Music, Robert Folk; Designer, Trevor Williams; Executive Producer, John Goldwyn; Co-Producer, Leonard Kroll; Production manager, Sascha Schneider; Assistant Directors, Don Heitzer, Roger Joseph Pugliese, Sandra M. Middleton, Jeff Stolow; Sound, Dale Johnston, David Kelson; Costumes, Bernie Pollack; Special Effects, Richard Ratliff; Songs by various artists; Technicolor; Panavision; 97 minutes; Rated PG-13; March release

CAST

Carey Mahoney	Steve Guttenberg
Hightower	Bubba Smith
Tackleberry	David Graf
Larvell Jones	Michael Winslow
Doug Fackler	Bruce Mahler
Laverne Hooks	Marion Ramsey
Kirkland	Colleen Camp
Pete Lassard	Howard Hesseman
Mauser	Art Metrano
Commandant Lassard	George Gaynes
Zed	Bob Goldthwait
Chloe	Julie Brown
Vinnie Schtulman	Peter Van Norden
Merchant	Tim Kazurinsky
Dooley	Ed Herlihy
Strunk	Sandy Ward
Proctor	Lance Kinsey
Jojo	Christopher Jackson
Jacko	Church Ortiz
Chief Hurst	George R. Robertson
Old Man Kirkland	Arthur Batanides
Mrs. Kirkland	Jackie Joseph
Ed Kirkland	Andrew Paris
Lamu	Monica Parker
Japanese Chef	Kenji Shintani
Mayor	Jennifer Darling
Mom	Lucy Lee Flippin
Kid	Jason Hervey
Nurse	Diana Bellamy
Man	Tim Haldeman
Bartender	Bert Williams
Jack	Pamela Matteson

and Julie Paris, Debra Dusay, Jim Boyce, Bufort L. McClerkins Jr., Conrad Hurtt, William Yamadera, Morris Beers

Michael Winslow, Lance Kinsey, Howard Hesseman, Peter Van Norden, Bubba Smith, Bruce Mahler, Steve Guttenberg, Marion Ramsey Top: Bubba Smith, Steve Guttenberg, Peter Van Norden Below: David Graf, Colleen Camp © *Warner Bros.*

THE PURPLE ROSE OF CAIRO

(ORION) Producer, Robert Greenhut; Director-Screenplay, Woody Allen; Photography, Gordon Willis; Designer, Stuart Wurtzel; Costumes, Jeffrey Kurland; Editor, Susan E. Morse; Music, Dick Hyman; Executive Producer, Charles H. Joffe; Associate Producers, Michael Peyser, Gail Sicilia; Production Manager, Michael Peyser; Assistant Directors, Thomas Reilly, James Chory; Songs by various artists; A Jack Rollins, Charles H. Joffe Production; Color and Black & White; 84 minutes; Rated PG; March release

CAST

Cecilia	Mia Farrow
Tom Baxter/Gil Shepherd	Jeff Daniels
Monk	Danny Aiello
Theatre Manager	Irving Metzman
Cecilia's Sister	Stephanie Farrow
Diner Boss	David Kieserman
Ticket Taker	Tom Degidon
Popcorn Seller	Mary Hedahl
Henry	Ed Herrmann
Jason	John Wood
Rita	Deborah Rush
Larry	Van Johnson
The Countess	Zoe Caldwell
Arturo	Eugene Anthony
Bandleader	Ebb Miller
Kitty Haynes	Karen Akers
Delilah	Annie Joe Edwards
Father Donnelly	Milo O'Shea
The Communist	Peter McRobbie
Olga	Camille Saviola
Usherette	Juliana Donald
Emma	Dianne Wiest
Raoul Hirsh	Alexander H. Cohen
Mr. Hirsh's Lawyer	John Rothman
Hollywood Executive	Raymond Serra
Press Agent	George J. Manos
Waiter	David Tice
Maitre D'	James Lynch
Variety Reporter	Sydney Blake
Gil's Agent	Michael Tucker
Drugstore Customer	Peter Von Berg
Music Store Owner	Loretta Tupper

and Elaine Grollman, Victoria Zussin, Mark Hammond, Wade Barnes, Joseph G. Graham, Don Quigley, Maurice Brenner (Diner Patrons), Paul Herman, Rick Petrucelli, Peter Castellotti (Penny Pitchers), Milton Seaman, Mimi Weddell (Ticket Buyers), Margaret Thompson, George Hamlin, Helen Hanft, Leo Postrel, Helen Miller, George Martin, Crystal Field (Movie Audience), Ken Champin, Robert Trebor (Reporters), Benjamin Rayson, Jean Shevlin, Albert S. Bennett, Martha Sherrill, Gretchen MacLane, Edwin Bordo (Movie Goers), Andrew Murphy (Policeman #1), Thomas Kubiak (Policeman #2), David Weber (Photo Double), Glenne Headley, Willie Tjan, Lela Ivey, Drinda La Lumia (Hookers)

Right: Zoe Caldwell, Van Johnson
Top: Mia Farrow, Jeff Daniels
© Orion

Milo O'Shea, Deborah Rush, John Wood, Edward Herrmann

Mia Farrow, Danny Aiello

QUEEN KELLY

(KINO INTERNATIONAL) Producer, Gloria Productions for United Artists; Director-Screenplay, Eric Von Stroheim; Photography, Gordon Pollock, Paul Ivano; Editor, Viola Lawrence; Designer, Harold Miles; Costumes, Max Ree; Music, Adolph Tandler; Dates of production: Nov. 1, 1928–Jan. 21, 1929; Unfinished Von Stroheim masterwork; Black and White; 96 minutes; Not Rated; March release

CAST

Kitty Kelly	Gloria Swanson
Queen Regina	Seena Owen
Prince Wolfram	Walter Byron
Prince's Adjutant	Wilhelm Von Brincken
Mother Superior	Madge Hunt
Valet	Wilson Benge
Lackey	Sidney Bracey
Maid	Lucille Van Lent
Maid	Ann Morgan
Jan Bloehm Vryheid	Tully Marshall
Kelly's Aunt	Florence Gibson
Kali	Mme. Sul Te Wan
Coughdrops	Ray Daggett

**Right, Below Right, and Below Left:
Gloria Swanson
© Kino International**

Gloria Swanson (L)

Gloria Swanson

27

RETURN OF THE JEDI

(20th CENTURY-FOX) Producer, Howard Kazanjian; Directo
Richard Marquand; Screenplay, Lawrence Kasdan, George Luca
Story-Executive Producer, George Lucas; Designer, Norman Re
nolds; Photography, Alan Hume; Editors, Sean Barton, Marcia Luca
Duwayne Dunham; Visual Effects, Richard Edlund, Dennis Mure
Ken Ralston; Costumes, Aggie Guerard Rodgers, Nilo Rodis-Jamer
Creatures, Phil Tippett, Stuart Freeborn; Sound, Ben Burtt; Musi
John Williams; Co-Producers, Robert Watts, Jim Bloom; Assista
Directors, David Tomblin, Roy Button, Michael Steele; Productio
Managers, Miki Herman, Patricia Carr; Special Effects, Roy Arboga
A Lucasfilm Ltd. Production; DeLuxe Color; Dolby Stereo; 1.
minutes; Rated PG; March release

CAST

Luke Skywalker	Mark Ham
Han Solo	Harrison Fo
Princess Leia	Carrie Fish
Lando Calrissian	Billy Dee Willian
See Threepio (C-3PO)	Anthony Danie
Chewbacca	Peter Mayhe
Anakin Skywalker	Sebastian Sha
Emperor	Ian McDiarm
Yoda	Frank C
Darth Vader	David Prow
Voice of Darth Vader	James Earl Jor
Ben (Obi-Wan) Kenobi	Alec Guinne
Artoo Detoo (R2-D2)	Kenny Bak
Moff Jerjerrod	Michael Penningt
Admiral Piett	Kenneth Coll
Bib Fortuna	Michael Car
Wedge	Denis Laws
Admiral Ackbar	Tim Ro
General Madine	Dermot Crowl
Mon Mothma	Caroline Blakist
Wicket	Warwick Da
Paploo	Kenny Bak
Boba Fett	Jeremy Bullo
Oola	Femi Tay
Sy Snootles	Michele Grus
Fat Dancer	Claire Davenp
Teebo	Jack Pur
Logray	Mike Edmor
Chief Chirpa	Jane Bus
Nicki	Nicki Rea
Ewok Warriors	Malcom Dixon, Mike Cott
Stardestroyer Controllers	Adam Bareham, Jonathan Oli
Stardestroyer Captains	Pip Miller, Tom Manni

and Toby Philpott, Mike Edmonds, David Barclay, Michael McC
mick, Deep Roy, Simon Williamson, Hugh Spirit, Swin Lee, Mich
Quinn, Richard Robinson

Left: Carrie Fisher, Harrison Ford
Top: Billy Dee Williams
Below: Carrie Fisher, Mark Hamill
© 20th Century-Fox

Harrison Ford, Mark Hamill, Peter Mayhew

Kenny Baker

Anthony Daniels,
Peter Mayhew,
Carrie Fisher

THE SLUGGER'S WIFE

(COLUMBIA) Producer, Ray Stark; Director, Hal Ashby; Screenplay, Neil Simon; Photography, Caleb Deschanel; Designer, Michael Riva; Editors, George Villasenor, Don Brochu; Music, Patrick Williams; Music Producers, Quincy Jones, Tom Bahler; Songs by various artists; Executive Producer, Margaret Booth; Production Manager, Jerry Baerwitz; Assistant Directors, Frank Bueno, Don Yorkshire; Costumes, Ann Roth; Metrocolor; Dolby Stereo; 114 minutes; Rated PG-13; March release

CAST

Darryl Palmer	Michael O'Keefe
Debby Palmer	Rebecca De Mornay
Burly De Vito	Martin Ritt
Moose Granger	Randy Quaid
Manny Alvarado	Cleavant Derricks
Aline Cooper	Lisa Langlois
Gary	Loudon Wainwright III
Marie De Vito	Georgann Johnson
Coach O'Brien	Danny Tucker
Tina Alvarado	Lynn Whitfield
Guard	Al Garrison
Nurse	Nicandra Hood
Sherry	Ginger Taylor
Peggy	Kay McClelland
Paloma	Julie Kemp
Chuck	Dennis Burkley
Lola	Alisha Das
Preacher	Dan Biggers
Iris Granger	Justine Thielemann
Mr. Davis	Marc Clement

and Tina Kincaid, Martha Harrison, Becky Pate, Richard Alan Reiner, Valerie Mitchell, Edwin H. Cipot, Stephen H. Stier, David R. Yood, Wallace G. Merck, Johnny B. Watson, Jr., Alex Hawkins, Mort Schwartz, John B. Sterling, George Stokes, Harmon L. Wages, John W. Bradley, Jerome Olds, Starshower, Erby Walker, Phillipe Fontanelli, Steve Daniels, Jr., Henry J. Rountree, George Jack Klarman, Collin Fagan, David M. Pallone, Kevin James Barnes, John Lawhorn, Douglas Garland Nave, Bill G. Fite, Al Hrobosky, Mark Fidrych, Pete Van Wieren, Ernie Johnson, Skip Caray, Nick Charles, Chico Renfroe, Anthony Peck, Corey B. McPherrin, Paul S. Ryden, Charles Darden, John Buren Solberg, Brad Nessler

Left: Michael O'Keefe, Randy Quaid, Cleavant Derricks
Top: Lisa Langlois
Below: Michael O'Keefe, Rebecca De Mornay
© *Columbia*

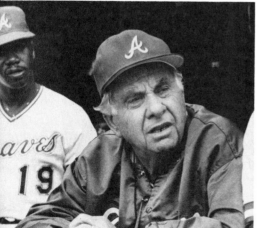

Cleavant Derricks, Martin Ritt

Loudon Wainwright III, Rebecca De Mornay

THE AVIATOR

(MGM/UA) Producers, Mace Neufeld, Thomas H. Brodex; Director, George Miller; Screenplay, Marc Norman; Based on book by Ernest Gann; Photography, David Connell; Designer, Brenton Swift; Editor, Duane Hartzell; Associate Producer, Dan Tana; Music, Dominic Frontiere; Production Manager, Nick Anderson; Assistant Directors, John Powditch, Zoran Budak, Mladen Cernjak; Special Effects, John Thomas, William Orr; Costumes, Patricia Smith; Metrocolor; Dolby Stereo; 96 minutes; Rated PG; April release

CAST

Edgar Anscombe	Christopher Reeve
Tillie Hansen	Rosanna Arquette
Moravia	Jack Warden
Bruno Hansen	Sam Wanamaker
Jerry Stiller	Scott Wilson
Evelyn Stiller	Tyne Daly
Rose Stiller	Marcia Strassman
Old Man	Will Hare
Student Pilot	Robert Peirce
George Hansen	Glenn Neufeld
Daniel Hansen	Franco Lasic
Probosky	Ron Travis
Carson	Jeff Harding
Counterman	Paul Reid Roman
Customer	Paul Lichtman
First Officer	Timothy Stack
Second Officer	Larry B. Williams

Right: Rosanna Arquette, Christopher Reeve
Below Right: Christopher Reeve
© MGM/UA

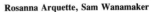

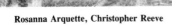

Rosanna Arquette, Christopher Reeve

Rosanna Arquette, Sam Wanamaker

ENORMOUS CHANGES AT THE LAST MINUTE

(FILM FORUM) Producer, Mirra Bank; Directors, Ellen Hovde, in association with Muffie Meyer ("Virginia's Story"), Mirra Bank, Ellen Hovde ("Faith's Story"), Mirra Bank ("Alexandra's Story"); Screenplay, John Sayles, Susan Rice; Based on the stories of Grace Paley; Photography, Tom McDonough; A production of ABC Video Enterprises, Inc., in association with Ordinary Lives, Inc.; Co-Producer, Larry Benes; ABC Executive, Liz Oliver; Distributed by TC Films International; Color; 115 minutes; Not Rated; April release.

CAST

"Virginia's Story"
Virginia .... Ellen Barkin
Larry .... David Strathairn
Ann .... Ron McLarty
Mrs. Raftery .... Sudie Bond

"Faith's Story"
Faith .... Lynn Milgrim
Ricardo .... Jeffrey DeMunn
.... Zvee Scooler
Ma .... Eda Reiss Merin
Mrs. Hegel-Shtein .... Fay Bernardi

"Alexandra's Story"
Alexandra .... Maria Tucci
Dennis .... Kevin Bacon
Doc .... John Wardwell
George .... Lou Criscuolo

Maria Tucci, Kevin Bacon
© *Film Forum*

CAT'S EYE

(MGM/UA) Producer, Martha J. Schumacher; Director, Lewis Teague; Screenplay, Stephen King; Photography, Jack Cardiff; Editor, Scott Conrad; Designer, Giorgio Postiglione; Costumes, Clifford Capone; Creatures Created by Carlo Rambaldi; Music, Alan Silvestri; and, Donald Summer; Visual Effects, Barry Nolan; Special Effects, Jeff Jarvis; Co-Producer, Milton Subotsky, International Film Corporation; Songs by various artists; Technicolor; Dolby Stereo; J-D-C Widescreen; 94 minutes; Rated PG-13; April release

CAST

Our Girl .... Drew Barrymore
Morrison .... James Woods
Donatti .... Alan King
Dussner .... Kenneth McMillian
Norris .... Robert Hays
Sally Ann .... Candy Clark
Hugh .... James Naughton
Junk .... Tony Munafo
McCann .... Court Miller
Mr. Milquetoast .... Russell Horton
Mrs. Milquetoast .... Patricia Benson
Lady .... Mary D'Arcy
Drunk Businessman .... James Rebhorn
Traitor .... Jack Dillon
Mrs. McCann .... Susan Hawes
Marilyn .... Shelly Burch
Westlake .... Sal Richards
Albert .... Jesse Doran
Garcia .... Patricia Kalember
Ducky .... Mike Starr
Man .... Charles Dutton

Right Center: Alan King, James Woods, Tony Munafo
© *MGM/UA*

Drew Barrymore

LADYHAWKE

(WARNER BROS./20th CENTURY-FOX) Producers, Richa
Donner, Lauren Schuler; Director, Richard Donner; Screenplay, E
ward Khmara, Michael Thomas, Tom Mankiewicz; Story, Edwa
Khmara; Photography, Vittorio Storaro; Editor, Stuart Baird; Design
Wolf Kroeger; Music, Andrew Powell; Costumes, Nana Cecchi; Pr
duction Manager, Mario Pisani; Production Manager-Assistant Dire
tor, Anthony Waye; Assistant Directors, Luciano Sacripanti, Te
Madden, Peter Bennet, Mauro Sacripanti; Special Effects, Jo
Richardson; Visual Effects, Richard A. Greenberg; Technicolor; Tec
novision; Dolby Stereo; 124 minutes; Rated PG-13; April release

CAST

Phillipe	Matthew Broder
Navarre	Rutger Ha
Isabeau	Michelle Pfeif
Imperius	Leo McK
Bishop	John Wo
Marquet	Ken Hutchi
Cezar	Alfred Mol
Fornac	Giancarlo Pr
Jehan	Loris Lo
Mr. Pitou	Alessandro Se
Insane Prisoner	Charles Borror
Innkeeper	Massimo Sarchi
Mrs. Pitou	Nicolina Pap
Lieutenant	Russell K

and Don Hudson, Gregory Snegoff, Gaetano Russo, Rod Dand, Ste
no Horowitzo, Paul Tuerpe, Venatino Venantini, Marcus Berensfo
Valerie O'Brien, Nana Cecchi

Left: Rutger Hauer, Matthew Broderick
Below Left: Matthew Broderick (L.)
Below: Michelle Pfeiffer
© Warner Bros./20th Century-Fox

Matthew Broderick (L.)

Rutger Hauer, Michelle Pfeiffer

Elke Sommer, Christopher Plummer

LILY IN LOVE

(NEW LINE CINEMA) Producer, Robert Halmi; Director, Karoly
Makk; Screenplay, Frank Cucci; Photography, John Lindley; Editor,
Norman Gay; Music, Szabolcs Fenyes, Irwin Fisch; Vocals, Holly
Sherwood; Designer, Tamas Vayer; Costumes, Clifford Capone; Exec-
utive Producers, Robert Halmi, Jr., Peter Bacso; Associate Producer,
Robert E. Altman; A Players Associates Film; Color; 100 minutes;
Rated PG-13; April release

CAST

Fitzroy Wynn/Roberto Terranova	Christopher Plummer
Lily Wynn	Maggie Smith
Alicia Braun	Elke Sommer
Jerry Silber	Adolph Green
Fedor	Szabo Sandor
Igor	Janos Kende
Rosanna	Rosetta LeNoire
Producer	Merwin Goldsmith
Young Actor	David Purdham
Young Actresses	Beatrix Porter, Jennifer Babtist
Chauffeur	Aron Lustig
Miklos	Janos Xantus
Pista	Istvan Butykai
Ivan	Gyorgy Feher
Actress	Ildiko Kishonti

Maggie Smith, Christopher Plummer
Above: Christopher Plummer, Adolph Green

33

STICK

(UNIVERSAL) Producer, Jennings Lang; Director, Burt Reynolds; Screenplay, Elmore Leonard, Joseph C. Stinson; Based on the novel by Elmore Leonard; Photography, Nick McLean; Designer, James Shanahan; Editor, William Gordean; Executive Producer, Robert Daley; Associate Producer, David Gershenson; Costumes, Norman Salling; Music, Barry De Vorzon, Joseph Conlan; Executive Co-producer, William Gordean; Production Managers, Larry Powell, Peter V. Herald; Assistant Directors, Jim Van Wyck, Jerry Ketcham, Aldric Porter; Sound, Don Hall; Special Effects, Cliff Wenger, Sr., Eric Roberts, Cliff Wenger, Jr.; Songs by various artists; Technicolor; Dolby Stereo; 109 minutes; Rated R; April release

CAST

Stick	Burt Reynolds
Kyle	Candice Bergen
Barry	George Segal
Chucky	Charles Durning
Rainy	Jose Perez
Cornell	Richard Lawson
Nestor	Castulo Guerra
Moke	Dar Robinson
Firestone	Alex Rocco
Luis	David Reynoso
Katie	Tricia Leigh Fisher
Bobbi	Sachi Parker
Avilanosa	John A. Garcia
Lionel	Don L. Moyer
Tourist at Bar	Joey Pouliot
Luisa Rosa	Phanie Napoli
Edgar	Lamar Jackson
Harvey	Dudley Remus

and Jorge Gil, Armand Grossman, Ignacio Menocal, Jesus Menocal, Dave Cadiente, Carlos Cervantes, Richard L. Duran, Thomas Rosales, Jr., Bert Rosario, April Clough, Deanna Lund, Augie Neves, Evie Sands, Lenny Geer, Monica Lewis, John Keller, Bernie Knee, Tommy Mercer, Don Goldie Orchestra, Tim Rossovich

Top Right: Burt Reynolds
© *Universal*

A TEST OF LOVE

(UNIVERSAL) Producer, Don Murray; Director, Gil Brealey; Scre play, John Patterson, Chris Borthwick; From the true story "Ann Coming Out" by Rosemary Crossley, Anne McDonald; Annie's Na tion by Anne McDonald; Photography, Mick Van Bornemann; Mu Simon Walker; Editor, Lindsay Frazer; Assistant Directors, Ge Letts, Judith Fox; Assistant Producer, Ian Adkins; Designers, Rok Perkins, Mike Hudson; Sound, Rodney Simmons; Eastmancolor; minutes; Rated PG; April release

CAST

Jessica Hathaway	Angela Punch McGre
David Lewis	Drew Forsy
Sally Clements	Liddy Cl
Vera Peters	Monica Maug
Sister Waterman	Philippa Ba
Annie O'Farrell	Tina Arhoi
Dr. John Monroe	Mark Bu
Harding	John Fraw
Dr. Rowell	Wallas Ea
Mrs. O'Farrell	Lyn Collingw
Mr. O'Farrell	Laurie Dob
Bill Hathaway	Carl Blea
Mrs. Arnold	Esme Melv
Mrs. Hathaway	Judith Grat
Hopgood	Alastair Dun
Metcalf	Simon Chilv
Douglas	James Wr
Judge	Charles Ting
Timmy	Brett Reyn
Stephen	Matthew Simp
Noelene	Andrea Mi
Dennis	Dean Ge
Mark	Craig Hargrea
Philip	Steven McCa

and Jane Neilson, Jenny Warner, Pattie Alexeff, Louise Dunne, J Parker, Catherine Vincenzini, Russell Taylor, Joy Westmore, Sutherland, Bill Bennett, John Larking, Michael Edgar, Tom Star vic, Nicky Coghill, Stewart Bates, Philip Stammers, Colin Willia Maureen Bailey, Ann Morgan, Wayne Cull, Jennifer Hearne, K Wise, Jeanine O'Donnell, Jenny Jarman Walker, Kim Bilston, El McKenner, Kathy Kerry, Sue Dukic

Tina Arhondis, Angela Punch McGregor
© *Universal*

1918

(CINECOM INTERNATIONAL) Producers, Lillian Foote, Ross Milloy; Director, Ken Harrison; Screenplay, Horton Foote; Photography, George Tirl; Designer, Michael O'Sullivan; Costumes, Van Ramsey; Executive Producers, Lewis Allen, Peter Newman; Co-producer, Walker Stuart; Associate Producer, Jim Crosby; Production Manager-Assistant Director, Dennis Bishop; Assistant Director, Terri Martin; Sound, John Pritchett; Color; 91 minutes; Not rated; April release

CAST

Horace Robedaux	William Converse-Roberts
Elizabeth Robedaux	Hallie Foote
Mrs. Vaughn	Rochelle Oliver
Mr. Vaughn	Michael Higgins
Brother	Matthew Broderick
Bessie	Jeannie McCarthy
Sam	Bill McGhee
Mr. Thatcher	L.T. Felty
Bessie	Horton Foote, Jr.
Stanley	Tom Murrel
Bill	Phillip Smith
Mrs. Gregory	Norma Allen
Mrs. Cunningham	Margaret Spaulding
Ruth Amos	Carol Goodheart
Gladys Maud	Buffy Carrol
Verna	Betty Murphy
Dan	Frost O. Myers
Mrs. Boone	Peggy Feury
Irma Sue	Belinda Jackson
R. White	Randy Moore
Country Woman	Janice Woodson
Davis	Gil Glasco
Harry	Nick Jordon
Clyde	Jerry Biggs
Mrs. Drayton	Cynthia Rogers
Mary Beth	Anna Harrison
Constance	Lisa Howard
Aunt Inez	Nancy Harrison
Straggler	Allan Alexander

Right: William Converse-Roberts, Hallie Foote
© *Cinecom International*

Matthew Broderick
Top Right: Jeannie McCarthy, Rochelle Oliver, Hallie Foote

Hallie Foote, William Converse-Roberts

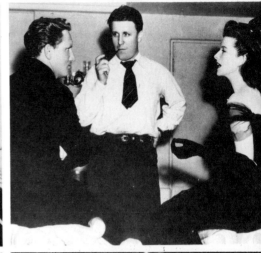

George Stevens, George Stevens, Jr.

GEORGE STEVENS: A FILMMAKER'S JOURNEY

(CASTLE HILL) Producer-Director-Screenplay, George Stevens, J
Associate Producer, Toni Vellani; Co-Producer-Editor, Susan Wir
low; Original Music, Carl Davis; Color; 110 minutes; Rated I
Equivalent; May release.

CAST

The on-camera commentary of: Fred Astaire, Warren Beatty, Fra
Capra, Katharine Hepburn, John Huston, Rouben Mamoulian, J
McCrea, Joseph L. Mankiewicz, Alan J. Pakula, Hal Roach, Gin
Rogers, Fred Zinnemann
The performances on film of: Jean Arthur, Fred Astaire, Montgome
Clift, Brandon DeWilde, James Dean, Douglas Fairbanks, Jr., Ca
Grant, Katharine Hepburn, Rock Hudson, Sam Jaffe, Alan Ladd, J
McCrea, Fred MacMurray, Jack Palance, Millie Perkins, Gin
Rogers, Elizabeth Taylor, Spencer Tracy, Max von Sydow, Shel
Winters

Above: George Stevens, Ginger Rogers, James Stewart
Top: Spencer Tracy, George Stevens, Katharine Hepburn
Top Left: James Dean, George Stevens
Left Center: Elizabeth Taylor, James Dean, George Stevens
© Castle Hill

BREWSTER'S MILLIONS

(NIVERSAL) Producers, Lawrence Gordon, Joel Silver; Director, alter Hill; Screenplay, Herschel Weingrod, Timothy Harris; Based the novel by George Barr McCutcheon; Photography, Ric Waite; esigner, John Vallone; Editors, Freeman Davies, Michael Ripps; stumes, Marilyn Vance; Music, Ry Cooder; Executive Producer-oduction Manager, Gene Levy; Associate Producer, Mae Woods; sistant Directors, Beau Marks, Emmitt-Leon O'Neil; Sound, Jim ebb; Technicolor; Dolby Stereo; 97 minutes; Rated PG

CAST

ontgomery Brewster	Richard Pryor
ike Nolan	John Candy
gela Drake	Lonette McKee
rren Cox	Stephen Collins
arley Pegler	Jerry Orbach
ward Roundfield	Pat Hingle
arilyn	Tovah Feldshuh
pert Horn	Hume Cronyn
B. Donaldo	Joe Grifasi
uck Fleming	Peter Jason
orge Granville	David White
rris Baxter	Jerome Dempsey
gene Provost	David Wohl
elvin	Ji-Tu Cumbuka
ller	Milt Kogan
vino	Carmine Caridi
adimir	Yakov Smirnoff
orty King	Rick Moranis
trid	Gloria Charles
uise	Yana Nirvana
dy	Grand Bush

d Conrad Janis, Rosetta Le Noire, Joseph Leon, Robert Ellenstein, ni Santoni, Alan Autry, Joseph G. Medalis, Malachy McCourt, ger Til, Allan Miller, Mike Hagerty, Kelly Yaegermann, Regina oks, Allan Graf, Archie Hahn, Jeff Mylett, Richard Hochberg, R.D. ll, Frank Slaten, Lin Shaye, Wesley Thompson, Strawn Bovee, Matt nders, Kip Waldo, Shaka Cumbuka, Brad Sanders, Bill McConnell, argot Rose, Joel Weiss, Candy Jennings, Bennie Dobbins, Gary exander, Joey Banks, Steven Benson, Mike Paciorek, Ken Medlock, bbie T. Robinson, Ken Knighten, Hank Robinson, Art Reichle

Right: John Candy, Richard Pryor
Top: Richard Pryor
© *Universal*

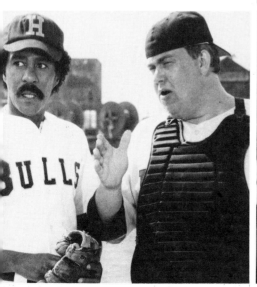

Richard Pryor, John Candy

Richard Pryor, John Candy

RAMBO: FIRST BLOOD PART II

(TRI-STAR) Producer, Buzz Feitshans; Director, George P. Cosmatos; Screenplay, Sylvester Stallone, James Cameron; Story, Kevin Jarre; Based on characters created by David Morrell; Music, Jerry Goldsmith; Photography, Jack Cardiff; Editors, Mark Goldblatt, Mark Helfrich; Costumes, Tom Bronson; Designer, Bill Kenney; Executive Producers, Mario Kassar, Andrew Vajna; Associate Producer, Mel Dellar; Production Manager, Fred Rollin; Assistant Directors, Fred Rollin, Patrick Kinney; Sound, Frederick J. Brown, Michele Sharp, Denise Horta, Rob Young; Technicolor; Panavision Widescreen; Dolby Stereo; 95 minutes; Rated R; May release

CAST

Rambo	Sylvester Stallone
Trautman	Richard Crenna
Murdock	Charles Napier
Podovsky	Steven Berkoff
Co	Julia Nickson
Ericson	Martin Kove
Tay	George Kee Cheung
Banks	Andy Wood
Vinh	William Ghent
Yushin	Vojo Goric
Kinh	Dana Lee
Gunboat Capt	Baoan Coleman
Lifer	Steve Williams
Prison Guard	Tony Munafo
Russian Pilot	Tom Gehrke

and Don Collins, Christopher Grant, John Sterlini, Alain Hocquenghem, William Rothlein (P.O.W.'s)

Left: Sylvester Stallone
© *Tri-Star*

Richard Crenna, Sylvester Stallone

Sylvester Stallone, Top Left: Richard Crenna, Top Right: Julia Nickson

LITTLE TREASURE

(TRI-STAR) Producer, Herb Jaffe; Director-Screenplay, Alan Sharp; Photography, Alex Phillips; Designers, Jose Rodriguez, Granada & Enrique Estevez; Editor, Garth Craven; Music, Leo Kottke; Executive Producers, Joanna Lancaster, Richard Wagner; Associate Producer, Theodore R. Parvin; Production Manager, Ricardo Frera; Assistant Directors, Ramiro Jaloma, Jose Luis Ortega; Sound, Claude Hitchcock; Special Effects, Laurencio Cordero; Choreographers, Joanne Divito, Chea Collette; Songs by various artists; Metrocolor; 95 minutes; Rated R; May release

CAST

Margo	Margot Kidder
Eugene	Ted Danson
Teschemacher	Burt Lancaster
Norman Kane	Joseph Hacker
Evangelina	Malena Doria
Joseph	John Pearce
Sadie	Gladys Holland
Charlie	Bill Zuckert
Chuck	James Hall

and Leonora Llausas, Ricardo Gallarzo, Rodolfo De Alexandre, Enrique Lucero, George Belanger, Patrick Welch, Julia Williams, Glenda Moore, Walter Eggen, Dieter Koll, Roberta Rose, Carol Marie, Samantha Swan, Chea Collette, Lupe Ontiveros, Juaquin Martinez, Deborah Fallender, Enrique Castillo, Burt Sharp, Dyana Ortelli, Tony Melendez, Mitch Carter

Left and Below: Margot Kidder, Ted Danson
© *Tri-Star*

Burt Lancaster, Margot Kidder   Burt Lancaster, Margot Kidder, Ted Danson

RUSTLERS' RHAPSODY

(**PARAMOUNT**) Producer, David Giler; Director-Screenplay, Hugh Wilson; Photography, Jose Luis Alcaine; Editor, John Victor Smith; Music, Steve Dorff; Designer, Gil Parrondo; Costumes, Wayne Finkelman; Executive Producer, Jose Vicuna; Associate Producer, Michael Green; Assistant Directors, Michael Green, Luis Gomez Valdivieso, Roberto Parra; Production Manager, Fransisco Lara; Sound, David Hyde; Special Effects, Antonio Parra; Songs, Steve Dorff, Milton Brown, Snuff Garrett, Nancy Masters; A David Giler/Walter Hill Production; Metrocolor; Panavision; 88 minutes; Rated PG; May release

CAST

Rex O'Herlihan	Tom Berenger
Peter	G. W. Bailey
Miss Tracy	Marilu Henner
Colonel Ticonderoga	Andy Griffith
Railroad Colonel	Fernando Rey
Colonel's Daughter	Sela Ward
Bob Barber	Bob Barber
Jim	Brant Van Hoffman
Jud	Christopher Malcolm
Blackie	Jim Carter
Sheepherders	Paul Maxwell, Manuel Pereiro
Sheepherder's Wife	Margarita Calahorra
Town Doctor	Billy J. Mitchell
Town Sheriff	John Orchard
Sheepherder in saloon	Emilio Linder
Bartender	Alan Larson
Saloon Owner	Thomas Abbot
Real Estate Broker	Elmer Modlin
Town Boy	Juan Miguel Manrique
Minister	Dennis Vaughan

and Eduardo Garcia, Ignacio Carreno, Alicia F. Cavada, Jose Sacristan, Tabare Carballo, Solier Fagundez, George Bullock, Roman Ariz-avaretta, Jorge Brito, Eugenio Serrano, Miguel Garcia, Francisco Gomez, Basilio Escudero, Gabriel Laguna, Camilo Vila, Hal Burton

Top:Andy Griffith, Patrick Wayne, Fernando Rey
Top Right: Marilu Henner, Tom Berenger, Wildfire,
Sela Ward Below: G. W. Bailey, Tom Berenger
© *Paramount*

Tom Berenger, Marilu Henner

CODE OF SILENCE

(ORION) Producer, Raymond Wagner; Director, Andy Davis; Screenplay, Michael Butler, Dennis Shryack, Mike Gray; Story, Michael Butler, Dennis Shryack; Music, David Frank; Photography, Frank Tidy; Designer, Maher Ahmed; Editors, Peter Parasheles, Christopher Holmes; Production Manager, John G. Wilson; Assistant Directors, James A. Dennett, Richard Feld; Sound, Scott Smith; Costumes, Jay Hurley, Mickey Antonetti, Jennifer Jobst; Special Effects, Bob Shelley, Bob Shelley Jr.; Astro Color/DeLuxe Color; 102 minutes; Rated R; May release

CAST

Eddie Cusack	Chuck Norris
Luis Comacho	Henry Silva
Commander Kates	Bert Remsen
Tony Luna	Mike Genovese
Felix Scalese	Nathan Davis
Cragie	Ralph Foody
Pirelli	Allen Hamilton
Victor Comacho	Ron Henriquez
Nick Kopalas	Joseph Guzaldo
Diana Luna	Molly Hagan
Brennan	Ron Dean
Spider	Wilbert Bradley
Dorato	Dennis Farina
Music	Gene Barge
Pompas	Mario Nieves
Efren	Miquel Nino
Doc	Ronnie Barron
Kobas	Joe Kosala
Gamiani	Lou Damiani
Partida	Nydia Rodriquez Terracina
Sanchez	Andre Marquis
"Prowler" Rep	John Mahoney
Hoods	Dennis Cockrum, Zaid Farid
Officer Johnson	Howard Jackson
Angel	Alex Stevens
Coroner	Les Podewell
Molly Luna	Trish Schaefer
Mother	Martha Oton
Eenie	Jack Kandel
Vito	Jemes Fierro
Samo	Tom Letuli

and Don Pike, Jeff Hoke, Gary T. Pike, Catalina Caceres, Frank Strocchia, Shirley Kelly, Angela Zimm, Jack Decker, Sue Kelly, Michael E. Bradley, Sally Anne Waranch, Jerry Tullos

Above and Top: Chuck Norris © *Orion*

42

A FLASH OF GREEN

(PECTRAFILM) Producer, Richard Jordan; Director-Screenplay-
otography-Editor, Victor Nunez; Lighting, Gus Holzer; Music,
arles Engstrom; Sound, Stewart Lippe; Costumes, Marilyn Wall-
se, Dana Moser; Executive Producer, Sam Gowan; Co-Producer,
merican Playhouse; Production Manager, Greg Hausch; Assistant
rector, Kerry McKenney; Special Effects, Don Baker; M3 Effects,
nema Research; Color by Du Art; 121 minutes; Not rated; June
ease

CAST

nmy Wing	Ed Harris
t Hubble	Blair Brown
no Bliss	Richard Jordan
ian Haas	George Coe
tchie	Joan Goodfellow
ckie Halley	Jean De Baer
nt Middie	Helen Stenborg
roy Shannard	William Mooney
ris Rohl	Isa Thomas
al Sinnat	Bob Murch
ss Halley	John Glover
n Haas	Joan MacIntosh
rklund	Bob Harris
t Sinnat	Nancy Griggs
lly Ann Lesser	Linda Lee Larsen
rt Lesser	Michael Doyle
m Jennings	Joe Carioth
llie Bliss	Maggie Beistle

d Maggie Klekas, Charles Kahlenberg, Phil Hunt, Gregory Jones,
ad Wallace, Margaret Bachus, Gene Densmore, Bill Schaaf, Jerry
ark

**Right: Richard Jordan, Ed Harris
Top: Ed Harris
© *Spectrafilm***

Blair Brown

Blair Brown, Ed Harris

COCOON

(20th CENTURY-FOX) Producers, Richard D. Zanuck, Dav
Brown, Lili Fini Zanuck; Director, Ron Howard; Screenplay, To
Benedek; Story, David Saperstein; Photography, Don Peterman; D
signer, Jack T. Collis; Editors, Daniel Hanley, Michael J. Hill; Musi
James Horner; Costumes, Aggie Guerard Rodgers; Special Effec
Visual Effects, Industrial Light & Magic, Joseph Unsinn, Ken Ralsto
Mitch Suskin; Cocoons-Dolphin Effects, Robert Short Production
Inc.; Alien Creatures-Effects, Greg Cannom; Creature Consultar
Rick Baker; Associate Producer, Robert Doudell; Production Manage
Robert Doudell; Assistant Directors, Jan R. Lloyd, Hans Beimle
Sound, Richard Church; Special Music-Dance Coordinator, Gw
Verdon; Alien Choreography, Caprice Rothe; DeLuxe Color; Pa
avision; 117 minutes; Rated PG-13; June release

CAST

Art Selwyn	Don Amech
Ben Luckett	Wilford Briml
Joe Finley	Hume Cron
Walter	Brian Dennel
Bernie Lefkowitz	Jack Gilfo
Jack Bonner	Steve Guttenbe
Mary Luckett	Maureen Staplet
Alma Finley	Jessica Tan
Bess McCarthy	Gwen Verde
Rose Lefkowitz	Herta Wa
Kitty	Tahnee Wel
David	Barret Oliv
Susan	Linda Harris
Pillsbury	Tyrone Power, J
John Dexter	Clint Howa
Pops	Charles Lampk
Doc	Mike Nom
Lou Pine	Jorge C
DMV Clerk	Jim R
Smiley	Charles Rainsbu
Aliens	Wendy Cooke, Pamela Presco
	Dinah Sue Rowley, Gabriella Sincla
Teller	Cyndi Vici
Doctor	Russ Whee
Reverend	Harold Bergm
Waitress	Ivy Thay
Dock Master	Fred Broders
Salvatore	Mark Cheresni
Realtor	Bette Sho
Coast Guard 1st Class BM	Mark Simps
Coast Guard 2nd Class BM	Robert Slacum, J
Detective	Rance Howa
Woman	Jean Speeg
Band Leader	Charles Voelk
Jasper	Irving Kro
Policemen	Clarence Thomas, Ted Scien

1985 Academy Awards for Best Supporting Actor (Don Ameche), Best Visual Effects

Left: Hume Cronyn Top: Gwen Verdon, Don Ameche
© 20th Century-Fox

Brian Dennehy, Mike Nomad, Tyrone Power, Jr.

**Brian Dennehy, Tyrone Power, Jr.,
Steve Guttenberg, Tahnee Welch**

Steve Guttenberg, Tahnee Welch, Tyrone Power, Jr.
Top: Wilford Brimley, Maureen Stapleton
Center: Jessica Tandy, Hume Cronyn

Steve Guttenberg, Tahnee Welch
Top: Gwen Verdon, Don Ameche
Center: Herta Ware, Jack Gilford

45

THE GOONIES

(WARNER BROS.) Producers, Richard Donner, Harvey Bernha
Director, Richard Donner; Screenplay, Chris Columbus; Story, Stev
Spielberg; Photography, Nick McLean; Designer, J. Michael Ri
Editor, Michael Kahn; Music, Dave Grusin; Executive Produce
Steven Spielberg, Frank Marshall, Kathleen Kennedy; Product
Managers, Robin S. Clark, James Herbert; Assistant Directors, D
Kolsrud, Patrick Cosgrove; Sound, Willie Burton; Costumes, Rich
LaMotte; Special Effects, Matt Sweeney; Technicolor; Panavisi
Dolby Stereo; 111 minutes; Rated PG; June release

CAST

Mickey	Sean As
Brand	Josh Bro
Chunk	Jeff Col
Mouth	Corey Feldn
Andy	Kerri Gre
Stef	Martha Plimp
Data	Ke Huy Q
Sloth	John Matus
Jake	Robert D
Francis	Joe Pantoli
Mama Fratelli	Anne Ram
Rosalita	Lupe Ontive
Mrs. Walsh	Mary Ellen Trai
Mr. Walsh	Keith Wal
Mr. Perkins	Curtis Han
Troy	Steve Ar

and Paul Tuerpe, George Robotham, Charles McDaniel, Elaine Co
McMahon, Michael Paul Chan, George Nicholas McLean, Bill Br
ley, Jeb Adams, Eric Briant Wells, Gene Ross, Max Segar, Hew
Dennis Arnold, Jack O'Leary, Patrick Cameron, Erwin Harvey,
Grossman

**Left: Kerri Green, Josh Brolin, Corey Feldman,
Sean Astin, Ke Huy-Quan, Jeff B. Cohen, Martha Plimpton
Top: Jeff B. Cohen, Sean Astin, Corey Feldman, Ke Huy-Qu
© Warner Bros.**

Kerri Green, Josh Brolin

**Sean Astin, Kerri Green, Ke Huy-Quan, Martha Plimpton
Corey Feldman, Josh Brolin Above: Jeff B. Cohen,
Feldman, Huy-Quan, Astin**

"Hungry for Profit"

HUNGRY FOR PROFIT

Producer-Reporter, Robert Richter; Photography, Burleigh Wartes; Editor, Peter Kinoy; Associate Producer, Audrey Zimmerman; Associate Editor, Tom Crawford; Sound, Felipe Borrero, Ralph Arlyck; Documentary; 85 minutes; Not rated; June release

PALE RIDER

(WARNER BROS.) Producer-Director, Clint Eastwood; Screenplay, Michael Butler, Dennis Shryack; Photography, Bruce Surtees; Dener, Edward Carfagno; Editor, Joel Cox; Music, Lennie Niehaus; Costumes, Glenn Wright; Sound, C. Darin Knight; Executive Producer, Fritz Manes; Associate Producer, David Valdes; Assistant Ditors, David Valdes, L. Dean Jones, Jr., Matt Earl Beesley; Special Effects, Chuck Gaspar; Technicolor; Panavision; Dolby Stereo; 115 minutes; Rated R; June release

CAST

Preacher	Clint Eastwood
Hull Barret	Michael Moriarty
Sarah Wheeler	Carrie Snodgress
Josh LaHood	Christopher Penn
Coy La Hood	Richard Dysart
Megan Wheeler	Sydney Penny
Club	Richard Kiel
Spider Conway	Doug McGrath
Stockburn	John Russell
McGill	Charles Hallahan
Jagou	Marvin J. McIntyre
Ma Blankenship	Fran Ryan
Jake Blankenship	Richard Hamilton
Gossage	Graham Paul
Eddie Conway	Chuck LaFont
Teddy Conway	Jeffrey Weissman
Mason	Allen Keller
Ulam	Tom Oglesby
Ulrik Lindquist	Herman Poppe
Miss Gossage	Kathleen Wygle
Tobe Henderson	Terrence Evans
Biggs	Jim Hitson
Bossy	Loren Adkins
Miner Tom	Tom Friedkin
Deputy Folke	S. A. Griffin
Deputy Grissom	Jack Radosta
Deputy Kobold	Robert Winley
Deputy Mather	Billy Drago
Deputy Sedge	Jeffrey Josephson
Deputy Tucker	John Dennis Johnston

and Mike Adams, Clay Lilley, Gene Hartline, R. L. Tolbert, Cliff Happy, Ross Loney, Larry Randles, Mike McGaughy, Gerry Gatlin, Boyd Nelson, Jay K. Fishburn, George Orrison, Milton Murrill, Mike Munsey, Keith Dillin, Wayne Van Horn, Fritz Manes, Glenn Wright

Clint Eastwood

Top Right: Clint Eastwood
© *Warner Bros.*

PERFECT

(COLUMBIA) Producer-Director, James Bridges; Screenplay, Aaron Latham, James Bridges; Based on Articles in *Rolling Stone* by Aaron Latham; Photography, Gordon Willis; Designer, Michael Haller; Editor, Jeff Gourson; Costumes, Michael Kaplan; Music, Ralph Burns; Co-Producer, Jack Larson; Executive Producer-Production Manager, Kim Kurumada; Associate Producer, Joan Edwards; Assistant Directors, Albert Shapiro, Marty Ewing; Sound, Gordon Ecker; Choreographers, Jerry Jackson, Natalie Brown, Kim Connell; Special Effects, Stan Parks; Songs by various artists; Technicolor; Panavision; Widescreen; Dolby Stereo; 125 minutes; Rated R; June release

CAST

Adam	John Travolta
Charlie	Stefan Gierasch
Mark Roth	Jann Wenner
Frankie	Anne De Salvo
Peckerman	Murphy Dunne
Joe McKenzie	Kenneth Welsh
Mrs. McKenzie	Laurie Burton
Mary	Ann Travolta
Nanette	Nannette Pattee-Francini
Robin	Robin Samuel
Robert	Robert Parr
Sterling	Rosalind Ingledew
Randy	Chelsea Field
Steve	Dan Lewk
Linda	Laraine Newman
Sally	Marilu Henner
Roger	Mathew Reed
Jessie	Jamie Lee Curtis
Matt	Roger Menache
Shotsy	Charlene Jones
Eddie	John Wesley
Jeff	Lee Nicholl
Billy	Stacy Bayne
Bobby	Tracy Bayne
Martha	Julie Fulton
Tod	Ken Sylk
Dita	Murphy Cross
Melody	Ronnie Claire Edwards

and Ramey Ellis, Alma Beltran, Perla Walter, Gina Morelli, John Napierala, Philippe Delgrange, Tom Schiller, Paul Kent, Michael Laskin, Robert Stark, Andrea Adams, Kurek Ashley, Paul Barresi, Leslie Borkin, Candy Ann Brown, Brent Carlton, Eileen Finney, Christian Letelier, Donna Perkins, Jill Schachne, Mario Marin, David Paymer, Jim Vanko, Laura Owens, Beth Herzhaft, Anson Downes, Renee Tetro, Joan Edwards, Sam Travolta, Clarke Wilson, Kim Connell, Kim Isaacson, Wendy Shawn, Dan Peterson, Doug Campbell, Gregory Hormel, Daniel Dayan, Annick Romain, Steven Solberg, Susan Burritt, John Michael Kelly, Bruce Savin, Jean Lubin, Kai Maxwell, Kevin Boyle, Frank Cavestani, Brian MaGuire, Elaine Perkins, Marlene Cramer, Bob Henry, Rick Avery, Chere Bryson

Top Right: Jamie Lee Curtis, John Travolta
© *Columbia*

Jann Wenner, Anne De Salvo, John Travolta

Jamie Lee Curtis

RETURN TO OZ

(UENA VISTA) Producer, Paul Maslansky; Director, Walter Murch; creenplay, Walter Murch, Gill Dennis; Based on the books "The Land Oz" and "Ozma of Oz" by L. Frank Baum; Music, David Shire; otography, David Watkin; Designer, Norman Reynolds; Editor, slie Hodgson; Executive Producer, Gary Kurtz; Production Man-r; Stephen Lanning; Associate Producer, Colin Michael Kitchens; sistant Directors, Michael Murray, Ray Corbett; Mime Movement, ns Maar; Costumes, Raymond Hughes, William R. McPhail; Crea-e Design, Lyle Conway, Tim Rose; Special Effects, Ian Wingrove; ymation, Will Vinton Productions Inc.; Produced in Association h Silver Screen Partners II; Presented by Walt Disney Pictures; hnicolor; Dolby Stereo; 110 minutes; Rated PG; June release

CAST

Worley/The Nome King	Nicol Williamson
rse Wilson/Princess Mombi	Jean Marsh
rothy	Fairuza Balk
nt Em	Piper Laurie
cle Henry	Matt Clark
Tok	Michael Sundin/Tim Rose
ice	Sean Barrett
lina	Mak Wilson
ice	Denise Bryer
k Pumpkinhead	Brian Henson/Stewart Larange
ce	Brian Henson
mp	Lyle Conway/Steve Norrington
ice	Lyle Conway
recrow	Justin Case
wardly Lion	John Alexander
Man	Deep Roy
na	Emma Ridley
d Wheeler/Nome Messenger	Pons Maar
o	Tansy

Susan Dacre, Geoff Felix, David Greenaway, Swee Lim, Sophie rd, Fiona Victory, Rachel Ashton, Robbie Barnett, Ailsa Berk, er Elliott, Roger Ennals, Michele Hine, Mark Hopkins, Colin aping, Ken Stevens, Philip Tan, Robert Thirtle, John Alexander, ce Boa, Nichola Roche, Cheryl Brown, Alison Lynn, Sarah White

**Right: Jean Marsh Top: John Alexander,
Deep Roy, Fairuza Balk, Justin Case, Brian Henson/
Stewart Larange, Michael Sundin/Tim Rose © Buena Vista**

Fairuza Balk

**Fairuza Balk, Nicol Willamson
Above: Fairuza Balk, Lyle Conway/Steve Norrington**

PRIZZI'S HONOR

(20th CENTURY-FOX) Producer, John Foreman; Director, J
Huston; Screenplay, Richard Condon, Janet Roach; From the nove
Richard Condon; Photography, Andrzej Bartkowiak; Designer, De
Washington; Editors, Rudi Fehr, Kaja Fehr; Music, Alex North; (
tumes, Donfeld; Production Managers, Donald C. Klune, Thomas }
Kane; Assistant Directors, Benjy Rosenberg, Christopher Gri
Special Effects, Connie Brink; Sound, Dennis Maitland, Kim M
land; DeLuxe Color; Dolby Stereo; Panavision; 129 minutes; Rate
June release

CAST

Charley Partana	Jack Nicho
Irene Walker	Kathleen Tu
Eduardo Prizzi	Robert Lo
Angelo "Pop" Partanna	John Rand
Don Corrado Prizzi	William Hic
Dominic Prizzi	Lee Richar
Filargi "Finlay"	Michael Lom
Maerose Prizzi	Anjelica Hu
Plumber	George Santop
Lt. Hanley	Lawrence Tie
Peaches Altamont	C. C. H. Pou
Amaliz Prizzi	Ann Selepe
Phil Vittimizzare	Vic Po
Bluestone	Dick O'
Casco Vascone	Sully B
Theresa Prizzi	Antonia Vasc
Opera Singer	Tomasino Ba
Don's Bodyguard	John Cal
Gallagher	Murray
Marxie Heller	Joseph Ru
Bocca	Ray S
Gomsky	Seth A
Presto Ciglione	Dominic B
Beulah	Teddi Si

Left: Kathleen Turner, Jack Nicholson
© *20th Century-Fox*

Academy Award for Best Supporting
Actress (Anjelica Huston)

Anjelica Huston, Jack Nicholson

Kathleen Turner, Jack Nicholson Top Left: Anjelica Huston
Top Right: Lee Richardson, William Hickey, Robert Loggia
Right Center: Jack Nicholson

ST. ELMO'S FIRE

(COLUMBIA) Producer, Lauren Shuler; Director, Joel Schumacher; Screenplay, Joel Schumacher, Carl Kurlander; Photography, Stephen H. Burum; Designer, William Sandell; Editor, Richard Marks; Costumes, Susan Becker; Music, David Foster; Executive Producers, Ned Tanen, Bernard Schwartz; Production Manager, Ray Hartwick; Assistant Directors, Gary Daigler, Katterli A. Frauenfelder; Choreographer, Kenny Ortega; Special Effects, Peter Albiez; Songs by various artists; Metrocolor; Panavision; Dolby Stereo; 110 minutes; Rated R; June release

CAST

Kirbo	Emilio Estevez
Billy	Rob Lowe
Kevin	Andrew McCarthy
Jules	Demi Moore
Alec	Judd Nelson
Leslie	Ally Sheedy
Wendy	Mare Winningham
Mr. Beamish	Martin Balsam
Dale Biberman	Andie MacDowell
Mrs. Beamish	Joyce Van Patten
Felicia	Jenny Wright
Wally	Blake Clark
Howie Krantz	Jon Cutler
Ron Dellasandro	Matthew Laurance
Judith	Gina Hecht
Naomi	Anna Maria Horsford

and Patrick Winningham, Andy Scott, Christian Iraberen, Daniele Iraberen, Bennet Bowman, James Carrington, Kaaren Lee, Nora Meerbaum, Don Moss, Whip Hubley, Michele Winding, Jim Turner, Mario Machado, Judy Kain, Seth Jaffe, Jeffrey Lampert, Elizabeth Arlen, Scott Nemes, Bernadette Birkett, Vincent J. Isaac, Dean R. Miller, Jamison Anders, Cindi Dietrich, David Lain Baker, Daniel Eden, Laurel Page, Thom Bierdz, J. T. Solomon, Reid Rondell

Right: Andie MacDowell, Emilio Estevez Top: Ally Sheedy, Judd Nelson, Emilio Estevez, Demi Moore, Rob Lowe, Mare Winningham, Andrew McCarthy Below: Andrew McCarthy, Demi Moore © Columbia

Andrew McCarthy, Emilio Estevez, Judd Nelson, Rob Lowe

Mare Winningham, Demi Moore, Ally Sheedy

SILVERADO

(COLUMBIA) Producer-Director, Lawrence Kasdan; Screenplay, Lawrence Kasdan, Mark Kasdan; Photography, John Bailey; Designer, — Random; Editor, Carol Littleton; Music, Bruce Broughton; Costumes, Kristi Zea; Executive Producers, Charles Okun, Michael Grillo; Associate Producer, Mark Kasdan; Production Manager, Charles —n; Assistant Director, Michael Grillo; Stephen Dunn, Sound, —vid Ronne; Special Effects, Roy Arbogast; Technicolor; Super Techniscope; Dolby Stereo; 133 minutes; Rated PG-13; June release

CAST

—en	Kevin Kline
—nett	Scott Glenn
—e	Kevin Costner
—	Danny Glover
—riff Langston	John Cleese
—uty Kern	Todd Allen
—uty Block	Kenny Call
—nah	Rosanna Arquette
—rad	Rusty Meyers
— Parker	Zeke Davidson
— Parker	Lois Geary
—b	Brian Dennehy
—la	Linda Hunt
—k	Jeff Goldblum
—Kendrick	Ray Baker
—a	Joe Seneca
—	Lynn Whitfield
—ee	Jeff Fahey
—e	Patricia Gaul
—ebe	Amanda Wyss
—	Earl Hindman
—ie	Tom Brown
—dley	Jim Haynie
—y	Richard Jenkins

Marvin J. McIntyre, Brad Williams, Sheb Wooley, Jon Kasdan, — Thurman, Meg Kasdan, Dick Durock, Gene Hartline, Autry Ward, —b Kasdan, James Gammon, Troy Ward, Roy McAdams, Jerry —gs, Sam Gauny, Ken Farmer, Bill McIntosh, Charlie Seybert, Jane —uchamp, Jerry Block, Ben Zeller, Pepe Serna, Ted White, Ross —ey, Walter Scott, Bob Terhune

Right: Danny Glover, Scott Glenn Top: Danny Glover —vin Costner, Scott Glenn, Kevin Kline Below: Linda Hunt, Kevin Kline, Scott Glenn, Brian Dennehy © *Columbia*

Dick Durock, Danny Glover

Scott Glenn, Tom Brown

BACK TO THE FUTURE

(UNIVERSAL) Producers, Bob Gale, Neil Canton; Director, Robert Zemeckis; Screenplay, Robert Zemeckis, Bob Gale; Photography, Dean Cunde; Designer, Lawrence G. Paull; Editor, Arthur Schmidt, Harry Keramidas; Music, Alan Silvestri; Executive Producers, Steven Spielberg, Frank Marshall, Kathleen Kennedy; Production Managers, Dennis E. Jones, Jack Grossberg; Assistant Directors, David McGiffert, Pamela Eilerson; Visual Effects, Industrial Light & Magic; Makeup, Ken Chase; Costumes, Deborah L. Scott; Special Effects, Kevin Pike; Choreographer, Brad Jeffries; Songs by various artists; Technicolor; Panavision; Dolby Stereo; 116 minutes; Rated PG-13; July release

CAST

Marty McFly	Michael J. Fox
Dr. Emmett Brown	Christopher Lloyd
Lorraine Baines	Lea Thompson
George McFly	Crispin Glover
Biff Tannen	Thomas F. Wilson
Jennifer Parker	Claudia Wells
Dave McFly	Marc McClure
Linda McFly	Wendie Jo Sperber
Sam Baines	George DiCenzo
Stella Baines	Frances Lee McCain
Mr. Strickland	James Tolkan
Skinhead	Jeffrey Jay Cohen
3-D	Casey Siemaszko
Match	Billy Zane
Marvin Berry	Harry Waters
Goldie Wilson	Donald Fullilove
Babs	Lisa Freeman
Betty	Cristen Kauffman
Clocktower Lady	Elsa Raven
Pa Peabody	Will Hare
Ma Peabody	Ivy Bethune
Sherman Peabody	Jason Marin
Peabody daughter	Katherine Britton
Milton Baines	Jason Harvey
Sally Baines	Maia Brewton
Dixon	Courtney Gains

and Richard L. Duran, Jeff O'Haco, Johnny Green, Jamie Abbott, Norman Alden, Read Morgan, Sachi Parker, Robert Krantz, G. Riley, Karen Petrasek, Tommy Thomas, Granville "Danny" Young, David Harold Brown, Lloyd L. Tolbert, Paul Hanson, Lee Brownfield, Robert DeLapp, Huey Lewis

1985 Academy Award for Best Sound Effects Editing

Michael J. Fox, Christopher Lloyd Top: Michael J. Fox © UNIVERSAL

Michael J. Fox, Christopher Lloyd Top: Claudia Wells, Michael J. Fox

Top Left: Taran, Princess Eilonwy Below: Dallben,
Hen Wen, Taran © *Buena Vista*

THE BLACK CAULDRON

(BUENA VISTA) Producer, Joe Hale; Directors, Ted Berman,
Richard Rich; Based on The Chronicles Of Prydain series by Lloyd
Alexander; Music, Elmer Bernstein; Executive Producer, Ron Miller;
Additional Dialogue, Rosemary Anne Sisson, Roy Edward Disney;
Story, David Jonas, Vance Gerry, Ted Berman, Richard Rich, Joe
Hale, Al Wilson, Roy Morita, Peter Young, Art Stevens; Production
Managers, Don Hahn; Assistant Directors, Mark Hester, Terry Noss,
Randy Paton; Character Design, Andreas Deja, Mike Ploog, Phil
Nibbelink, Al Wilson, David Jonas; Produced in association with Silver
Screen Partners II; Presented by Walt Disney Pictures; Technicolor;
Super Panavision; Widescreen; Dolby Stereo; 80 minutes; Rated PG;
July release

CAST (VOICES)

Taran	Grant Bardsley
Eilonwy	Susan Sheridan
Dallben	Freddie Jones
Fflewddur	Nigel Hawthorne
King Eidilleg	Arthur Malet
Gurgi/Doli	John Byner
Orddu	Eda Reiss Merin
Orwen	Adele Malis-Morey
Orgoch	Billie Hayes
Creeper	Phil Fondacaro
The Horned King	John Hurt

and Lindsay Rich, Brandon Call, Gregory Levinson, Peter Renaday,
Wayne Allwine, Steve Hale, James Almanzar, Phil Fondacaro, Phil
Nibbelink, Jack Laing

Taran, Gurgi Above: The Creeper

56

THE EMERALD FOREST

(20th CENTURY-FOX) Producer-Director, John Boorman; Screenplay, Rospo Pallenberg; Photography, Philippe Rousselot; Designer, Simon Holland; Editor, Ian Crafford; Sound, Ron Davis; Choreography, Jose Possi; Music, Junior Homrich, Brian Gascoigne; Costumes, Christel Boorman, Clovis Bueno; Co-Producer, Michael Dryhurst; Executive Producer, Edgar F. Gross; Assistant Directors, Barry Langley, Michael Higgins, Jerry Daly, Jaime Schwartz, Edson Mendonca; Special Effects, Raph Salis; Production Manager, Roberto Bakker; Presented by Embassy Films Associates; Eastmancolor; Panavision, Widescreen; Dolby Stereo; 115 minutes; Rated R; July release

CAST

Bill Markham	Powers Boothe
Jean Markham	Meg Foster
Young Tommy	William Rodriquez
Young Heather	Yara Vaneau
Heather	Estee Chandler
Tomme	Charley Boorman
Kachiri	Dira Paes
Uwe Werner	Eduardo Conde
Padre Leduc	Ariel Coelho
Ferreira	Peter Marinker
Costa	Mario Borges
Trader	Atilia Iorio
Frenchman	Babriel Archanjo
Carlos	Gracindo Junior
Rico	Arthur Muhlenberg
Paulo	Chico Terto
Wanadi	Rui Polanah
Uluru	Maria Helena Velasco
Caya	Tetchie Agbayani
Mapi	Paulo Vinicius
Kamanpo	Aloisio Flores
Monkey	Joao Mauricio Carvalho
Kachiri's Cousins	Isabel Bicudo, Patricia Prisco
Tequi	Silvana De Faria
Jacareh	Claudio Moreno

and Alexandre Fontez, Antioni Japones, Candido Silveira, Diocelio Nascimento, Fabio Da Silveira, Fernando Pires, Haroldo Da Silva Rampolha, Itakati Croaia, Jorge Luiz Coelho De Mello, Jose Ademir Dos Santos, Marcos Tuantagno, Meszuita, Nilson Accioly, Sergio Martins, Wanderley, Wladimir Oliveiro, Ana Lucia Dos Reis, Elidia Moraes, Elisette Costa Oliveira, Ivan Barbosa Freitas, Jurema Carvalho, Walkiria De Freitas, Antonio Rodriquez Neto, Coluene Kodwel, Benilto Gomes, Fernando Pires, Guot Macido, Iran Magalhaes, Jandir Carvalho Leite, Jose Maria Carvalho, Wellison De Azvedo Santos, Jose Maria Gomes De Silva, Luiz Carlos Felix, Luiz Fernando Machado, Luiz Roberto DeVeiro, Marcelo Toneao, Ricardo Costo De Souza, Ronaldo Alves, Sergio Espirito Santo

Top Right: Charley Boorman, Dira Paes
Below: Charley Boorman © *20th Century-Fox*

Charley Boorman, Powers Boothe

Rui Polonah

NATIONAL LAMPOON'S EUROPEAN VACATION

(WARNER BROS.) Producer, Matty Simmons; Director, Amy Heckerling; Screenplay, John Hughes, Robert Klane; Story, John Hughes; Photography, Bob Paynter; Editor, Pembroke Herring; Music, Charles Fox; Designer, Bob Cartwright; Co-Producer, Stuart Cornfeld; Production Manager, William Lang; Assistant Directors, Don French, Ian Higginbotham; Sound, Tony Dawe; Special Effects, Richard Richtfeld; Costumes, Graham Williams; Musical Staging, Gillian Lynn; Songs by various artists; Technicolor; Panavision; 95 minutes; Rated PG-13; July release

CAST

Clark W. Griswald	Chevy Chase
Ellen Griswald	Beverly D'Angelo
Audrey Griswald	Dana Hill
Rusty Griswald	Jason Lively
Kent	John Astin
Game Show Hostesses	Sheila Kennedy, Tricia Lange
Mr. Froeger	Paul Bartel
Mrs. Froeger	Cynthia Szigeti
The Froegers' Son	Malcolm Danare
The Froegers' Daughter	Kevi Kendall
Jack	William Zabka
Stewardess	Wendy Goldman
Court Announcer	Angus MacKay
Princess Di	Julie Wooldridge
Prince Charles	Peter Hugo
Queen Elizabeth	Jeanette Charles
Taxi Driver	Derek Deadman
Hotel Manager	Mel Smith
Hotel Manager's Mother	Gwen Nelson
Mrs. Garland	Elizabeth Arlen
Mr. Garland	David Gers
Desk Clerk	Jacques Herlin
Assistant Manager	Jacques Maury
Cherie	Sylvie Badala
Fritz Spritz	William Millowitsch
Helga Spritz	Erica Wackernagel
Claudia	Claudia Neidig
The Thief	Victor Lanoux
The Other Thief	Massimo Sarchielli
Rusty's California Girl	Moon Zappa

and Robbie Coltrane, Maureen Lipman, Paul McDowell, Ballard Berkeley, Eric Idle, Phillip Stubelle, Alice Sapritch, Isa Carol Horio, Isabelle Massard, Didier Pain, Jorge Krimer, Gloria Charles

Jason Lively, Dana Hill, Beverly D'Angelo, Chevy Chase
(also Left Center) Top: Chevy Chase © Warner Bros.

FRIGHT NIGHT

(COLUMBIA) Producer, Herb Jaffe; Director-Screenplay, Tom Holland; Photography, Jan Kiesser; Designer, John De Cuir, Jr.; Editor, Kent Beyda; Music, Brad Fiedel; Associate Producer-Production Manager, Jerry A. Baerwitz; Assistant Directors, Gerald Sobul, Carole Keligian; Visual Effects, Richard Edlund; Sound, Don Rush; Costumes, Bettylee Balsam; Special Effects, Michael Lantieri, Darrell Pritchett, Clayton Pinney, Albert Lannutti; Choreographer, Dorain Grusman; Creatures, Randall William Cook, Steve Johnson; Songs by various artists; Metrocolor; Panavision; Dolby Stereo; 105 minutes; Rated R; July release

CAST

Jerry Dandridge	Chris Sarandon
Charley Brewster	William Ragsdale
Amy Peterson	Amanda Bearse
Peter Vincent	Roddy McDowall
Evil Ed	Stephen Geoffreys
Billy Cole	Jonathan Stark
Judy Brewster	Dorothy Fielding
Detective Lennox	Art J. Evans
Cook	Stewart Stern
Jonathan	Robert Corff
Miss Nina	Pamela Brown

and Nick Savage, Ernie Holmes, Heidi Sorenson, Irina Irvine, Chris Hendrie, Prince A. Hughes

Top: Stephen Geoffreys, William Ragsdale, Amanda
Bearse, Chris Sarandon Below: Roddy McDowall
Top Right: Stephen Geoffreys, Chris Sarandon
Below: Amanda Bearse
© Columbia

Chris Sarandon, Amanda Bearse

Arnold Schwarzenegger, Brigitte Nielsen,
Ernie Reyes, Jr., Paul Smith

RED SONJA

(MGM/UA) Producer, Christian Ferry; Director, Richard Fleischer; Screenplay, Clive Exton, George MacDonald Fraser; Based on th character created by Robert E. Howard; Photography, Giusepp Rotunno; Editor, Frank J. Urioste; Music, Ennio Morricone; Costumes Danilo Donati; Executive Producer, A. Michael Lieberman; Associat Producer-Assistant Director, Jose Lopez Rodero; Production Manage Lucio Trentini; Assistant Directors, Mauro Sacripanti, Michel Ferry Special Effects, John Stirber; Technicolor-Metrocolor; J-D-C Wide screen; 89 minutes; Rated PG-13; July release

CAST

Kalifor	Arnold Schwarzenegge
Red Sonja	Brigitte Nielse
Queen Gedren	Sandahl Bergma
Falkon	Paul Smit
Tarn	Ernie Reyes, J
Ikol	Ronald Lace
Brytag	Pat Roac
Djart	Terry Richard
Varna	Janet Agre
Kendra	Donna Osterbuh
Handmaid	Lara Naszinsk
Father	Hans Meye
Mother	Francesca Romana Coluzz
Barlok	Stefanao Mior
Wizard	Tutte Lemko
Kyobo	Kiyoshi Yamazak
Swordmaster	Tad Horin

Top: Arnold Schwarzenegger, Brigitte Nielsen
(also below) Top Left: Brigitte Nielsen
Below: Sandahl Bergman

COMPROMISING POSITIONS

(PARAMOUNT) Executive Producer, Salah M. Hassanein; Producer-Director, Frank Perry; Screenplay, Susan Isaacs from her novel; Music, Brad Fiedel; Photography, Barry Sonnenfeld; Editor, Peter Frank; In color; Rated R; 98 minutes; August release

CAST

Judith Singer	Susan Sarandon
Lt. David Suarez	Raul Julia
Nancy Miller	Judith Ivey
Bob Singer	Edward Herrmann
Peg Tuccio	Mary Beth Hurt
Dr. Bruce Fleckstein	Joe Mantegna
Dicky Dunck	Josh Mostel
Brenda Dunck	Deborah Rush
Mary Alice Mahoney	Joan Allen
Phyllis Fleckstein	Anne DeSalvo

Judith Ivey, Susan Sarandon, Joan Allen
Top Right: Raul Julia, Susan Sarandon
Below: Susan Sarandon, Edward Herrmann
Right: Josh Mostel, Deborah Rush
© *Paramount*

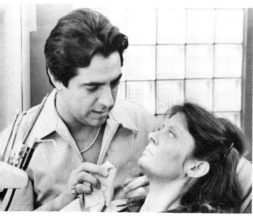

Joe Mantegna, Susan Sarandon

Judith Ivey, Susan Sarandon

61

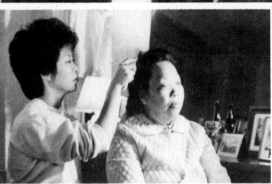

DIM SUM: A LITTLE BIT OF HEART

(ORION CLASSICS) Producers, Tom Sternberg, Wayne Wang, Danny Yung; Director, Wayne Wang; Screenplay, Terrel Seltzer; From an idea by Terrel Seltzer, Laureen Chew, Wayne Wang; Photography, Michael Chin; Editor, Ralph Wikke; Music, Todd Boekelheide; In English and Cantonese with sub-titles; Executive Producer, Vincent Tai; Associate Producer, Emily Leung; Art Director, Danny Yung; In color; Rated PG; 88 minutes; August release

CAST

Geraldine Tam	Laureen Chew
Mrs. Tam	Kim Chew
Uncle Tam	Victor Wong
Auntie Mary	Ida F. O. Chung
Julia	Cora Miao
Richard	John Nishio
Amy Tam	Amy Hill
Kevin Tam	Keith Choy
Old M. J. Players	Mary Chew, Nora Lee
Young M. J. Players	Joan Chen, Rita Yee
Bar Patron	George Wu
Eliza	Elsa Cruz Pearson
Linda Tam	Helen Chew
Baby Tam	Jarrett Chew

Top: Victor Wong, Laureen Chew, Kim Chew
Left Center: Laureen Chew, Kim Chew
© *Orion*

Victor Wong, Laureen Chew
(also above)

KEY EXCHANGE

20th CENTURY-FOX) Producers, Mitchell Maxwell, Paul Kurta; Director, Barnet Kellman; Screenplay, Kevin Scott, Paul Kurta; Based on play of same title by Kevin Wade; Photography, Fred Murphy; Designer, David Gropman; Editor, Jill Savitt; Costumes, Ruth Morley; Music, Mason Daring, Michael Jay, Kenny White; Song, Michael Jay, Tyche Chlanda; Choreographer, Sara Sugihara; Co-Executive Producer, Peer J. Oppenheimer; Executive Producers, Ronald Winston, Michael Pochna; Production Manager, Paul Kurta; Assistant Directors, Paula Mazur, Deborah L. Marrs; Sound, Maryte Kavaliauskas; Color; 90 minutes; Rated R; August release

CAST

Lisa	Brooke Adams
Carabello	Danny Aiello
Frank	Seth Allen
The Beauty	Kerry Armstrong
Marcy	Sandra Beall
Willie the Stage Manager	Peter Brinkerhoff
Lighting Technician	Ian Calderon
Mr. Simon	Keith Charles
A. D. Switcher	Roger S. Christiansen
Debbie	Debbie Copaken
Joane	John Cunningham
Piero	Ned Eisenberg
Mrs. Anderson	Alix Elias
Makeup Girl	Debra Engle
Interviewer	Gia Galeano
Amy	Terri Garber
Sal	Annie Golden
Gym Honey	Susanne Gregard
Party Girl	Robin Groves
Director	Barnet Kellman
Mayor Edward I. Koch	As Himself
Philip	Ben Masters
Roudaille Guy	Vincent McDonald
Loraine	Davenia McFadden
April	Nancy Mette
Chiropractor Woman	Deborah Offner
Eric	Peter Pucci
Cosmo Women	Maggie Renzi, Marisa Smith
Mr. Fanshaw	Rex Robbins
Slattery	Tony Roberts
Guard	Mary Lou Rosato
Lenny	Bill Smitrovich
Record Executive	John Spencer
Michael	Daniel Stern
Asst. Choreographer	Sara Sugihara
Mrs. Fanshaw	Holland Taylor
George	Eric Van Valkenberg
Hal	Rick Van Valkenberg
Man at party	John Venema
Aerobics Teacher	High Voltage
Mr. Anderson	Dan Ziskie

and Brad Brewer, Marvin Brown, Glenngo King, David Marin

Top Right: Tony Roberts, Daniel Stern, Brooke Adams
Below: Tony Roberts, Ben Masters
© *20th Century-Fox*

Brooke Adams, Daniel Stern, Ben Masters

Brooke Adams

PEE-WEE'S BIG ADVENTURE

(WARNER BROS.) Producers, Robert Shapiro, Richard Gilber Abramson; Director, Tim Burton; Screenplay, Phil Hartman, Pau Reubens, Michael Varhol; Executive Producer, William E. McEuen Photography, Victor J. Kemper; Designer, David L. Snyder; Editor Billy Weber; Costumes, Aggie Guerard Rodgers; Music, Danny Elfman; Assistant Director, Robert P. Cohen; In Technicolor and Dolby Stereo; Rated PG; 92 minutes; August release

CAST

Pee-Wee Herman	Himsel
Dottie	Elizabeth Daily
Francis	Mark Holto
Simone	Diane Salinge
Mickey	Judd Ome
Neighbor	Irving Hellma
Mario	Monte Land
Chip	Damon Marti
Chuck	Daryl Roac
Sgt. Hunter	Starletta DuPo
Butler	Toru Tanak
Mr. Buxton	Ed Herlih
Amazing Larry	Lou Cute
Madam Ruby	Erica Yoh
Large Marge	Alice Nun
Highway Patrolman	Bill Richmon
Trucker	Ed Griffit
Andy	Jon Harri
Hobo Jack	Carmen Filp
Tina	Jan Hook

and David Glasser, Gregory Brown, Mark Everett, Bill Cable, Pete Looney, Ralph Seymour, Raymond Martino, Simmy Bow, Joh Moody, John O'Neill, Alex Sharp, Chester Grimes, Luis Contreras Lonnie Parkinson, Howard Hirdler, Cassandra Peterson, Jason Hervey Bob McClurg, John Paragon, Susan Barnes, Zachary Hoffman, Lynn Stewart, George Sasaki, Richard Brose, Drew Seward, Brett Fellman Bob Drew, John Gilgreen, Noreen Hennessy, Phil Hartman, Michae Varhol, David Rothenberg, Pat Cranshaw, Sunshine Parker, Gille Savard, and special appearances by James Brolin, Morgan Fairchild Tony Bill, Twisted Sister

Pee-Wee Herman (also Top Left) © *Warner Bros.*

TEEN WOLF

(ATLANTIC) Producers, Scott M. Rosenfelt, Mark Levinson; Executive Producers, Thomas Coleman, Michael Rosenblatt; Director, Rod Daniel; Screenplay, Joseph Loeb III, Matthew Weisman; Photography, Tim Suhrstedt; Art Director, Chester Kaczenski; Editor, Lois Freeman-Fox; Music, Miles Goodman; A Wolfkill Production in color; Rated PG; 91 minutes; August release

CAST

Scott Howard	Michael J. Fox
Harold Howard	James Hampton
Lisa "Boof" Marconi	Susan Ursitti
Rupert "Stiles" Stilinsky	Jerry Levine
Lewis Erikson	Matt Adler
Pamela Wells	Lorie Griffin
Russell Thorne	James MacKrell
Mick McAllister	Mark Arnold
Coach Finstock	Jay Tarses
Chubby	Mark Holton
Kirk Lolley	Scott Paulin

Left: Michael J. Fox
Below Left: Jerry Levine
© *Atlantic*

Susan Ursitti, Michael J. Fox

Michael J. Fox, Jerry Levine

INVASION U.S.A.

(CANNON) Producers, Menahem Golan, Yoram Globus; Direc[tor,] Joseph Zito; Screenplay, James Bruner, Chuck Norris; Story, Aa[ron] Norris, James Bruner; Music, Jay Chattaway; Photography, Joao F[er]nandes; Designer, Ladislav Wilheim; Editors, Daniel Loewent[hal,] Scott Vickrey; Production Managers, Peter A. Runfolo, James Herb[ert;] Assistant Directors, David Anderson, Leonid Zisman; Costumes, F[???] Long; Special Effects, Gary F. Bentley; Special Effects Make-Up, T[om] Savini; Color; Dolby Stereo; 108 minutes; Rated R; September rele[ase.]

CAST

Matt Hunter	Chuck No[rris]
Rostov	Richard Ly[nch]
McGuire	Melissa Prop[het]
Nikko	Alexander Z[ale]
Tomas	Alex Co[???]
Cassidy	Eddie Jo[???]
Johnston	Jon De V[???]
Harper	James O'Sulli[van]
Mickey	Billy Dr[ago]
Castillo	Jaime Sanc[hez]
John Eagle	Dehl B[???]
Flynn	Stephen Ma[???]
Kurt	Shane McCa[???]
Adams	Martin Sha[???]
Koyo	James [???]
Clark Little Hawk	Nick Rar[???]
Detective Tom Green	Bernie McIner[ney]
Maria	Lorraine M[???]
Carlos	Anthony Marci[???]
Tonio	Michael Carm[???]
Victor	Mario Ernesto Sanc[???]
Cindy	Amanda Grah[???]
Angela	Teresa M. R[???]

and Nate Esformes, Tony Bolano, Marilyn Romero, Sheryl Bro[???] Dan Albright, Megan Blake, Jason Ehrlich, Charles Kahlenberg, R[???] dy Parks, Katherine Ann Payne, Bill Alexander, Peter Bannon, B[???] Shaw, Tom Mintier, Tranette Ledford-Furnad, Bob Varsha, Mor[???] Kaufman, Don Miller, Art Eckman, Jack Bell, Gene Griessman, B[???] Burns, Jeff Benninghofen, Bernard Barrow, Bruce Evers, Lisa St[???] Rene Rokk, Joe Frasca, Dan Fitzgerald, Robin Kinsey, Michael[???] Kelly, Ruben Rabasa, Raymond Rosario, Howard Jackson, Tim T[???] ers, Kevin Maggiore, Andy Stahl, Chondra Wolle, Jana Camp, Tom[???] Nowell, Wallace Wilkinson, Bob Hannah, Laura Whyte, Jenn[???] Sullivan, Dick Tirschel, Alex Malenky, Gerry Murphy, Robert Ro[???] guez, Maria Doest, Afif Yordi, Tarek Yordi, Aaron Norris

**Left: Alexander Zale, Melissa Prophet
Top: Chuck Norris © Cannon**

Richard Lynch   Chuck Norris

AFTER HOURS

(WARNER BROS.) Producers, Amy Robinson, Griffin Dunne, Robert F. Colesberry; Director, Martin Scorsese; Screenplay, Joseph Minion; Photography, Michael Ballhaus; Editor, Thelma Schoonmaker; Costumes, Rita Ryack; Designer, Jeffrey Townsend; Music, Howard Shore; Associate Producer, Deborah Schindler; Production Manager, Michael Nozik; Assistant Directors, Stephen J. Lim, Christopher Griffin; Sound, Chat Gunter; Songs by various artists; Presented by The Geffen Company; Du Art Color; 97 minutes; Rated R; September release

CAST

Paul Hackett	Griffin Dunne
Marcy	Rosanna Arquette
June	Verna Bloom
Pepe	Thomas Chong
Kiki	Linda Fiorentino
Julie	Teri Garr
Tom the Bartender	John Heard
Neil	Cheech Marin
Gail	Catherine O'Hara
Waiter	Dick Miller
Horst	Will Patton
Mark	Robert Plunket
Lloyd	Bronson Pinchot

Rocco Sisto, Larry Block, Victor Argo, Murray Moston, John P. Coriglia, Clarke Evans, Victor Bumbalo, Bill Elverman, Joel Jason, Gerald Carr, Clarence Felder, Henry Baker, Margo Winkler, Victor Magnotta, Robin Johnson, Stephen J. Lim, Frank Aquilino, Maree Catalano, Paula Raflo, Rockets Redglare

Top: Griffin Dunne
Top Right: Linda Fiorentino, Griffin Dunne
Below: Griffin Dunne, Rosanna Arquette
© *Warner Bros.*

Griffin Dunne, Teri Garr

MAXIE

(ORION) formerly "Free Spirit"; Producer, Carter DeHaven; Director, Paul Aaron; Screenplay, Patricia Resnick; Based on "Marion's Wall" by Jack Finney; Photography, Fred Schuler; Editor, Lynzee Klingman; Music, Georges DeLerue: Designer, John Lloyd; Costumes, Ann Roth; Executive Producers, Rich Irvine, James L. Stewart; Production Manager, Tom Joyner; Assistant Directors, David Sosna, Robert Yannetti; Sound, David MacMillian; Choreography, Matthew Diamond; Visual Effects, Bill Taylor; In association with Elsboy Entertainment; DeLuxe Color; Dolby Stereo; 98 minutes; Rated PG; September release

CAST

Jan/Maxie	Glenn Close
Nick	Mandy Patinkin
Mrs. Lavin	Ruth Gordon
Bishop Campbell	Barnard Hughes
Miss Sheffer	Valerie Curtin
Father Jerome	Googy Gress
Cleopatra Director	Michael Ensign
Commercial Director	Michael Laskin
Art Isenberg	Lou Cutell
Bartender	Nelson Welch
E. T. Reporter	Leeza Gibbons
Ch. 4 Announcer	Evan White
Mr. Chu	Harry Wong
Policeman	Charles Douglas Laird
Asst. Director	David Sosna
Charity Patron	Hugo Stanger
Trainer	John O'Neill
Usher	Eddie Wong
Exercise Class Lady	Pauline Bluestone
Mr. San Francisco	Cyril Magnin
Reporter	Michael Jordan
Magazine Attendant	Alan Gin
Al the Dog	Nelson

and Glen Chin, Nancie Kawata, Conan Lee (Movie Patrons)

Right: Mandy Patinkin, Glenn Close
Top: Valerie Curtin, Mandy Patinkin, Glenn Close
Below: Ruth Gordon © *Orion*

KEROUAC

(DAYBREAK) formerly "Jack Kerouc's America;" Producer-Dir tor, John Antonelli; Screenplay, John Tytell, John Antonelli, Fr Cervarich; Photography, Jerry Jones; Co-Producer-Editor, Will I rinello; Sound, Gene Doherty; Songs by various artists; Execu Producer, Marilyn Smith; Documentary; 78 minutes; Not rated; S tember release

CAST

Narrator	Peter Coy
Jack Kerouac	Jack Cou
Dean Moriarty	David Andr
Morley	Jonah Pear
Japhy Ryder	John Rouss
Lucian Carr	Patrick Tur
Ship Mate	Michael Wa
Young Kerouac	Seth Golds
Father	Leon Bene

and Margaret Lafonton, Cindy Alwan, Jennifer Tofflemire, Patti ter, Diane Potter, Ron Wills, Kurt Deibel, Bob Smith, Adam W Richard Casselman, Michelle DeFors, Constance Johnson, Wen Walker

Jack Coulter © *Daybreak*

PLENTY

th CENTURY-FOX) Producers, Edward R. Pressman, Joseph
p; Director, Fred Schepisi; Screenplay, David Hare; Based on play
ame title by David Hare; Photography, Ian Baker; Music, Bruce
eaton; Editor, Peter Honess; Designer, Richard MacDonald; Cos-
es, Ruth Myers; Executive Producer, Mark Seiler; Associate Pro-
er, Roy Stevens; Assistant Directors, David Tringham, Michael
enson, Ken Shane; Sound, Peter Pennell, John Mitchell; Special
cts, Effects Associates, Ltd.; An RKO Pictures Presentation; Tech-
lor; Panavision Widescreen; Dolby Stereo; 124 minutes; Rated R;
tember release

CAST

an	Meryl Streep
on	Andre Maranne
ar	Sam Neill
mond Brock	Charles Dance
ncey	Tristram Jellinek
el Manager	Peter Forbes-Robertson
ctor	Hugo De Vernier
y—Dead	James Taylor
Leonard Darwin	John Gielgud
ce Park	Tracey Ullman
dlicott	Ian Wallace
dall	Andy De La Tour
chael	Hugh Laurie
ry	Mitch Davies
ncer	Christopher Fairbank
da	Lindsay Ingram
stair	Richard Hope
ck	Sting
z Group	Terry Lightfoot and his band
mmittee Chairman	Roddy Maude-Roxby
ley	Andrew Seear
ce Officer	Roger Rowland
Committee Man	John Kidd
count Tampan	James Snell
count Executive	Michael Johnson
ent	Bernard Brown
ent's Assistant	Rupert Vansittart
use Wife in advert	Beth Morris
Salesman	Geoffrey Larder
Charles Curry	Tim Seely
ung Diplomat	Jasper Jacob
ck's Maid	Karen Lewis
Aung	Burt Kwouk
ne. Aung	Pik Sen Lim
eign Office Asst	Nicholas Frankau
l at dinner party	Clare McIntyre
ian Servant	Ali Refaie
est	William Hoyland
lio Producer	Roger Ashton-Griffiths
Men	Jeffrey Wickham,
	Matthew Guinnes, John Rees
lio Interviewer	Alexander John
gley	Lyndon Brook
Andrew Charleson	Ian McKellen
ss Simpson	Joan Blackham
nch Farmer	John Serret

Top: Meryl Streep, Sam Neill
Below: Tracey Ullman, Meryl Streep, Charles Dance
Right: Sting, Meryl Streep
Above Right: Charles Dance, Meryl Streep, John Gielgud
© *20th Century-Fox*

AGNES OF GOD

(COLUMBIA) Producers, Patrick Palmer, Norman Jewison; Director, Norman Jewison; Screenplay, John Pielmeier from his play of same title; Photography, Sven Nykvist; Music, Georges Delerue; Designer, Ken Adam; Editor, Antony Gibbs; Costumes, Renee April; Art Director, Carol Spier; Associate Producers, Charles Milhaupt, Bonnie Palef-Woolf; Assistant Directors, John Board, Madeleine Henrie, David Bailey; In Metrocolor and Dolby Stereo; Rated PG13; 98 minutes; October release

CAST

Dr. Martha Livingston	Jane Fonda
Mother Ruth Miriam	Anne Bancroft
Sister Agnes	Meg Tilly
Dr. Livingston's Mother	Anne Pitoniak
Detective Langevin	Winston Rekert
Father Martineau	Gratien Gelinas
Justice Joseph Leveau	Guy Hoffman
Monsignor	Gabriel Arcand
Eve LeClaire	Francoise Faucher
Eugene Lyon	Jacques Tourangeau
Sister Marguerite	Janine Fluet
Sister Anne	Deborah Grover
Sister Susanna	Michele George
Sister Jeannine	Samantha Langevin
Sister David Marie	Jacqueline Blais
Sister Therese	Francoise Berd
Sister Elizabette	Mimi D'Estee
Sister Geraldine	Rita Tucket
Sister Madeline Marie	Lillian Graham
Sister Genevieve	Norma Dell'Agnese
Sister Luke	Muguette Moreau
Sister Mary Joseph	Janice Bryan
Sister Paul	Agnes Middleton
Housekeeper	France Arbour
Receptionist	Laurel Lyle
Librarian	Victor Desy
Young Prostitute	Charlotte Laurier
Paramedic	Gerry Huckstep
Newscaster	Marc Denis

Top: Meg Tilly, Jane Fonda
Right Center: Jane Fonda, Meg Tilly, Anne Bancroft
© *Columbia*

Anne Bancroft, Jane Fonda (also top)

CODE NAME: EMERALD

(GM/UA) Producer, Martin Starger; Director, Jonathan Sanger; Screenplay, Ronald Bass, based on his Novel "The Emerald Illusion"; Photography, Freddie Francis; Editor, Stewart Linder; Music, John Addison; Designer, Gerard Viard; Costumes, Jean Zay; Sound, Daniel Brisseau; Co-Producers, Jonathan Sanger, Howard Alston; Production Manager, Philippe Modave; Assistant Directors, Paolo Barzman, Marc Guy; Presented by NBC Productions; Metrocolor; Panavision; 93 minutes; Rated PG; October release

CAST

s Lang	Ed Harris
gen Brausch	Max von Sydow
lter Hoffman	Horst Buchholz
st Ritter	Helmut Berger
ire Jouvet	Cyrielle Claire
dy Wheeler	Eric Stoltz
onel Peters	Patrick Stewart
Geoffrey Macklin	Graham Crowden
or Seitz	George Mikell
ter Trager	Gabriel Barylli
ann	Peter Bonke
rick Callaghan	Tony Rohr
dre	Henri Lambert
lloughby	Ray Armstrong
mine	Julie Jezequel
ny Doctor	Oscar Quitak
rie Claude	Katia Tchenko
chelle	Didier Sandre
rty	Peter Whitman
	Ed Wiley
dame Farrel	Jenny Cleve
o Taxi Driver	Daniel Breton
cker	Vincent Grass
son Guards	Christophe Merian, Bruno Vieillard
ver	Stanislas Robiolles
autiful Girl	Valerie Vandeville
sign	Steve Foster
chel Jouvet	Alexandre Viros

Helmut Berger, Max von Sydow, Ed Harris, Horst Buchholz
Top Right: Ed Harris, Cyrielle Claire Below: Max von Sydow,
Eric Stoltz, Ed Harris © MGM/UA

COMMANDO

(20th CENTURY-FOX) Producer, Joel Silver; Director, Mark Lester; Screenplay, Steven E. de Souza; Story, Joseph Loeb III, Matt ew Weisman, Steven E. de Souza; Photography, Matthew F. Leone Designer, John Vallone; Editor, Mark Goldblatt, John F. Link, Gle Farr; Music, James Horner; Costumes, Bob Harris, Enid Harris; Ass ciate Producers, Joseph Loeb III, Matthew Weisman; Production Ma ager, Larry Kostroff; Assistant Directors, Beau E. L. Marks, K. Colwell, Brad Yacobian; Co-Associate Producers, Stephanie Broc Robert Kosberg; Special Effects, Henry Millar; Song, Andy Tayl Michael Des Barres; DeLuxe Color; Dolby Stereo; 88 minutes; Rated October release

CAST

Matrix	Arnold Schwarzenegg
Cindy	Rae Dawn Cho
Arius	Dan Heda
Bennett	Vernon We
General Kirby	James Ols
Sully	David Patrick Ke
Jenny	Alyssa Mila
Cooke	Bill Du
Lawson	Drew Sny
Leslie	Sharon Wy
Forrestal	Michael DeLa
Jackson	Bob Mir
Harris	Mike Ada
Diaz	Carlos Cervant
Soldier	Lenny Julia
Henriques	Charles Mesha
Flight Attendants	Chelsea Field, Julie Hay
Latin Man	Hank Ca
Cates	Walter Sc
Biggs	Gregory W. Ela
Security Guard	George Fish
Galleria Officer	Phil Ada
Girl in bed	Ava Cad
Boy in bed	Mikul Rob
Vega	Branscombe Richmo
Fred	Matt Lande
Daryl	Peter DuPe
Kirby's Driver	Tom Simm

and Bill Paxton, Richard Royce, John Reyes, Billy Cardenas, Edwa Reyes, Vivian Daily, Thomas Rosales, Jr., Ronald C. McCarty, J Painter

Left: David Patrick Kelly, Arnold Schwarzenegger, Vernon Wells, Dan Hedaya, Charles Meshack Top: Arnold Schwarzenegger, Alyssa Milano © *20th Century-Fox*

Arnold Schwarzenegger   Rae Dawn Chong

DEATH WISH 3

(CANNON) Producers, Menahem Golan, Yoram Globus; Co-producer-Director, Michael Winner; Screenplay, Michael Edmonds; Based on characters created by Brian Garfield; Music, Jimmy Page; Photography, John Stanier; Designer, Peter Mullins; Editor, Arnold Crust; Associate Producer, Michael Kagan; Assistant Director, Alan Hopkins; Art Director, David Minty; Costumes, Peggy Farrell; Rated R; In color and Dolby Stereo; 90 minutes; October release

CAST

Paul Kersey	Charles Bronson
Kathryn Davis	Deborah Raffin
Richard Striker	Ed Lauter
Bennett	Martin Balsam
Fraker	Gavan O'Herlihy
Giggler	Kirk Taylor
Hermosa	Alex Winter
Angel	Tony Spiridakis
Cuban	Ricco Ross
Tulio	Tony Britts
Hector	David Crean
Chaco	Nelson Fernandez
Punks at car	Alan Cooke, Bob Dysinger
Garcia	Topo Grajeda
Female Punk	Barbie Wilde
Lieutenant	Ron Hayes
Street Punk	Jerry Phillips
Rodriguez	Joseph Gonzalez
Charlie	Francis Drake
Eli Kaprov	Leo Kharibian
Mrs. Kaprov	Hana-Maria Pravda
Emil	John Gabriel
Mrs. Emil	Mildred Shay
Used Car Seller	Kenny Marino
Mugging Victim	Birdie M. Hale
Maria	Mirina Sirtis
Interns	Hayward Morse, Ronald Fernee
Rape Victim	Sandy Grizzle
Nurses	Dinah May, Steffanie Pitt
Fraker's Lawyer	Billy J. Mitchell
TV Newscaster	Lee Patterson
Protesting Lady	Olivia Ward
Lt. Sterns	Manning Redwood

Left: Ed Lauter, Charles Bronson
Top: Charles Bronson, Joseph Gonzalez
© *Cannon*

Martin Balsam

Gavan O'Herlihy

Peter Coyote, Glenn Close

JAGGED EDGE

(COLUMBIA) Producer, Martin Ransohoff; Director, Richard Mar
quand; Screenplay, Joe Eszterhas; Photography, Matthew F. Leonetti;
Designer, Gene Callahan; Editors, Sean Barton, Conrad Buff; Cos
tumes, Ann Roth; Music, John Barry; Assistant Directors, Michael
Daves, Alan B. Curtiss; Associate Producer, Michele Connors-Raley;
Art Director, Peter J. Smith; In Metrocolor and Dolby Stereo; Rated R;
108 minutes; October release

CAST

Page Forrester	Maria Mayenze
Thomas Krasny	Peter Coyote
Policemen	Dave Austin, Richard Partlow
Frank Martin	Lance Henriksen
Greg Arnold	William Allen Young
Dr. Goldman	Ben Hammer
Jack Forrester	Jeff Bridges
Andrew Hardesty	James Karen
Scott Talbot	Sanford Jensen
Austin Lofton	Woody Eney
Carl Siegal	Al Ruscio
Assistant D. A.	Sharon Haniar
First Judge	Sarah Cunningham
Teddy Barnes	Glenn Close
Ms. Barnes' Secretary	Ann Walker
Ted Fitzpatrick	James Winker
Richard Duffin	Bruce French
David Barnes	Brandon Call
Jenny Barnes	Christina Hutter
Butler	John Furlong
Stablehand	Karen Wonnell
City Editor	Sharon Madden
Virginia Howell	Leigh Taylor-Young
Matthew Barnes	Guy Boyd
Mrs. Stiles	Phyllis Applegate
Sam Ransom	Robert Loggia
Dan Hislan	Michael Dorn
Dr. Holloway	John Clark

and Louis Giambalvo (Fabrizi), John Dehner (Judge Carrigan), David
Wiley (Court Clerk), Jay Crimp (Ms. Barnes' Assistant), Mike Mitch
ell (Bailiff), Diane Erickson (Eileen), Marshall Colt (Bobby Slade),
Walter Brooke (Duane), Karen Austin (Julie Jensen), Bill Gratton (Jury
Foreman), Joyce Shank (TV Interviewer), Dean Webber (Newscaster),
John X. Heart, Brenda Huggins, Richard Marion, Edwina Moore, Sue
Rihr, Suzanne Lodge, Judith Siegfried, Sally Train, Abigail Van Alyn,
Terry Wills, Biff Yeager

Top Left: Jeff Bridges, Glenn Close
Below: Glenn Close, Robert Loggia, Jeff Bridges,
Jay Crimp Top Right: Robert Loggia, Glenn Close
© Columbia

THE JOURNEY OF NATTY GANN

(BUENA VISTA) Producer, Mike Lobell; Director, Jeremy Kagan; Screenplay, Jeanne Rosenberg; Photography, Dick Bush; Editor, David Holden; Designer, Paul Sylbert; Music, James Horner; Costumes, Albert Wolsky; Associate Producers, Jeanne Rosenberg, Les Kimber; Production Manager, Les Kimber; Assistant Directors, Michael Steele, Tom Rowe, Patrice Leung; A Lobell-Bergman Production; Produced in association with Silver Screen Partners II; Sound, Leslie Shatz; Special Effects, Dennis Dion; Technicolor; Dolby Stereo; 105 minutes; Rated PG; October release

CAST

Natty Gann	Meredith Salenger
Harry	John Cusack
Sol Gann	Ray Wise
Connie	Lainie Kazan
Sherman	Scatman Crothers
Parker	Barry Miller
Farm Woman	Verna Bloom
Charlie Linfield	Bruce M. Fischer
Logging Boss	John Finnegan
Employment Agent	Jack Rader
Buzz	Matthew Faison
Frankie	Jordon Pratt
Louis	Zachary Ansley

and Campbell Lane, Max Trumpower, Doug MacLeod, Gary Chalk, Dwight McFee, Peter Anderson, Corliss M. Smith, Jr., Hagan Beggs, Jan Black, Ray Michal, Clint Rowe, Frank C. Turner, Jack Ackroyd, Grant Heslov, Gary Riley, Scott Andersen, Ian Tracey, Jennifer Michas, Wally Marsh, Kaye Grieve, Hannah Cutrona, Gabrielle Rose, Marie Klingenberg, Stephen E. Miller, Robert Clothier, Don Davis, Alex Diakun, Tom Heaton, Harvey M. Miller, Sheelah Megill, Jeff Ramsey, Gary Hendrickson, Wally Beeton, Doug Boyd, Bryan Coure, Al MacIntosh, Lorne LaRiviere, Bob Storms, Paula-Marie Moody, John Hock

Right: Ray Wise, Meredith Salenger
Top: Meredith Salenger, John Cusack
© Buena Vista

Meredith Salenger, Ray Wise

Meredith Salenger, John Cusack

MARIE

(MGM/UA) Producer, Frank Capra, Jr.; Director, Roger Donaldso. Screenplay, John Briley; Based on book "Marie: A True Story" by Pete Maas; Executive Producer, Elliot Schick; Photography, Chris Menge Editor, Neil Travis; Art Director, Ron Foreman; Music, Francis La Costumes, Joe Tompkins; Assistant Director, Bob Howard; A Dino D Laurentiis Production in Technicolor, and J-D-C Widescreen; Rate PG13; 112 minutes; October release

CAST

Marie Ragghianti	Sissy Space
Eddie Sisk	Jeff Danie
Kevin McCormack	Keith Szarabajl
Charles Traughber	Morgan Freema
Fred Thompson	Himse
Toni Greer	Lisa Bane
FBI Agent	Trey Wilso
Deputy Attorney General	John Cullu
Governor Blanton	Don Hoo
Charlie Benson	Graham Beck
Murray Henderson	Macon McCalma
Virginia	Collin Wilcox Paxto
Dante Ragghianti	Robert Green Benson I
Therese Ragghianti	Dawn Carme
Ricky Ragghianti	Shane Wex
Dave Ragghianti	Vincent Irizar
Bill Thompson	Michael P. Mora
Jack Lowery	Clarence Feld
Sherry Lomax	Lisa Foste
Arnold Hurst	Charles Kahlenbe
Tommy Prater	Joe Su
Bernie Weinthal	R. Pickett Bug
Singer at rally	Jane Powe

and David Eddings, Tom Story (Detectives), George Gray, Mac Pirk (Doctors), Leon Rippy (Gary), Timothy Carhart (Clayton), Fia Port (Rape Victim), Phil Markert (Judge), Ivan Green (Foreman), Sara Hunley (Stenographer), Edward Carr (George), Ruby L. Wilson (Ros Stephen Henderson (Cooper's Husband), Lorenzo Allen (Prisoner), I Herb Harton (Polygraph Operator), John-Michael Maas (Chris), Ala Sader (Professor), J. Michael Hunter (Bartender), Carla Cantrel (Marilyn), Jeff Marcum, James Fields, Billy McIntyre, Jerry Rushing Larry Brinton, Drue Smith, Dwight Lewis, Chip Arnold

Left: Sissy Spacek, Jeff Daniels
Top: Lisa Banes, Sissy Spacek, Collin Wilcox-Paxton
© MGM/UA

Dawn Carmen, Sissy Spacek, Don Hood

John Cullum, Fred Thompson

REMO WILLIAMS:
THE ADVENTURE BEGINS . . .

ORION) Producer, Larry Spiegel; Director, Guy Hamilton; Screenplay, Christopher Wood; Based on "The Destroyer" series by Richard Sapir, Warren Murphy; Photography, Andrew Laszlo; Designer, Jackson De Govia; Editor, Mark Melnick; Music, Craig Safan; Co-producer, Judy Goldstein; Executive Producers, Dick Clark, Mel Bergman; Consultant, Stanley J. Corwin; Production Manager, John H. Clarke; Assistant Directors, Alex Hapsas, Richard L. Espinoza, Joseph Ray; Sound, James J. Sabat; Costumes, Ellen Mirojnick; Special Effects, Andy Evans; Songs by various artists; DeLuxe Color; Dolby Stereo; Rated PG-13; October release

CAST

Remo Williams	Fred Ward
Chium	Joel Grey
Harold Smith	Wilford Brimley
Conn MacCleary	J. A. Preston
General Scott Watson	George Coe
George Grove	Charles Cioffi
Major Rayner Fleming	Kate Mulgrew
Stone	Patrick Kilpatrick
Jim Wilson	Michael Pataki
Private Damico	Cosie Costa

and Davenia McFadden, J. P. Romano, Joel J. Kramer, Frank Ferrara, Marv Albert, Ray Woodfork, Phil Neilson, Webster Whinery, Frank Simpson, Dodi Kenan, Reginald Veljohnson, Jon Polito, Gene LeBell, Michael M. Ryan, Jeff Allin, Will Jeffries, Sebastian Ligarde, Roger Dudney, Duane B. Clark, John Christianson, Phil Culotta, Tom McBride, Andrew MacMillan, Wendy Gazelle, Suzy Snyder, William Buckey

**Top: Fred Ward, Joel Grey, Kate Mulgrew
Below: Grey, Ward Top Right: Wilford Brimley,
Fred Ward, J. A. Preston Below: Ward, Grey
© Orion**

Fred Ward

SWEET DREAMS

(TRI-STAR) Producer, Bernard Schwartz; Director, Karel Reisz; Screenplay, Robert Getchell; Co-producer, Charles Mulvehill; Photography, Robbie Greenberg; Designer, Albert Brenner; Editor, Malcolm Cooke; Costumes, Ann Roth; Music, Charles Gross; Songs by Patsy Cline from original recordings; Assistant Director, Patrick Crowley; Choreographer, Susan Scanlan; Art Director, David M. Haber; Soundtrack album on MCA Records; in Technicolor and Dolby Stereo; Rated PG13; 115 minutes; October release

CAST

Patsy Cline	Jessica Lange
Charlie Dick	Ed Harris
Hilda Hensley	Ann Wedgeworth
Randy Hughes	David Clennon
Gerald Cline	James Staley
Woodhouse	Gary Basaraba
Otis	John Goodman
Wanda	P. J. Soles
Girl Singer	Terri Gardner
Sylvia Hensley	Caitlin Kelch
John Hensley	Robert L. Dasch
Older Julie	Courtney Parker
Baby Randy	Colton Edwards
Madrine	Holly Filler
Arthur Godfrey	Bruce Kirby
Owen Bradley	Jerry Haynes
Big Bill Shawley	Kenneth White
Announcer at Opry	Stonewall Jackson
Biker	Jake T. Robinson
Old Man in jail	Boxcar Willie
Bartender	Tony Frank
Cowboy Copas	Charlie Walker
Hawkshaw Hawkins	Frank Knapp, Sr.
TV Technician	Richard J. Kidney
Recording Engineer	Jack Slater
Sergeant	Carlton Cuse
Skip Cartmill	John E. Davis
Stone	John Walter Davis
Baby Nurse	Toni Sawyer
Plastic Surgeon	Robert Rothwell
Surgery Nurse	Patricia Allison
Girls at fair	Missy Proulx, Aleda Pope

**Right: Ed Harris, Jessica Lange,
David Clennon Top: Jessica Lange
© Tri-Star**

Ann Wedgeworth, Jessica Lange

Jessica Lange, Ed Harris

THIEF OF HEARTS

(PARAMOUNT) Producers, Don Simpson, Jerry Bruckheimer; Director-Screenplay, Douglas Day Stewart; Photography, Andrew Laszlo; Designer, Edward Richardson; Editor, Tom Rolf; Music, Harold Faltermeyer; Costumes, Michael Kaplan; Associate Producer, Tom Jacobson; Production Managers, Tom Jacobson, Michael Grillo; Assistant Directors, Michael Grillo, Stephen P. Dunn; Sound, Keith A. Wester, Crew Chamberlain; Special Effects, Michael Lantieri; Metrocolor; Panavision; Dolby Stereo; 100 minutes; Rated R; October release

CAST

Scott Muller	Steven Bauer
Mickey Davis	Barbara Williams
Ray Davis	John Getz
Buddy Calamara	David Caruso
Janie Pointer	Christine Ebersole
Marty Morrison	George Wendt
Sweeny	Alan North
Nicole	Romy Windsor
Security Guard	Joe Nesnow
Parking Attendant	Gordon Pulliam
Scott	Vince Deadrick, Jr.
College Girls	Annette Sinclair, Aleana Downs
Ad-Libbers	Jane Marla Robbins, Ray Hassett, Marsha Wolfe, Brenda Currin

Right: Barbara Williams, Steven Bauer
© *Paramount*

**John Getz, Barbara Williams, Steven Bauer
Above: Steven Bauer, David Caruso**

**Barbara Williams, Christine Ebersole
Above: John Getz, George Wendt**

UFORIA

(UNIVERSAL) Producer, Gordon Wolf; Director-Screenplay, John Binder; Photography, David Myers; Designer, William Malley; Editor, Dennis M. Hill; Music, Richard Baskin; Co-Producer, Susan Spinks; Executive Producers, Melvin Simon, Barry Krost; Production Manager, Joseph M. Ellis; Assistant Directors, Anthony Brand, Irwin Marcus; Associate Producer, Jeanne Field; Sound, Kirk Francis; Costumes, Betsy Heimann, Thomas Ed Sunly; Songs by various artists; Deluxe Color; Panavision; 100 minutes; Rated PG; October release

CAST

Arlene	Cindy Williams
Brother Bud	Harry Dean Stanton
Sheldon	Fred Ward
Naomi	Beverly Hope Atkinson
George Martin	Harry Carey, Jr.
Delores	Diane Diefendorf
Emile	Robert Gray
Gregory	Ted Harris
Toby	Darrell Larson
Celia Martin	Peggy McKay
Colonel	Hank Worden
Brother Roy	Alan Beckwith

and Andrew Winner, Pamela Lamont, Herman Lee Montgomery, Joe Unger, Constance Pfeifer, Stephanie Kohl, Esther Sutherland, Morgan Ames, Erik Stern, James Deeth, Terry Brannon, Wayne Kruse, Russell L. Matheny, Robert A. Weisler, Jennifer Robb, Ashley Robb, Charlotte Stewart, Marji Martin, Pamela Mathews, Angela Newell, James Hartley, Rolaine Knight, Kirk Francis, Julie Wakefield, William Callaway, Torben Torp-Smith, Karen Stern, Jordon Hahn, Kedric Wolfe, Claudia Sloan, Dennis L. McArthur, Nick Edwards, Sharon Rae Oberg, Rodney W. Bergen, McAdoo Greer, Sally Russell, Gene Edwards, Tony Santoro, Cris E. Reese, Dwayne Smith, Terry Wilson, Frank De La Rosa, Phil Lee, Gary Rowles, Snuff Walden, Tony Braunagle, Oma Drake, Monalisa Young, Terry Young, Mindy Sterling, Herman Lee Montgomery

Right: Fred Ward, Cindy Williams
Top: Cindy Williams
© *Universal*

Fred Ward, Cindy Williams, Harry Dean Stanton

THE GIG

Producer, I. Cohen; Director-Screenplay, Frank D. Gilroy; Photography, Jeri Sopanen; Editor, Rick Shaine; Music, Warren Vache; Sound, Eric Taylor, Hal Levinsohn; Assistant Director, Ken Ornstein; Associate Producer, Scott Hancock; Costumes, Linda Benedict; Songs by various artists; Presented by McLaughlin, Piven, Vogel, Inc.; Color; 92 minutes; Not rated; November release

CAST

Marty Flynn	Wayne Rogers
Marshall Wilson	Cleavon Little
Jack Larmon	Andrew Duncan
Aaron Wohl	Jerry Matz
Arthur Winslow	Daniel Nalbach
Gil Macrae	Warren Vache
Abe Mitgang	Joe Silver
Rick Valentine	Jay Thomas
George Pappas	Stan Lachow
Lucy	Celia Bressack
The Blonde	Georgia Harrell
Vincent Amati	Michael Fischetti
Laura Macrae	Susan Egbert
Janet Larmon	Karen Ashley
Mrs. Winslow	Virginia Downing
The Driver	Chuck Wepner
Miss Gersh	Annie Korzen
Joanne Larmon	Lisa Biesele
Billy Larmon	Victor Murdock
Sylvia	Nancy Parker
Assistant	Mark Polycan
Director	Joel Rooks
Mr. Oglivie	Edward Stevlingson
Mitgang's Grandson	Patrick Beesmer
Taxi Driver	Ramon J. Dunn
Clarinet Student	Todd Myer
Bartender	John Pekovich
Arthur's Patient	Miriam Smith

Right: Cleavon Little, Daniel Halbach, Warren Vache, Andrew Duncan, Jerry Matz, Wayne Rogers **Top:** Daniel Nalbach, Andy Duncan, Warren Vache

Cleavon Little

Wayne Rogers

ELENI

(WARNER BROS.) Producers, Nick Vanoff, Mark Pick, Nichola
Gage; Director, Peter Yates; Screenplay, Steve Tesich; From the boc
"Eleni" by Nicholas Gage; Photography, Billy Williams; Designe
Roy Walker; Costumes, Tom Rand; Editor, Ray Lovejoy; Music
Bruce Smeaton; Associate Producer, Nigel Wooll; Sound, Ivan Sha
rock; Special Effects, Kit West, Jeffrey Clifford; Assistant Directors
Chris Newman, Derek Cracknell; Marcia Gay; Presented by CB
Productions; Color; 117 minutes; Rated PG; November release

CAST

Eleni	Kate Nelliga
Nick	John Malkovic
Katina	Linda Hui
Katis	Oliver Cotto
Spiro	Ronald Picku
Grandmother	Rosalie Crutchle
Joan	Glenne Head
Ana (Czechoslovakia)	Dimitra Arli
Christos	Steve Plyt
Grandfather	Peter Woodthor
Lukas	Jon Rumne
Lukas' Wife	Alison Kir
Antoni	Leon Lisse
Tasso	Stefan Gry
Nikola	Andrea Laska
Olga	Lisa Ro
Fotini	Claudia Goug
Alexandra	Maria Calver
Glykeria	Anhoula Vra
Katina's Son	Noam Alm
New York Secretary	Arlene Mazero
Sidney Cohn	Michael Zelnik
Nick's Son	Keram Malicki-Sanch
Nick's Daughter	Adrienne Poco
Minister of Justice	Anthony Stamboulie
Ana (Greece)	Christana Frage

and Michael Chesden, Niguel Pedregosa, Vic Tablian, John Easthar
Georgia Clarke, Avril Clark, Athena Voyatzis, Aaron Schwartz, Pat
cia Carroll Brown, Theresa Tora, Lisa Jakub

**Left: Linda Hunt, Kate Nelligan, Maria
Calvente, Lisa Rose Top: Lisa Rose, Maria Calvente,
Kate Nelligan, Andreas Laskaris, Claudia Gough**
© *Warner Bros.*

John Malkovich   **Kate Nelligan**

Ronald Pickup, Kate Nelligan, Oliver Cotton Top Left: John Malkovich
Below: Oliver Cotton, John Malkovich Top Right: Kate Nelligan

ROCKY IV

(MGM/UA) Producers, Irwin Winkler, Robert Chartoff; Direct[or], Screenplay, Sylvester Stallone; Photography, Bill Butler; Design[er], Bill Kenney; Editors, Don Zimmerman, John W. Wheeler; Costum[e], Tom Bronson; Music, Vince DiCola, Bill Conti; Executive Produc[er], James D. Brubaker, Arthur Chobanian; Production Manager, Jo [A], May-Pavey; Assistant Directors, Duncan Henderson, Chris Ry[], Sound, Chuck Wilborn; Special Effects, Howard Jensen; Choreog[ra]phy, Michael McKensie Pratt; Songs by various artists; Presented [by] United Artists; Metrocolor; Panavision; 91 minutes; Rated PG; Nove[m]ber release

CAST

Rocky Balboa	Sylvester Stall[one]
Adrian	Talia Sh[ire]
Paulie	Burt Yo[ung]
Apollo Creed	Carl Weath[ers]
Ludmilla	Brigitte Niel[sen]
Duke	Tony Bu[rton]
Nicoli Koloff	Michael Pa[taki]
Drago	Dolph Lundg[ren]
Sports Announcer	R. J. Ad[ams]
American Commentator #2	Al Band[y]
Russian Government Official	Dominic Ba[]
Rocky Jr.'s Friend	Daniel Bro[]
The Godfather of Soul	James Bro[wn]
Maid	Rose Mary Cam[]
KGB Driver	Jack Carpe[r]
Russian Cornerman	Mark Delessan[]
Russian Referee	Marty Den[]
Las Vegas Referee	Lou Fili[]
Manual Vega	James "Cannonball" Gr[]
Interviewer	Dean Hamm[]
Rocky Jr.	Rocky Kra[]
Russian Ring Announcer	Sergei Le[]
KGB Agent	Anthony Maffat[]
Mrs. Creed	Sylvia M[]
Limo Driver	Dwayne Mc[]
Commentator #1	Stu Na[]
Ring Announcer	LeRoy Nein[]
Caretaker	George Pip[]
Igor Rimsky	George Ro[]
American Commentator #1	Barry Tompl[]
Commentator #2 in Las Vegas	Warner W[]
Sico The Robot (Voice)	Robert Doorn[]

and Richard Blum, Gerald Berns, Ray Glanzmann, Julie Inouye, [] rick Pankhurst, Jean Thoreau, Jim Bullock, Frank D'Annibale, R[] Dursy, Rick Kelley, Craig Schaefer, Jeff Austin, Leslie Morris, [] Giovane, Julio Herzer, George Spaventa, Rolf Williams, Jim Ho[] (Reporters)

Left: Sylvester Stallone
© MGM/UA

Sylvester Stallone, Talia Shire

Burt Young, Tony Burton, Sylvester Stallone

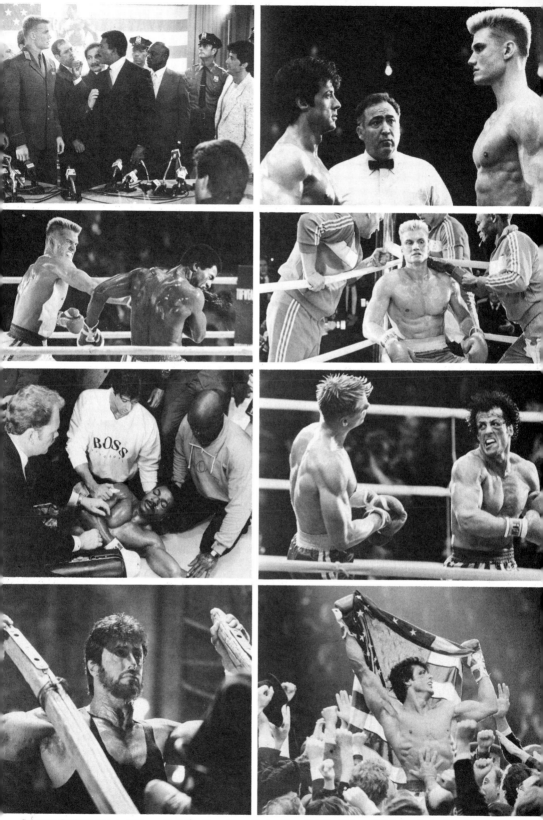

Sylvester Stallone Above: Stallone, Carl Weathers, Tony Burton Top: Brigitte Nielsen, Dolph Lundgren, Weathers, Burton, Stallone Below: Lundgren, Weathers Top Right: Stallone, Marty Denkin, Lundgren Below: Lundgren Bottom Right: Stallone Above: Lundgren, Stallone

KING SOLOMON'S MINES

(CANNON GROUP, INC.) Producers, Menahem Golan, Yoram Globus; Director, J. Lee Thompson; Screenplay, Gene Quintano, James R. Silke; Based on the novel by H. Rider Haggard; Music, Jerry Goldsmith; Photography, Alex Phillips; Designer, Luciano Spadoni; Editor, John Shirley; Associate Producer, Rony Yacov; Assistant Directors, Miguel Gil, Wynton Tavill, Neal Sundstrom, Steve Ghigorimbo; Sound, Eli Yarkoni; Costumes, Tony Pueo; Production Manager, Joe Pollini; Color; J-D-C Widescreen; 100 minutes; Rated PG-13; November release

CAST

Quatermain	Richard Chamberlain
Jessie	Sharon Stone
Colonel Bockner	Herbert Lom
Dogati	John Rys-Davies
Umbopo	Ken Gampu
Gagoola	June Buthelezi
Scragga	Sam Williams
Kassam	Shai K. Ophir
Mapaki Chief	Fidelis Che A
Dorfman	Mick Lesley
Shack	Vincent Van Der Byl
Hamid	Bob Greer
Bushiri	Oliver Tengende
German Pilot	Neville Thomas
Dari	Bishop McThuzen
Rug Carrier	Isiah Murert

and Rocky Green, Calvin Johns, Isaac Mabhikwa, Innocent Choga, Brian Kagure, Stanley Norris (Silent Ones), Anna Ditano (Dogati Girl), Andrew Whaley (German)

Right: Richard Chamberlain
Top: John Rhys-Davies, Sharon Stone
© Cannon Group

Herbert Lom
Above: Richard Chamberlain, Sharon Stone

Sharon Stone, Richard Chamberlain
Above: Richard Chamberlain, Sharon Stone

SMOOTH TALK

(SPECTRAFILM) Producer, Martin Rosen; Director, Joyce Chopra; Screenplay, Tom Cole; Based on Story by Joyce Carol Oates; Music Director, James Taylor; Music, Bill Payne, Russell Kunkel, George Massenburg; Photography, James Glennon; Editor, Patrick Dodd; Designer, David Wasco; Costumes, Carol Oditz; Associate Producer, Timothy Marx; Executive Producer, Lindsay Law; Production Manager, Mary Ensign; Assistant Directors, Timothy Marx, Gail Mezey Morris; Songs by various artists; A Goldcrest Presentation; A Nepenthe/American Playhouse Production; Color; 92 minutes; Rated PG-13; November release

CAST

Arnold Friend	Treat Williams
Connie	Laura Dern
Catherine	Mary Kay Place
June	Elizabeth Berridge
Harry	Levon Helm
Jill	Sarah Inglis
Laura	Margaret Welch
Ellie	Geoff Hoyle
Jeff	William Ragsdale
Eddie	David Berridge
Pick-Up Driver	Cab Covay
Dan	Michael French
Laura's Mother	Joy Carlin
Bobby King	Mark McKay
Tall Boys	Carl Mueller, David O'Neill, Craig Caddell
Tall Creeps	Darian Alioto, Gary Harris
Saleslady	Sally Schuab
Laura's Dad	William Desmond
Leroy	Michael Vaughn
Beach Boys	Rob Blair, Edgar Kahn
Eddie's Friend	Spenser Mains

Right: David Berridge, Laura Dern
Top: Laura Dern, Margaret Welch
© *Spectrafilm*

Laura Dern, Treat Williams

Treat Williams, Laura Dern

TARGET

(WARNER BROS.) Producers, Richard D. Zanuck, David Brown; Director, Arthur Penn; Screenplay, Howard Berk, Don Peterson; Story, Leonard Stern; Photography, Jean Tournier; Designer, Willy Holt; Editors, Stephen A. Rotter, Richard P. Cirincione; Music, Michael Small; Production Managers, Bernard Farrel, William Watkins; Assistant Directors, Alain Tasma, Vincent Macheras; Costumes, Marie-Francoise Perochon; Sound, Bernard Bats; Special Effects, Rene Albouze; Songs by various artists; Technicolor; Panavision; 117 minutes; Rated R; November release

CAST

Walter Lloyd	Gene Hackman
Chris Lloyd	Matt Dillon
Donna Lloyd	Gayle Hunnicutt
Lise	Victoria Fyodorova
Carla	Ilona Grubel
Schroeder	Herbert Berghof
Taber	Josef Sommer
Clay	Guy Boyd
The Colonel	Richard Munch
Mason	Ray Fry
Glasses	Jean-Pol Dubois
Young Agent	Werner Pochath
Older Agent	Ulrich Haupt
Ross	James Selby
Howard	Ric Krause
Black Man	Robert Liensol
Proprietress	Jany Holt
Nurse	Catherine Rethi
Squat Man Henke	Tomas Hnevsa
Switchboard Operator	Charlotte Bailey
Secretary	Veronique Guillaud
Madison Hotel Clerk	Jacques Mignot
Forklift Operator	Brad Williams
Tour Director	Randy Moore
Ballard	Jean-Pierre Stewart

Right: Matt Dillon, Gene Hackman Above: Ilona Grubel, Dillon Top: Dillon, Hackman, Ray Fry
© *CBS*

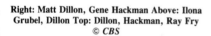

Gene Hackman, Matt Dillon

Matt Dillon, Gayle Hunnicutt, Gene Hackman

WHITE NIGHTS

OLUMBIA) Producers, Taylor Hackford, William S. Gilmore; rector, Taylor Hackford; Screenplay, James Goldman, Eric Hughes; ry, James Goldman; Photography, David Watkin; Designer, Philip rrison; Editors, Fredric Steinkamp, William Steinkamp; Choreogra- y, Twyla Tharp; Music Supervisor, Phil Ramone; Music, Michel lombier; Songs by various artists; Additional Choreography, Roland it, Gregory Hines, Mikhail Baryshnikov; Costumes, Evangeline rrison; Associate Producer, Bill Borden; In Charge of Production, nis Holt; Production Manager, Neville C. Thompson; Assistant rectors, Ray Corbett, Kieron Phipps, Anthony Aherne; Sound, Clive nter; Special Effects, Martin Gutteridge, Ian Wingrove, Garth Inns; :trocolor; Dolby Stereo; 135 minutes; Rated PG-13; November re- se

CAST

kolai "Kolya" Rodchenko	Mikhail Baryshnikov
ymond Greenwood	Gregory Hines
lonel Chaiko	Jerzy Skolimowski
lina Ivanova	Helen Mirren
ne Wyatt	Geraldine Page
rya Greenwood	Isabella Rossellini
ynn Scott	John Glover
ptain Kirigin	Stefan Gryff
uck Malarek	William Hootkins
nbassador Smith	Shane Rimmer
llerina	Florence Faure
ot	David Savile
-Pilot	Ian Liston
ght Engineer	Benny Young
wardesses	Hilary Drake, Megumi Shimanuki
. Asher	Daniel Benzali
ild Ballerina	Maria Werlander
ornik	Galina Pomerantzeva
jB	Sergei Rousakov, Alexander Naumov
ench Girlfriend	Maryam D'Abo
arles	Marc Sinden
roline	Josephine Buchan
ss	Helene Denbey
urnalists	Susannah Morley, Elisa Tornqvist
aiko's Driver	Jiri Stanislav
jB Agents	Edward Ochagavia, Marc Michalsky
licopter Pilot	Michael Petrovich
camilla	Andreas Markos

985 Academy Award for Best Original Song ("Say You, Say Me")

Right: Geraldine Page
Top: Mikhail Baryshnikov, Gregory Hines
© Columbia Pictures

Mikhail Baryshnikov, Helen Mirren

Gregory Hines, Isabella Rossellini

ONE MAGIC CHRISTMAS

(BUENA VISTA) Producer, Peter O'Brian; Director, Phillip Borsos; Screenplay, Thomas Meehan; Story, Thomas Meehan, Phillip Borsos, Barry Healey; Executive Producer, Phillip Borsos; Associate Producer, Michael MacDonald; Photography, Frank Tidy; Design, Bill Brodie; Editor, Sidney Wolinsky; Music, Michael Conway Baker; Assistant Director, Tony Lucibello; Art Director, Tony Hall; Costumes, Olga Dimitrov; In Dolby Stereo and DeLuxe Color; A Walt Disney Production; Rated G; 100 minutes; November release

CAST

Ginny Grainger	Mary Steenburgen
Jack Grainger	Gary Basaraba
Gideon	Harry Dean Stanton
Caleb Grainger	Arthur Hill
Abbie Grainger	Elizabeth Harnois
Cal Grainger	Robbie Magwood
Betty	Michelle Meyrink
Eddie	Elias Koteas
Harry Dickens	Wayne Robson
Santa Claus	Jan Rubes
Molly Monaghan	Sarah Polley
Frank Crump	Graham Jarvis
Herbie Conklin	Timothy Webber
Mrs. Monaghan	Joy Thompson-Allen
Mr. Noonan	John Friesen
Mrs. Noonan	Debra McGrath
Noonan Children	Julie Beaulieu, Jeremy Dingle
Bank Teller	Jane Schoettle
Bank Manager	Damir Andrei
Gil in bank	Amah Harris
Mrs. Claus	Rita Tuckett
Garage Mechanic	Sam Malkin

and Garreth Bennett, John E. Johnson, Alf Humphreys, Gary Bush, Robin McCulloch, Robert King, Rodger Barton, Genevieve Appleton

Top Right: Arthur Hill, Mary Steenburgen, Robbie Magwood, Elizabeth Harnois, Gary Basaraba Below: Harry Dean Stanton, Elizabeth Harnois © *Walt Disney Productions*

Robbie Magwood, Elizabeth Harnois
Above: Elizabeth Harnois

Elizabeth Harnois, Arthur Hill, Robbie Magwood

BRAZIL

(UNIVERSAL) Producer, Arnon Milchan; Director, Terry Gilliam; Screenplay, Terry Gilliam, Tom Stoppard, Charles McKeown; Photography, Roger Pratt; Editor, Julian Doyle; Music, Michael Kamen; Designer, Norman Garwood; Special Effects, George Gibbs; Model Effects, Richard Conway; Costumes, James Acheson, Ray Scott; Co-Producer, Patrick Cassavetti; Production Manager, Graham Ford; Assistant Director, Guy Travers; Sound, Bob Doyle; Songs by various artists; Technicolor; Dolby Stereo; 131 minutes; Not rated; December release

CAST

Sam Lowry	Jonathan Pryce
Tuttle	Robert De Niro
Ida Lowry	Katherine Helmond
Kurtzmann	Ian Holm
Spoor	Bob Hoskins
Jack Lint	Michael Palin
Warren	Ian Richardson
Helpmann	Peter Vaughan
Jill Layton	Kim Greist
Dr. Jaffe	Jim Broadbent
Mrs. Terrain	Barbara Hicks
Lime	Charles McKeown
Dowser	Derrick O'Connor
Shirley	Kathryn Pogson
Spiro	Bryan Pringle
Mrs. Buttle	Sheila Reid
TV Interviewer/Salesman	John Flanagan
Technician	Ray Cooper
Mr. Buttle	Brian Miller
Boy Buttle	Simon Nash
Girl Buttle	Prudence Oliver
Arrest Official	Simon Jones
Bill-Dept. of Works	Derek Deadman
Charlie-Dept. of Works	Nigel Planer
M.O.I. Lobby Porter	Gordon Kaye
Neighbor	Tony Portacio
Samurai Warrior	Winston Dennis
Telegram Girl	Diana Martin
Dr. Chapman	Jack Purvis
Alison/Barbara Lint	Elizabeth Spender
Porter-Information Retrieval	Antony Brown
Typist	Myrtle Devenish
Holly	Holly Gilliam
Basement Guard	John Pierce Jones
Old Lady with dog	Ann Way
Burning Trooper	Terry Forrestal
Black Maria Guards	Don Henderson, Howard Lew Lewis
Interview Official	Oscar Quitak
Cell Guard	Patrick Connor
Priest	Roger Ashton-Griffiths

**Right: Kim Greist Above: Michael Palin,
Jonathan Pryce Top: Katherine Helmond,
Jonathan Pryce** © *Universal*

Robert De Niro

Jonathan Pryce

A CHORUS LINE

(COLUMBIA) Producers, Cy Feuer, Ernest Martin; Director, Richard
Attenborough; Screenplay, Arnold Schulman; Music, Marvin Hamlisch; Lyrics, Edward Kleban; Arranger-Conductor, Ralph Burns; Costumes, Faye Poliakin; Designer, Patrizia Von Brandenstein; Editor,
John Bloom; Photography, Ronnie Taylor; Choreography, Jeffrey Hornaday; Based on the stage play "A Chorus Line," Conceived, Choreog-
raphed and Directed by Michael Bennett; Book, James Kirkwood,
Nicholas Dante; Executive Producer, Gordon Stulberg; Associate Pro-
ducer-Production Manager, Joseph M. Caracciolo; Assistant Directors,
Robert Girolami, Louis D'Esposito; Sound, Chris Newman; Dance
Music, Joseph Joubert, Robert E. Wooten, Jr.; Assistant Choreogra-
phers, Brad Jeffries, Gregg Burge, Helene Phillips, Vicki Regan, Troy
Garza; Presented by Embassy Film Associates/Polygram Pictures;
Technicolor; Panavision; Widescreen; Dolby Stereo; 113 minutes;
Rated PG-13; December release

CAST

Zach	Michael Douglas
Cassie	Alyson Reed
Sheila	Vicki Frederick
Paul	Cameron English
Morales	Yamil Borges
Richie	Gregg Burge
Val	Audrey Landers
Maggie	Pam Klinger
Don	Blane Savage
Mark	Michael Blevins
Connie	Jan Gan Boyd
Tricia	Sharon Brown
Judy	Janet Jones
Bebe	Michelle Johnston
Larry	Terrence Mann
Al	Tony Fields
Kristine	Nicole Fosse
Mike	Charles McGowan
Greg	Justin Ross
Bobby	Matt West
Robbie	Pat McNamara
Doorman	Sammy Smith
Boy with headband	Timothy Scott
Girl in yellow trunks	Bambi Jordan
Cab Driver	Mansoor Najee-Ullah
Dancer with gum	Peter Fitzgerald
Advertising Exec	John Hammil
Posterman	Jack Lehner
Taxi Passenger	Gloria Lynch
Misfit Boy Dancer	Gregg Huffman

and Richard DeFabees, Melissa Randel, Jeffrey Cornell, Karen Prunc-
zik, Jennifer Kent (Reject Dancers), Dancers: Eric Aaron, Khandi
Alexander, Annemaire, David Askler, Michele Assaf, Bryant Bald-
win, Buddy Balou, Carol Baxter, Tina Bellis, Robin Brown, Id
Broughton, Anna Bruno, Brian Bullard, Cheryl Burr, Bill Bushnell,
Roxann Cabalero, Sergio Cal, Joe Anthony Cavise, Linda Cholodenko,
Cheryl Clark, Christine Colby, Alexander Cole, Anne Connors, Lesli
Cook, Alice Cox, Frank Cruz, Amy Danis, Kim Darwin, Gary-Michael
Davies, John DeLuca, Anita Ehrler, Rickee Farrell, Denise Faye,
Penny Fekany, Felix, Angel Ferreira, Scott Fless, Ed Forsyth, William
Gabriner, David Gibson, Sandra Gray, Darrell Greene, Michael Scott
Gregory, Tonda Hannum, Niki Harris, Laura Johnson, D. Michael
Heath, Sonya Hensley, Dawn Herbert, Linda Hess, Regina Hood,
Craig Innes, Cindy Lauren Jackson, Reed Jones, Bob Kellet, Barbara
Kovac, Stanley Kramer, Andrew Kraus, Wayde Laboissoniere,
Michael Lafferty, Brett Larson, Barbara LaVorato, Rodney Alan
MaGuire, Mia Malm, Monique Mannen, Celia Marta, Frank Mastrocco-
la, Liz McLellan, Nancy Melius, Gwendolyn Miller, Brad Miskel,
Gregory Mitchell, Debi A. Monahan, Edd Morgan, Bob Morrisy,
Charles Murray, Ron Navarre, Arleen Ng, Reggie O'Gwyn, Alan
Onickel, Lorena Palacios, Peggy Parten, Keri Lee Pearsall, Helen
Phillips, Lacy Phillips, Richard Pierlon, Scott Plank, Rhett Pyle, Bub-
ba Dean Rambo, Vicki Regan, Daryl Richardson, Tia Riebling,
Michael Rivera, Debbie Roche, Leora Ron, Adrian Rosario, Elissa
Rosati, Patricia Ruck, Michelle Rudy, Mark Ruhala, George Russell,
Lynne Savage, Ann Louise Schaut, Jeanna Schweppe, Kimry Smith,
Jodi Sperduto, Ty Stephens, Leslie Stevens, Mary Ellen Stuart, Wil-
liam Sutton, Scott Taylor, Kirby Tepper, Christopher Todd, Evelyn
Tosi, David Vernon, Linda Von Germer, Bobby Walker, James Wal-
ki, Robert Warners, Marsha Watkins, Faruma Williams, Melanie Win-
ter, Scott Wise, Lily Lee Wong, Leslie Woodies, Barbara Yeager

Top Left: Alyson Reed, Michael Douglas
Below: Auditions © *Embassy Films*

Michelle Johnston

Matt West, Vicki Frederick
Above: Nicole Fosse (L), Michael Blevins
Top: Gregg Burge

Audrey Landers Above: Yamil Borges,
Charles McGowan Top: Alyson Reed,
Terrence Mann © Embassy

THE COLOR PURPLE

(WARNER BROS.) Producers, Steven Spielberg, Kathleen Kennedy, Frank Marshall, Quincy Jones; Director, Steven Spielberg; Screenplay, Menno Meyjes; Based on the novel by Alice Walker; Photography, Allen Daviau; Designer, J. Michael Riva; Editor, Michael Kahn; Music, Quincy Jones; Costumes, Aggie Guerard Rodgers; Executive Producers, Jon Peters, Peter Guber; Production Manager, Gerald R. Molen; Assistant Directors, Pat Kehoe, Richard Alexander Wells, Victoria Elizabeth Rhodes; Sound, Willie Burton; Special Effects, Matt Sweeney; Choreographer, Claude Thompson; Songs by various artists; An Amblin Entertainment Presentation; DeLuxe Color; Panavision, 155 minutes; Rated PG-13; December release

CAST

Albert	Danny Glover
Celie	Whoopi Goldberg
Shug Avery	Margaret Avery
Sofia	Oprah Winfrey
Harpo	Willard Pugh
Nettie	Akosua Busia
Young Celie	Desreta Jackson
Old Mr	Adolph Caesar
Squeak	Rae Dawn Chong
Miss Millie	Dana Ivey
Pa	Leonard Jackson
Grady	Bennet Guillory
Preacher	John Patton, Jr
Reverend Samuel	Carl Anderson
Corrine	Susan Beaubian
Buster	James Tillis
Mayor	Phillip Strong
Swain	Larry Fishburne
Adam	Peto Kinsaka
Olivia	Lelo Masamba
Odessa	Margaret Freeman
Young Harpo	Howard Starr
Young Olivia	Daphanie Oliver
Young Adam	Jadili Johnson
Young Tashi	Lillian Njoki Distefano
Daisy	Donna Buie
Store Clerk	Leon Rippy
Mailman	John R. Hart
Road Gang Leader	Davids Thomas
Caller-Africa	Thamsanqa R. Nguber
Loretta	Carrie Murray
Boy	Marcus Covington
Boo	Marcus Lile
Emma	April Myers

and Juliet Poe, Katie Simon, Ethel Taylor (Church Sisters), Maurice Moore, Lechanda Latharp (Children), Saunders Sonny Terry, Greg Phillinganes, Roy Gaines (Jook Joint Musicians), Paulinho Da Costa, Nana Yaw Asiedu, Clarence Avant, Bayo Martin, Ndugu Chancler, Jeffrey Kwashi, Pete Munzhi, Aniijia Rae Schockley (African Musicians)

Left: Desreta Jackson (L) Above: Danny Glover (L) and top with Okasua Busia © *Warner Bros.*

Danny Glover, Whoopi Goldberg

Whoopi Goldberg, Oprah Winfrey, Willard Pugh

Willard Pugh, Oprah Winfrey Above: Margaret
Avery Top: Adolph Caesar, Danny Glover
Below: Margaret Avery, Danny Glover

Whoopi Goldberg, Danny Glover Above: Oprah
Winfrey, Willard Pugh Top: Danny Glover
Below: Oprah Winfrey

FOOL FOR LOVE

(CANNON) Producers, Menahem Golan, Yoram Globus; Director, Robert Altman; Screenplay, Sam Shepard; Photography, Pierre Mignot; Editor, Luce Grunewaldt, Steve Dunn; Designer, Stephen Altman; Music, George Burt; Songs, Sandy Rogers, Louise Kircher, Billy Joe Shaver, Waylon Jennings; Associate Producers, Scott Bushnell, Mati Raz; Production Manager, Allan Nicholls; Production Executive, Jeffrey Silver; Assistant Directors, Ned Dowd, Steve Dunn, Sound, Catherine D'Hoir, Daniel Brisseau; Costumes, Kristine Flones Czeski; Color; 107 minutes; Rated R; December release

CAST

Eddie	Sam Shepard
May	Kim Basinger
Old Man	Harry Dean Stanton
Martin	Randy Quaid
May's Mother	Martha Crawford
Eddie's Mother	Louise Egol
Teenage May	Sura Co
Teenage Eddie	Jonathan Skinner
Young May	April Russel
The Countess	Deborah McNaughton
Mr. Valdez	Lon H

**Left: Sam Shepard Left Center:
Randy Quaid © *Cannon Films***

Kim Basinger

**Kim Basinger, Sam Shepard
Above: Harry Dean Stanton**

ENEMY MINE

(20th CENTURY-FOX) Producer, Stephen Friedman; Director, Wolfgang Petersen; Screenplay, Edward Khmara; Based on story by Barry Longyear; Music, Maurice Jarre; Photography, Tony Imi; Editor, Hannes Nikel; Designer, Rolf Zehetbauer; Costumes, Monika Bauert; Aliens created and designed by Chris Wala; Executive Producer, Stanley O'Toole; Production Managers, Harry Nap, Walter Pucker, Scott Woodehouse; Assistant Directors, Bert Batt, Gerd Huber, Robert Hotrek; Sound, Christian Schubert; Visual Effects, Don Dow; Special Effects, Bob MacDonald, Jr.; A Kings Road Entertainment Production; DeLuxe Color; Arriflex Widescreen; Dolby Stereo; 108 minutes; Rated PG-13; December release

CAST

Davidge	Dennis Quaid
Jeriba the Drac	Louis Gossett, Jr.
Stubbs	Brion James
Arnold	Richard Marcus
Morse	Carolyn McCormick
Wommis	Bumper Robinson
Dead Drac	Jim Mapp
Wooster	Lance Kerwin
Jonathan	Scott Kraft
Bates	Lou Michaels
Wilson	Andy Geer
Bates	Henry Stolow
Copper	Herb Andress
Base Guy	Danmar
Medic	Mandy Hausenberger
Sampson	Emily Woods
Zack	Barry Stokes
Front Dracs	Tony Moore, Kevin Taylor
Bravo	Colin Gilder
Panzer	Charly Huber
Eggett	Ulrich Gunther
Kemp	Frank Henson
Airbreath	Jazzer Jeyes
Walker	Doug Robinson
Hensler	Mark McBride
Ils	Balog Menyert

Top: Dennis Quaid, Brion James
Right: Quaid, Louis Gossett, Jr.
Below: Gossett, Quaid
© 20th Century-Fox

Louis Gossett, Jr., Dennis Quaid

THE JEWEL OF THE NILE

(20th CENTURY-FOX) Producer, Michael Douglas; Director, Lewis Teague; Screenplay, Mark Rosenthal, Lawrence Konner; Based on characters created by Diane Thomas; Photography, Jan DeBont; Designers, Richard Dawking, Terry Knight; Editors, Michael Ellis, Peter Boita; Music, Jack Nitzche; Costumes, Emma Porteous, Raymond Hughes; Co-Producers, Joel Douglas, Jack Brodsky; Production Manager, Bernard Mazauric; Assistant Directors, Kuki Lopez, Bruce Moriarity; Choreographer, Billy Goodson; Special Effects, Nick Allder, Philip Knowles; Optical Effects, Robin Browne, John Fletcher; Sound, Les Wiggins, Sandy MacRae; Songs by various artists; Technicolor; Widescreen; Dolby Stereo; 105 minutes; Rated PG; December release

CAST

Jack	Michael Douglas
Joan	Kathleen Turner
Ralph	Danny DeVito
Omar	Spiros Focas
Holy Man	Avner Eisenberg
Tarak	Paul David Magid
Barak	Howard Jay Petterson
Karak	Randall Edwin Nelson
Arak	Samuel Ross Williams
Sarak	Timothy Daniel Furst
Rachid	Hamid Fillali
Gloria	Holland Taylor
Le Vasseur	Guy Cuevas
Missionary	Peter De Palma
Pirate	Mark Daly Richards
Nubian Chief	Sadeke Colobanane
Nubian Wrestler	Hyacinthe N'Iaye
Rock Promoter	Daniel Peacock
Omar Officer	Benyahim Ahed
Station Master	Alaoui Hassen
Ticket Seller	Makoula Ahmed
Old Man in Sug	Akasby Mohamed
F-16 Pilot	Zaouis Abdelmajid
Fire Walker	Ted Buffington

and Flora Alberti, Patricia Poullair (Society Matrons), Ziraoui Mustapha, Baji Abdelmajid, Kachela Mohammed, Attif Mohammed, Hilal Abdellatif, Ben Abadi Mohammed Fillali (Omar's Elite Guards), National Dance Company of Senegal (Nubian Dancers)

**Right: Kathleen Turner, Avner
Eisenberg, Michael Douglas
Top: Michael Douglas, Kathleen
Turner, Danny DeVito
© 20th Century-Fox**

Michael Douglas, Kathleen Turner

Spiros Focas

98

MURPHY'S ROMANCE

(COLUMBIA) Producer, Laura Ziskin; Director, Martin Ritt; Screen-play, Harriet Frank, Jr., Irving Ravetch; Based on the novella by Max Schott; Photography, William A. Fraker; Designer, Joel Schiller; Editor, Sidney Levin; Costumes; Joe I. Tompkins; Music, Carole King; Songs Performed by Carole King, David Sanborn/Produced by Lou Adler; Production Manager, George Justin; Assistant Directors, Jim Van Wyck, Aldric La-auli Porter; Associate Producers, George Justin, Jim Van Wyck; Special Effects, Dennis Dion; Choreographer, Ken Rinker; A Martin Ritt/Fogwood Films, Ltd. Production; Metrocolor; Panavision; 103 minutes; Rated PG-13; December release

CAST

Emma Moriarty	Sally Field
Murphy Jones	James Garner
Bobby Jack Moriarty	Brian Kerwin
Jake Moriarty	Corey Haim
Freeman Coverly	Dennis Burkley
Margaret	Georgann Johnson
Bessie	Dortha Duckworth
Albert	Michael Prokopuk
Harry Le Beau	Billy Ray Sharkey
Don Forrest	Michael Crabtree
Wanda	Anna Levine
Amos Abbott	Charles Lane
Rex Boyd	Bruce French
Jesse Pinker	John C. Becher
Ed Hite	Henry Slate
Len	Tom Rankin
Mrs. Willis	Peggy McCay
Allie	Carole King
Auctioneer	Ted Gehring
Henry Bass	Joshua Ravetch
Thomas	Eugene Cochran
Lucius Holt	Gene Blakely
Doris	Sherry Lynn Amorosi
	Patricia Ann Willoughby
Ray Trucker	Mike Casper

and C. Ray Cook, Hugh Burritt, Michael Friel, Art Royer, Marian Robson, Irving Ravetch, Michael Hungerford, John Higgenbotham, Sasha Meyer, Ron Nix, Johnny Ray Anthony, Paul E. Pinnt

Right: Brian Kerwin, Sally Field
Top: Sally Field, James Garner
© *Columbia Pictures*

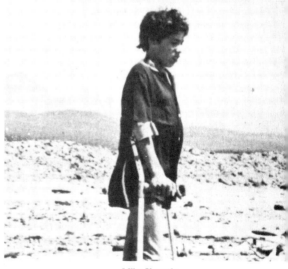

HERO

(MIRROR FILMS) Producer-Director-Screenplay, Alexandre Rock-well; Photography, Robert Yeomans, Alexandre Rockwell; Sound, Anne Abbot, Mark Wilson; Assistant Camera, Sheila O'Neil; Script, Christine Legoff; Production Manager, Timothy Rockwell; Editors, Alexandre Rockwell, Christine Legoff, Lizzie Borden; Music, Rolling Stones, Judy Garland, David Bowie, Mader, Jayne Blis Nodland, Jan Hassle, David Hykes, Charlie Hayden; Executive Producer, Benny Ray; Associate Producers, Tim Rockwell, Christoph Holch; Color; 104 minutes; Not rated; December release

CAST

Paul	Paul Rockwell
Kim	Kim Flowers
Mika	Mika Yamada
Cody	William "Cody" Maher
Hawk	William "Bluehouse" Johnson
Hair Dress	Lorna Scott
Teacher	Alexandre Bull

Mika Yamada

RUNAWAY TRAIN

(CANNON) Producers, Menahem Golan, Yoram Globus; Director, Andrei Konchalovsky; Screenplay, Djordje Milicevic, Paul Zindel, Edward Bunker; Based on a screenplay by Akira Kurosawa; Photography, Alan Hume; Music, Trevor Jones; Editor, Henry Richardson; Designer, Stephen Marsh; Associate Producer, Mati Raz; Executive Producers, Robert Whitmore, Henry Weinstein, Robert A. Goldston; Production Executive, Sue Baden-Powell; Production Manager, Christopher Pearce; Assistant Directors, Jack Cummins, Nancy King; Sound, Susumu Tokunow; Costumes, Kathy Dover; Special Effects, Keith Richins, Rick Josephson; Color; 111 minutes; Rated R; December release

CAST

Manny	Jon Voight
Buck	Eric Roberts
Sara	Rebecca DeMornay
Frank Barstow	Kyle T. Heffner
Ranken	John P. Ryan
Dave Prince	T. K. Carter
Eddie MacDonald	Kenneth McMillan
Ruby	Stacey Pickren
Conlan	Walter Wyatt
Jonah	Edward Bunker
Al Turner	Reid Cruikshank
Short Con	Michael Lee Gogin
Tall Con	John Bloom
Old Con	Norton E. Warden
Cat Con	John Otrin
Queen Con	Norman Alexander Gibbs
Announcer	Wally Ros
Boxer	Daniel Trejo
Trainer	Big Yank
Black Guard	Tom "Tiny" Lister
Prison Guard	Dana Belgard
Sue Majors	Diane Erickson
Pulasky	Larry John Meyers
Foreman Cassidy	Don McLaughlin
Fireman Wright	Vladimir Bibic
Rogers	William Tregoe, Jr

and Dennis Ott, Don Pugsley, John Fountain, (Guards), Loren Janes (Engineer), Obie Weeks (Brakeman), John Clay Scott (Conductor), Robert M. Klempner (Cushman), Carmen Filpi (Signal Maintainer), Phillip Earl, Tom Keenan (Crewmen), Tony Epper (Hitman), Jerr Brainum (Bodybuilder), Duey Thomasick (Emergency Worker)

**Jon Voight and Top with
Eric Roberts, Rebecca DeMornay**

Jon Voight © *Cannon Films*

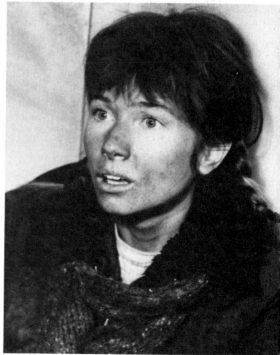

**Eric Roberts, and top with
Rebecca DeMornay, Jon Voight**

Rebecca DeMornay © *Cannon Films*

THE TRIP TO BOUNTIFUL

(ISLAND PICTURES) Producers, Sterling VanWagenen, Horton Foote; Director, Peter Masterson; Screenplay, Horton Foote; Based on his play, "The Trip to Bountiful"; Music, J. A. C. Redford; Photography, Fred Murphy; Editor, Jay Freund; Designer, Neil Spisak; Costumes, Gary Jones; Production Manager-Assistant Director, Stephen McEveety; Assistant Director, Michael Schilz; Sound, John Pritchett; Executive Producers, Sam Grogg, George Yaneff; Line Producer, Dennis Bishop; A FilmDallas/Bountiful Film Partners Production; Color; 106 minutes; Rated PG: December release

CAST

Mrs. Watts	Geraldine Page
Ludie Watts	John Heard
Jessie Mae	Carlin Glynn
Sheriff	Richard Bradford
Thelma	Rebecca De Mornay
Roy	Kevin Cooney
Rosella	Mary Kay Mars
Ticket Man #1	Norman Bennett
Ticket Man #2	Harvey Lewis
Ticket Agent, Houston	Kirk Sisco
Billy Davis	Dave Tanner
Stationmaster, Gerard	Gil Glasgow
Bus Driver #1	Jerry Nelson
Bus Passenger	Wezz Tildon
Downstairs Neighbor	Peggy Ann Byers
Mexican Man	David Romo

Geraldine Page received an Academy Award for Best Actress of 1985

Left: Geraldine Page
© Island Pictures

John Heard, Carlin Glynn, Rebecca DeMornay

Rebecca DeMornay, Geraldine Page
(also above)

TROUBLE IN MIND

(ALIVE FILMS) Producers, Carolyn Pfeiffer, David Blocker; Director-Screenplay, Alan Rudolph; Photography, Toyomichi Kurita; Editors, Tom Walls, Sally Coryn Allen; Designer, Steven Legler; Music, Mark Isham; Vocals, Marianne Faithfull; Costumes, Tracy Tynan; Executive Producer, Cary Brokaw; Assistant Director, Bruce Chevillat, Arthur Anderson, Kenneth Collins; Sound, Ron Judkins, Robert Jackson, Richard Portman, Dody Dorn; Special Effects, Bob Burns; Songs by various artists; An Island Alive and Terry Glinwood Presentation; In association with Embassy Home Entertainment; Color; 111 minutes; Rated R; December release

CAST

Hawk	Kris Kristofferson
Coop	Keith Carradine
Georgia	Lori Singer
Wanda	Genevieve Bujold
Solo	Joe Morton
Hilly Blue	Divine
Lt. Gunther	George Kirby
Nate Nathanson	John Considine
Rambo	Dirk Blocker
Leo	Albert Hall
Fat Adolph	Gailard Sartin
Mardy Skoog	Robert Gould
Sonja Nathanson	Antonia Dauphin
Elmo	Billy Silva
Spike	Caitlin Ferguson
Sector Rep. Pete Regis	Allan Nicholls
Marie La Mer	Debra Dusay
Bunny	Elizabeth Kaye
Biff	Rick Tutor
Eve Lamour	Joanne Klein
Nancy Lamour	Jill Klein
Long Militia	William Hall
Short Militia	David Kline
Maria	Andrea Stein
McBride	David McIntyre
Stevo Zarque	Steve Danton
Trixie	Mara Scott-Wood
Chiene	Robert Kim
Ho	Robert Lee
Slick	Matt Almond
Tammy Regis	Tracey Kristoferson

and Ron Ben Jarrett (Bouncer), William Earl Ray, Steven Ross (Prison Guards), Patricia Tyler (Soldier), Toni Cross (Bartender), Sarah Yvonne Murray (Samaritan), Carl Sander (Wealthy Man), Judy Lynne Gratton (Wealthy Woman), Stuart Manne (Little Ceasar), B. J. Alexander (Snookums), Danielle Aubuchon (Shana), Nanci Anton (Eva), Barry Press (Salesman), J. Morgan Armstrong (Mo), Frank Gargani (Ginny), Felix Casares (Scholar), David Quintera (Blackie), R. Fox (Officer Clark), M. James Clark (Officer Fox), Raymond Kemp (Lucky Bill), James Etue (Shamus), Frances Diamond (Diamond), Patti Dobrowolski (Vega), Pamela Gray (Dot), Lee Ann Fuji (Rose), Karen Gottberg, Shelle Renee, Susan Catherine, Sheri Ann Nye, Jabus Wesson (Les Filles De La Nuit), Jabus Wesson (Pud), J. R. Smith (Jingles), James Fulgium (Flip), Terry Morgan (Pimp), James Crabtree (Fireman), Tammy Wolfe (Guide), Stephen Sneed (Bellboy), Greg Walker (Bull), Greg Elam (Skinny), Rock Walker (Rocko), Mickey Alzola (Leapy), Bill McIntosh (Cosmo)

**Top Right: Kris Kristofferson, Keith
Carradine, Lori Singer
Below: Lori Singer, Genevieve Bujold**
© *Alive Films*

**Kris Kristofferson, Lori Singer
Above: Kristofferson, Divine**

TWICE IN A LIFETIME

(YORKIN) Producer-Director, Bud Yorkin; Screenplay, Colin Wel-
land; Photography, Nick McLean; Editor, Robert Jones; Designer,
William Creber; Music, Pat Metheny; Title Song, Paul McCartney;
Executive Producer, David Salven; Production Manager, David
Salven; Associate Producer, David Yorkin; Assistant Director, Tommy
Thompson, William Cosentino; Costumes, Bernie Pollack; Sound,
Darin Knight; Color; 111 minutes; Rated R; December release

CAST

Harry	Gene Hackman
Audrey	Ann-Margret
Kate	Ellen Burstyn
Sunny	Amy Madigan
Helen	Ally Sheedy
Keith	Stephen Lang
Jerry	Darrell Larson
Nick	Brian Dennehy
Jim	Chris Parker
Joanne	Rachel Street
Chris	Kevin Bleyer
Patty	Micole Mercurio
Ollie	Doris Hugo Drewien
Carlos	Lee Corrigan
Jake	Ralph Steadman
Rick	Rod Pilloud
Markos	Art Cahn
Susie	Anne Ludlum
Nancy	Evelyn Purdue
Dan	Gayle Bellows
Dolores	Kit Harris

and George Catalano, Tawnya Pettiford, Mary Ewald, Daniel Mahar,
Aaron Collar, Gary Kowalski, Keith Nicholai, Ken Clark, Audrey
Rod, Loretta Adair, Eileen Cornwell, Mary Thielen, Denise Aiumu,
Junior Barber

Right: Gene Hackman, Brian Dennehy
Top: Ann-Margret, Gene Hackman
© Yorkin Co.

Ally Sheedy, Gene Hackman
Above: Ellen Burstyn, Hackman

Gene Hackman, Ally Sheedy, Ellen Burstyn
Above: Amy Madigan, Burstyn, Sheedy

Susan Tyrrell, Barry Pearl, Rory Calhoun,
Betsy Russell in "Avenging Angel" © *New World*

Bronson Pinchot, Samm-Art Williams, Michael
Berz in "Hot Resort" © *Cannon Group*

THE ANNIHILATORS (New World) Producers, Allan C. Pedersen, Tom Chapman; Director, Charles E. Sellier, Jr.; Screenplay, Brian Russell; Photography, Henning Schellerup; Editor, Dan Gross; Music, Bob Summers; Art Director, Simon Gittins; Assistant Director, Leon Dudevoir; Associate Producer/Second Unit Director, Perry Husman; In color; Rated R; 84 minutes; January release. CAST: Christopher Stone (Bill), Andy Wood (Woody), Lawrence Hilton-Jacobs (Garrett), Gerrit Graham (Ray), Dennis Redfield (Joe), Paul Koslo (Roy Boy), Cavanaugh Yelling (Leon), Bruce Evers (Jessee), Tom Harper (Doc), Lonnie Smith (Virgil), Josh Patton (C.C.), Jim Antonio (Hawkins), Bruce Taylor (Capt. Lombard)

AVENGING ANGEL (New World) Producers, Sandy Howard, Keith Rubinstein, Director, Robert Vincent O'Neil; Screenplay, Robert Vincent O'Neil, Joseph M. Cala; Associate Producers, Joel Soisson, Michael Murphey; Production Executives, John Tarnoff, David Hirsch; Production Manager, Hugh McCallum; Assistant Directors, Betsy Pollock, Sandy Collister, Charles W. Gordon; Photography, Peter Lyons Collister; Art Director, Steve Marsh; Set, Patti Hall; Editor, John Bowey; Costumes, Nedra Watt, Shirlene Williams; Special Effects, Greg Landerer, Gary Bentley; Color; 93 minutes; Rated R; January release. CAST: Betsy Russell (Angel/Molly), Rory Calhoun (Kit Carson), Robert F. Lyons (Detective Andrews), Susan Tyrrell (Solly), Ossie Davis (Captain Moradian), Barry Pearl (Johnny Glitter), Ross Hagen (Ray Mitchell), Tim Rossovich (Teddy Butts), Estee Chandler (Cindy), Steven Mr. Porter (Yo-Yo Charlie), Paul Lambert (Arthur Gerrard), Frank Doubleday (Miles Gerrard), Richard DeHaven (Terry), Tracy Robert Austin (Pat), Michael A. Andrews (Mike), Karin Mani (Janie Soon Lee), Carol Bressler (Professor Garfield), and LeRoy Daniels, Bill Cakmis, Joseph Michael Cala, Billy Beck, Liz Sheridan, Tony Lorea, Laura Burkett, Robert Tessier, Jan Peters, Hoke Howell, Edward Blackoff, Dick Valentine, Paul Mousie Garner, Jeanne Lucas, Charlene Jones, Claudia Templeton, Howard Honig, Debi Sue Voorhees, Charlene Shires, Richard Acunto, Jessica O'Neil

FANDANGO (Warner Bros.) Producer, Tim Zinnemann; Director-Screenplay, Kevin Reynolds; Executive Producers, Frank Marshall, Kathleen Kennedy; Music, Alan Silvestri; Photography; Art Director, Peter Lansdown Smith; Editor, Arthur Schmidt; Associate Producers, Barrie M. Osborne, Pat Kehoe; Assistant Directors, Pat Kehoe, Bob Roe; Costumes, Michele Neely, Art Brouillard; Special Effects, Larry

Kevin Costner, Suzy Amis,
Sam Robards in "Fandango"
© *Warner Bros.*

Cavanaugh; Choreographer, Mike Haley; Dolby Stereo; In Technicolor; Dolby Stereo; 91 minutes; Rated PG; January release. CAST: Kevin Costner (Gardner Barnes), Judd Nelson (Phil Hicks), Sam Robards (Kenneth Waggener), Chuck Bush (Dorman), Brian Cesak (Lester), Marvin J. McIntyre (Truman Sparks), Suzy Amis (The Girl), Glenne Headly (Trelis), Pepe Serna (Mechanic), Elizabeth Daily (Judy), Robyn Rose (Lorna), Stanley Grover (Dad), Jane A. Johnston (Mom), and Don Brunner, Michael Conn, Michael Maxwell Katz, Dana Halsted, Karl Wickman, Michael M. Vendrell, Bill Warren, Bill Evridge, Margaret Nelson, Manley Adams, Ken Fagen, Bill Silver, Ben Graham, Jewel Watson, Allan Keown

HOT RESORT (Cannon Group) Producers, Menahem Golan and Yoram Globus; Director, John Robins; Screenplay, John Robins, Boaz Davidson & Norman Hudis; Story, Paul Max Rubenstein; Photography, Frank Flynn; Editors, Brent Schoenfeld, Dory Lubliner; Production Manager-Assistant Director, Roger La Page; Production Supervisor, Rami Alon; Production Coordinator, Patty Goulden, Patricia Doherty, Jane Morrissey; Sound, Jakob Goldstein; Songs, David Powell, Ken Brown; Color by TVC; Rated R; 93 minutes; January release CAST: Bronson Pinchot (Brad), Tom Parsekian (Marty), Michael Berz (Kenny), Daniel Schneider (Chuck), Marcy Walker (Franny), Debra Kelly (Liza), Samm-Art Williams (Bill Martin), Frank Gorshin (Mr. Green), Zora Rasmussen (Mrs. Green), David Lipman (Mr. Bray, Jr.), Jerome Collamore (Mr. Bray, Sr.), Stephen Stucker (Bobby Williams), William Tucker (Andrew), Michael Craig (Bo Bo), Linda Kenton (Geraldine), Charles Mayer (Mr. Labowitz), Mae Questel (Mrs. Labowitz), James Dietz (Peter), Charles McCaughan (Daryl), Tudi Wiggins (Sarah), Stephen Strimpell (Cruse), Janis Hall (Rita), Casey Nye (Vicki), Cynthia Lee (Alive), Dana Kaminsky (Melanie), Anna Nicholas (Jeannie), Maureen Quinn (Susan), Victoria Barrett (Jane), Peter Sugar (Maitre'D), David Whitfield (Sam), and We Covina, Geoffrey Gormley, Steve Heineman, Christopher Littlefield, Karl Brandes, Arthur Cooper, Paul Gaigelas, Biff Green, Jim Green, Eddy Hernandez, Robert Hernandez, David Lill, Charlie Sumner, Bob "Wags" Waggener

KADDISH (Ways and Means) Producer-Director-Editor, Steve Brand; Photography, Robert Achs; Music, Andy Statman; Documentary; 92 minutes; Not rated; January release

THE MUTILATOR (Marvin Films) formerly "Fall Break"; Producers, OK Productions, Buddy Cooper; Directors, Buddy Cooper, John S. Douglas; Screenplay, Buddy Cooper; Photography, Peter Schnall; Editor, Stephen Mack; Music, Michael Minard; Production Manager, Tamara Bally; Assistant Directors, Richard Garber, M. Walker Pearce; Sound, Larry Loewinger; Special Makeup Effects, Mark Shostrom, Anthony Showe, Edward Ferrell; Designer, Stephen Davis; Associate Producer, Neil B. Whitford; Movielab color; 86 minutes; No rating; January release. CAST: Matt Mitler, Ruth Martinez, Bill Hitchcock, Frances Raines, Morley Lampley, Connie Rogers, Jack Chatham, Ben Moore, Pamela Weddle Cooper, Trace Cooper

"The Party Animal"
© *Manson International*

Eric Douglas, Betsy Russell, Jerry Dinome
in "Tomboy" © *Crown International*

[TH]E PARTY ANIMAL (International Film Marketing) Producers, [Al]an C. Fox, Bryan England, Mark Israel, David Beaird; Director-[Scr]eenplay, David Beaird; Editor, Susan Jenkins; Story, Alan C. Fox, [Da]vid Beaird; Photography, Bryan England; Music Consultant, Steve [Sm]ith; Associate Producers, Terrie Cohen, Charles A. Duncombe, Jr.; [As]sistant Directors, Gerald Michenaud, Marty Schiff; Production Man-[ag]er, Charles A. Duncombe, Jr.; Songs by various artists; Color; 78 [mi]nutes; Rated R; January release. CAST: Matthew Causey (Pondo), [Ti]m Carhart (Studley), Robin Harlan (Natasha), Jerry Jones (Elbow), [Ha]nk Galati (The Professor), Luci Roucis (Sophia), Joan Dykman (The [Nu]rse), Barbara Baylis (Madame), Frannie James (Dean), Leland [Co]oke (Secretary), Billi Gordon (New Dean), Suzanne Ashley [(Mi]randa), and Julie Casey, Rachel Frantz, Donna Robb, Debbie Ross, [Li]sa Toothman Wolfe, Deanna Olivier, Debbie Elliott, Melinda [Ste]vens, Judi Evans, Merrie Lawson, Adrian Nandory, Mary Beth [Lo]mbardi, Herman Simon, Michael Listorti, Rick Wilson, Mary Tall-[ma]n, Ron Seigel, Mary Tallman, Herman Simon, Vic Anthony, Louis [Ol]iviar, Brandy Bushell, Wendy Payette, Cherly Frasure, Mari Rene, [Te]ri French, Patti Tippo, Kelly Garrett, Cory Titus, Mauretania Bal-[lar]d, Roberta Royer, Debi Bonsall, Jan Tarmy, Wendy Hart, Andrea [Ha]nna, Tracy Schaut Somers, Marcia Deppa, Christine Reedy, Trish [Th]aut, Margaret Aylward, Vic Anthony, Steve Raimonde, Jason [Ch]arles, Jean Robert, Swayne Johnson, Karen Bankhead, Adrian Nan-[dor]y, Marilynn Celeste, The Untouchables

[TH]E PLAGUE DOGS (Nepenthe Productions) Producer-Director-[Wr]iter, Martin Rosen; based on the novel by Richard Adams; Directors [of] Animation, Tony Guy, Colin White; Music, Patrick Gleeson; An-[im]ated; Color; 86 minutes; Rated PG; January release. VOICES: John [Hu]rt (Snitter), James Bolan (The Tod); Christopher Benjamin (Rowf)

[RA]PE/CRISIS (Cinema Guild) Producers, the Criminal Justice Cen-[ter,] Sam Houston State University, Victor Strechter, Larry Hoover, [Ter]ry Dowling; Director-Writer, Gary T. McDonald; Photography, [Ar]t Guthrie; Sound, Wayne Bell; Editor, McDonald; Consultants, [Syl]via Callaway, Sherri Goode, Jef Schroeder; Documentary; Color; [30] minutes; January release. CAST: Carla Phillips (Becky), David [Co]ll (Bob), Suzanne Chesshire (Laurie), Jennifer Johanos (Joan), [Tit]us Sharp (David), Sheila Tesar (Sharon)

[SU]PERSTITION formerly "The Witch" (Almi Pictures) Producers, [Ma]rio Kassar, Andrew Vajna, Penaria Corp., Ed Carlin, John D. [Sch]wartz, Robert L. J. Lewis; Director, James W. Roberson; Screen-[pla]y, Michael Sajbel, Bret Plate, Brad White, Donald G. Thompson; [fro]m story "The Witch" by Sajbel; Photography, Lee Madden; Editor, [—] Rabinowitz; Music, David Gibney; Sound, Ron Judkins; Assistant [Dir]ector, Jan S. Ervin; Production Manager, Michael Bennett; Design-[er,] Penny Hadfield, Cricket Rowland; Special Effects Make-Up, Bill [Mu]nns, Steve LaPorte, David B. Miller; CFI color; 84 minutes; No [rati]ng; January release. CAST: James Houghton (Rev. David Thomp-[son]), Albert Salmi (Insp. Sturgess), Lynn Carlin (Melinda Leahy), [Lar]ry Pennell (George Leahy), and Maylo McCaslin, Heidi Bohay, [Bil]ly Jacoby, Jacquelyn Hyde, Kim Marie, Stacy Keach Sr., Joshua [Ca]dman, Robert Symonds, Carole Goldman, John Alderman, Johnny [Do]ran, Bennett Liss, Casey King

TOMBOY (Crown International) Producers, Marilyn J. Tenser, Michael D. Castle; Director, Herb Freed; Screenplay, Ben Zelig; Pho-tography, Daniel Yarussi; Editor, Richard E. Westover; Music Super-vision, Michael Lloyd; Assistant Directors, Stephen Mann, Robin Jones; Art Director, Randy Ser; Costumes, Kristin Nelson; Songs, Al Kasha, Joel Hirschhorn, Michael Lloyd, Pat Robinson, Harriet Shock; Color by DeLuxe; 91 minutes; Not rated; January release. CAST: Betsy Russell (Tommy Boyd), Jerry Dinome (Randy Starr), Kristi Somers (Seville Ritz), Richard Erdman (Chester), Philip Sterling (Earl De-larue), Eric Douglas (Ernie Leeds, Jr.), Paul Gunning (Frankie), Toby Iland (Harold), E. Danny Murphy (Pimples), Rory Barish (Jennifer), Cynthia Ann Thompson (Amanda), Cory Hawkins (Carlos), Shane McCabe (Goodley), Aaron Butler (Tod), Dennis Hayden (Bartender), Danna Garen (Girl in Hall), Alicia Hollinger (Girl at Party), Carey Shearer (Lanky Kid), Friday (Bumper), Jacqueline Jacobs (Wilde Abandon)

TOO SCARED TO SCREAM (The Movie Store) Producer, Mike Connors; Director, Tony Lo Bianco; Executive Producer, Ken Norris; Screenplay, Glenn Leopold, Neal Barbera; Photography, Larry Pizer; Editors, Ed Beyer, Michael Economou; Music, George Garvarentz; Sound, Doug Holman; Design, Lilly Kilvert; Assistant Director, Mike Haley; Associate Producer, A. Kitman Ho; CFI Color; Rated R; 104 minutes; January release. CAST: Mike Connors (Lt. Dinardo), Anne Archer (Kate), Leon Isaac Kennedy (Frank), Ian McShane (Hardwick), Ruth Ford (Irma), John Heard (Lab Technician), Carrie Nye (Graziel-la), Maureen O'Sullivan (Mother), Murray Hamilton (Jack), Ken Nor-ris (Mike)

WALKING THE EDGE (Empire Pictures) Producers, Manfred Mentz, Cinema Overseas Distributors, Sergei Goncharoff, Marketing Film; Director, Norbert Meisel; Screenplay, Curt Allen; Photography, Ernie Poulos; Editor, Warren Chadwick; Music, Jay Chattaway; Sound, Don Summer; Assistant Director, David Watkinson; Designers, Dana Roth, Kim Buckley; Special Effects, Don Power; United color; 93 minutes; No rating; January release. CAST: Robert Forster (Jason Walk), Nancy Kwan (Christine), Joe Spinell (Brusstar), A Martinez (Tony), Aarika Wells (Julia), Wayne Woodson (McKee), James McIn-tire (Jimmy), Russ Courtney (Leon), Frankie Hill (Delia), Doug Toby (Danny), Howard Honig (Ron)

Maureen O'Sullivan, Mike Connors, Ian McShane
in "Too Scared to Scream" © *The Movie Store*

Lillie the Sad One in "Streetwise"
© *Angelica Films*

**Sheree Wilson, Stephen Geoffreys
in "Fraternity Vacation"** © *New World*

STREETWISE (Angelika Films) Producer, Cheryl McCall; Director-Photography, Martin Bell; Editor, Nancy Baker; Music, Tom Waits; Sound, Keith Desmond; Associate Editors, Jonathan Oppenheim, Meredith Birdsall; A film by Martin Bell, Mary Ellen Mark and Cheryl McCall; Documentary; Color; 92 minutes; Not Rated; February release. CAST: Alabama, Annie, Antoine, Baby Gramps, Biker Kim, Black Junior, Breezy, Buddha, Butch, Calvin, Chrissie, Dawn, DeWayne, Drugs, Eddie, Erica, Floyd, J. R., James, Jimi, John, Juan, Justin, Kim, Kevin, Lillie, Lora Lee, Lulu, Melissa, Michele, Mike, Munchkin, Patrice, Patti, Peehole, Rat, Red Dog, Roberta, Russ, Sam, Shadown, Shellie, Smurf, Sparkles, Tiny (Erin), Tracy, White Junior, William

BLUE HEAVEN (Five Point) Producer, Elaine Sperber; Co-producers, Kathleen Dowdey, Jed Dannenbaum; Executive Producer, Mr. Dannenbaum; Directed-Written-Edited by Kathleen Dowdey; Photography, Kees Van Oostrem; Art Director, Howard Cummings; Music, Fonda Feingold; Associate Producer, Elaine Gilner Friedman; In DuArt Color; Not rated; 111 minutes; February release. CAST: Leslie Denniston (Carol), James Eokhouse (Tony), Lisa Sloan, Marsha Jackson, Bruce Evers, Brenda Bynum, Merwin Goldsmith

THE DUNGEONMASTER (Empire) Producer, Charles Band; Directors, Rosemarie Turko, John Buechler, Charles Band, David Allen, Steve Ford, Peter Manoogian, Ted Nicolaou; Screenplay, Allen Actor; Photography, Mac Ahlberg; Editors, Marc Leif, Ted Nicolaou; Sound, Doug Arnold, Ike Magal, Ann Krupa; Designer, Julie Stroh; Music, Richard Band, Shirley Walker; Associate Producer, Debra Dion; Assistant Directors, Matia Karrell, Debbie Pinthus, John Dahl, David Warfield, Michaelle Noble, Caren Singer, Betsy Magruder; Costumes, Kathie Clar; Special Effects Makeup, John Buechler; CFI Color; 73 minutes; Rated PG-13; February release. CAST: Jeffrey Byron (Paul Bradford), Richard Moll (Mestema), Leslie Wing (Gwen), Blackie Lawless (Heavy Metal), Danny Dick (Slasher)

FAST FORWARD (Columbia) Producer, John Patrick Veitch; Director, Sidney Poitier; Screenplay, Richard Wesley; Story, Timothy March; Executive Producer, Melville Tucker; Photography, Matthew F. Leonetti, A.S.C., Designer, Michael Baugh; Editor, Harry Keller; Executive Music Producer, Quincy Jones; Music, Tom Scott, Jack Hayes; Choreography, Rick Atwell, Felix, Aimee Covo, Robin Summerfield, Pamela Poitier, Gary Porter, Charlie Washington; Production Manager, Richard Stenta; Assistant Directors, Candace Allen, Roger Joseph Pugliese; Costumes, Winnie D. Brown, Violette W. Jones;

Songs by various artists; Metrocolor; Dolby Stereo; 110 minutes; Rate PG; February release. CAST: John Scott Clough (Matt), Don Frankli (Michael), Tamara Mark (June), Tracy Silver (Meryl), Cindy McGe (Francine), Gretchen F. Palmer (Valerie), Monique Cintron (Rita) Debra Varnado (Debbie), Noel Conlon (Mr. Stanton), Karen Kopir (Susan), Irene Worth (Ida), Sam McMurry (Clem), Michael De Lorenzo (Caesar), Doris Belack (Mrs. Gilroy), David White (M Sabol), Robin Bach (Mark Dalton), Constance Towers (Jessie), Phyll Ehrlich (Landlady), Bobbi Jordon (Mrs. Stanton), Robert Do Qui (M Hughes), and Val De Vargas, Panos Christi, Paul Ryan, Steve Beach Tony Cuen, Keith Nisonoff, Hugo Huizar, Derrick Brice, Kenne Jezek, Laura O'Banion, Regan Patno, Dorian Sanchez, Linda Talcot Scott Wilder, David Le Bell, Rick Collitti, Bob Giovane, Micha Rougas, Jack Heller, Kevin Jay, Vince Cannon, Lisa Maurer, Bc Lippre, David Martinson, Jef Scott Band, Living Daylights, Dynam Breakers

FEAR CITY (Zupnik-Curtis Enterprises Inc.) Producer, Bruc Cohn Curtis; Director, Abel Ferrara; Screenplay, Nicholas St. Joh Photography, James Lemmo; Editors, Jack Holmes, Anthony Redma Music, Dick Halligan; Color; 93 minutes; Rated R; February releas CAST: Tom Berenger (Matt Rossi), Billy Dee Williams (Wheeler Jack Scalia (Nicky), Melanie Griffith (Loretta), Rossano Brazzi (Ca mine), Rae Dawn Chong (Leila), Joe Santos (Frank), Michael V. Gazz (Mike), Jan Murray (Goldstein), Janey Julian (Ruby), Daniel Farald (Sanchez)

FRATERNITY VACATION (New World) formerly "Wendell"; Pr ducers, Robert C. Peters, Boris Malden, Christopher Nelson; Directo James Frawley; Screenplay, Lindsay Harrison; Music, Brad Fiede Photography, Paul Ryan; Designer, Roberta Neiman; Assistant Dire tors, William Carroll, Mitchell Bock; Costumes, Tracy Tynan; Speci Effects, Roger George and Co.; Color; 89 minutes; Rated PG; Februa release. CAST: Stephen Geoffreys (Wendell Tvedt), Sheree J. Wilsc (Ashley Taylor), Cameron Dye (Joe Gillespie), Leigh McCloske (Charles "Chas" Lawlor III), Tim Robbins (Larry "Mother" Tucker Matt McCoy (J. C. Springer), Amanda Bearse (Nicole Ferret), Joh Vernon (Chief Ferret), Nita Talbot (Mrs. Ferret), Barbara Crampto (Chrissie), Kathleen Kinmont (Marianne), Max Wright (Milla Tvedt), Julie Payne (Naomi Tvedt), Franklyn Ajaye (Harry), Charl Rocket (Madman Mac), Britt Ekland (Evette), Denise Beaumo (Hooker Smith), Frances McCaffrey (Hooker Jones), and Roger Beb stock, Millicent Hawkins, Sheridan Batson, Penny Sathews, Auro Rodriguez, Roberta Whitewood

**Michael DeLorenzo, Gretchen Palmer, John Scott
Clough, Tamara Mark in "Fast Forward"**
© *Columbia*

**Britt Ekland, Tim Robbins, Cameron Dye,
Stephen Geoffreys in "Fraternity Vacation"**
© *New World Pictures*

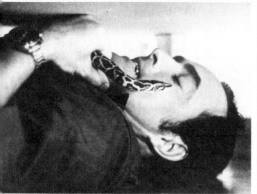

"The G. I. Executioner"
© *Troma Team*

Michelle Pfeiffer, Jeff Goldblum
in "Into the Night" © *Universal*

E G.I. EXECUTIONER (Troma Team) formerly "Wit's End"; ʿied Vol. 27 as "Dragon Lady"

AVENLY BODIES (MGM/UA) Producers, Robert Lantos, Ste- n J. Roth; Director, Lawrence Dane; Screenplay, Lawrence Dane, ᴎ Base; Photography, Thomas Burstyn; Choreography, Brian Foley; ꜱigner, Lindsey Goddard; Music Director, Paul Hoffert; Costumes, e Ganton; Associate Producer, Andras Hamori; Production Mana- Gerry Arbeid; Assistant Director, Mac Bradden; Songs by various ꜱts; Color by Medallion; Dolby Stereo; 89 minutes; Rated R; Febru- release. CAST: Cynthia Dale (Samantha), Richard Rebiere (Steve), ꜱter George Alton (Jack), Laura Henry (Debbie), Stuart Stone ꜱl), Patricia Idlette (KC), Pam Henry (Patty), Linda Sorensen (TV ꜱts; Reiner Schwartz (TV Director), Cec Linder (Walter), Micki ᴑre (TV Reporter), Sean Sullivan (Salesman), Mac Bradden (Nick), ʜael Tait (Mr. Howard), Murray Westgate (Coach Hudson), Elena ꜱoba (Babysitter), Sugar Bouche (Stripper), and Andrew Douglas, ᴎ Foley, Fay Foley, Howard Barish, Eric Fink, Reg Dreger, Anne y, Don Hennessy, Debarah Kimmet, Joanne Bates, Marsha Levine

ʿO THE NIGHT (Universal) Producers, George Folsey Jr., Ron ꜱlow; Director, John Landis; Screenplay, Ron Koslow; Executive ꜱlucer, Dan Allingham; Photography, Robert Paynter B.S.C.; De- ꜱohn Lloyd; Editor, Malcolm Campbell; Music, Ira Newborn; ʿals, B. B. King; Costumes, Deborah Nadoolman; Associate Pro- ꜱers, David Sosna, Leslie Belzberg; Assistant Directors, David Sos- Robert Simon; Special Effects, Mike Wood; Songs by various ꜱts; Technicolor; 115 minutes; Rated R; February release. CAST: Goldblum (Ed Okin), Michelle Pfeiffer (Diana), Stacey Pickren ꜱn Okin), Carmen Argenziano (Stan), Dan Aykroyd (Herb), Cal ꜱrthington (Himself), Ali Madani (Hasi), Jake Steinfeld (Larry), ꜱe McGill (Charlie), Joe Stephen Fink (Don), Kathryn Harrold ꜱistie), Paul Mazursky (Bud Herman), Houshang Touzie (Hamid), ᴵ Perkins (Mr. Williams), Jim Henson (Man on Phone), David ꜱvie (Colin Morris), Art Evans (Jimmy), Bud Abbott (Chic), Lou ꜱtello (Wilbur), Bela Lugosi (Count Dracula), Lon Chaney, Jr. (The ꜱfman), Pete Ellis (Himself), Roger Vadim (Monsieur Melville), ꜱard Farnsworth (Jack Caper), Vera Miles (Joan Caper), Irene ꜱs (Shaheen Parvizi), Clu Gulager (Federal Agent), and Andrew

Marton, Sue Dugan, Elizabeth Solorzano, Robert Paynter, David Croenberg, Robert Moberly, John Hostetter, Dick Balduzzi, Richard Franklin, Wes Dawn, Christopher George, Michael Zand, Hadi Sad- jadi, Beruce Gramian, John Landis, Hope Clarke, Eric Lee, Sue Bow- ser, Waldo Salt, Viola Kates Stimpson, DeeDee Pfeiffer, Rick Baker, Colin Higgins, Daniel Petrie, David Sosna, Mark Levine, William B. Kaplan, Jonathan Kaufer, Saul Kahan, Rory Barish, Jean Pelton, Jonathan Lynn, Paul Bartel, Bill Taylor, Jim Bentley, Slavka, Erica Sakai, Don Siegel, Peggy Sands, Robert Traynor, Domingo Ambriz, Amy Heckerling, Robert LaBassiere, Yacub Salih, Jack Roberts, Dian Roberts, Reid Smith, Rusdi Lane, Lawrence Kasden, Hassan Ildari, Zoreh Ramsey, Beulah Quo, Patricia Gaul, Jonathan Demme, Tracy Hutchinson, Gene Whittington, Eddy Donno, Carl Gottlieb, Alma Beltran

LOST IN AMERICA (Warner Bros.) Producer, Marty Katz; Direc- tor, Albert Brooks; Screenplay, Albert Brooks, Monica Johnson; Pho- tography, Eric Saarinen; Editor, David Finfer; Music, Arthur B. Rubin- stein; Designer, Richard Sawyer; Costumes, Cynthia Bales; Special Effects, Dick Albain; Executive Producer, Herb Nanas; Production Manager, Marty Katz; Assistant Directors, Michael Daves, Robert Doherty; Sound, Bill Nelson; Presented by The Geffen Company; Songs by various artists; Technicolor; Panavision; 91 minutes; Rated R; February release. CAST: Albert Brooks (David Howard), Julie Hagerty (Linda Howard), Maggie Roswell (Patty), Hans Wagner (Hans), Michael Greene (Paul Dunn), Tom Tarpey (Brad Tooley), Raynold Gideon (Ray), Garry K. Marshall (Casion Manager), Donald Gibb (Ex-Convict), Ernie Brown (Pharmacist), Art Frankel (Employment Agent), Candy Ann Brown (David's Secretary), Joey Coleman (Skip- py), and Sylvia Farrel, Tina Kincaid, Brandy Rubin, Michael Greene, Robert Hughes, John Di Fusco, Michael Cornelison, Radu Gavor, John C. Reade, Pat Garrison, Byron Tong, Gayle Lanza, Charles Boswell, Zeke Manners, Bea Manners, Mark Sydney, David Katz, Raul Flores, Herb Nanas

A MARRIAGE Producer, David Greene; Director-Screenplay, Sandy Tung; Photography, Benjamin David; Music, Jack Waldman; Pre- sented by the Film Society of Lincoln Center and the Department of Film of the Museum of Modern Art; 90 minutes; No rating; February release. CAST: Ric Gitlin (Ted), Isabel Glasser (Nancy), Jane Darby (Jane), Jack Rose (Mark)

Richard Rebiere, Cynthia Dale
in "Heavenly Bodies"
© *MGM/UA Entertainment*

Julie Hagerty, Albert Brooks
in "Lost in America"
© *Geffen Film Co.*

**Lynn Massie, Wendy Gregory
in "Seventeen"**

**Doug McKeon, Kelly Preston
in "Mischief" © 20th Century-Fox**

JOEY (Satori) Producer-Director-Screenplay, Joseph Ellison; Executive Producer, Frank Lanziano; Story, Ellen Hammill; Photography, Oliver Wood; Editor, Christopher Andrews; Music, Jim Roberge; Associate Producer, Jeffrey Silver; Sound-Music Editor, Greg Sheldon; Created by Frank Lanziano; Color; 99 minutes; Not Rated; February release. CAST: Neill Barry (Joey), James Quinn (Joey's Father), Elisa Heinsohn (Janie), Linda Thorson (Principal O'Neill), Ellen Hammill (Bobbie), Rickey Ellis (John), Dee Hourican (Bonnie), Dan Grimaldi (Ted), Frankie Lanz (Himself)

THE LOST EMPIRE (JGM Enterprises) Producer-Director-Screenplay, Jim Wynorski; Photography, Jacques Haitkin; Editor, Larry Bock; Music, Alan Howarth; Sound, Mark Ulano; Designer, Wayne Springfield; Special Animated Effects, Steve Neill; Production Manager, Max Bloom; Assistant Director, Betsy Magruder; Co-Producers, Alex Tabrizi, Robert Greenberg; Associate Producer, Raven de la Croix; Presented by Harwood Productions; DeLuxe color; 83 minutes; Rated R; February release. CAST: Melanie Vincz (Angel Wolfe), Raven de la Croix (Whitestar), Angela Aames (Heather), Paul Coufos (Rick), Bob Tessier (Koro), Angus Scrimm (Dr. Sin Do), Blackie Dammett (Krager), Linda Shayne (Cindy), Angelique Pettyjohn (Whiplash), Kenneth Tobey (Cop), Garry Goodrow (Doctor), and Art Hern, Annie Gaybis, Gary Don Cox, Jason Stuart, Tom Rettig

VISION QUEST (Warner Bros.) Producers, Jon Peters, Peter Guber; Director, Harold Becker; Screenplay, Darryl Ponicsan; Based on a novel by Terry Davis; Executive Producers, Stan Weston, Adam Fields; Music, Tangerine Dream; Photography, Owen Roizman; Designer, Bill Malley; Editor, Maury Winetrobe; Costumes, Susan Becker; Assistant Directors, Thomas Mack, Bill Elvin; Special Effects, Joe Mercurio; Songs by various artists; Technicolor, Dolby Stereo; 108 minutes; Rated R; February release. CAST: Matthew Modine (Louden Swain), Linda Fiorentino (Carla), Michael Schoeffling (Kuch), Ronny Cox (Louden's Dad), Harold Sylvester (Tanneran), Charles Hallahan (Coach), J. C. Quinn (Elmo), Daphne Zuniga (Margie Epstein), R. H. Thomson (Kevin), Gary Kasper (Otto), Raphael Sbarge (Schmoozler), Forest Whitaker (Balldozer), Frank Jasper (Shute), Roberts Blossom (Grandpa), James Gammon (Kuch's Dad), Judith Hansen (Elsie), and Fred Miles, Sean Morgan, Cash Stone, Ken Pelo, Kevin Kahl Lease, Tony Christianson, Jay Bonnett, Ted Collins, Paul Spangenberg, Darrell Driggs, David Haugen, Tom Elkins, Ron Silverman, Jana Marie Hupp, Madonna

MISCHIEF (20th Century-Fox) formerly "Heart and Soul"; Producers, Sam Manners, Michael Nolin; Director, Mel Damski; Screenplay, Noel Black; Photography, Donald E. Thorin; Editor, Nick Brown; Music, Barry De Vorzon; Songs by various artists; Color; 97 minutes; Rated R; February release. CAST: Doug McKeon (Jonathan), Catherine Mary Stewart (Bunny), Kelly Preston (Marilyn), Chris Nash (Gene), D. W. Brown (Kenny), Jami Gertz (Rosalie), Maggie Blye (Claire Miller), Graham P. Jarvis (Mr. Travis), Terry O'Quinn (Claude Harbrough), Darren Ewing (Ted), Dennis L. O'Connell (T. J.), Bill McGuire (Mr. Hewitt), Bryce Kasson (Robbie), Andrew Ream (Harry Horner), Julie Noble (Mrs. McCauley)

SEVENTEEN Producers-Directors-Photographers-Editors, Joel DeMott, Jeff Kreines; Producer, Peter Davis; Documentary; 120 minutes; Not rated; February release

TORCHLIGHT (UCO Films) Producer, Joel Douglas; Director, Tom Wright; Story-Screenplay, Pamela Sue Martin, Eliza Moorman; Photography, Alex Philips; Theme song music, Carly Simon; Color; minutes; Rated R; February release. CAST: Pamela Sue Martin (Lillian), Steve Railsback (Jake), Ian McShane (Sidney)

BABY . . . SECRET OF THE LOST LEGEND (Touchstone) Producer, Jonathan T. Taplin; Director, B. W. L. Norton; Screenplay, Clifford & Ellen Green; Music, Jerry Goldsmith; Photography, John Alcott; Editors, Howard Smith, David Bretherton; Executive Producer, Roger Spottiswoode; Designer, Raymond G. Storey; Associate Producer-Production Manager, E. Darrell Hallenbeck; Assistant Directors, Steve McEveety, Craig A. Beaudine; Special Effects, Roland Tantin; Costumes, Susie S. McEveety; Dinosaurs Created and Engineered, Isidoro Raponi & Roland Tantin; Technicolor; Supertechniscope; Dolby Stereo; 135 minutes; Rated PG; March release. CAST: William Katt (George Loomis), Sean Young (Susan Matthews-Loomis), Patrick McGoohan (Dr. Eric Kiviat), Julian Fellowes (Nigel Jenkins), Kyalo Mativo (Cephu), Hugh Quarshie (Kenge Obe), Olu Jacobs (Colonel Nsogbu), Eddie Tagoe (Sgt. Gambwe), Edward Hardwicke (Dr. Pierre Dubois), Julian Curry (Etienne), and Alexis Meless, Susie Nottingham, Stephane Krora, Anthony Sarfoh, Jeannot Banny, Roger Carlton, Therese Taba, and Mark Mangini, George Budd (Dinosaur Voices)

FRIDAY THE 13TH—A NEW BEGINNING (Paramount) Producer, Timothy Silver; Director, Danny Steinmann; Screenplay, Martin Kitrosser, David Cohen, Danny Steinmann; Music, Harry M.

**Linda Fiorentino, Matthew Modine
in "Vision Quest"
© Warner Bros.**

**Sean Young, William Katt
in "Baby"
© Touchstone**

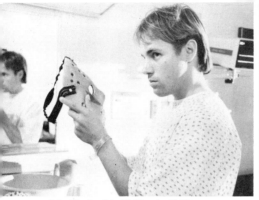

John Shepherd in "Friday the 13th"
© *Paramount*

Peter Coyote, Carol Wayne
in "Heartbreakers" © *Orion*

dini; Executive Producer, Frank Mancuso, Jr.; 92 minutes; Rated R; arch release. CAST: John Shepherd (Tommy Jarvis), Shavar Ross eggie), Melanie Kinnaman (Pam), Richard Young (Dr. Peters), rnon Washington (George), Jerry Pavlon (Jake), Juliette Cummins obin), Tiffany Helm (Violet), Debbisue Voorhees (Tina), John bert Dixon (Eddie), Mark Venturini (Victor), Dominic Brascia ey), Richard Lineback (Carl Dodd), Marco St. John (Sheriff Tuck-, Carol Lacatell (Ethel), Ron Sloan (Junior), Caskey Swain (Duke nson), Dick Wieand (Roy), Sonny Shields (Raymond), Bob De none (Male Nurse), Todd Bryant (Neil), Curtis Conaway (Les), rey Parker (Pete), Anthony Barille (Vinnie), Rebecca Wood-Sharke ana), Ric Mancini (Mayor Cobb), Miguel A. Nunez, Jr. (Demon), e Fields (Anita), Corey Feldman (Tommy at 12), Susanne Bateman urse Yates), and Tom Morga

IOULIES (Empire Pictures) Producer, Jefery Levy; Director, ca Bercovici; Screenplay, Mr. Bercovici, Mr. Levy; Photography, ac Ahlberg; Music, Richard Band, Shirley Walker; Color; 88 nutes; Rated PG-13; March release. CAST: Peter Liapis (Jonathan aves), Lisa Pelikan (Rebecca), Michael Des Barres (Malcolm aves), Jack Nance (Wolfgang), Peter Risch (Grizzel), Tamara De eaux (Greedigut), Scott Thomson (Mike), Ralph Seymour (Mark), ariska Hargitay (Donna), Keith Joe Dick (Dick), David Dayan ldie), Victoria Catlin (Anastasia), Charlene Cathleen (Robin), Robbi esee (Temptress)

ARTBREAKERS (Orion) Producers, Bob Weis, Bobby Roth; ector-Screenplay, Bobby Roth; Photography, Michael Ballhaus; usic, Tangerine Dream; Editor, John Carnochan; Executive Produc-, Lee Muhl, Harry Cooper, Joseph Franck; Production Manager, l Rapp; Assistant Directors, Jack Baran, Michael Pariser; Special ects, Eric Allard; Costumes, Betsy Jones; Songs by various artists; A hro Films Presentation; 95 minutes; Rated R; March release. CAST: er Coyote (Blue), Nick Mancuso (Eli), Carole Laure (Liliane), Max il (King), James Laurenson (Terry Ray), Carol Wayne (Candy), nie Rose (Libby), Kathryn Harrold (Cyd), George Morfogen (Max), ry Hardin (Warren Williams), Henry Sanders (Reuven), Walter kewicz (Marvin), and Terry Wills, Annie O'Neill, Michelle Davi-a, Claire Malis, Carmen Argenziano, Adele Corey, Tina Chappel, tin Leir, Scott Wade, Alfonse Ruggiero, Howard Shatsky

HELLHOLE (Arkoff International) Producers, Louis S. Arkoff, Billy Fine; Director, Pierre De Moro; Screenplay, Vincent Mongol; Story-New Dialogue, Lance Dickson; Additional Dialogue, Mark Evan Schwartz; Photography, Steven Posey; Editor, Steve Butler; Music, Jeff Sturges; Sound, Jerry Wolfe; Assistant Director, D. K. Miller; Production Manager, Tony Lopez; Special Effects, Dale Martin; Special Make-Up, Donn Markel; A Hellhole Production; DeLuxe Color; 95 minutes; Rated R; March release. CAST: Ray Sharkey (Silk), Judy Landers (Susan), Marjoe Gortner (Dr. Dane), Richard Cox (Ron), Edy Williams (Vera), Terry Moore (Sidnee Hammond), Mary Woronov (Dr. Fletcher), Robert Darcy (Brad), Martin Beck (Monroe), Cliff Emmich (Dr. Blume), Lynn Borden (Mom), Dyanne Thorne (Crysta), Mae Campbell (Daisy), Martin West (Rollins), Pamela Ward (Tina), Curtis Taylor (Jim), Jan Stratton (Nurse Soto), Carole Ita White (Nurse Turner), Rochelle Firestone (Darla), Sammy Thurston (Beat Woman), and Marneen Fields, Lamya Derval, Natalie Main, Marie LaMarre, Judith Geller, Ann-Leizabeth Chatterton, Loyda Ramos, Ingrid Oliu, Charley M. Morgan, Tanya Russell, Lynne Bell, Juliet Rohde, Annette Claudier, Larraine Blanc Rosner, Joel Bennett, Kristina Kirstin, DeVera Marcus, Renee Vicary, Lauri Creach, Sherry Peterson, Dan Bradley, Tony Lopez, Margarita Nosalt, Michele Laurent, James Paola

JAMES JOYCE'S WOMEN (Universal) Producer, Fionnula Flanagan; Director, Michel Pearce; Screenplay-Adaption, Fionnula Flanagan; From the Life and Works of James Joyce; Photography, John Metcalfe; Editor, Arthur Keating, Dan Perry; Assistant Director, Barry Blackmore; Sound, Kieran Horgan; Special Effects, Gerry Johnston; Co-Producer, Garrett O'Connor; Associate Producers, Patrick Flanagan, Ann Kirch; Based on the stage production "James Joyce's Women" Directed by Burgess Meredith; Music, Noel Kelehan, Arthur Keating, Vincent Kilduff, Garrett O'Connor; A Rejoycing Company Production; 91 minutes; Not Rated; March release. CAST: Fionnula Flannagan (Nora Barnacle Joyce/Sylvia Beach/Harriet Shaw Weaver/ Gerty MacDowell/The Washerwoman/Molly Bloom), Timothy E. O'Grady (The Interviewer), Chris O'Neill (James Joyce), Tony Lyons (Leopold Bloom), Paddy Dawson (Stannie Joyce), Martin Dempsey (The Father), Gerald Fitzmahony (First Gossip), Joseph Taylor (Second Gossip), Rebecca Wilkinson (Washerwoman), Gladys Sheehan (Washerwoman), Gabrielle Keenan (Cissy Caffrey), Michele O'Connor (Ed Boardman), Thomas Kitt (Jacky Caffrey), Brian Dunn (Tommy Caffrey), Zoe Blackmore (Young Girl), and Peter Kerr (Tenor)

Peter Coyote, Nick Mancuso, Carole Laure
in "Heartbreakers" © *Orion*

Gerty McDowell
in "James Joyce's Women"
© *Universal*

111

Lori Loughlin, Shannon Presby
in "The New Kids" © *Columbia*

Murry Langston, Linda Blair
in "Night Patrol" © *New World*

THE NEW KIDS (Columbia) Producers, Sean S. Cunningham, Andrew Fogelson; Director, Sean S. Cunningham; Screenplay, Stephen Gyllenhaal; Story, Stephen Gyllenhaal, Brian Taggert; Photography, Steven Poster; Editor, Pete Smith; Editor, Rita Roland; Music, Lalo Schifrin; Associate Producer-Production Manager, Barbara De Fina; Assistant Directors, Brian Frankish, Harry Bring; Special Effects, J. B. Jones; Sound, Howard Warren; Costumes, Molly Maginnis; Songs by various artists; Metrocolor; 90 minutes; Rated R; March release. CAST: Shannon Presby (Loren), Lori Loughlin (Abby), James Spader (Dutra), John Philbin (Gideon), David H. MacDonald (Moonie), Vincent Grant (Joe Bob), Theron Montgomery (Gordo), Eddie Jones (Charlie), Lucy Martin (Aunt Fay), Eric Stoltz (Mark), Paige Lyn Price (Karen), Court Miller (Sheriff), Tom Atkins ("Mac" MacWilliams), Jean DeBaer (Mary Beth MacWilliams), Robertson Carricart (Debuty), Brad Sullivan (Colonel Jenkins), Chad Wiggins (Chad Bob), and John Archie, Alex Panas, Toni Crabtree, Fred Buch, Ilse Earl, Billy Barzee, Greg Gilbert, John LeMay, Noel Rego, Don Kehr, Tim Waldrip, Margaret Welsh, Artie Maleschi, Jeff Moldovan, Courtney Brown, Mike Kirton, Jay Amor, Mark Mercury, Betty Raymond

NIGHT PATROL (New World) Producer, Bill Osco; Director, Jackie Kong; Screenplay, Murry Langston, Bill Levey, William Osco, Jackie Kong; Photography, Juerg Walthers, Hanania Baer; Editor, Miss Kong; 87 minutes; Rated R; March release. CAST: Murry Langston (Melvin), Linda Blair (Sue), Pat Paulsen (Kent), Jaye P. Morgan (Kate), Jack Riley (Dr. Ziegler), Billy Barty (Captain Lewis), Pat Morita (The Rape Victim), Sidney Lassick (Peeping Tom)

PORKY'S REVENGE! (20th Century-Fox) Producer, Robert L. Rosen; Director, James Komack; Screenplay, Ziggy Steinberg; Based on characters created by Bob Clark; Photography, Robert Jessup; Designer, Peter Wooley; Editor, John W. Wheeler; Music, Dave Edmunds; Costumes, Ray Summers; Sound, Howard Warren; Executive Producers, Melvin Simon, Milton Goldstein; Production Manager, Kurt Neumann; Assistant Director, David M. Whorf, Mary Lou MacLaury; Special Effects, J. B. Jones; Songs by various artists; Presented by Melvin Simon Productions and Astral Bellevue Pathe Inc.; DeLuxe Color; Panavision; 94 minutes; Rated R; March release. CAST: Dan Monahan (Pee Wee), Wyatt Knight (Tommy), Tony Ganios (Meat), Mark Herrier (Billy), Kaki Hunter (Wendy), Scott Colomby (Brian), Nancy Parsons (Ms. Balbricker), Chuck Mitchell (Porky), Rose McVeigh (Miss Webster), Fred Buch (Mr. Dobbish), Wendy Feign

(Blossom), Eric Christmas (Mr. Carter), Ilse Earl (Mrs. Morris), Kimberly Evenson (Inga), Bill Hindman (Coach Goodenough), Nan Hassinger (Grandmother), and Heidi Helmer, Nancy Valen, Don Rosae, Adrienne Walbridge, Doreen Murphy, Laura Tracy, San Mielke, William Fuller, Tom Bishop, James Cassidy, Ron Campbe Kimberly Kerwin, Julie Morgan, Lou Nelson, Jody Wilson, Jim Pa Eilers, Fred Waugh, Marc Mercury, Mal Jones, Mark Harris, M Johnston, Bert Sheldon, Michael Sandler, Elizabeth Hipwell, Elai Berman, Wanda the Chimp, Pep and Country Bands

THE SECRET OF THE SWORD (Atlantic) Producer, Arthur Nadel; Directors, Ed Friedman, Lou Kachivas, Marsh Lamore, B Reed, Gwen Wetzler; Screenplay, Larry Ditillo, Bob Forward; Exec tive Producer, Lou Scheimer; Presented by Filmation; Animation; 1 minutes; Rated G; March release. VOICES: John Erwin, Melen Britt, Alan Oppenheimer, Linda Gary, George Dicenzo, Erika Schei er, Erik Gunden

VARIETY (Horizon Films) Producer, Renee Shafransky; Direct Bette Gordon; Screenplay, Kathy Acker; Original Story, Miss Gord Photography, Tom Dicillo, John Foster; Editor, Ila Von Haspe Music, John Lurie; 100 minutes; Not Rated; March release. CAS Sandy McLeod (Christine), Will Patton (Mark), Richard Davids (Louie), Luis Guzman (Jose), Nan Goldin (Nan), and Lee Tucker, Pe Rizzo, Mark Boone Jr.

THE SURE THING (Embassy) Producer, Roger Birnbaum; Direct Rob Reiner; Screenplay, Steven L. Bloom, Jonathan Roberts; Photo raphy, Robert Elswit; Editor, Robert Leighton; Executive Produc Henry Winkler; Co-Producer, Andrew Scheinman; Production Mar ger, Steve Nicolaides; Assistant Directors, Thomas Lofaro, Bri James Ellis, Sam Epstein; Costumes, Durinda Wood; Set, Lisa Fisch Special Effects, John Frazier, Jeff Wischnack; Color by DeLuxe; Son by various artists; 94 minutes; Rated PG-13; March release. CAS John Cusack (Walter "Gib" Gibson), Daphne Zuniga (Alison Bra bury), Anthony Edwards (Lance), Boyd Gaines (Jason), Tim Robbi (Gary Cooper), Lisa Jane Persky (Mary Ann Webster), Viveca Lindf (Professor Taub), Nicollette Sheridan (The Sure Thing), Marcia Cha tie (Julie), Robert Anthony Marcucci (Bobby), Sarah Buxton (Sharo Lorrie Lightle (Lucy), Joshua Cadman (Jimbo), and Krystal Richar John Putch, Steve Pink, Tracy Reiner, Marty Layton, Amy Resnic Robert Bauer, Frantz Turner, Garry Goodrow

Dan Monahan, Kimberly Evenson
in "Porky's Revenge"
© *20th Century-Fox*

John Cusack, Daphne Zuniga
in "The Sure Thing"
© *Embassy*

Richard Farnsworth, Sylvester, Melissa
Gilbert, Michael Schoeffling in "Sylvester"
© Columbia

"Zombie Island Massacre"
© Picnic Productions

YLVESTER (Columbia) Producer, Martin Jurow; Director, Tim
unter; Screenplay, Carol Sobieski; Photography, Hiro Narita; De-
gner, James W. Newport; Editors, Howard Smith, Suzanne Pettit,
avid Garfield; Costumes, Sharon Day; Music, Lee Holdrige; Produc-
n Manager, Don Goldman; Assistant Directors, Pat Crowley, Rick
idney; Songs by various artists; from Rastar; Color; Dolby Stereo; 103
inutes; Rated PG; March release. CAST: Richard Farnsworth (Fos-
r), Melissa Gilbert (Charlie), Michael Schoeffling (Matt), Constance
wers (Muffy), Pete Kowanko (Harris), Yankton Hatten (Grant),
ane Sherwin (Seth), Chris Pedersen (Red), Angel Salazar (Tommy
hn), Arliss Howard (Peter), Shizuko Hoshi (Mrs. Daniels), Richard
mison (Capt. Marsh), James Gammon (Steve), Ariane de Vogue
riane), Norman Bennett (Lenny), Sam Laws (Sammy), Victoria
allegos (Sandy) and Nigel Casserley, Barbara Brumley, Dabney
arrett Munson, Helmut Graetz, Earl John McElroy, Brian T. O'Con-
r, Stuart Silbar, Maggie Wise Riley, J. P. Robertson, Michael
borne, Linda Snead, Dan Lufkin

UST IN THE DUST (New World) Producers, Allan Glaser, Tab
unter; Director, Paul Bartel; Screenplay, Philip John Taylor; Photog-
phy, Paul Lohmann; Editor, Alam Toomayan; Music, Peter Matz;
signer, Walter Pickette; Costumes, Dona Granata; Production Man-
er, John J. Smith; Assistant Directors, Michael Schroeder, Dennis
hite; Sound, Frank Meadows; Executive Producer, James C. Katz;
ecial Effects, A & A Special; Choreography, Stan Mazin; CFI Color;
Fox Run Production; 85 minutes; Rated R; March release. CAST:
b Hunter (Abel), Divine (Rosie), Lainie Kazan (Marguerita), Geof-
y Lewis (Hard Case), Henry Silva (Bernardo), Cesar Romero (Father
rcia), Gina Gallego (Ninfa), Nedra Voltz (Big Ed), Courtney Gains
ed Dick), and Pedro Gonzalez-Gonzalez, Woody Strode, Daniel
shman, Al Cantu, Ernie Shinagawa, Clinton S. Doran, Pit Ginsburg

ARK TWAIN (Harbour Towns Films) Producer-Director, Will
nton; Screenplay, Susan Shadburne; Editors, Kelley Baker, Michael
ll, Will Vinton; Music, Billy Scream; Character Design, Barry
ce; Set Design, Joan C. Gratz, Don Merkt; Claymation, William L.
sterman, Tom Gasek, Mark Gustafson, Craig Bartlett, Bruce
Kean; Executive Producer, Hugh Kennedy Tirrell; Color; 90
nutes; Not Rated; March release. VOICES: James Whitmore (Mark
ain), Michele Mariana (Becky Thatcher), Gary Krug (Huck Finn),
is Ritchie (Tom Sawyer)

ZOMBIE ISLAND MASSACRE (Troma Inc.) Producer, David
Broadnax; Director, John N. Carter; Screenplay, William Stoddard,
Logan O'Neil; Original Story, Mr. Broadnax, Mr. O'Neil; Photogra-
phy, Robert M. Baldwin; Editor, John N. Carter; Music, Harry Man-
fredini; Executive Producers, Michael Malagiero, Abraham Dabdoub;
Associate Producers, Dennis Stephenson, Umberto Dileo; Production
Manager, Robert Russell; Costumes, Unique Fashions, Mr. T; Assis-
tant Directors, Dwight Williams, Harvey Portee; Special Effects, Steve
Kirshoff; Song, Di Reggae Picnic, Harry Manfredini, NJRS; TVC
Color; 86 minutes; Rated R; March release. CAST: David Broadnax
(Paul), Rita Jenrette (Sandy), Tom Cantrell (Steve), Diane Clayre
Holub (Connie), George Peters (Whitney), Ian McMillian (Joe), Den-
nis Stephenson (Tour Guide), Debbie Ewing (Helen), Kristina Wetzel
(Barbie), Harriet Rawlings (Ethel), Christopher Ferris (Matt), Ralph
Monaco (Jerry), Deborah Jason (Donna), Tom Fitzsimmons (Ed),
Bruce Sterman (Hogan), Luba Pinus (Simmons), Emmett Murphy
(George), Trevor Reid (Voodoo Priest), Mignon Lowe (Voodoo
Priestess), Oscar Lawson (Creature)

WHAT SEX AM I? (HBO/Cinemax) Producers, Joseph Feury, Mil-
ton Justice, Mary Beth Yarrow; Director, Lee Grant; Photography,
Fred Murphy; Editors, Joanne Burke, Stephanie Palewski; Sound,
Maryte Kavaliauskus; Associate Producer, Prudence Glass Greenblatt;
Assistant Director-Production Manager, Joseph Feury; A Joseph Feury
Production; Produced in consultation with National Gender Counseling
Referrals, Janus Information Facility, San Francisco; Documentary; Du
Art Color; 60 minutes; Not rated; March release. CAST: Lee Grant
(Narrator)

LOVELINES (Tri-Star) Producers, Hal Taines, Michael Lloyd; Di-
rector, Rod Amateau; Screenplay, Chip Hand, William Hillman; Story,
Hand Hillman, Lloyd; Photography, Duke Callaghan; Art Director,
Robert K. Kinoshita; Editors, David Bretherton, Fred A. Chulack;
Associate Producer, Chip Hand; Music, Various Artists; Associate
Producer, Gary Hudson; Assistant Directors, Laura Andrus, Nicholas
Batchelor; In Metrocolor and Dolby Stereo; Rated R; 93 minutes;
March release. CAST: Greg Bradford (Rick), Mary Beth Evans (Piper),
Michael Winslow (J.D.), Don Michael Paul (Jeff), Tammy Taylor
(Priscilla), Stacey Toten (Cynthia), Robert DeLapp (Beagle), Frank
Zagarino (Godzilla), Todd Bryant (Hammer), Jonna Lee (Lisa), Robin
Watkins (Theresa), Claudia Cowan (Brigit), Lynn Cartwright (Mrs.
Woodson), Albert Szabo (Prof. Fromawitz), David Jolliffe (Tongue),
Miguel Ferrer (Dragon), Sherri Stoner (Suzy), Sarah Buxtom (Cathy),
Joyce Jamison (Mary), Shecky Greene (M.C.), Gary Morgan, Mar-
guerite Kimberley, Kelley Jean Browser, Michael Lloyd, Paul Val-
entine (Vandermeer), Conrad Palmisario, Robert Fiacco, James Davis
Trenton, Ernest Robinson, Aimee Eccles

Divine, Tab Hunter, Lainie Kazan
in "Lust in the Dust"
© New World

Mary Beth Evans, Greg Bradford
in "Lovelines"
© Tri-Star

113

Marin Kanter, Diane Lane, Laura Dern
in "Ladies and Gentlemen, the Fabulous Stains"

Vanity (center) in "The Last Dragon"
© Tri-Star

LADIES AND GENTLEMEN, THE FABULOUS STAINS (Paramount) Producer, Joe Roth; Director, Lou Adler; Screenplay, Rob Morton; Photography, Bruce Surtees; Executive Producer, Lou Lombardo; 87 minutes; Not rated; March release. CAST: Diane Lane (Corinne Burns), Ray Winstone (Billy), John "Fee" Waybill (Lou Corpse), Christine Lahti (Corinne's Aunt), David Clennon (Corinne's Agent), Barry Ford (Lawnboy), Laura Dern (Jessica McNeil), Marin Kanter (Tracy Burns), Paul Simonon (Johnny), Paul Cook (Danny), Steve Jones (Steve)

THE LAST DRAGON (Tri-Star) Producer, Rupert Hitzig; Director, Michael Schultz; Screenplay, Louis Venosta; Photography, James A. Contner; Designer, Peter Larkin; Editor, Christopher Holmes; Music, Misha Segal; Costumes, Robert de Mora; Executive Producer, Berry Gordy; Associate Producer-Production Manager, Joseph Caracciolo; Assistant Directors, Thomas Reilly, Ken Ornstein; Special Visual Effects, Rob Blalack, Praxis Filmworks, Inc.; Martial Arts Choreography, Torrance Mathis, Ron Van Clief, Ernie Reyes, Sr.; Choreography, Lester Wilson; Special Effects, Gary Zeller; Songs by various artists; Technicolor; Dolby Stereo; 109 minutes; Rated PG-13; March release. CAST: Taimak (Leroy), Vanity (Laura), Chris Murney (Eddie), Julis J. Carry, II (Sho'Nuff), Faith Prince (Angela), Leo O'Brien (Richie), Mike Starr (Rock), Jim Moody (Daddy Green), Glen Eaton (Johnny Yu), Ernie Reyes, Jr. (Tai), Roger Campbell (Announcer), Ester Marrow (Mama Green), Keshia Knight (Sophia), Jamal Mason (Roy), B. J. Barie (Jackie), Henry Yuk (Hu Yi), Michael G. Chin (Lu Yi), Fredric Mao (Du Yi), Thomas Ikeda (Master), W. H. Macy (J. J.), Trulie MacLeod (Margo), Gary Aprahamian (Jason), and Sarita Allen, Jacqui Lee Smith, Jodi Moccia, Sal Russo, Chazz Palminteri, Frank Renzulli, Andre Brown, David Claudio, Kirk Taylor, Shonte, Janet Bloem, Lisa Loving, Lou David, Verne Williams, Captain Haggerty, Robert Silver, Clayton Prince, Brandon Schultz, Carl Payne, Torrance Mathis, Jeffrey Ward, William Taylor, Anthony Cortino, Sebastian Hitzig, Kim Chang, Derek Schultz, Rhonda Silberstein, Peter Traina, Freddie Stroble, Jack Meeks, Joe Dabenigno, Soo Ginn Lee, Scott Coker, Julian Villanueva

DELIVERY BOYS (New World) Producers, Craig Horrall, Per Sjostedt; Director-Screenplay, Ken Handler; Photography, Larry Revene; Assistant Director, Per Sjostedt; Executive Producer, Chuck Vincent; Production Manager, David Larkin; Designer, George Brown;

Costumes, The Bob Pusilo Studio; Editor, Gary Karr; Choreographer Nelso Vasquez, Jody Oliver; Color; 94 minutes; Rated R; April releas CAST: Joss Marcano (Max), Tom Sierchio (Joey), Jim Soriero (Co rad), Nelson Vasquez (Izzie), Victor Colicchio (Tony), Naylon Mitc ell (Jazz Mace), Ralph Cole Jr. (Wild Man), Jody Oliver (Angelina Deckard Fontanes (Paulie), Lisa Vidal (Tina), Kelly Nichols (Eliz beth), Jerome Bynder (Septimus), Kuno Sponholz (Dr. Schmid Frank Canzano (Elmer), and Craig Horrall, Taija Rae, Suzanne Rem Lawrence, Deborah Quayle, Yvette Edelhart, Anthony Matte Geralynn Gerard, Joey Faye, Carolyn Green, Veronica Hart, Annabe Gurwitch, Jeff Nielsen, Mario Van Peebles, Samantha Fox, Jose Maldonado, Rob Roy, Jo-Ann Marshall, Naima Eriksen, Scott Bake Carlos Jiminez, John Debello, Crist Swann, Sammy Luquis, Rodn Harvey, Frank Lynn, Alex Wood, George Ovalle, Richie Pinero, Jo Roman, Angel Valentin, Eddie Gonzalez, Pablo Vasquez, Israel Cre po, Eddie Roman, Marilyn Randall, Galli Horacio, Kenji Takabayash Paul Vargas, Jorge Gonzalez, Andre De Lise, Kevin Rogers, Elizabe Stern, Susan Mitchell, Linda Ipanema, John Eitel, Michael Mason

GIRLS JUST WANT TO HAVE FUN (New World) Produce Chuck Russell; Director, Alan Metter; Screenplay, Amy Spies; Exec tive Producer, Stuart Cornfeld; Associate Producer, Robert F. Lyo Designer, Jeffrey Staggs; Production Manager, Britt Lomond; Ass tant Directors, Daniel Schneider, Stan Zabka, Roger LaPage, Richa Muessel; Photography, Thomas Ackerman; Editor, Lorenzo D Stefano; Sound, Alvin Susumu Tokunow; Choreographers, Otis Sall Bill Goodson, Steve LaChance; Gymnastics Coordinator, Chu Gaylord; Music, Thomas Newman; Costumes, Betty Pecha Madde Special Effects, Robert Calvert, Court Wizard; Color; Dolby Stereo; minutes; Rated PG; April release. CAST: Sarah Jessica Parker (Jan Glenn), Lee Montgomery (Jeff Malene), Morgan Woodward (J. Sands), Jonathan Silverman (Drew), Helen Hunt (Lynne Stone), Hoc Gagnier (Natalie Sands), Ed Lauter (Colonel Glenn), Shannen Dohe (Maggie Malene), Biff Yeager (Mr. Malene), Ian Giatti (Zacha Glenn), Margaret Howell (Mrs. Glenn), Terence McGovern (Ir Kristi Somers (Rikki), Lee Arone (Mrs. Lemsky), Shaun Bry (Dave), Charene Cathleen (Patty), Mark Caso (Wolf), Deanna Cla (Tiffany), and Candace Daly, Olive Dunbar, Stuart Fratkin, La Gelman, Valerie Grear, Noreen Hennesy, Steve LaChance, Mil Phineas Newborn III, Jim Ruttman, Sharon Shayne, Susan Styles, W. Smith, Cecilie A. Stuart, Michael Higgins, Alison Brown

Tom Sierchio, Jim Soriero
in "Delivery Boys"
© New World

Lee Montgomery, Sarah Jessica Parker
in "Girls Just Want to Have Fun"
© New World

Deborah Goodrich, Clayton Rohner, Joyce Hyser
in "Just One of the Guys" © *Columbia*

Toni Hudson, Lee Montgomery
in "Prime Risk" © *Almi*

JUST ONE OF THE GUYS (Columbia) Producer, Andrew Fogelson; Director, Lisa Gottlieb; Screenplay, Dennis Feldman, Jeff Franklin; Story, Dennis Feldman; Photography, John McPherson; Designer, Paul Peters; Editor, Lou Lombardo; Executive Producer, Jeff Franklin; Associate Producers, Don McFarlane, Peck Prior; Music, Tom Scott; Production Manager, Don Goldman; Assistant Directors, Bill Scott, Dennis Capps; Choreography, Jennifer Stace; Costumes, George Little, Linda Matthews; Special Effects, John Frazier; Songs by various artists; Metrocolor; 100 minutes; Rated PG-13; April release. CAST: Joyce Hyser (Terry), Clayton Rohner (Rick), Billy Jacoby (Buddy), Toni Hudson (Denise), William Zabka (Greg), Leigh McCloskey (Kevin), Sherilyn Fenn (Sandy), Deborah Goodrich (Deborah), Arye Gross (Willie), Robert Fieldsteel (Phil), Stuart Charno (Reptile), John Apicella (Coach Morrison), Kenneth Tigar (Mr. Raymaker), Steve Basil (Mark), J. Williams (Julian), Don Blanton (Jimmy), Ramon Chavez (Mr. Mendosa), Frank Sprague (Mr. Grasso), Emily Ragsdale (English Teacher), Richard Blake (Janitor), Mickey Finn (Security Guard), Stacy Blythe (Linda), Anthony Galde (Ralph), Linda Kelly (Betty), Kim Norwitz (Jill), Kim Studer (Beth), Joseph Easterwald (Freshman), Katy Boyer (Jeanine), and Troy Clegg, Randy Bowers, Brain Melrose, Tony Brock, Jay Davis, John Coury, James Michael Zavala, J. Williams

MOVERS AND SHAKERS (MGM/UA) Producers, Charles Grodin, William Asher; Director, William Asher; Screenplay, Charles Grodin; Photography, Robbie Greenberg; Editor, Tom Benko; Music, Ken and Mitzie Welch; Color; 80 minutes; Rated PG; April release. CAST: Walter Matthau (Jon Mulholland), Charles Grodin (Herb Derman), Vincent Gardenia (Saul Gritz), Tyne Daly (Nancy Derman), Bill Macy (Fred Spokane), Gilda Radner (Livia Machado), Earl Boen (Marshall), Michael Lerner (Arnie), Joe Mantell (Larry), William Prince (Louis Martin), Nita Talbot (Dorothy), Sandy Ward (Doctor)

MOVING VIOLATIONS (20th Century-Fox) Producers, Joe Roth, Harry Ufland; Director, Neal Israel; Screenplay, Neal Israel, Pat Proft; Story, Paul and Sharon Boorstin; Photography, Robert Elswit; Editor, Tom Walls; Music, Ralph Burns; Designers, Virginia Field, Gregory Pickrell; Costumes, Darryl LeVine; Sound, James S. La Rue; Co-Producer, Robert Israel; Executive Producers, Pat Proft, Doug Draizin; Production Manager, Ann Kindberg; Associate Producer, Richard Dwyer; Assistant Directors, Irby Smith, James F. Behnke; Special Effects, Rick H. Josephsen; DeLuxe Color; 90 minutes; Rated PG-13; April release. CAST: John Murray (Dana Cannon), Jennifer Tilly (Amy Hopkins), James Keach (Deputy Halik), Brian Backer (Scott Greeber), Ned Eisenberg (Wink Barnes), Clara Peller (Emma Jean), Wendie Jo Sperber (Joan Pudillo), Nedra Volz (Mrs. Loretta Houk), Fred Willard (Terrence "Doc" Williams), Lisa Hart Carroll (Dep. Virginia Morris), Nadine Van Der Velde (Stephanie McCarthy), Ben Mittleman (Spencer Popadophalos), Victor Campos (Raoul Bienveneda), Willard Pugh (Jeff Roth), Sally Kellerman (Judge Nedra Henderson), and Joseph Alfasa, Elizabeth Arlen, Billy Beck, Charles Bergansky, Anne Betancourt, Mitch Brown, Don Cheadle, Darlene Chehardy, William Forward, Kym Herrin, Vince Howard, Jim Hudson, Alvin Ing, Neal Israel, Robert Israel, Freeman King, John Lykes, Danny Mauna, Mark Mauna, Mike McManus, R. A. Mihailoff, Jamie Mizada, Tom McFadden, Gregory W. Norberg, Jimmy Ortega, Dedee Pfeiffer, Karen Philipp-Proft, David Pierce, Casey Sander, Robert Saurman, Jess Sofer

PRIME RISK (Almi Pictures, Inc.) Producer, Herman Grigsby; Director-Screenplay, Michael Farkas; Photography, Mac Ahlberg; Editor, Bruce Green; Music, Phil Marshall; Designer, Christopher Henry; Costumes, Bernadette O'Brien; Executive Producer, Bernard Farkas; Associate Producer, James Reed; Assistant Directors, John R. Woodward, Gary A. Lowe; Sound, Linda Dove; Production Manager, Tony Lopez; Special Effects, Special Effects Systems, Gary F. Bentley, John Pospisil; Color; 100 minutes; Rated PG-13; April release. CAST: Toni Hudson (Julie Collins), Lee Montgomery (Michael Fox), Samuel Bottoms (Bill Yeoman), Clu Gulager (Paul Minsky), Keenan Wynn (Dr. Lasser), Lois Hall (Dr. Holt), Rick Rakowski (John), John Lykes (Vance), James O'Connell (Terry), Randy Pearlman (Ed), Timothy Rice (Albert), Roy Stuart (Mr. Fox), Helen Duffy (Mrs. Fox), Christopher Murphy (Tony), and Caron Tate, Cathey Paine, Art Scholl, Rick Warner, Biff Yeager, Tony Roque, Dale Stein, Bruce Elliott, Michael Willis, Carol Bennett, Dick Valentine, Carey Scott

PUMPING IRON II: THE WOMEN (Cinecom International) Producer-Director-Concept, George Butler; Written by Charles Gaines, George Butler; Based on their book "Pumping Iron II: The Unprecedented Woman"; Photography, Dyanna Taylor; Editors, Paul Barnes, Susan Crutcher; 107 minutes; Not Rated; April release. CAST: Lori Bowen, Carla Dunlap, Bev Francis, Rachel McLish, Kris Alexander, Lydia Cheng, Steve Michalik, Steve Weinberger, Randy Rice

James Keach, Sally Kellerman
in "Moving Violations"
© *20th Century-Fox*

Carla Dunlap in "Pumping Iron II"
© *Cinecom International*

Brent Huff, Emilia Lesniak, Sho Kosugi
in "9 Deaths of the Ninja" © *Crown*

Marcello Rollando, Ronald Hunter, George Stover
in "Two for the Money"

9 DEATHS OF THE NINJA (Crown International) Producer, Ashok Amritraj; Director-Screenplay, Emmett Alston; Photography, Roy H. Wagner; Music, Cecile Colayco; Designer, Rodell Cruz; Choreographers, Douglas Nierras, Alan Amiel; Executive Producers, Vijay Amritraj, Robert L. Friedman, Sidney Balkin; Associate Producers, Shelley E. Reid, Charo Santos Concio; Production Manager, Aurelio Navarro; Assistant Directors, Jun Amazan, Tim Bismark; Special Effects, Danilo Dominquez; Costumes, Margaret Rose; Editors, Mr. Alston, Mr. Ordonnez, Mr. Waters, Tim Bismark; DeLuxe Color; 94 minutes; Rated R; April release. CAST: Sho Kosugi (Spike Shinobi), Brent Huff (Steve Gordon), Emilia Lesniak (Jennifer Barnes), Blackie Dammett (Alby the Cruel), Regina Richardson (Honey Hump), Vijay Amritraj (Rankin), Lisa Friedman (Tour Guide), Kane Kosugi (Kane), Shane Kosugi (Shane), Bruce Fanger (Dr. Wolf), Sonny Erang (Rahji), David Brass (Tex), Aiko Cownden (Marisa Lee), Jennifer Crumrine (Amanda), Helen McNeely (Mrs. Garcia), Protacio Dee (Feng Fu), Judy Blye (Wo Pee/Woo Wee), and Joji Nagai, Ken Watanabe, Victor Ordonez, Leah Navarro, Ric Segreto, Ron Milhench, Jacques Gervais, Warren Maclean, Susan Meyer, Sam Lombardo, Nancy Keaton, James Crumrine, Emebet Aigaz, Des Ayallew

TWO FOR THE MONEY (Bonner Films) Producer, Mary Holland; Director, Lee Bonner; Screenplay, Lee Bonner, Leif Elsmo; Photography, David Insley; Designer, Vincent Perania; Editors, Lee Bonner, Randy Aitken; Music, John Palumbo; Assistant Director, Leif Elsmo; Production Manager, Terri Trupp; Color; 75 minutes; Not Rated; April release. CAST: Ronald Hunter (Walter), Sean Murphy (Betsy), Steve Beauchamp (Skipper), Peter Walker (Oliver), Hans Kramm (Bartender), and Joseph Cimino, Art Donovan, Marcello Rollando, George Stover (Gangsters)

WILDROSE (Troma, Inc.) Producer, Sandra Schulberg; Director-Co-Producer, John Hanson; Screenplay, John Hanson, Eugene Corr; Story, John Hanson, Sandra Schulberg; Photography, Peter Stein; Editor, Arthur Coburn; Music, Cris Williamson, Bernard Krause, Gary Remal; Executive Producer, New Front Films; Color; 95 minutes; Not Rated; April release. CAST: Lisa Eichhorn (June Lorich), Tom Bower (Rick Ogaard), Jim Cada (Pavich), Cinda Jackson (Karen), Dan Nemanick (Ricotti), Lydia Olson (Katri Sippola), Bill Schoppert (Timo Maki), James Stowell (Doobie), Stephen Yoakam (Billy), and Vienna Maki, Frankie Smoltz, Clinton Maxwell, Ernest Tomatz, Marie Nelson, Father Frank Perkovich, People of the Mesabi Range and Bayfield, Wisconsin

DELTA PI (Pegasus) formerly "Mugsy's Girls"; Producers, Leonard Shapiro, Kevin Brodie; Direction and Screenplay, Kevin Brodie; Executive Producers, J. Don Harris, Frederick Kunel; Photography, Paul Lohmann; Editor, Bill Parker; Music, Nelson Kole; In CFI Color; Rated R; 90 minutes; April release. CAST: Ruth Gordon (Mugs), Laura Branigan, Joanna Dierek, Estrelita, Rebecca Forstadt, Candace Pandolfo (Girls), Eddie Deezen (Lane), James Marcel (Shaun)

THE GALAXY INVADER (Moviecraft Entertainment) Director-Screenplay-Editor-Story, Don Dohler; Photography Paul E. Loeschke; Music, Norman Naplock, Led & Silver; Assistant Director, Anne Frith; Special Effects, David Donoho; Alien Design and Creation, John Cosentino; Color; 80 minutes; Rated PG; April release. CAST: Richard Ruxton (Joe), Faye Tilles (Carol), George Stover (J.J.), Greg Dohler (David), Anne Frith (Ethel), Richard Dyszel (Dr. William Tracy), Kim Dohler (Annie), Theresa Harold (Vickie), Don Leifert (Frank), Glenn Barnes (Alien)

SANFORD MEISNER: THE THEATER'S BEST KEPT SECRET (Columbia) Producer, Kent Paul; Directed, Photographed and Edited by Nick Doob; Creative Adviser-Interviewer, Stephen Harvey; Music, Skip Kennon; Executive Producer, Sydney Pollack; In color, black and white; Not rated; 60 minutes; April release. A documentary profile of veteran drama coach Sanford Meisner featuring interviews with Robert Duvall, Peter Falk, Bob Fosse, Lee Grant, Anne Jackson, David Mamet, Tony Randall, Mark Rydell, Mary Steenburgen, Frances Sternhagen, Gwen Verdon, Jon Voight, Eli Wallach, Joanne Woodward, Gregory Peck, Vivian Matalon, Suzanne Pleshette, Elia Kazan

FUTURE COP (Empire Pictures) Producer-Director, Charles Band; Screenplay, Paul De Meo, Danny Bilson; Photography, Mac Ahlberg; Special Effects Make-up, John Buechler; Music, Mark Ryder, Phil Davies; Deluxe Color; 85 minutes; Rated PG-13; May release. CAST: Tim Thomerson (Jack Deth), Helen Hunt (Leena), Michael Stefani (Whistler), Art Le Fleur (McNulty), Biff Manard (Hap Ashby)

GOTCHA! (Universal) Producer, Paul G. Hensler; Director, Jeff Kanew; Screenplay, Dan Gordon; Story, Paul G. Hensler, Dan Gordon; Photography, King Baggot; Designer, Norman Newberry; Editor, Michael A. Stevenson; Music, Bill Conti; Costumes, April Ferry; Supervising Producer, Peter MacGregor-Scott; Executive Producer, Michael I. Levy; Production Manager, P. M. Scott; Assistant Directors, Jim Simons, Jerry Ketchum; Sound, Colin Charles, Thomas

Glenn Barnes, George Stover
in "The Galaxy Invader"

Tom Bower, Lisa Eichhorn
in "Wildrose"
© *Red Ghosts Films*

Nick Corri, Anthony Edwards
in "Gotcha!" © *Universal*

Billy Dee Williams, John Cassavetes
in "Marvin and Tige" © *Castle Hill*

ausey; Special Effects, Fred Z. Gebler; Songs by various artists; echnicolor; 97 minutes; Rated PG-13; May release. CAST: Anthony dwards (Jonathan), Linda Fiorentino (Sasha), Nick Corri (Manolo), lex Rocco (Al), Marla Adams (Maria), Klaus Loewitsch (Vlad), hristopher Rydell (Bob), Brad Cowgill (Reilly), Kari Lizer (Muffy), d Christie Claridge, David Wohl, Irene Olga Lopez, Bernard iegel, Muriel Dubrule, Tiina Maria, Francis LeMaire, Marie Carlan, Ayshea Leigh, Danny Tolkan, Maxmilian Ruethlein, Roland itschke, Dan Van Husen, Traudl Haas, Manfred Tummler, Erich hwartz, Christel Merian, Georg Tryphon, Reggie, Tom Deininger, irk Vogeley, Susanna Bonasewicz, Karl Spanner, Dragomir anojevic, Berno Kurten, Bernward Buker, Elke Knittel, Kristina asari, Dante Di Loreto

GRACE QUIGLEY" (Cannon) Carried 1985 as "The Ultimate olution of Grace Quigley" CAST: Katharine Hepburn, Nick Nolte

YMKATA (MGM/UA) Producer, Fred Weintraub; Director, Robert louse; Screenplay, Charles Robert Carner; Based on the novel by Dan yler Moore; Photography, Godfrey Godar; Designer, Veljko Despoto- c; Editor, Robert A. Ferretti; Music, Alfi Kabiljo; Associate Pro- icer, Rebecca Poole; Production Managers, Richard Delabio, Boris regoric, Dgorjan Tozija; Assistant Directors, Vladimir Spindler, reg Logan, Brana Srdic, Kathy McGinnis; Special Effects, Peter awson, Terry Glass, Steve Purcell; Costumes, Drago Habazin; Met- color; 90 minutes; Rated R; May release. CAST: Kurt Thomas onathan Cabot), Tetchie Agbayani (Princess Rubali), Richard Norton amir), Edward Bell (Paley), John Barrett (Gomez), Conan Lee lao), Bob Schott (Thorg), Buck Kartalian (The Kahn), Eric Lawson olonel Cabot), and Sonny Barnes, Tadashi Yamashita, Sharan Lea, aniel Price, Peter Buntic, T. Vukusic, Pai Kim, Lou Baldovine, Matt eaumont, Bill Britt, Bruce Crete, Martin Ellis, Tony Fletcher, Jim ibson, Colin Handley, John Hooper, Blake Johnson, Kerry Long, acy Noles, Jonas Patricko, Monty Wells, Mark Wickman, Chip right, Margo Bartow, Debbie Beckin, Larry Bisonnette, Brent isonnette, Ray Downing, Carla Hill, Pam Lewis, Teresa Marineau, ecky Palachuk

ERE COME THE LITTLES (Atlantic) Producers, Jean Chalopin, ndy Heyward, Tetsuo Katayama; Director, Bernard Deyries; Screen- ay, Woody Kling; From a book by Jon Peterson; Executive Produc- s, Jean Chalopin, Andy Heyward; Voice Recording Director, Wally

Burr; Animation Directors, Tsukasa Tannai, Yoshinobu Michihata; Associate Producers, Kohi Takeuchi, Yuji Toki; Associate Director, Nobu Tomizawa; Assistant Director, Sunao Katabuchi; Designer, Mutsuo Koseki; Photography, Hajime Hasegawa, Kenichi Kobayashi; Editor, Masatoshi Tsurubuchi; Music, Haim Saban, Shuki Levy; Color; 90 minutes; Rated G; May release. VOICES: Jimmy E. Keegan (Henry Bigg), Bettina Bush (Lucy Little), Donovan Freberg (Tom Little), Hal Smith (Uncle Augustus), Gregg Berger (William Little), Patricia Parris (Helen Little), Alvy Moore (Grandpa Little), Robert David Hall (Dinky Little), Mona Marshall (Mrs. Evans)

MARVIN AND TIGE (Castle Hill) Producer, Wanda Dell; Director, Eric Weston; Screenplay, Wanda Dell, Mr. Weston; Based on the novel by Frankcina Glass; Photography, Brian West; Editor, Fabien Dahlen Tordjmann; Music, Patrick Williams; Color; 104 minutes; Rated PG; May release. CAST: John Cassavetes (Marvin Stewart), Billy Dee Williams (Richard Davis), Denise Nicholas-Hill (Vanessa Jackson), Gibran Brown (Tige Jackson), Fay Hauser (Brenda Davis), and Georgia Allen, Jerry Penson, Charles Darden, May K. Pearce, Lou Walker, Rob Narke, Danny Nelson, Jennie Fleming, Frank Hart, Tami Dash

NIGHT TRAIN TO TERROR (Visto International) Producer, Jay Schlossberg-Cohen; Directors, John Carr, Schlossberg-Cohen, Philip Marshak, Tom McGowan, Gregg Tallas; Screenplay, Philip Yordan; Photography, Susan Maljan; Editors, Evan Stoliar, Steve Nielson; Music, Ralph Ives; Effects, William Stromberg; Animation, Anthony Doublin, Stromberg; United Color; 93 minutes; Rated R; May release. CAST: John Phillip Law (Harry Billings), Cameron Mitchell (Detective Stern), Marc Lawrence (Weiss/Dieter), Charles Moll (James Hansen/Orderly), Meridith Haze (Gretta Connors), Ferdy Mayne (God), Lu Sickler (Devil)

ALMOST YOU (20th Century-Fox) Producer, Mark Lipson; Director, Adam Brooks; Screenplay, Mark Horowitz; Photography, Alexander Gruszynski; Editor, Mark Burns; Music, Jonathan Elias; Color; 96 minutes; Rated R; May release. CAST: Brooke Adams (Erica), Griffin Dunne (Alex), Karen Young (Lisa), Marty Watt (Kevin), Christine Estabrook (Maggie), Josh Mostel (David), Laura Dean (Jeannie), Dana Delany (Susan), Miguel Pinero (Ralph), Joe Silver (Uncle Stu), Joe Leon (Uncle Mel), Spalding Gray (Travel Agent)

Kurt Thomas, Tetchie Agbayani
in "Gymkata"
© *MGM/UA Entertainment Co.*

Marty Watt, Laura Dean
in "Almost You"
© *20th Century-Fox*

117

Daniel Roebuck, Cindy Ann Thompson
in "Cavegirl" © Crown International

Joe Don Baker in "Final Justice"
© Arista Films

CAVEGIRL (Crown International) Producer-Director-Screenplay-Photography, David Oliver; Adapted from a Screenplay by Phil Groves; Editor, Robert Field; Music, Jon St. James; Costumes, Pam Lovancher, Cher Slater; Sound, Ken Willingham, Walt Martin, Bayard Carey; Associate Producer, Reed Fenton; Assistant Director, Jack Isgro; Color; 90 minutes; Rated R; May release. CAST: Daniel Roebuck (Rex), Cindy Ann Thompson (Eba), Saba Moor (Saba), Jeff Chayette (Argh), Darren Young (Dar), Charles Mitchell (Char), Cynthis Rullo (Aka), Tom Hamil (Casey), Bill Adams (Bill), Chris Noble (Hank), Bill Sehres (Ralph), Sydni King (Karen), Stacey Swain (Brenda), Larry Gabriel (Professor), Valerie Greybe (Attila), David Castro (Catso), Bob Vern (Oben), Kent Jorgensen (Jorge)

FINAL JUSTICE (Arista Films, Inc.) Producer-Director-Screenplay, Greydon Clark; Photography, Nicholas von Sternberg; Music, David Bell; Executive Producer, Louis George; Color; 90 minutes; Rated R; May release. CAST: Joe Don Baker (Thomas Jefferson Geronimo III), Venantino Venantini (Joseph Palermo), Patrizia Pellegrino (Gina), Helena Abella (Maria), Bill McKinney (Chief Wilson), Rossano Brazzi (La Manna)

FLETCH (Universal) Producers, Alan Greisman, Peter Douglas; Director, Michael Ritchie; Screenplay, Andrew Bergman; Based on the novel by Gregory McDonald; Photography, Fred Schuler; Designer, Boris Leven; Editor, Richard A. Harris; Costumes, Gloria Gresham; Music, Harold Faltermeyer; Associate Producer, Gordon A. Webb; Production Manager, Gordon A. Webb; Assistant Directors, Wolfgang Glattes, Larry Rapaport; Sound, Robert Shoup, Karen Spangenberg; Songs by various artists; Technicolor; Dolby Stereo; 96 minutes; Rated PG; May release. CAST: Chevy Chase (Fletch), Joe Don Baker (Chief Karlin), Dana Wheeler-Nicholson (Gail Stanwyk), Richard Libertini (Walker), Tim Matheson (Alan Stanwyk), M. Emmet Walsh (Dr. Dolan), George Wendt (Fat Sam), Kenneth Mars (Stanton Boyd) Geena Davis (Larry), Grace Gaynor (Mrs. Underhill), and Bill Henderson, William Traylor, George Wyner, Tony Longo, Larry Flash Jenkins, Ralph Seymour, Kareen Abdul-Jabbar, James Avery, Reid Cruickshanks, Bruce French, Burton Gilliam, David Harper, Chick Hearn, Alison LaPlaca, Joe Praml, William Sanderson, Penny Santon, Robert Sorrells, Beau Starr, Nico DeSilva, Peggy Doyle, Rick Garcia, Freeman King, Loraine Shields, Bill Sorrells, Arnold Turner, Roger Ammann, Mary Battilana, Henry Hank Bleeker, Donald Chaffin, Darren Dublin, Kristine M. Gossman, Irene Olga Lopez, Merv Maruyama

OUT OF CONTROL (New World) Producers, Fred Weintraub, Daniel Grodnik; Director, Allan Holzman; Screenplay, Sandra Weintraub Roland, Vicangelo Bullock; Photography, John A. Alonzo; Music, Hawk, Susan Justin; Editors, Robert Ferretti, Allan Holzman; Executive Producers, Paul Lichtman, Arnold Fishman; Production Manager, Richard DeLabio; Sound, John Stein; Songs by various artists; A Jordan Film/Incovent Production; Color; 78 minutes; Rated R; May release. CAST: Martin Hewitt (Keith), Betsy Russell (Chrissie), Claudia Udy (Tina), Andrew J. Lederer (Elliot), Cindi Dietrich (Robin), Richard Kantor (Gary), Sherilyn Fenn (Katie), Jim Young (Cowboy), Zoenko Jelcio (Carlos) Mirko Satalic (Nick), Pavo Baienovic (Pete), Bill Farrington (George), Slobodan Dimitrijevic (Gypsy), Kapural Vjenceslav (McDuff), Ken Swerilas (Mr. Clarkson), Susan Justin (Debby), and Suzanne Stanford, Peter Buntic, Sylvo Farrington, Jorma Komulainen, Lentotilaus Oy, Esa Westerlund

RAPPIN' (Cannon Group) Producers, Menahem Golan, Yoram Globus; Director, Joel Silberg; Screenplay, Robert Litz, Adam Friedman; Photography, David Gurfinkel; Editors, Marcus Manton, Andy Horvitch, Bert Glatstein; Choreographer, Edmond Kresley; Music, Larry Smith, Michael Linn; Designer, Steve Miller; Associate Producer-Production Manager, Jeffrey Silver; Assistant Directors, Steven Felder, Tommy Burns; Costumes, Aude Bronson-Howard, Kevin Faherty; Songs by various artists; TVC Color; 92 minutes; Rated PG; May release. CAST: Mario Van Peebles (John Hood), Tasia Valenza (Dixie), Charles Flohe (Duane), Leo O'Brien (Allan), Eriq La Salle (Ice), Richie Abanes (Richie), Kadeem Hardison (Moon), Melvin Plowden (Fats), Harry Goz (Thorndike), Rony Clanton (Cedric), Edy Byrde (Grandma), and Ruth Jaroslow, Anthony Bishop, Fredric Mao, Michael Esihos, Rutanya Alda, Brandi Freund, Debra Greenfield, David Butler, Scott Peck, Clayton Hill, Joe Schad, Joe Marmo, William Mott, Tommy Ross, Harry Scanlon, Anthony Bradberry, Do Brockett, Thomas Clint Clutter, Carl Fred Robinson, Angela De Filippo, Lyn Philistine, Dan Caliguire, Warren Mills, Claudja Barry, Eugene Wilde, JoAnna Gardner, Tracy Marrow, David Storrs, Eric Garcia, Henry Garcia, Ernest Cunningan, Christopher Johnson, Jack Reese, Stacey O'Neal, Rosie Steave, Arlinda Dickens, Antoine Lundy, Steven Lundy, Trisco Pearson, Jessie Daniels, Charles Nelson, Will Cross, Salvador Irizarry, David Whitaker, Troion Whitaker, David Marshall

Chevy Chase in "Fletch"
© Universal

Richie Abanes, Eriq LaSalle, Tasia Valenza,
Mario Van Peebles, Melvin Plowden in "Rappin' "

Betsy Russell, Martin Hewitt
in "Out of Control" © *New World*

Barret Oliver, Amy Linker, Daniel Bryan
Corkill in "D.A.R.Y.L." © *Paramount*

THE PASSING (International Cinema) Producers-Screenplay, John Huckert, Mary Maruca; Director-Editor, John Huckert; Photography, ochi Melero, Richard Chisolm; Music, William-John Tudor; Special Effects, Mark Chorvinsky, Miguel Munoz; Sound, Dennis Towns, Dwayne Dell, David Masser; Color; 96 minutes; Not rated; May release. CAST: Welton Benjamin Johnson (Laviticus Rose), James Carroll Plaster (Ernie Neuman), John Huckert (Wade Carney), Lynn Odell (Monica)

THE ORACLE (Shapiro Entertainment) Producer, Walter E. Sear; Director, Roberta Findlay; Music, Walter E. Sear, Michael Litovsky; screenplay-Story, R. Allen Leider; Assistant Director, Rafael Guadalupe; A Reeltime Corp. production in color; Rated R; 94 minutes; May release. CAST: Caroline Capers Powers, Roger Neil, Victoria Dryden, Pam LaTesta, Chris Maria de Koron

KILLZONE (Films Around the World) Producer, Jack Marino; Director, David A. Prior; Photography, Victor Alexander; Music, Robert A. Higgins; Associate Producer, Thomas Baldwin; Editor, Victor Alexander; Screenplay, David A. Prior, Jack Marino; Assistant Director, T. E. Baldwin, Jr.; A Spartanfilms production in color; Not rated; 87 minutes; May release. CAST: Fritz Matthews, Ted Prior (Mitchell), David James Campbell (Crawford), Daniel Kong (Ling), Richard Massery (Lucas), William Joseph Zipp (Manley), Lawrence Jdy (Matthews), Richard Brailford (Johnson), Ron Pace (Hillbilly), Jack Marino (Harry), Tom Baldwin (Hillbilly's Son), Sharon Young (Harry's Wife), Richard Bravo (Gunman), James Edward Everett (Co-Pilot), Terry St. Clair (McKenna's Wife), Kathleen Louise Marino McKenna's Daughter)

FUTURE-KILL (IFM) Presented by Magic Shadows; Executive Producer, Don Barker; Producers, Gregg Unterberger, John H. Best; Associate Producers, Ronald W. Moore, Edwin Neal, Terri Smith; screenplay-Direction, Ronald W. Moore; In color; Rated R; 85 minutes; May release. CAST: Edwin Neal, Marilyn Burns

LIFEFORCE (Tri-Star) Producers, Menahem Golan, Yoram Globus; Director, Tobe Hooper; Screenplay, Dan O'Bannon, Don Jakoby; based on a novel by Colin Wilson; Music, Henry Mancini, Michael Kamen; Designer, John Graysmark; Photography, Alan Hume; Editor, John Grover; Special Effects, John Gant; Costumes, Carin Hooper; Choreographer, Adrian Hedley; Associate Producer, Michael J. Kagan; roduction Manager, Basil Somner; Assistant Directors, Richard Hoult, Melvin Lind, Tim Reed, Tony Aherne, Paul Lowin; Eastman Color; Dolby Stereo; J-D-C Widescreen; 101 minutes; Rated R; June release. CAST: Steve Railsback (Carlsen), Peter Firth (Caine), Frank Finlay (Fallada), Mathilda May (Space Girl), Patrick Stewart (Dr.

Armstrong), Michael Gothard (Bukovsky), Nicholas Ball (Derebridge), Aubrey Morris (Sir Percy), Nancy Paul (Ellen), John Hallam (Lamson), and John Keegan, Christopher Jagger, Bill Malin, Jerome Willis, Derek Benfield, John Woodnutt, James Forbes-Robertson, Peter Porteous, Katherine Schofield, Owen Holder, Jamie Roberts, Russell Sommers, Patrick Connor, Sidney Kean, Paul Cooper, Chris Sullivan, Milton Cadman, Rupert Baker, Gary Hildreth, Edward Evans, Nicholas Donnelly, Peter Lovstrom, Julian Firth, Carl Rigg, Elizabeth Morton, Geoffrey Frederick, David English, Emma Jacobs, Michael John Paliotti, Brian Carroll, Richard Oldfield, Christopher Barr, Burnell Tucker, Thom Booker, Michael Fitzpatrick, Richard Sharpe, John Golightly, William Lindsay, David Beckett, Sydney Livingstone, Ken Parry, John Edmunds, Haydn Wood

D.A.R.Y.L. (Paramount) Producer, John Heyman; Director, Simon Wincer; Screenplay, David Ambrose, Allan Scott, Jeffrey Ellis; Photography, Frank Watts; Editor, Adrian Carr; Music, Marvin Hamlisch; Co-Producers, Burtt Harris, Gabrielle Kelly; Color; Panavision; Dolby Stereo; 100 minutes; Rated PG; June release. CAST: Mary Beth Hurt (Joyce Richardson), Michael McKean (Andy Richardson), Kathryn Walker (Ellen), Colleen Camp (Elaine), Josef Sommer (Dr. Stewart), Barret Oliver (D.A.R.Y.L.), Daniel Bryan Corkill (Turtle), Steve Ryan (Howie), Amy Linker (Sherie)

DEMON LOVER DIARY (DeMott/Kreines Films) Producer-Director-Photography-Editor, Joel DeMott; Documentary; 90 minutes; Not rated; June release. CAST: Joel DeMott, Don Jackson, Jerry Younkins, Jeff Kreines, Mark Rance, Ray Poll, Carol Lasowski, Ted Nugent, Kyra Nash, Bill Baetz, Val Mayerik

DOCUMENT OF THE DEAD (Roy Frumkes Productions, Ltd.) Producer-Director-Screenplay, Roy Frumkes; Photography, Reeves Lehman; Editor, Dennis Werner; 66 minutes; Not Rated; June release

HOTEL NEW YORK (World Artists) Producer, Zanzibar Productions; Director, Jackie Raynal; Screenplay, Suzanne Fenn, Jackie Raynal; Dialogue, Gary Indiana, Jackie Raynal; Photography, Babette Mangolte; Editor, Suzanne Fenn; Sound, Helene Kaplan, Paul Bang; Music, Lee Erwin; Assistant Directors, Melvie Arslanian, Silvie de la Riviere; 60 minutes; Not rated; June release. CAST: Sid Geffen (Sid), Jackie Raynal (Loulou), Gary Indiana (Gary), Jim Dratfield (Organist/Young Lover), Donna Geffen (Golf Widow), Peter Gerard (Neighbor), Tom Baker (Mario), Suzanne Fenn (Brigitte), Sandee Zeig (Marget)

Joe Don Baker (L) in "Final Justice" © *Arista*

Steve Railsback, Patrick Stewart, Peter Firth
in "Lifeforce." © *Tri-Star*

**Lori Loughlin, C. Thomas Howell
in "Secret Admirer" © Orion**

SECRET ADMIRER (Orion) Producer, Steve Roth; Director, David Greenwalt; Screenplay, Jim Kouf, David Greenwalt; Music, John Hammer; Photography, Victor J. Kemper; Designer, William J. Cassidy; Editor, Dennis Virkler; Costumes, Mary Vogt; Executive Producer-Production Manager, C. O. Erickson; Co-Producer, Jim Kouf; Assistant Directors, L. Andrew Stone, Robert Engelman III; Associate Producer, Lynne Oblinger Bigelow; Special Effects, Allen Hall; Technicolor; Panavision; 98 minutes; Rated R; June release. CAST: C. Thomas Howell (Michael Ryan), Lori Loughlin (Toni), Kelly Preston (Debora), Dee Wallace Stone (Connie), Cliff De Young (George), Leigh Taylor-Young (Elizabeth), Fred Ward (Lou), Casey Siemaszko (Roger), Geoffrey Blake (Ricardo), Rodney Pearson (Kirkpatrick), Courtney Gains (Doug), Jeffrey Jay Cohen (Barry), Scott McGinnis (Steve), Cory Haim (Jeff), Michael Menzies (Mr. Simpson), Michael Moore (Leon), John Terlesky (Rick), and Keith Mills, Ken Lerner, Dermott Downs, Doug Savant, Leslie Allan, Gypsi De Young, Janet Carroll, Mike Toto, Ron Burke, Arvid Malnaa, Ernie Brown

BOMBS AWAY (Shapiro Entertainment) Producers, Bruce Wilson, Bill Fay; Director-Story, Bruce Wilson; Screenplay, Bruce Wilson, Ed Mast; Photography, Marty Openheimer; Editor, Skets McGrew; Designer, Richard Johnson; Production Manager, Bill Fay; Costumes, Julie Reed, Jody Silverman; Sound, Bob Marts; Executive Producer, Chris Pearce; Associate Producers, Patricia Fay, Thom Fermstad; Assistant Directors, James Carroll, Bob Allen, Lynn Wegenka; Special Effects, Tim Buck; Presented by The Nexus Group; Color; 91 minutes; Not rated; June release. CAST: Michael Huddleston (Kabale), Pat McCormick (Dispatcher), Michael Santo (P.R. Ransom), Ben Tone (Col.), Lori Larson (Susan), John Tristao (J.J.), Susan Ludlow (Lilian), Richard Hawkins (Max), Jane Bray, Don Matt (Lieutenants), Cheri Sorenson (Dispatcher), Don Hibbard (Uncle Ken), Elizabeth Kaye (Reporter), Jeannie Barker, Mara Scott Wood (Wives), Tom O'Connell (Father), Marguerite Hogue (Granny), and Rod Pilloud, Jeff Prather, Ron Timmons, George Jay, Scott Honeywell, Barbara Benediti, Allan Pruzan, Doug York, Tamu Gray, Robert Hyde, Irv Goddard, M Davis, Bill Ontiveros, Jane Muirhead, Ken Flectcher, George Peckham, Ed Sampson, Jeanne Fay, Annie Zanatta, Chris Fay, Jane Adams, Valerie Porter, Paula Sorse, "Mary", Jerry Harper, Dick Arnold, Nancy Driver, Jordan Wilson, Lara McNight, Martin Wilson, Chris Keene, Annie Koerner, Mike McGrady, Gene Stone, Stewart Ballenger

SAM'S SON (New World) Screenplay-Director, Michael Landon; color; Rated PG; 110 minutes; No other credits available; June release CAST: Eli Wallach, Anne Jackson, Timothy Patrick Murphy, Hallie Todd, Jonna Lee, Michael Landon

THE ZOO GANG (New World) Executive Producer, Kerry Herscl Produced, Written and Directed by Pen Densham, John Watson; Co Producer, Richard Barton Lewis; Story, Stuart Birnbaum, Davi Dashev, John Watson, Pen Densham; Editor, James Symons; Photog raphy, Robert New; Music, Patrick Gleeson; Designer, Steve Legle Assistant Directors, Scott Maitland, Nick Batchelor; In C.F.I. Colo Rated PG13; 96 minutes; June release. CAST: Jack Earle Haley (Litt Joe), Ben Vereen (Leatherface), Tiffany Helm (Kate), Jason Gedric (Hardin), Eric Gurry (Danny), Marc Price (Val), Gina Battist (Bobbi Darwyn Swayle (Goose), Glen Mauro, Gary Mauro (Twins), Bobb Jacoby (Ricky), Ramon Bieri (Jack), Ty Hardin (Dean), Tiny Wel (Hank), Ramon Chavez (Cop), Masequa Myers (Nurse), Willia Reynolds (Fire Chief), Bruce Lee (Will), Living Dolls (Band)

BEFORE STONEWALL: THE MAKING OF A GAY AND LES BIAN COMMUNITY (Cinema Guild) Producers, Robert Rose berg, John Scagliotti, Greta Schiller for Before Stonewall, Inc.; Dire tor, Greta Schiller; Co-Director, Robert Rosenberg; Editor, B: Daughton; Research Director, Andrea Weiss; Photography, Sandi Si: sel, Jan Kraepelin, Cathy Zheutlin; Executive Producer, John Scagliot i; Associate Producer, Ann-Marie Forte; Sound, Lori Seligman, Ro Ramsing, J.T. Tagaki; Photo Animation, Lauren Helf; In Associatic with The Center for the Study of Filmed History; Best America Independent Feature Film, Filmex 1985; Documentary; Color; 8 minutes; Not rated; June release. CAST: Rita Mae Brown (Narrator Richard Bruce Nugent, Harry Otis, Donna Smith, Harry Hay, Mab Hampton, Ted Rolfs, Allen Ginsberg, Barbara Grier, Chuck Rov lands, George Buse, Hank Vilas, Johnnie Phelps, Ricky Streiker, Ji Kepner, Carroll Davis, Dr. Evelyn Hooker, Barbara Gittings, Paul F Clarke, Frank Kameny, Red Jordan Arobateau, Martin Duberman Dorothy (Smilie) Hillaire, Teddie Boutte, Jackie Cachero, Aud Lorde, Marge Summit, Lisa Ben, Maua Adele Ajanaku, Jheri, Nanc (Bunny) MacCulloch, Ann Bannon, Craig Rodwell, Jose Sarria, Rev erend Grant Gallup, Ivy Bottini

SECRET HONOR (Cinecom International) Producer-Directo Robert Altman; Screenplay, Donald Freed, Arnold M. Stone; Photog raphy, Pierre Mignot; Editor, Juliet Weber; 90 minutes; Not rated; Jur release. CAST: Philip Baker Hall (Richard M. Nixon)

AMERICAN FLYERS (Warner Bros.) Producers, Gareth Wiga Paula Weinstein; Director, John Badham; Screenplay, Steve Tesic Photography, Don Peterman; Designer, Lawrence G. Paull; Edito Frank Morriss; Music, Lee Ritenour, Greg Mathieson; Associate Pr ducer, Gregg Champion; Production Manager, Wallace Worsle Assistant Directors, Jerry Ziesmer, Tena Yatroussis, Bryan Denega Costumes, Marianna Elliott; Panavision; Widescreen; Technicolo Dolby Stereo; 114 minutes; Rated PG; July release. CAST: Kev Costner (Marcus), David Grant (David), Rae Dawn Chong (Sarah Alexandra Paul (Becky), Janice Rule (Mrs. Sommers), Luca Bercovi (Muzzin), Robert Townsend (Jerome), John Amos (Dr. Conrad), Dc Johnson (Randolph), John Garber (Belov), Jennifer Grey (Leslie Katherine Kriss (Vera), and James Terry, Jessica Nelson, Tom Law rence, Brian Drebber, Judy Jordan, Jan Speck, Greg Walker, Si Frohlich, John J. Caraccioli, Barbara Hinchcliffe, Bobby Anderso Peter Boyles, K. C. Carr, Martin Chenoweth, Jim Flanagin, Stev Burch, Kate Sullivan, Gregg Hayden Bilson II, Christine Blackwell Michael Harshberger, Craig Manning, Brad Peterman, Chris Ziesme Eddie Mercks, Emanuel Alongi, Scott Christopher, Ray Hilliard, Bria Searchinger, John Barvik, Wesley Falker, Fritz Johnston, Bruc Thompson, Jown Bowen, Lindsay Hankins, Scott Noakes, Splinte Wrenn

**Ben Tone, Pat McCormick
in "Bombs Away" © Shapiro Entertainment**

**Jason Gedrick, Kate Haskell
in "The Zoo Gang" © New World**

River Phoenix, Neek, Jason Presson,
Ethan Hawke in "Explorers" © Paramount

Richard Mulligan, Lewis Smith
in "The Heavenly Kid" © Orion

EXPLORERS (Paramount) Producers, Edward S. Feldman, David Bombyk; Director, Joe Dante; Screenplay, Eric Luke; Photography, John Hora; Designer, Robert F. Boyle; Editor, Tina Hirsch; Special Make-Up Effects, Rob Bottin; Music, Jerry Goldsmith; Executive Producer, Michael Finnell; Associate Producer-Production Manager, om Jacobson; Assistant Directors, Pat Kehoe, Carol Green; Costumes, Rosanna Norton; Visual Effects, Industrial Light & Magic; Songs by various artists; Technicolor; Panavision; Dolby Stereo; 110 minutes; Rated R; July release. CAST: Ethan Hawke (Ben Crandall), River Phoenix (Wolfgang Muller), Jason Presson (Darren Woods), Ricardo (Wak/Starkiller), Leslie Rickert (Neek), James Cromwell (Mr. Muller), Dana Ivey (Mrs. Muller), Bobby Fite (Steve Jackson), Meshach Taylor (Gordon Miller), and Bradley Gregg, George Olden, Chance Schwass, Brooke Bundy, Tricia Bartholome, Eric Luke, Caliesin Jaffe, Karen Mayo-Chandler, Robert F. Boyle, John P. Navin ., Mary Hillstead, Simone Blue, Christa Denton, Angela Lee, Deb-ah A. Paddock, Elaine Pagnozzi. VOICES: Frank Welker, Fred Newman, Joanie Gerber, Belinda Balaski, Roger Behr, Roger Peltz, Neil Ross, Marilyn Schreffler, Bill Ratner, Jane Kean, Robert Holt, Jay Lewart

THE HEAVENLY KID (Orion) Producer, Mort Engelberg; Director, Cary Medoway; Screenplay, Cary Medoway, Martin Copeland; Photography, Steven Poster; Designer, Ron Hobbs; Editor, Christopher Greenbury; Music, Kennard Ramsey; Executive Producers, Gabe Sumner, Stephen G. Cheikes; Production Manager, Al Salzer; Assistant Directors, David Whorf, Robert Simon; Special Visual Effects, Louis Schwartzberg; Special Effects, R. J. Hohman; Costumes, Mary Lou Byrd; Songs by various artists; Deluxe Color; Panavision; Dolby Stereo; 92 minutes; Rated PG-13; July release. CAST: Lewis Smith (Bobby), Jason Gedrick (Lenny), Jane Kaczmarek (Emily), Richard Mulligan (Rafferty), Mark Metcalf (Joe), Beau Dremann (McIntyre), Stephen Gregory (Gallo), Anne Sawyer (Sharon), Nancy Valen (Melissa), Chad Wiggins-Grady (Jerry), Scott Stone (Frank), Rooney Kerwin (Suburbanite), Will Knickerbocker (Max), Harold Bergman (Mr. Finley), and Donna Rosae, Barney Johnston, Lit Connah, Bill Ash, Willie Woods, Jody Sharlow, David Stidham, Kevin L. Clarit, T. R. Durphy, Debra Gallagher, Lynne Griffin, Stacy Koolick, Christopher Greenbury

THE LEGEND OF BILLIE JEAN (Tri-Star) formerly "Fair Is Fair"; Producer, Rob Cohen; Director, Matthew Robbins; Screenplay, Mark Rosenthal, Lawrence Konner; Photography, Jeffrey L. Kimball; Designer, Ted Haworth; Music, Craig Safan; Editor, Cynthia Scheider; Costumes, Donna Linson; Executive Producers, Jon Peters, Peter Gruber; Co-Producers, Lawrence Konner, Mark Rosenthal; Associate Producer, Lori Weintraub; Production Manager, Tony Wade; Assistant Directors, Tom Mack, Mark Radcliffe; Special Effects, Ken Pepiot, Michael Arbogast; Songs by various artists; Metrocolor; Panavision; Dolby Stereo; 96 minutes; Rated PG-13; July release. CAST: Helen Slater (Billie Jean), Keith Gordon (Lloyd), Christian Slater (Binx), Richard Bradford (Pyatt), Peter Coyote (Ringwald), Martha Gehman (Ophelia), Yeardley Smith (Putter), Dean Stockwell (Muldaur), Barry Tubb (Hubie), Mona Fultz (Donna Davy), and John M. Jackson, Rodney Rincon, Caroline Williams, Rudy Young, Bobby Fite, Kim Valentine, Robby Jones, Janet Smalley, Charles Redd, Joshua Butts, Ray Hanna, Tony Slowik, Celia Newman, B. J. Thompson, Steve Uzzell, Robert Scott Cate, Jim Miller, Lauren Hartman, Rod Pilloud, John Wolfshohl, David Lee Morgan, Barbara Durham, Cass Gabriel, Thomas M. Jarrett, Forrest Patton, Antony Peraino, Kenneth Beall, Robert Wassell, Sage Parker, John Edson, Cathleen Sutherland, Angela Churchill, Stephanie Shook, Sharon-Marie Stolar, Peter Bonanno, Sharon Holmin, Joy Swan, Kathryn Childers, J. C. Minter, Kenneth Searle, Al Geatano, Sonya Robbins

THE MAN WITH ONE RED SHOE (20th Century-Fox) Producer, Victor Drai; Director, Stan Dragoti; Screenplay, Robert Klane; Based on the motion picture screenplay by Francis Veber, Yves Robert; Photography, Richard H. Kline; Designer, Dean E. Mitzner; Editor, Bud Molin, O. Nicholas Brown; Music, Thomas Newman, Michael Masser; Costumes, William Ware Theiss; Sound, Willis D. Burton; Special Effects, Alan E. Lorimer; Associate Producers, Jack Sanders, Bill Wilson, Xavier Gelin; Production Manager, Henry Kline; Assistant Directors, William Beasley, Alan B. Curtiss; DeLuxe Color; Panavision; 92 minutes; Rated PG; July release. CAST: Tom Hanks (Richard), Dabney Coleman (Cooper), Lori Singer (Maddy), Charles Durning (Ross), Carrie Fisher (Paula), Ed Herrmann (Brown), Jim Belushi (Morris), Irving Metzman (Virdon), Tom Noonan (Reese), Gerrit Graham (Carson), David L. Lander (Stemple), Ritch Brinkley (Hulse), Frank Hamilton (Edgar), Dortha Duckworth (Natalie), David Ogden Stiers (Conductor), and Julius J. Carry III, Stephen Bradley, Art La Fleur, Richard F. McGonagle, George Martin, Patricia Gaul, Charles Levin, Dan Resin, Tom Rayhall, Victoria Carroll, Mark Robman, Charles Walker, David Selburg, Lisa Raggio, Ivy Bethune, C. Richard Clark, Tom Chiu, Damita Jo Freeman, Jeff Ware, Noel De Souza, Daniel Ziskie, Sam Sako

Helen Slater, Keith Gordon
in "Legend of Billie Jean"
© Tri-Star

Jim Belushi, Lori Singer, Tom Hanks
in "The Man with One Red Shoe"
© 20th Century-Fox

Paul O'Shea, Derek Hardwick
in "Among the Cinders" © New World

Terry Alexander, Lori Cardille, Jarlath Conroy
in "Day of the Dead" © Dead Films

AMONG THE CINDERS (New World) Producer, John O'Shea; Director, Rolf Haedrich; Screenplay, Rolf Haedrich, John O'Shea; Based on the novel by Maurice Shadbolt; Photography, Rory O'Shea; Designer, Gerry Luhman; Costumes, Ulla-Britt Soederlund; Editors, Inge Behrens, John Kiley; Music, Jan Preston; Associate Producer, Craig Walters; Production Manager, Roi McGregor; Assistant Directors, Lee Tamahori, Terry Pearce; Color; 90 minutes; Rated R; July release. CAST: Paul O'Shea (Nick Flinders), Derek Hardwick (Hubert Flinders), Yvonne Lawley (Beth Flinders), Rebecca Gibney (Sally), Amanda Jones (Glenys), Bridget Armstrong (Helga), Maurice Shadbolt (Frank)

DAY OF THE DEAD (United Film Distribution Company) Producer, Richard P. Rubinstein; Director-Screenplay, George A. Romero; Photography, Michael Gornick; Special Make-Up Effects, Tom Savini; Designer, Cletus Anderson; Music, John Harrison; Executive Producer, Salah M. Hassanein; Production Manager, Zilla Clinton; Editor, Pasquale Buba; Costumes, Barbara Anderson; Assistant Directors, John Harrison, Katarina Wittich, Annie Loeffler; Special Effects, Steve Kirshoff, Mark Mann; Color; 102 minutes; Rated PG-13; July release. CAST: Lori Cardille, Terry Alexander, Joseph Pilato, Jarlath Conroy, Antone DiLeo, G. Howard Blar, Ralph Marrero, John Amplas, Phillip G. Kellams, Taso N. Stavrakis, Gregory Nicotero, Richard Liberty, Howard Sherman, Don Brockett, William Cameron, Deborah Carter, Winnie Flynn, Debra Gordon, Jeff Hogan, Barbara Holmes, David Kindlon, Bruce Kirkpatrick, William Andrew Laczko, Susan Martinelli, Kim Maxwell, Barbara Russell, Gene A. Saraceni, John Schwartz, Mark Tierno, Michael Trcic, John Vulich

AMERICAN NINJA (Cannon) Producers, Menahem Golan, Yoram Globus; Director, Sam Firstenberg; Screenplay, Paul DeMielche; Associate Producers-Story, Avi Kleinberger, Gideon Amir; Photography, Hanania Baer; Editor, Michael J. Duthie; Designer, Adrian H. Gorton; Music, Michael Linn; In TVC Color; Assistant Directors, Ron Tal, Ricardo DeGuzman, Gene Rose Singson, Pepito Diaz; Rated R; 95 minutes; August release. CAST: Michael Dudikoff (Joe), Guich Koock (Hickock), Judie Aronson (Patricia), Steve James (Jackson), John Fujioka (Shinyuki), Don Stewart (Ortega), John LaMotta (Rinaldo), Tadashi Yamashita (Black Star Ninja), Phil Brock (Charley), Tony Carreon (Older Colombian), Roi Vinzon (Younger Colombian), Manolet Escudero, Gregg Rocero, Berto Spoor, Michael Hackbart (Bodyguards), Jerry Bailey (Head Hijacker), Rohy Batliwala, James Gaines, Steve Cook, Brian Robilliard, Zenon Gil (Truck Drivers), Willie Wil-

liams, Christian Hoss (Barrack Soldiers), Estrella Antonio (House keeper), Joey Galvez (MP Arresting Officer), Nick Nicholson (Duty Officer), Eric Hahn (Supply Sergeant), Jacob Mendoza (Fat Driver) Avi Charupe (Joe's Father), Esther Zewko (Joe's Mother), Doug Ivan Richard Norton, Kenny Lesco

ALMONDS AND RAISINS (TeleCulture) Produced and Written by David Elstein, Russ Karel; Director, Russ Karel; Based on a treatmen by Wolf Mankowitz; Photography, Jacee Laskus; Editor, Christophe Barnes; Music, Don Altman; Narrator, Orson Welles; In black an white; Not rated; 90 minutes; August release. With Herschel Bernardi Joseph Green, Zvee Schooler, Seymour Rechzeit, Leo Fuchs, Miriam Kressyn, David Opatashu

DOOR TO DOOR (Castle Hill) Executive Producer, Robert H Goodman; Producer, Ken Wales; Director, Patrick Bailey; Photogra phy, Reed Smoot; Screenplay, Peter Baloff, Dave Wollert; Editor Michael Brown; In color; Rated PG 90 minutes; August release. CAST: Ron Leibman (Larry Price), Arlis Howard (Leon Spencer), Jane Kaczmarek (Katherine Holloway), Ala Austin (Jimmy Lupus)

DREAMS COME TRUE (Troma) Producer, Carlton J. Albright Associate Producer, David Platt; Director, Max Kalmanowicz; Photog raphy, John Drake; Written by Steve Kinjerski; Special Visual Effects Ed Darino; Presented by Lloyd Kaufman, Michael Herz; In color; Rate R; 90 minutes; August release. CAST: Michael Sanville (Lee), Stepha nie Shuford (Robyn), David Platt (Gary), Nancy Baldwin (Mom), Be Kenyon (Foreman), Richard France (Uncle Smit), Catherine Heena (Reporter), Robert Heise (Police Chief), Jim Lehnedorf (Lt.), Mar Schumerth (Swanson), Don Braun (Fred), Virginia Cox (Mrs. Brad ley), Gay Strandemo (Dorothy), Ken Charlton (Stan), Steve Charlto (Svenson), Nan Ducklow (Head Nurse), Juoffroy-Lucien Rade (Maitre d'), Tom Snider (Swanson Kid), Raymond Zagorski (Guard) Wilbert Hooten, Jr. (Pizza Guy), Darice Clewell (Admissions Nurse Mike Aspen (Bank Guard), Julie Bigger (Marilyn), Kevin Cox (To Trucker), Philip Harris (News Cameraman), Tony Iorio (Tony), Co rine Conrad (Waitress), Nancy Schwieger (Doctor)

BIOHAZARD (21st Century) Producer-Director-Screenplay, Fre Olen Ray; Additional Dialogue, T. L. Lankford, Miriam L. Preisse Photography, Paul Elliott, John McCoy; Editor, Miriam L. Preisse Jack Tucker; Music, Eric Rasmussen, Drew Neumann; Sound, Re Baille, Craig Tomlin; Executive Producers, Art Schweitzer, T. L

"Dreams Come True"
© Troma Team

"The Hills Have Eyes II"
© Castle Hill

Chuck Hemingway, Joe Rubbo, Charles Schillaci,
Allan J. Kayser in "Hot Chili" © *Cannon*

Fisher Stevens, Danielle von Zerneck, John Stockwell
in "My Science Project" © *Touchstone Films*

ankford; Assistant Director, Donald E. Jackson; Special Effects
1ake-Up, Jon McCallum; Monster, Kenneth J. Hall; Special Effects
nimation, Bret Mixon; Co-Producer, Ray Guttman; Associate Pro-
ucers, Richard Hench, Miriam L. Preissel; A Viking Films Pro-
uction; Color; 79 minutes; Not rated. CAST: Aldo Ray (Gen. Ran-
olph), Angelique Pettyjohn (Lisa), William Fair (Mitchell), Frank
1cDonald (Mike), David Pearson (Reiger), Christopher Ray (Bio-
1onster), Charles Roth (Jack), Carroll Borland (Rula), Arthur Payton
Dr. Williams), Richard Hench (Roger), Loren Crabtree (Jenny)

HE HILLS HAVE EYES II (Castle Hill) Producers, Barry Cahn,
eter Locke; Direction-Screenplay, Wes Craven; In color; Rated PG;
0 minutes; August release. CAST: Michael Berryman (Pluto), Kevin
lair (Roy), John Bloom (The Reaper), Janus Blythe (Rachel/Ruby),
eter Frechette (Harry), Robert Houston (Bobby), Tamara Stafford
Cass)

OT CHILI (Cannon) Producers, Menahem Golan, Yoram Globus;
ssociate Producer, Jonathan Debin; Screenplay, Menahem Golan,
illiam Sachs; Director, William Sachs; In color; Not rated; August
lease. CAST: Charles Schillaci, Allan J. Kayser, Joe Rubbo, Chuck
emingway, Taafe O'Connell, Victoria Barrett, Louisa Moritz, Flo
errish, Bea Fiedler

HE BRIDE (Columbia) Producer, Victor Drai; Director, Franc
oddam; Screenplay, Lloyd Fonvielle; Editor, Michael Ellis; Photog-
phy, Stephen H. Burum; Music, Maurice Jarre; Dolby Stereo; In
olor; Rated PG-13; 119 minutes; August release. CAST: Sting (Fran-
nstein), Jennifer Beals (Eva), Anthony Higgins (Clerval), Clancy
rown (Viktor), David Rappaport (Rinaldo), Geraldine Page (Mrs.
auman), Alexei Sayle (Magar), Phil Daniels (Bela), Veruschka
Countess), Quentin Crisp (Dr. Zalhus), Gary Elwes (Josef), Tom
aull (Paulus), Ken Campbell (Pedlar), Guy Rolfe (Count), Andrew
e la Tour (Priest), Tony Haygarth (Tavern Keeper)

HE MAN WHO ENVIED WOMEN (First Run Features) Written
d Directed by Yvonne Rainer; Editors, Yvonne Rainer, Christine
Goff; Photography, Mark Daniels; In color, black and white; Not
ed; 125 minutes; August release. CAST: William Raymond (Jack
eller #1), Larry Loonin (Jack Deller #2), Trisha Brown (Trisha),
ckie Raynal (Jackie)

MY SCIENCE PROJECT (Buena Vista) Producer, Jonathan Taplin;
Direction-Screenplay, Jonathan Betuel; Photography, David M.
Walsh; Editor, C. Timothy O'Meara; Music, Peter Bernstein; In Dolby
Stereo, Panavision Widescreen, and color; Rated PG; 95 minutes;
August release. CAST: John Stockwell (Michael Harlan), Danielle Von
Zerneck (Ellie Sawyer), Fisher Stevens (Vince Latello), Raphael
Sbarge (Sherman), Richard Masur (Det. Nulty), Barry Corbin (Lew
Harlan), Ann Wedgeworth (Dolores), Dennis Hopper (Bob Roberts)

LOOSE SCREWS (Concorde/Cinema Group) Producer, Maurice
Smith; Director, Rafal Zielinski; Screenplay, Michael Cory; Additional
Dialogue, Phil Keuber; Photography, Brian Foley; Editor, Stephan
Fanfara; Music, Fred Mollin; Designer, Judith Lee; Associate Produc-
ers, Mike Dolgy, Terrea Oster; Production Manager, Ken Gord; Assis-
tant Directors, Bill Cummings, Merv Prokop, Geoffrey Pilo; Sound,
Nolan Roberts; Costumes, Nancy Kaye; Special Effects, Randy
Daudlin; Songs by various artists; Color; 76 minutes; Rated R; August
release. CAST: Brian Genesse (Brad Lovett), Lance Van Der Kolk
(Steve Hardman), Alan Deveau (Hugh G. Rection), Jason Warren
(Marvin Eatmore), Cyd Belliveau (Mona Lott), Karen Wood (Gail
Poulet), Annie McAuley (Nikki Mystroke), Mike McDonald (Principal
Arsenault), Liz Green (Tracy Gratehead), Debora Lobbin (Miss Von
Blow), Carolyn Tweedle (Teacher), Stephanie Sulik (Claudia), Terrea
Oster (Wendy), Wayne Fleming (Pig Pen M.C.), Cindy Fidler, Susan
Irvine (Bathtub Girls), Ken Toylor (Principal Hardbutt), Beth Gondek
(Candy Barr), and Mack Dolgy, Yuri Sudjito, Kimberly Brooks,
Robert Toppin, Kim Cayer, Lila Durette, Melissa Madden, Kelly
Hollingsworth, Michelle Burley, Julie Forbes, Nancy Vacheresse,
Laura Potter, Ron Clifford, Robert Vasil, Carl Bauer, David Baldwin,
Greta Shepherd, Phil Myatin, Jane Mansell, Gregory Smith, Sarah
Stranks, Ted Tanyock, James Gale, Lucy Laronde, Antonio Dileo,
Ernesto Camera, Graham Gautier, Don Patterson, Janette Scott, Babs
Morello, Angela Jensen, Lisa Maggiore, Antonella DiMartino

OCEAN DRIVE WEEKEND (Troma) Executive Producer, Dwight
South; Producer, Marvin Almeas; Direction and Screenplay, Bryan
Jones; Presented by Lloyd Kaufman, Michael Herz; Songs performed
by The Drifters, The Rivieras, The Tams, The Showmen, Ron and
Karen; Rated PG13; In color; 77 minutes; August release. CAST:
Charles Redmond, Robert Peacock, P. J. Grethe, Sharon Brewer, Tony
Freeman, Jon Kohler

"The Man Who Envied Women"
© *First Run Features*

Jennifer Beals, Sting
in "The Bride"
© *Columbia*

Michelle Meyrink, Gabe Jarrett, Val Kilmer,
Mark Kamiyama in "Real Genius" © *Tri-Star*

Alyson Court, Benjamin Barrett, Big Bird
in "Sesame Street Presents: Follow That Bird"
© *Warner Bros.*

THE PROTECTOR (Golden Harvest) Executive Producer, Raymond Chow; Producer, David Chan; Direction and Screenplay, James Glickenhaus; Editor, Evan Lottman; Photography, Mark Irwin; Music, Ken Throne; In color; Rated R; 95 minutes; August release. CAST: Jackie Chan, Danny Aiello, Roy Chiao, Victor Arnold, Kim Bass, Richard Clarke, Saun Ellis, Ronan O'Casey, Bill Wallace

REAL GENIUS (Tri-Star) Producer, Brian Grazer; Director, Martha Coolidge; Screenplay, Neal Israel, Pat Proft, Peter Torokvei; Story, Neal Israel, Pat Proft; Photography, Vilmos Zsigmond; Design, Josan F. Russo; Executive Producer, Robert Daley; Music, Thomas Newman; Associate Producer, Sam Crespi-Horowitz; Editor, Richard Chew; Assistant Directors, Steve McEveety, Joseph P. Moore, Michael J. Schilz; In Metrocolor and Dolby Stereo; Rated PG; 105 minutes; August release. CAST: Val Kilmer (Chris), Gabe Jarret (Mitch), Robert Prescott (Kent), William Atherton (Prof. Hathaway), Ed Lauter (CIA Man Decker), Patti D'Arbanville (Sherry), Severn Darden (Dr. Meredith), Stacy Peralta, Daniel Addes, Andres Aybar, Louis Giambalvo, Charles Shull, Beau Billingslea, Charles Parks, Sean Frye, Joann Willette, Ina Gould, Nadine Vix, Paul Tulley, Chip Johnson, Monte Landis, Randolph Dreyfuss, Jonathan Gries, John Shepherd Reid, Tom Swerdlow, Mark Kamiyama, Michelle Meyrink, Martin Gundersen, Brett Miller, Dean Devlin, Deborah Foreman, Corki Grazer, Jeanne Mori, David Ursin, Joe Dorsey, Will Knox, Kevin Hurley

THE RETURN OF THE LIVING DEAD (Orion) Producer, Tom Fox; Executive Producers, John Daly, Derek Gibson; Screenplay-Director, Dan O'Bannon; Story, Rudy Ricci, John Russo, Russell Streiner; Music, Matt Clifford; Co-Producer, Graham Henderson; Photography, Jules Brenner; Design, William Stout; Editor, Robert Gordon; Assistant Director, David M. Robertson; Art Director, Robert Howland; In CFI Color and DeLuxe Prints; Rated R; 91 minutes; August release. CAST: Clu Galager (Burt), James Karen (Frank), Don Calfa (Ernie), Thom Mathews (Freddy), Beverly Randolph (Tina), John Philbin (Chuck), Jewel Shepard (Casey), Miguel Nunez (Spider), Brian Peck (Scuz), Linnea Quigley (Trash), Mark Venturini (Suicide), Jonathan Terry (Col. Glover), Cathleen Cordell (His Wife), Drew Deighan, James Dalesandro (Paramedics), John Durbin, David Bond (Radio Corps), Bob Libman (Tac Squad Captain), John Stuart West, Michael Crabtree, Ed Krieger (Riot Cops), Robert Craighead, Paul Cloud (Cops), Leigh Drake (Dispatcher), Derrick Brice, Terrence M. Houlihan, Allan Trautman, Robert Bennett, Jerome Daniels Coleman, Cherry Davis

ROCK & RULE (MGM/UA) Director, Clive A. Smith; Screenplay, Peter Sauder, John Halfpenny; Story, Patrick Loubert, Peter Sauder; Photography, Lenora Hume; Score, Patricia Cullen; Producers, Patrick Loubert, Michael Hirsh; A Nelvana Production in color and animation; Rated PG; 85 minutes; August release. CAST: Don Francks (Mok), Paul Le Mat (Omar), Susan Roman (Angel), Catherine O'Hara (Aunt Edith), Sam Langevin (Mok's Computer)

SESAME STREET PRESENTS: FOLLOW THAT BIRD (Warner Bros.) Producer, Tony Garnett; Executive Producer, Joan Ganz Cooney; Director, Ken Kwapis; Screenplay, Tony Geiss, Judy Freudberg; Music, Van Dyke Parks, Lennie Niehaus; In Dolby Stereo and color; Rated G; 85 minutes; August release. CAST: Sesame Street Muppets, Caroll Spinney, Jim Henson, Frank Oz, Sandra Bernhard, John Candy, Chevy Chase, Joe Flaherty, Waylon Jennings, Dave Thomas

THE STUFF (New World) Executive Producer, Larry Cohen; Producer, Paul Kurta; Director-Screenplay, Larry Cohen; Photography, Paul Glickman; Editor, Armond Lebowitz; Associate Producer, Barry Shils; Assistant Directors, Mark Croll, Jenny Fitzgibbons, Harvey Waldman; Costumes, Tim D'Arcy; Designer, Larry Lurin; A Larco Production in color; Rated R; 93 minutes; August release. CAST: Michael Moriarty (David), Andrea Marcovicci (Nicole), Garrett Morris (Chocolate Charlie), Paul Sorvino (Col. Spears), Scott Bloom (Jason), Danny Aiello (Vickers), James Dixon (Postman), Alexander Scourby (Evans), Russell Nype (Richards), Gene O'Neill (Scientist), Cathy Schultz (Waitress), Jim Dukas (Gas Attendant), Peter Hock (State Trooper), Colette Blonigan (Jason's Mother), Frank Telfer (Jason's Father), Brian Bloom (Jason's Brother), Marilyn Staley (Stud Girl), Beth Teagarden (Investigator)

SUMMER RENTAL (Paramount) Producer, George Shapiro; Executive Producer, Bernie Brillstein; Director, Carl Reiner; Screenplay, Jeremy Stevens, Mark Reisman; Music, Alan Silvestri; Designer, Peter Wooley; Editors, Bud Molin, Lee Burch; Photography, Ric Waite; In color; Rated PG; 88 minutes; August release. CAST: John Candy (Jack Chester), Richard Crenna (Al Pellet), Rip Torn (Scully), Karen Austin (Sandy Chester), Kerri Green (Jennifer Chester), Joey Lawrence (Bobby), Aubrey Jene (Laurie Chester), John Larroquette (Don Moore), Richard Herd (Angus MacGloughlin), Santos Morales (Cortez), Carmine Caridi (Ed)

Clu Gulager, James Karen, Thom Mathews
in "Return of the Living Dead"
© *Orion Pictures*

Andrea Marcovicci, Michael Moriarty, Scott
Bloom in "The Stuff" © *New World*

John Candy, Rita Wilson, Tom Hanks
in "Volunteers" © *Tri-Star*

Richard Crenna, Pierrino Mascarino, John Candy
in "Summer Rental" © *Paramount*

VOLUNTEERS (Tri-Star) Producers, Richard Shepherd, Walter F. Parkes; Director, Nicholas Meyer; Story, Keith Critchlow; Screenplay, Ken Levine, David Isaacs; Associate Producer, Theodore R. Parvin; Photography, Ric Waite; Designer, James Schoppe; Editors, Ronald Roose, Steven Polivka; Music, James Horner; Assistant Director, Elie John; Art Director, Jose Rodriguez Granada; In Metrocolor; Rated R; 106 minutes; August release. CAST: Tom Hanks (Lawrence Bourne III), John Candy (Tom Tuttle), Rita Wilson (Beth Wexler), Tim Thomerson (John Reynolds), Gedde Watanabe (At Toon), George Plimpton (Mr. Bourne), Ernest Harada (Chung Mee), Allan Arbus (Albert), Xander Berkeley (Kent), Ji-Tu Cumbaka (Cicero), Guillermo Del Rio (Sumo Guard), Jacqueline Evans (Aunt), Pamela Gual (Tammy), Phillip Guilmant (Yale President), Chick Hearn (Announcer), Virginia Kiser (Evelyn), Clyde Kusatsu (Souvana), Jude Mussetter (Bootsy), Carlos Romano (Beatty), Duncan Ross (Noble), Shakti (Lucille), Toru Tanaka, Lonnie Wun (Sumo Guards), Harry Yorku (Ai o)

THE SEVEN MAGNIFICENT GLADIATORS (Cannon) Producers, Menaheam Golan, Yoram Globus; Director, Bruno Mattei; Screenplay, Claudio Fragasso; Photography, Silvano Ippolitti; Music, Ennio Morricone; Designer, Amedeo Mellone; Costumes, Pierro Rizzo; Production Manager, Marcello Berni; Assistant Directors, Claudio Fragasso, Domenico B. Attista, Remo Odevaine; Sound, Candido Raini; Special Effects, Paolo Ricci; Executive Producer, Alexander Hacohen; color; 86 minutes; Rated PG; August release. CAST: Lou Ferrigno (Han), Brad Harris (Scipio), Sybil Danning (Julia), Dan Vadis (Nicerote), Carla Ferrigno (Pandora), Mandy Rice-Davies (Lucilla), Yehuda Efroni (Emperor), Emillia Messina (Golia), Sal Borchese (Glafiro), Marina Rocchi (Cornelia), Antonella Giacomini (Fabia), Cesarina Taccani (Morena), Franco Daddi (Neomio), Mark Urban (Dario), Kendal Kaldwell (Anacora), Giovanni Cianfriglia (Festo), Roberto Mura (Venox), Francoise Perrot (Martina), Renata Roggero (Mora), Kim McKay (Livia), Pino Mattei (Dex), Raul Cabrera (Elenio), Omero Capanna (Elios)

WARNING SIGN (20th Century-Fox) Producer, Jim Bloom; Director, Hal Barwood; Screenplay, Hal Barwood, Matthew Robbins; Photography, Dean Cundey; Designer, Henry Bumstead; Editor, Robert Lawrence; Music, Craig Safan; Costumes, Aggie Guerard Rodgers; Executive Producer, Matthew Robbins; Associate Producer-Production Manager, Robert Latham Brown; Assistant Directors, Nick Marck, Pope Goodwin; Special Effects, J. Kevin Pike; Sound, Michael Evje; A Barwood/Robbins Production; DeLuxe Color; Panavision; 100 minutes; Rated R; August release. CAST: Sam Waterston (Cal Morse), Kathleen Quinlan (Joanie Morse), Yaphet Kotto (Mjr. Connolly), Jeffrey De Munn (Dan Fairchild), Richard Dysart (Dr. Nielsen), G. W. Bailey (Tom Schmidt), Jerry Hardin (Vic Flint), Rick Rossovich (Bob), Cynthia Carle (Dana), Scott Paulin (Capt. Walston), Kavi Raz (Dr. Ramesh Kapoor), Keith Szarabajka (Tippett), Jack Thibeau (Pisarczyk), J. Patrick McNamara (Aide), Tom McFadden (Grazio), Kyle Heffner, Meshach Taylor (Technicians), Lori Hallier (TV Reporter), and Jeannie Epper, Gilbert Smith, Nancie Kawata

WEIRD SCIENCE (Universal) Producer, Joel Silver; Direction-Screenplay, John Hughes; Photography, Matthew F. Leonetti; Designer, John W. Corso; Editors, Mark Warner, Christopher Lebenzon, Scott Wallace; Music, Ira Newborn; Costumes, Marilyn Vance; Associate Producer, Jane Vickerilla; Assistant Directors, Deborah Love, Rob Corn; Art Director, James Allen; Choreography, Jerry Evans; In Technicolor and Dolby Stereo; Rated PG13; 94 minutes; August release. CAST: Anthony Michael Hall (Gary), Kelly LeBrock (Lisa), Ilan Mitchell-Smith (Wyatt), Bill Paxton (Chet), Suzanne Snyder (Deb), Judie Aronson (Hilly), Robert Downey (Ian), Robert Rusler (Max), Vernon Wells (Lord General), Britt Leach (Al), Barbara Lang (Lucy), Michael Berryman (Mutant Biker), Ivor Barry (Henry), Anne Bernadette Coyle (Carmen), Suzy J. Kellems (Gymnast), John Kapelos, Fred D. Scott, Vince Monroe Townsend, Chino Williams, Jill Whitlow, Theodocia Goodrich, Doug MacHugh, Pamela Gordon

YEAR OF THE DRAGON (MGM/UA) Producer, Dino De Laurentiis; Director, Michael Cimino; Screenplay, Michael Cimino, Oliver Stone; Based on novel of same title by Robert Daley; Photography, Alex Thomson; Editor, Francoise Bonnot; Music, David Mansfield; Designer, Wolf Kroeger; Costumes, Marietta Ciriello; Assistant Director, Brian Cook; Art Director, Vicki Paul; In J-D-C Widescreen and Dolby Stereo; In Technicolor; Rated R; 136 minutes; August release. CAST: Mickey Rourke (Stanley White), John Lone (Joey Tai), Ariane (Tracy Tzu), Leonard Termo (Angelo Rizzo), Ray Barry (Louis), Caroline Kava (Connie), Eddie Jones (William), Joey Chin (Ronnie), Victor Wong (Harry), K. Dock Yip (Milton), Pao Han Lin (Fred), Way Dong Woo, Jimmy Sun (Elders), Daniel Davin (Francis), Mark Hammer (Commissioner), Dennis Dun (Herbert), Jack Kehler (Alan), Steven Chen (Tony), Paul Scaglione (Teddy), Joseph Bonaventura (Lagnese), Tony Lip (Lenny), Jilly Rizzo (Schiro), Fabia Drake, Tisa Chang (Nuns), Gerald Orange (Bear), Fan Mui Sang, Yukio Yamamoto, Doreen Chan, Harry Yip, Dermot McNamara, Vallo Benjamin, Myra Chen, Aileen Ho, Sammy Lee

Kathleen Quinlan, Sam Waterston, Jeffrey
DeMunn in "Warning Sign"
© *20th Century-Fox*

Mickey Rourke, John Lone
in "Year of the Dragon"
© *MGM/UA Entertainment*

125

Geoff Edholm, David Schachter
in "Buddies" © *New Line*

Rae Dawn Chong, Darrell Larson
in "City Limits" © *Atlantic Releasing*

BUDDIES (New Line Cinema) Producer-Director-Screenplay-Editor, Arthur J. Bressan, Jr.; Photography, Carl Teitelbaum; Music, Jeffrey Olmsted; Sound, Steve Hirsch; Executive Producer, Frederick Schminke; Associate Producer, John Hartis; Color; 81 minutes; Not rated; September release. CAST: Geoff Edholm (Robert Willow), David Schachter (David Bennett), Billy Lux (Edward), David Rose (Steve), Libby Saines (Mrs. Bennett), Damon Hairston (Gym Instructor), Tracy Vivat (Nurse), Susan Schneider (Sylvia Douglas), Joyce Korn (Lynn)

CITY LIMITS (Atlantic) Producers, Rupert Harvey, Barry Opper; Director, Aaron Lipstadt; Screenplay, Don Opper; Story, Aaron Lipstadt, James Reigle; Music, Mitchell Froom; Executive Producer, Warren Goldberg; A Sho Films/Videoform Pictures Presentation; Color; 85 minutes; Rated PG-13; September release. CAST: John Stockwell (Lee), Don Opper (Sammy), Kim Cattrall (Wickings), Norbert Weisser (Bolo), Rae Dawn Chong (Yogi), Darrell Larson (Mick), John Diehl (Whitey), Pamela Ludwig (Frankie), Tony Plana (Ramos), Danny De La Paz (Ray), Robby Benson (Carver), James Earl Jones (Albert)

CREATOR (Universal) Producer, Stephen Friedman; Director, Ivan Passer; Screenplay, Jeremy Leven; Based on novel "Creator" by Jeremy Leven; Photography, Robbie Greenberg; Editor, Richard Chew; Music, Sylvester Levay; Production Manager, Charles Mulvehill; Assistant Directors, Wolfgang Glattes, Larry Rapaport; Sound, Jeff Wexler; Costumes, Tom Dawson, Jennifer Parson; "Zeno" Designers, Michael & Richard Prather; Presented by Kings Road Productions; CFI Color; 114 minutes; Rated R; September release. CAST: Peter O'Toole (Harry), Mariel Hemingway (Meli), Vincent Spano (Boris), Virginia Madsen (Barbara), David Ogden Stiers (Sid), John Dehner (Paul), Karen Kopins (Lucy), Kenneth Tiger (Pavlo), Elsa Raven (Mrs. Mallory), Lee Kessler (Mrs. Pruitt), Rance Howard (Mr. Spencer), Ellen Geer (Mrs. Spencer), Ian Wolfe (Prof. Brauer), Mike Jolly (Boom-Boom), Burton Collins (Lyman), Judith Hanson (Karen), Doug Cox (Arthur), Anthony Peck (Norman), Crawford Binion (Fred), Byrne Piven (Krauss), Vincent Cobb (Hamberg), Gary Bayer (Bovi), and Jordan Charney, William H. Bassett, Sandy Ignon, Jeff Corey, Michael McGrady, Eve McVeagh, Al Fann, Michael Green

DESERT WARRIOR (Concorde/Cinema Group) Producer-Director, Cirio H. Santiago; Screenplay, Frederick Bailey; Story, Ellen Collett; Photography, Richard Remias; Editor, George Saint; Music,

Chris Young; Designer, Paul Di Malentino; Costumes, Raymor Allen, Elvira Cannon; Co-Producer, Aomida Reynolds; Associate Pr ducer, John Carlos; Production Manager, Eugene Navarro; Assista Directors, J. M. Avalon, Joe Tower; Special Effects, Jesse St. Don nic; A Rodeo Production; DeLuxe Color; 85 minutes; Rated R; Septe ber release. CAST: Gary Watkins (Trace), Laura Banks (Stinge Lynda Wiesmeier (Arlie), Linda Grovenor (Spike), Joseph Anders (Scourge), Joe Zucchero (Whiz), Jack S. Daniels (Scag), Steve Parv (Bo), Nigel Hodge (Ambassador), Dennis Cole (Harlan), Don Gorde (Robot), Gary Taylor (Pug), Linda Obalil (Hazel), Henry Sherma (Sargent), Debbie Pusa, Cathy Leckie (Scum Women)

HARD ROCK ZOMBIES (Cannon) Producer-Director, Krish Shas; Screenplay, Krishna Shas, David Ball; Photography, Tom Ric mond; Editor, Amit Bose; Designer, Cynthia Sowder; Music, Pa Sabu; Special Effects, John Buechler; Executive Producer, Shas Patel; Associate Producers, Sigurjon Sighvatsson, Steve Golin; other credits available; September release. CAST: E. J. Curcio, Ge Andrews, Sam Mann, Mick McMains, Lisa Toothman, Jennifer Co Ted Wells, Jack Bliesener, Crystal Shaw

MATA HARI (Cannon) Producer, Rony Yacov; Director, Cur Harrington; Screenplay, Joel Ziskin; Photography, David Gurfink Music, Wilfred Josephs; Editor, Henry Richardson; Executive Produ ers, Menahem Golan, Yoram Globus; Production Manager, Sand Toth; Assistant Directors, Juan Carlos Gil Diaz, Vilmos Kolba; D signer, Tivadar Bertalan; Sound, Eliezer Yarkoni; Choreographe Senanda Kumar, Lucy Igaz; Costumes, Bermans & Nathans, Theat kunst, S.A.F.A.S.; Eastmancolor; 108 minutes; Not rated; Septemb release. CAST: Sylvia Kristel (Mata Hari), Christopher Cazeno (Kart), Oliver Tobias (Ladoux), Gaye Brown (Fraulein Doktor), Go fried John (Wolff), William Fox (Maitre Clunet), Michael Antho (Duke of Montmorency), Vernon Dobtcheff (Prosecutor), Antho Newlands (Baron Joubert), Brian Badcoe (General Messigny), Tu Lemkow (Ybarra), Taylor Ryan (Contessa), Tobias Rolt (Jean P vost), Victor Langley (Colonel Michaud), Nicholas Selby (V Jagow), Malcolm Terris (Von Krohn), Carlos Sutton (Captain Schl ser), and Neil Robinson, Derek De Lint, Agnes David, Odon Guja Ferenc Nemethy, Csaba Jakab, Erzsebet Cserhalmi, Matyas Uszti Gabor Nagy, Ferenc Bencze, Miklos B. Szekely, Laszlo Baran Lajos Mezei, Terez Bod, Laszlo Konter, Laszlo Ujlaki, Ildiko Moln Gabor Reviczky, Gyorgy Maday, Marta Bako, Vilmos Izsof, Las Nemeth, Magda Darvas, Andras Marton.

Toni, Meagan, Richie Havens
in "A Matter of Struggle"
© *Parallel Films*

Sylvia Kristel, Tobias Rolt
in "Mata Hari"
© *Cannon*

A MATTER OF STRUGGLE (Parallel Films) Producers, Saul Newton, Ralph Klein; Director-Editor, Joan Harvey; Photography, Mark Peterson, Jeff Wayman; Documentary; 90 minutes; Not rated; September release. CAST: Richie Havens

THE NINTH CONFIGURATION (New World) Producer-Director-Screenplay, William Peter Blatty; Based on the novel by William Peter Blatty; Photography, Gerry Fisher; Music, Barry De Vorzon; Designers, Bill Malley, J. Dennis Washington; Editor, Peter Taylor; Sound, Colin Charles; Executive Producer, William Paul; Associate Producer-Assistant Director, Tom Shaw; Costumes, Tom Bronson; Special Effects, Willard Flanagin; Songs by various artists; Metrocolor; Panvision; 105 minutes; Rated R; September release. CAST: Stacy Keach (Colonel Kane), Scott Wilson (Capt. Cutshaw), Jason Miller (Lt. Reno), Ed Flanders (Col. Fell), Neville Brand (Himself), George DiCenzo (Capt. Fairbanks), Moses Gunn (Maj. Nammack), Robert Loggia (Lt. Bennish), Joe Spinell (Spinell), Alejandro Rey (Lt. Gomez), Tom Atkins (Sgt. Krebs), Billy Blatty (Young Kane), and Steve Sandor, Richard Lynch, Mark Gordon, Bill Lucking, Stephen Powers, David Healy, William Paul, Tom Shaw, Gordon K. Kee, Bruce Boa, Linda Blatty, Marilyn Raymon, Hobby Gilman, Bobby Bass

Ed Flanders, Stacy Keach
in "The 9th Configuration" © *New World*

STAND ALONE (New World) Producer, Leon Williams; Director, Alan Beattie; Screenplay, Roy Carlson; Photography, Tom Richmond, Tim Suhrstedt; Editors, Fabien Dahlen Tordjmann; Designer, Pam Warner; Music, David Richard Campbell; Executive Producers, George Kondos, Daniel P. Kondos; Co-Producer, David Thomas; Associate Producers, Tamar Simon Hoffs, Fabien Dahlen Tordjmann; Assistant Directors, Fred Baron, Matt Hintlian; Special Effects, Paul Staples; Costumes, Darcee A. Frisch; Sound, David Brownlow, Peter Bentley; A Texas Star Production; Metrocolor; 94 minutes; Rated R; September release. CAST: Charles Durning (Louis), Pam Grier (Catherine), James Keach (Isgro), Bert Remsen (Paddie), Barbara Sammeth (Meg), Lu Leonard (Mrs. Whitehead), Luis Contreras (Lookout), Willard Pugh (Macombers), Bob Tzudiker (Farley), Mary Ann Smith (Nurse Warren), Cory "Bumper" Yothers (Gordie), Holly Hardman (Polly), Duane Tucker (Johnnie), Douglas Durning (Young Louis), and Annie O'Donnell, Eddie Hartes, Robert Covarrubias, Marty Zagon, Alan Marcus, Al Christy, Joe Alfasa, Mercedes Alberti, Gino de Fulgentis, Suzan Stadner, Kerry Nakagawa, Joey Miyashima, Ed Pansullo, Paul Anselmo, Bob Yothers, Alan Abelew, Jeffrey Leavitt, Jerry Anderson, Maryly Bucci, Nancy Kaine, Peter Dirlis, Denny Ferrugiaro, Thomas Rosales, Jr., Bill Silva, Del Zamora, Greg Lawrocki, Jerry L. Reed, Lisa Tauber, Chester Grimes, Caroline Swann, Sheila Silber

STREETWALKIN' (Concorde/Cinema Group) Producer, Robert Alden; Director, Joan Freeman; Screenplay, Joan Freeman, Robert Alden, Diane Gonciarz; Photography, Steven Fierberg; Music, Matthew Ender, Doug Timm; Song, Matthew Ender, Odette Springer; Editor, John K. Adams, Patrick Rand; Designer, Jeffery Robbins; Costumes, Karen Perry; Executive Producer, Roger Corman; Production Manager, Robert Zimmerman; Assistant Directors, Evan Dunsky, Lisa Gamble; Special Effects, Wilfred Caban; A Rodeo Production; DeLuxe color; 87 minutes; Rated R; September release. CAST: Melissa Leo (Cookie), Dale Midkiff (Duke), Leon Robinson (Jason), Julie Newmar (Queen Bee), Randall Batinkoff (Tim), Annie Golden (Phoebe), Antonio Fargas (Finesse), Deborah Offner (Heather), Khandi Alexander (Star), Julie Cohen (Tricia), Greg Germann (Creepy), Kirk Taylor (Spade), Jaison Walker (Willy), and Michael Torres, Bill Shuman, Ke Reno, Garth Gardner, Gary Klar, Samantha Fox, Kendal Kaldell, Conrad Roberts, Lyneise Williams, Tom Wright, Daniel Jardano, Richard Council, David Chandler, Tyra Janssen, J. S. Johnson, Kim Chan, Gordon Press, John Branagan, Annie Allman, Michael Russo

SUDDEN DEATH (Marvin Films, Inc.) Producers, Steven Shore, David Greene; Director-Screenplay, Sig Shore; Photography, Benjamin Davis; Editor, John Tintori; Costumes, Rosemary Ponzo; Sound, Steve Rogers, Dorielle Rogers; Assistant Directors, Ron Gorton, Jr., Steve Dealy; Special Effects, Wilfred Kaban; Executive Producer, Marvin Friedlander; Technicolor; 95 minutes; Rated R; September release. CAST: Denise Coward (Valarie Wells), Frank Runyeon (Marc Lowery), Jamie Tirelli (Willie), Robert Trumbull (Herbert), Rebecca Allen (Peggy), J. Kenneth Campbell (Kosakowski), Joe Maruzzo (Raphael), Arnold Mazer (Sailor), Gary Majchrzak (Reggie), Tony Wolfe (Driver), Doug McCoy (Cooch Elliot), Steve Wise (Bruce), Laura Gardner (Det. Carter), and Mischa Bogin, Tim Roselle, Barbara Frieden, Phil Soltanoff, Gerald Orange, Gary Auerbach, Ted Bouton, Ray Camparelli, Jeff Carpenter, Tara Cavanaugh, Derek Davis

THUNDER ALLEY (The Cannon Group, Inc.) Producer, William Ewing; Director-Screenplay, J. S. Cardone; Photography, Karen Grossman; Editor, Daniel Wetherbee; Music, Robert Folk, Ken Topolsky; Designer, Joseph T. Garrity; Executive Producers, Menahem Golan, Yoram Globus; Production Manager, Susan W. Dukow; Assistant Directors, David Womark, Tommy Burns, Larry Litton; Costumes, Dorothy Baca, David Baca; Songs by various artists; Metrocolor; Panavision; 111 minutes; Rated R; September release. CAST: Roger Wilson (Richie), Jill Schoelen (Beth), Scott McGinnis (Donnie), Cynthia Eilbacher (Lorraine), Clancy Brown (Weasel), Leif Garrett (Skip), Phil Brock (Butch), Brian Cole (Wolf), Bert Kramer (Father), Elizabeth Huddle (Mother), John Dragon (Brad), Randy Polk (Fatman), Carol Kottenbrook (Candy), Melanie Kinnaman (Star), and Don Saffer, Tiny Wells, Robert Curtin, Henry Max Kendrick, Susan McIver, Frederick Flynn, John O'Connor White, Cheryl A. Waters, Richard Rubio, Jack Leal, Jeff Martin, Emily Blanton, Wink Sargeant, Bob Milan, Mark Lehman, Paul Kosanovich, Jeff Martin, James Keeler, Scott G. Jamieson, Donald E. Jamieson, Tim J. Andersen, John A. Staples, Steven D. Coffman

WHEN NATURE CALLS (Troma, Inc.) Producers, Frank Vitale, Charles Kaufman; Director, Charles Kaufman; Screenplay-Story, Charles Kaufman, Straw Weisman; Photography, Mike Spera; Editor, Michael Jacobi; Designer, Susan Kaufman; Music, Arthur Custer; Executive Producer, Susan Thomases; Costumes, Ellen Lutter; Assistant Directors, Rex A. Piano, Per Sjostedt; Color; 85 minutes; Rated R; September release. CAST: David Orange (Greg), Barbara Marineau (Barb), Nicky Beim (Little Billy), Tina Marie Staiano (Bambi), David Strathairn (Weejun), and Willie Mays, Morey Amsterdam, Fred Blassie, Myron Cohen, Stanley Siegel, John Cameron Swayze, G. Gordon Liddy, Silas Davis, Mike Brancato, Patricia Clement, Scott Perrin, Ted Brooks, Amy Miller, The First Americans, Sture M. Sjostedt, Linda Johnson, Edith Blume, Justin Stevens, Dan Goldman, Ray Sundlin, Jerome Bates, Rob Ashley Bolwes, Adele Hudson, Lance Tooks, Dan Khoury, Isaac Permaul, Philip Tashjan, Grey Wolf, Marie Antoinette Rogers, Mort Kravitz, James Edwards, Rob Roy, Earl E. Ritchie, Tony Alexander, Celeste Anson, David O. Beim, Stephen Berger, George Calfa, John Clohessy, Linda Curtis, Guy Da Silva, Hank Davies, Eileen Dawson, K. T. Dawson, Yvonne Delet, Ray Gusweller, Frank Hartman, Jack Johnston, Robert Kaufman, Kevin M. Kennedy, Herb Kramer, R. J. De Mio, William De Mio, Elena De Rosa, Jim Flanagan, Bill Ford, Ray Frankowski, Naomi Gariele, Bruce Gorelich, Steve Gorelich, Howard Owen Godnick, Ronald Grant, Kenyatta Green, Liza Mitchell, Lorraine Orange, Robert Paz, Carl Pepi, Susan Pratt, Edward Quinn

Melissa Leo, Annie Golden
in "Streetwalkin' " © *Concorde*

SAVAGE ISLAND (Empire) formerly "Orinoco—Prison of Sex"; Producers, Robert Amante, Mark Alabiso; Directors, Edward Muller, Nicholas Beardsly; Screenplay, Michelle Tomski, Nicholas Beardsly; Editor, Michelle Tomski; Music, Mark Ryder, Phil Devies; In color; Rated R; 74 minutes; September release. CAST: Linda Blair (Daly), Anthony Steffen (Laredo), Ajita Wilson (Marie), Christina Lai (Muriel), Leon Askin (Luker)

EVILS OF THE NIGHT (Shapiro Entertainment) Producer-Director, Mardi Rustam; Screenplay, Mardi Rustam, Phillip D. Connors; Photography, Don Stern; Editor, Henri Charr; Music, Robert O. Ragland; Songs, Rod Burton, Richard Bellis; Executive Producer, Mohammed Rustam; Associate Producers, John Kasha, Jim Talmadge; Production Manager, Jeanne Van Cott; Assistant Directors, Richard Kanter, William Nettles; Sound, Gerald Wolfe; Color; 98 minutes; Rated R; October release. CAST: Neville Brand (Kurt), Aldo Ray (Fred), Tina Louise (Cora), John Carradine (Dr. Kozmar), Julie Newmar (Dr. Zarma), Karrie Emerson (Nancy), Bridget Holloman (Heather), G.T. Taylor (Connie), David Hawk (Brian), Keith Fisher (Ron), Tony O'Dell (Billy), Kelly Parsons (Laura Lee), and Scott Hunter, Laura Lee, Bonnie J. Karlyle, Susan Pastor, Kimberly Bleier, Kari Thompson, Diana Payne, Walter Zeri, Keith Johnson, Erika Marr

BETTER OFF DEAD (Warner Bros.) Producer, Michael Jaffe; Director-Screenplay, Savage Steve Holland; Photography, Isidore Mankofsky; Editor, Alan Balsam; Music, Rupert Hine; Executive Producers, Gil Friesen, Andrew Meyer; Presented by CBS Productions; An A & M Films Production; 98 minutes; Rated PG; October release. CAST: John Cusack (Lane Myer), David Ogden Stiers (Al Myer), Diane Franklin (Monique), Kim Darby (Jenny Myer), Amanda Wyss (Beth), Aaron Dozier (Roy), Curtis Armstrong (Charles)

THE BOYS NEXT DOOR (New World) Producers, Keith Rubenstein, Sandy Howard; Director, Penelope Speeris; Screenplay, Glen Morgan, James Wong; Photography, Arthur Albert; Editor, Andy Horvitch; Music, George S. Clinton, Geo; Associate Producers, Michael S. Murphey, Joel Soisson; Executive Producers, Mel Pearl, Don Levin; Production Manager, William Fay; Assistant Directors, Eric Jewett, Warren Lewis, Scott White, Michael A. Masciarelli, Steven Pomeroy; Designer, Jo-Ann Chorney; Sound, Craig Felburg; Costumes, Gail Viola; Special Effects, Joe Quinlivan; Songs by various artists; CFI Color; 91 minutes; Rated R; October release. CAST: Maxwell Caulfield (Roy Alston), Charlie Sheen (Bo Richards), Patti D'Arbanville (Angie), Christopher McDonald (Det. Mark Woods), Hank Garrett (Det. Ed Hanley), Paul C. Dancer (Chris), and Richard Pachorek, Lesa Lee, Kenneth Cortland, Moon Zappa, Dawn Schneider, Kurt Christian, Don Draper, Blackie Dammett, Phil Rubenstein, James Carrington, Grant Heslov, Michael Lewis, Leonard O. Turner, Vance Colvig, Jeff Prettyman, Claudia Templeton, Ron Ross, Carlos Guitarlos, Helen Brown, Hettie Lynne Hurtes, Sarah Lilly, Jimmy Ford, James Bershad, Joseph Michael Cala, Mark Tiffany, Marilou Conway, Mark Stanton, Kevin Kendall, Kenneth Gilman Sr., Carmen Filpi, Christina Beck, John Davey, Geof Brewer, Toby Iland, Richard Halpern, John Escobar, Ray Lykins, Jadie David, Texacala Jones, Pinkie Tessa, Maggie Ehrig, Tequila Mockingbird, Ted Quinn

CEASE FIRE (Cineworld Enterprises) Producer, William Grefe; Director, David Nutter; Screenplay, George Fernandez from his play "Vietnam Trilogy"; Photography Henning Schellerup; Editor, Julio Chaves; Music, Gary Fry; Sound, Henry Lopez; Designer, Alan Avchen; Assistant Director, Allan Harmon; Production Manager, Dean Gates; A Double Helix Films presentation of an E.L.F. Productions production; Executive Producers, George Fernandez, Ed Fernandez; Continental Color; 97 minutes; Rated R; October release. CAST: Don

David Ogden Stiers, Kim Darby, John Cusack, Scooter Stevens in "Better Off Dead" © CBS

Johnson (Tim Murphy), Lisa Blount (Paula Murphy), Robert F. Lyon (Luke), Richard Chaves (Badman), Rick Richards (Robbs), Chris Noe (Wendy), Jorge Gil (Sanchez), John Archie (Rafer), T. R. Durphy (Hartz), Buddy Bolan (Benny)

FLANAGAN (United Film) Producer, Mark Slater; Director, Sco Goldstein; Screenplay, Edmond Collins, Scott Goldstein; Photogra phy, Ivan Strasburg; Editor, Scott Vickery; Color; 100 minutes; Rate R; October release. CAST: Philip Bosco (James Flanagan), Geraldin Page (Mama), Linda Thorson (Andrea), William Hickey (Papa), Olym pia Dukakis (Mary), Brian Bloom (Danny), Steven Weber (Sean)

FLESH AND BLOOD (Orion) Producer, Gys Versluys; Directo Paul Verhoeven; Screenplay, Gerard Soeteman, Paul Verhoever Story, Gerard Soeteman; Photography, Jan De Bont; Editor, In Schenkkan; Music, Basil Poledouris; Designer, Felix Murcia; Cos tumes, Yvonne Blake; Sound, Tom Tholen, Ad Roest; Associate Pro ducer, Jose Vicuna; Production Managers, Remmelt Remmelts, Carlc Orengo; Special Effects, Joe Di Gaetano; Assistant Director, Jindr Markus; Puppetplay, Rien Baartmans, Joost Hilterman; Lyrics, Arthu Hamilton; DeLuxe Color; Technovision Widescreen; 126 minutes Rated R; October release. CAST: Rutger Hauer (Martin), Jennife Jason Leigh (Agnes), Tom Burlinson (Steven), Jack Thompson (Hawk wood), Fernando Hillbeck (Arnolfini), Susan Tyrrell (Celine), Rona Lacey (Cardinal), Brion James (Karsthans), John Dennis Johnsto (Summer), Simon Andreu (Miel), Bruno Kirby (Orbec), Kitty Cou bois (Anna), Marina Saura (Polly), Hans Veerman (Father George Jake Wood (Little John), Hector Alterio (Niccolo), Blanca Marsillac (Clara), Nancy Cartwright (Kathleen), Jorge Bosso (Sterz), Mario D Barros (Herman), Ida Bons (Roly Poly), and Jaime Segura, Bettin Brenner, Siobhan Hayes, Susan Beresford, Monica Luccetti

HERCULES II (Cannon) Producer, Alfred Pecoriello; Directo Lewis Coates; Photography, Alberto Spagnoli; Editor, Sergio Monta nari; Music, Pino Donaggio; Costumes, Adriana Spadaro; Designe Tony Gelleng; Production Manager, Vittorio Galiano; Assistant Direc tors, Giancarlo Santi, Massimo Galiano, Armando Valcauda; Soun Roberto Petrozzi; Special Effects, Giovanni Corridori; Technicolc Dolby Stereo; 90 minutes; Rated PG; October release. CAST: Lo Ferrigno (Hercules), Milly Carlucci (Urania), Sonia Viviani (Glaucia William Berger (King Minos), Carlotta Green (Athena), Claudio Ca sinelli (Zeus), Nando Poggi (Poseidon), Maria Rosaria Omaggi (Hera), Venantino Venantini (High Priest), Laura Lenzi (Flora), Mar

Charlie Sheen, Maxwell Caulfield in "The Boys Next Door" © New World Pictures

Maxwell Caulfield, Charlie Sheen in "The Boys Next Door" © New World

Lou Ferrigno in "Hercules II"
© *Cannon*

Blair Underwood, Sheila E.
in "Krush Groove" © *Warner Bros.*

ewton (Aphrodite), Cindy Leadbetter (Ilia), Raf Baldassarre
Atreus), Serena Grandi (Euryale), Era Robbins (Dedalos), Sandra
enturini (Teti), Andrea Nicole (Amazon), Alessandra Canale (Dei-
aira), Pamela Prati (Aracne), Cristina Basili (Little People)

RUSH GROOVE (Warner Bros.) formerly "Rap Attack"; Produc-
s, Michael Schultz, Doug McHenry; Director, Michael Schultz;
creenplay, Ralph Farquhar; Photography, Ernest Dickerson; Editors,
rry Bixman, Conrad M. Gonzalez; Music, Various Composers; Exec-
ive Producers, George A. Jackson, Robert O. Kaplan; Co-Producer,
heila E., Run-D.M.C., The Fat Boys, Kurtis Blow, Blair Underwood,
ew Edition

MIXED BLOOD (Sara Films/Cinevista) Producers, Antoine Gan-
ge, Steven Fierberg; Director-Screenplay, Paul Morrissey; Photogra-
y, Stefan Zapasnik; Editor, Scott Vickerey; Music, Andy "Sugar-
ated" Hernandez; Color; 98 minutes; Not rated; October release.
AST: Marilia Pera (Rita La Punta), Richard Ulacia (Thiago), Geral-
ne Smith (Toni), Rodney Harvey (Jose), Angel David (Juan the
ullet), Pedro Sanchez (Commanche), Linda Kerridge (Carol), Ulrich
err (The German), Marcelino Rivera (Hector), Yukio Yamamoto
aptain Kenzo), Susan Blond (Caterer)

RIVATE CONVERSATIONS (Punch) Producer-Director, Chris-
n Blackwood; Photography, Christian Blackwood; Editor, Donna
arino; Music, Alex North; In color; Not rated; 88 minutes; October
lease. A documentary about the making of the tv broadcast of "Death
a Salesman" with Arthur Miller, Dustin Hoffman, John Malkovich,
olker Schlondorff, Stephen Lang, Michael Ballhaus, Charles Durning

E-ANIMATOR (Empire Pictures) Producer, Brian Yurma; Direc-
r, Stuart Gordon; Screenplay, Dennis Paoli, William J. Norris, Stuart
ordon; Photography, Mac Ahlberg; Editor, Lee Percy; Music,
chard Band; Color; 86 minutes; Not rated; October release. CAST:
ffrey Combs (Herbert West), Bruce Abbott (Dan Cain), Barbara
rampton (Megan Halsey), David Gale (Dr. Carl Hill), Robert Samp-
n (Dean Halsey), Gerry Black (Mace), Carolyn Purdy-Gordon (Dr.
arrod), Peter Kent (Melvin the Re-Animated), and Barbara Pieters,
n Patrick Williams

CHOOL SPIRIT (Concorde/Cinema Group) Producers, Ashok
mritraj, Jeff Begun; Director, Alan Holleb; Screenplay, Geoffrey
ere; Photography, Robert Ebinger; Editor, Sonya Sones; Music,
m Bruner; Designer, Peter Knowlton; Executive Producers, Sidney

Balkin, Ken Dalton; Associate Producers, Vijay Amritraj, Chandru
Manghnani; Production Manager, Bill Tasgal; Assistant Directors,
Stephen Buck, Whitney Hunter; Costumes, Sarah Bardo; Special
Effects, Ken Solomon; DeLuxe Color; 90 minutes; Rated R; October
release. CAST: Tom Nolan (Billy Batson), Elizabeth Foxx (Judith
Hightower), Larry Linville (Pres. Grimshaw), John Finnegan (Pinky
Batson), Daniele Arnaud (Madeleine), Nick Segal (Gregg), Marta
Kober (Ursula), Roberta Collins (Helen Grimshaw), Frank Mugavero
(Lasky), Toni Hudson (Rita), Brian Mann (Barducci), David Byrd (The
Boss), Michael Miller (Chuck), Leslee Bremer (Sandy), Laurence
Haddon (Dr. Strohman), Liz Sheridan (Mrs. Kingman), Jay Scorpio
(Prof. Sylvester), Julie Gray (Kendall), Susan Schroder (Vania), David
Kendrick, Leslie Bohem, Bob Haag, Jimbo Goodwin (Gleaming
Spires), and Beach Dickerson, Cynthia Harrison, Karen Smythe, Helen
Vick, Pamela Ward, Diane Hoyes, Glen Mont, Freddy Ramos, Nuisa
Kato, Claudio Slon, Laura Lee Kasten, Marlene Janssen, Biff Yeagar,
Johnny Lee, Jay Cohen, Charles Dayton, Dina Russo, Becky Le Beau,
Jacki Easton, Jeff Yesko, Daniel Friedman, Katherine McBride, Deke
Anderson, Tony Balderama, Robert Briscoe, Sandra Grass, Theresa
Mesquita, Linda Carol, Kathi Pierce, Leslie Kelly

SOUTH BRONX HEROES (Continental Inc.) formerly "The Run-
aways" and "Revenge of the Innocents"; Producer, Director, William
Szarka; Screenplay, William Szarka, Don Schiffrin; Additional Dia-
logue, Marc Shmuger, Mario van Peebles; Photography, Eric Schmitz;
Editors, Jim Rivera, Eli Haviv, William Szarka; Music, Al Zima, Mitch
Herzog; Sound, Michael Trujillo; Assistant Director, Sean Ward; Pro-
duction Manager, George Szarka Sr.; Associate Producers, Jon Kurtis,
Don Schiffrin; A Zebra Prods. Ltd. and Walter Manley presentation;
Color; 85 minutes; Not rated; October release. CAST: Brendan Ward
(Paul), Mario van Peebles (Tony), Megan van Peebles (Chrissie),
Melissa Esposito (Michelle), Martin Zurla (Bennett), Jordan Abeles
(Scott), and Barry Lynch, Dan Lauria, Bo Rucker, Sean Ward

THERE WERE TIMES, DEAR A Presentation of the Northeastern
Gerontological Society, the New York Commission on Aging, and
Sardoz (Dorsey Pharmaceuticals and Sardoz Pharmaceuticals); Pro-
ducer, Lilac Productions; Director-Co-Producer, Linda Hope; Screen-
play, Harry Cauley; Photography, Brianne Murphy; Music, Jay Grus-
ka; Editor, Kenneth Miller; Executive Producer-Co-Producer, Flora
Lang; Medical Consultant, Jack Rowe, M.D.; Color; 60 minutes; Not
rated; October release. CAST: Shirley Jones (Susanne Millard), Len
Cariou (Bob Millard), Cynthia Eilbacher (Jenny), Dana Elcar (Don
Mason), Alan Haufrect (Dr. Rosen), Ina Balin (Marsha)

"School Spirit"
© *Concorde*

Tom Burlinson, Jennifer Jason Leigh
in "Flesh and Blood" © *Orion*

129

APPOINTMENT WITH FEAR (Galaxy) Producer, Tom Boutross; Director, Ramzi Thomas; Screenplay, Ramzi Thomas, Bruce Meade; Executive Producer, Moustapha Akkad; Associate Producer, M. Sanousi; Photography, Nicolas Von Sternberg; Art Director, David Gladstone; Editor, Paul Jasiukonis; Music, Andrea Saparoff; In color; Rated R; 96 minutes; October release. CAST: Michele Little (Carol), Michael Wyle (Bobby), Kerry Remsen (Heather), Douglas Rowe (Det. Kowalski), Garrick Dowhen (The Man), Deborah Sue Voorhees (Ruth), Pamela Bach (Samantha), Vincent Barbour (Cowboy), Mike Gomez (Little Joe), Danny Dayton (Norman), James Avery (Connors), Sergia Simone (The Woman), Steven B. Gregory (Young Man), Charlotte Speer (Mrs. Pierce), Hugo L. Stranger (Old Man), Gertrude M. Clement (Old Woman), Ilanga (Mime), P. Morgan Morrow (Nurse), John Escobar, Bruce Meade (Police)

PRAY FOR DEATH (American Distribution Group) Executive Producers, Moshe Diamant, Sunhil Shah, Moshe Barkat; Producer, Don Van Atta; Director, Gordon Hessler; Screenplay, James Booth; Photography, Roy H. Wagner; Editor, Bill Butler; Music, Thomas Chase, Steve Rucker; Martial Arts Choreography, Sho Kosugi; In color; Rated R; 92 minutes; November release. CAST: Sho Kosugi (Akira), Donna Kei Benz (Reiko), Kane Kosugi (Takeshi), Shane Kosugi (Tomoya), Michael Constantine (Newman), James Booth (Limehouse), Matthew Faison (Daley), Charles Gruber (Trumble), Parley Baer (Old Man), Norman Burton (Lt. Dalmain), Robert Ito (Koga)

TO LIVE AND DIE IN L.A. (New Century) Executive Producer, Samuel Schulman; Producer, Irving H. Levin; Director, William Friedkin; Screenplay, William Friedkin, Gerald Petievich; Based on novel by Gerald Petievich; Photography, Robby Muller; Co-producer, Bud Smith; Music, Wang Chung; Editor, Bud Smith; In Technicolor and Dolby Stereo; Rated R; 116 minutes; November release. CAST: William L. Petersen (Richard Chance), Willem Dafoe (Eric Masters), John Pankow (John Vukovich), Debra Feuer (Bianca Torres), John Turturro (Carl Cody), Darlanne Fluegel (Ruth Lanier), Dean Stockwell (Bob Grimes), Steve James (Jeff), Robert Downey (Thomas), Michael Greene (Jim), Christopher Allport (Max), Jack Hoar (Jack), Val DeVargas (Judge), Dwier Brown (Doctor), Michael Chong (Ling), Jackelyn Giroux (Claudia), Michael Zand (Terrorist), Bobby Bass, Dar Allen Robinson (FBI Agents), Anne Betancourt (Nurse), Katherine M. Louie (Ticket Agent), Edward Harrell (Guard), Gilbert Espinoza (Bartender), John Petievich, Zarko Petievich, Rick Dalton, Richard L. Lane, Jack Cota, Shirley J. White, Gerald H. Brownlee, David M. DuFriend, Ruben Garcia, Joe Duran, Buford McClerkins, Gregg Dandridge, Donny Williams, Earnest Hart, Jr., Thomas F. Duffy, Gerry Petievich, Mark Gash, Pat McGroarty, Brian Bradley, Jane Leaves

MACARONI (Paramount) Producers, Luigi and Aurelio De Laurentiis, Franco Committeri; Director, Ettore Scola; Screenplay, Ruggero Maccari, Furio Scarpelli, Ettore Scola; Photography, Claudio Ragona; Music, Armando Trovaioli; Editor, Carla Santarelli; Assistant Directors, Paola Scola, Alessandro Colizzi, Stefano Rubeo; Color; 104 minutes; Rated PG; November release. CAST: Jack Lemmon (Robert Traven), Marcello Mastroianni (Antonio Jasiello), Daria Nicolodi (Laura Di Falco), Isa Danieli (Carmelina Jasiello), Maria Luisa Santella (Doorkeeper), Patrizia Sacchi (Virginia), Bruno Esposito (Giulio Jasiello), Orsetta Gregoretti (Young Actress), Marc Berman, Jean Francois Perrier (Record Producers), Giovanna Sanfilippo (Maria), Fabio Tenore (Pasqualino), Marta Bifano (Luisella), Aldo De Martino (Cottone), Clotilde De Spirito (Villain's Mistress), Carlotta Ercolino (Journalist), Vincenza Gioioso (Donna Amalia), Ernesto Mahieux (Young Actor), Giovanni Mauriello (Driver), Alfredo Mingione (Manager), Daniela Novak (Fiancee), Umberto Principe (Michele Vitale), Giovanni Riccardi (Eugenio), Corrado Taranto (Alberto)

MATTER OF HEART (Horizon) Producer, Michael Whitney; Director, Mark Whitney; Concept-Screenplay, Suzanne Wagner; Music,

John Pankow, William Petersen, John Turturro
in "To Live and Die in L.A." *MGM/UA*

John Adams; Executive Producer, George Wagner; Consultant, Sa Francis; Color; 107 minutes; Not rated; November release. CAST: D Marie-Louise von Franz, Sir Laurens van der Post, Barbara Hanna Dr. Liliane Frey, Prof. C. A. Meier, Dr. Gerhard Adler, Josep Henderson, Dr. Joseph Wheelwright, Jane Wheelwright, Aniela Jaffi Dieter Baumann, Hilde Kirsch, Dr. James Kirsch, Mary Bancro Prof. Tadeus Reichstein, Baroness von der Heydt, Michael Fordhar Heinrich Fierz

CONTRARY WARRIORS (Rattlesnake Productions) Produce Connie Poten, Pamela Roberts, Beth Ferris; Photography, Steph Lighthill; Editor, Jennifer Chinlund; Music, Todd Boekelheide; Na rator, Peter Coyote; In color; Not rated; 60 minutes; November releas A documentary about The Crow Indians in Montana.

FEVER PITCH (MGM/UA) Producer, Freddie Fields; Direct Screenplay, Richard Brooks; Photography, William A. Fraker; D signer, Raymond G. Storey; Editor, Jeff Jones; Music, Thomas Dolb Production Manager, Jack Terry; Assistant Directors, Jerry Balle Ken Collins, Susan Norton; Sound, Al Overton, Jr.; Special Effec William Balles; Costumes, Michael Hoffman, Aggie Lyon; Songs various artists; Metrocolor; Panavision; 96 minutes; Rated R; Nove ber release. CAST: Ryan O'Neal (Taggart), Catherine Hicks (Fl Giancarlo Giannini (Charley), Bridgette Andersen (Amy), Ch Everett (Dutchman), John Saxon (Sports Editor), Hank Greensp (Publisher), William Smith (Panama Hat), Keith Hefner (Sweene Rafael Campos (Rafael), Patrick Cassidy (Soldier), Cherie Mich (Rose O'Sharon), Tom Schanley (Scanlon), William Prince (Mitche Tony March, Stu Black (Bodyguards), Johnny Sekka (Chocolat Steve Danton (Towel Boy), Timothy Blake (Babs), Pearl Shear (M Applebaum), Chad McQueen (Prisoner), Bobby Jacoby (Gam-a-te Boy), Heidi Sorenson (Airport Attendant), Lonny Chin (Miss Cas blanca), D. P. Bentley (High Roller), Joseph Bernard (Bernstei Selma Archerd (Sister Theresa), and Bill Caplan, Sid Sakowic Leonard Sacks, John Kirby, Alan Buchdahl, Mary Asta, Benita E llamy, Jimmie Spades, Bill Willard, Sandy Oshatz, Marc Lefkowi Lynn Parker, Tim Scott, Gary Pagett, Mark Mitchell, Steven Clo Rita Cox, Carol Crotta, Steven Horn, Gordon Jones, Bob Keiss Robert Lutz, Allan Malamud, Kevin Modesti, Fred Robledo, Willi Schorr, Mel Albert, Jose Aldana, John Beyrooty, Bud Furillo, T Liotta, Len Miller, Jim Murray, Diane Shah, Jeff Silverman, R Tosches, Scott A. Zamost

Marcello Mastroianni, Jack Lemmon
in "Macaroni" © *Paramount*

Giancarlo Giannini, Ryan O'Neal
in "Fever Pitch"
© *MGM/UA Entertainment*

"Louie Bluie"
© *Superior Pictures*

Kim Myers, Mark Patton
in "A Nightmare on Elm Street Part 2"
© *New Line Cinema*

RINGO Producers, Lech Kowalski, Ann S. Barish; Director, Lech Kowalski; Photography, Raffi Ferrucci; Editor, Val Kuklowsky; Music, Chuck Kentis; Presented by Kasba Productions, Newell Media I, Ann S. Barish; Documentary; 80 minutes; Not rated; November release. CAST: John Spacely

LOUIE BLUIE (Corinth Films) Producer-Director, Terry Zwigoff; Photography, John Knoop, Chris Li; Editor, Victoria Lewis; Music, various composers; Documentary; 60 minutes; Not rated; November release. CAST: Howard Armstrong "Louis Bluie" (Fiddle and Mandolin), Yank Rachell (Mandolin), Ted Bogan (Guitar), Ikey Robinson (Banjo), Tom Armstrong (Bass)

REBEL LOVE (Troma) Producer, John Quenelle; Director-Screenplay, Milton Bagby, Jr.; Photography, Joseph A. Whigham; Editor, Mellena Bridges; Music, Bobby Horton; Designer, Bill Teague; Associate Producer, Shirley Fulton Crumley; Assistant Directors, Philip B. Peters, Gordon McGee, De Anna Cataldo; Sound, Tommy Dilbeck; Costumes, Deborah Brunson; Special Effects, Vern Hyde; Presented by Lloyd Kaufman, Michael Herz; Color; 88 minutes; Not rated; November release. CAST: Jamie Rose (Columbine Cromwell), Terence Knox (McHugh/Hightower), Fran Ryan (Granny Plug), Carl Spurlock (Sergeant), Rick Waln (Corporal), Larry Larson (Aaron Cromwell), Charles Hill (The Captain), Harry Howell (General Mason), Thom Bossom, Jr. (Pompeii)

STARCHASER: THE LEGEND OF ORIN (Atlantic) Producer-Director, Steven Hahn; Screenplay, Jeffrey Scott; Music, Andrew Belling; Editor, Donald W. Ernst; Animation Directors, Mitch Rochon, Sung-Gil Kim; Designers, Louis Zingarelli, Thomas Warkentin, Timothy Callahan, Roy Allen Smith; Executive Producers, Thomas Coleman, Michael Rosenblatt; Associate Producers, Daniel Pia, Christine Danzo; Key Animators, Yoon Young Sang, Jung Yul Song, Bill Kroyer; DeLuxe Color; Widescreen 3-D; Dolby Stereo; 101 minutes; Rated PG; November release. VOICES: Joe Colligan (Orin), Carmen Argenziano (Dagg), Noelle North (Elan/Aviana), Anthony Delongis (Zygon), Les Tremayne (Arthur), Tyke Caravelli (Silica), Ken Samson (Magreb), John Moschitta, Jr. (Auctioneer/Z. Gork), Atwood (Shooter), Mona Marshall (Kallie), Tina Romanus (Aunt Bella, and Ryan MacDonald, John Garwood, Joseph Dellasorte, Philip Clarke, Mike Winslow, Thomas H. Watkins, Daryl T. Bartley, Barbera Harris & Co.

A NIGHTMARE ON ELM STREET Part 2 FREDDY'S REVENGE (New Line Cinema) Producer, Robert Shaye; Director, Jack Sholder; Screenplay, David Chaskin; Photography, Jacques Haitkin; Music, Christopher Young; Editor, Arline Garson; Freddy Krueger's Make-Up, Kevin Yagher; Special Effects, A & A Special Effects/Dick Albain; Transformation Effects, Mark Shostrom; Co-Producer, Sara Risher; Executive Producers, Stephen Diener, Stanley Dudelson; Line Producers, Michael Murphey, Joel Soisson; Color; 85 minutes; Rated R; November release. CAST: Mark Patton (Jesse Walsh), Kim Myers (Lisa Poletti), Robert Rusler (Grady), Clu Gulager (Mr. Walsh), Hope Lange (Mrs. Walsh), Marshall Bell (Coach Schneider), Melinda O. Fee (Mrs. Poletti), Thom McFadden (Mr. Poletti), Sydney Walsh (Kerry), Hart Sprager (Teacher), Steve Eastin (Policeman), Christie Clark (Angela), Robert Englund (Freddy Krueger)

STEPHEN KING'S SILVER BULLET (Paramount) Producer, Martha Schumacher; Director, Daniel Attias; Screenplay, Stephen King; Based on the novelette "Cycle of the Werewolf" by Stephen King; Photography, Armando Nannuzzi; Editor, Daniel Loewenthal; Music, Jay Chattaway; Costumes, Clifford Capone; Designer, Giorgio Postiglione; Creatures, Carlo Rambaldi; Associate Producer-Production Manager, John A. Eckert; Assistant Directors, John Kretchmer, Bruce Moriarty; Sound, Richard Goodman; Songs by various artists; Technicolor; J-D-C Widescreen; 95 minutes; Rated R; November release. CAST: Gary Busey (Uncle Red), Everett McGill (Rev. Lowe), Corey Haim (Marty Coslaw), Megan Follows (Jane Coslaw), Robin Groves (Nan Coslaw), Leon Russom (Bob Coslaw), Terry O'Quinn (Sheriff Joe Haller), Bill Smitrovich (Andy Fairton), Joe Wright (Brady Kincaid), Kent Broadhurst (Herb Kincaid), Heather Simmons (Tammy Sturmfuller), James A. Baffico (Milt Sturmfuller), Rebecca Fleming (Mrs. Sturmfuller), Lawrence Tierney (Owen Knopfler), William Newman (Virgil Cuts), Sam Stoneburner (Mayor O'Banion), Lonnie Moore (Billy McLaren), Rick Pasotto (Aspinall), Cassidy Eckert (Girl), Wendy Walker (Stella Randolph), Michael Lague (Boyfriend), Myra Mailloux (Mother), William Brown (Bobby Robertson), Herb Harton (Elmer Zinneman), David Hart (Pete Sylvester), Graham Smith (Porter Zinneman), Paul Butler (Edgar Rounds), Crystal Field (Maggie Andrews), Julius LeFlore (Smokey), Roxanne Aalam (Uncle Red's Girl), Pearl Jones (Mrs. Thayer), Ish Jones, Jr. (Mr. Thayer), Steven White (Outfielder), Conrad McLaren (Mac), Tovah Feldshuh (Older Jane's Voice), Everett McGill (Werewolf), James Gammon (Arnie Westrum)

Jamie Rose, Terence Knox
in "Rebel Love"
© *Troma Team*

Megan Follows, Gary Busey, Corey Haim
in "Silver Bullet"
© *Paramount*

131

Jim Carrey, Lauren Hutton
in "Once Bitten" © *Samuel Goldwyn*

ONCE BITTEN (Samuel Goldwyn) Producers, Dimitri Villard, Robby Wald, Frank E. Hildebrand; Director, Howard Storm; Screenplay, David Hines, Jeffrey Hause, Jonathan Roberts; Story, Dimitri Villard; Photography, Adam Greenberg; Music, John Du Prez; Editor, Marc Grossman; Designer, Gene Rudolf; Choreography, Joanne Divito, Randy Grazio; Costumes, Jill Ohanneson, Harold O'Neal; Special Effects, Court Wizard; Associate Producer, Russell Thacher; Production Manager, Don Behrns; Assistant Directors, Gene Sultan, Nicholas Batchelor, Robert Altshuler; Executive Producer, Samuel Goldwyn, Jr.; Songs by various artists; Metrocolor; 97 minutes; Rated PG-13; November release. CAST: Lauren Hutton (Countess), Jim Carrey (Mark Kendall), Karen Kopins (Robin Pierce), Cleavon Little (Sebastian), Thomas Ballatore (Jamie), Skip Lackey (Russ), Jeb Adams (World War I Ace Vampire), Joseph Brutsman (Confederate Vampire), Stuart Charno (Cabin Boy Vampire), Robin Klein (Flowerchild Vampire), Glen Mauro, Gary Mauro (Twin Vampires), Carey More (Moll Flanders Vampire), Peter Elbling (Bookseller), Richard Schaal (Mr. Kendall), Peggy Pope (Mrs. Kendall), Anna Mathias (Daphne), Kate Zentall (Tanya), Laura Urstein (Darlene), Megan Mullally (Suzette), Garry Goodrow (Wino), Dan Barrows (Harry), Alan McRae (Man in Drag), Philip Linton (Boy In Shower), and Ruth Silveira, Ron Vernan, Terry Wills, Dee Dee Rescher, Opelene Bartley, Dominick Brascia, Nancy Hunter, Don Richey, Anthony Storm, Casey Storm, Maria Vidal, Rainbow Shalom, Kimberlye Gold, Nancy Scher, Kelly Salloum

RAINBOW BRITE AND THE STAR STEALER (Warner Bros) Producers, Jean Chalopin, Andy Heyward, Tetsuo Katayama; Directors, Bernard Deyries, Kimio Yabuki; Screenplay-Voice Director, Howard R. Cohen; Story, Jean Chalopin, Howard R. Cohen; Music, Haim Saban, Shuki Levy; Lyrics, Howard R. Choen; Executive Producers, Jean Chalopin, Andy Heyward; Associate Producers, Victor Villegas, Alan Lee; Designer, Rich Rudish; Character-Background Designers, Laureen Burger, Rich Lynes, John Calmette, J. Kenton Manning; Special Effects, Kou Yamamoto, Masayuki Nakajima; Editors, Yutaka Chikura, Izumi Okada; A presentation of Hallmark Properties; A Dic Enterprises Production; Technicolor; Dolby Stereo; 97 minutes; Rated G; November release. VOICES: Bettina (Rainbow Brite), and Patrick Fraley, Peter Cullen, Robbie Lee, Andre Stojka, David Mendenhall, Rhonda Aldrich, Les Tremayne, Mona Marshall, Jonathan Harris, Marissa Mendenhall, Scott Menville, Charles Adler, David Workman

AMATEUR HOUR (Kaufman) Producer, Susan Kaufman; Director, Stanford Singer; Screenplay, Mr. Singer, Kevin McDonough; Photography, Lisa Rinzler; Art Director, Ann Williams; Editor, Richard King; Music, Cengiz Yaltkaya; In color; Not rated; 85 minutes; November release. CAST: Adam Nathan (Paul Pierce), Julie Hanlon (Donna Rose), John MacKay (John Reid), Walt Willey (Bill Johnson), Sau Alpiner (Frank Romance), Mikhail Druhan (Miss Murphy), Michael Griffith (Marcel Pederewsky), Guillermo Gonzalez (Rico)

GRUNT! THE WRESTLING MOVIE (New World) Executive Producer, James G. Robinson; Producers, Don Normann, Anthony Randell; Director, Allan Holzman; Screenplay, Roger D. Manning; Photography, Eddie van der Enden; Editors, Allan Holzman, Barry Zetlin; Music, Susan Justin; Assistant Director, Kristine Peterson; In Technicolor; Rated R; 90 minutes; November release. CAST: Jeff Dial (Lesley), Robert Claudini (Tweed), Marilyn Dodds Farr (Sweet Lola), Greg Magio Schwartz, Bill Grant, Steve Cepello, Dick Murdock, Exotic Adrian Street, John Tolos, Wally George, Victor Rivera, Count Billy Varga, Duck's Breath Mystery Theatre

STITCHES (International Film Marketing) Producers, William B. Kerr, Robert P. Marcucci; Director, Alan Smithee; Screenplay, Michel Coquette, Michael Paseornek; Photography, Hector R. Figueroa; Editor, John Duffy; Music, Bob Floke; Costumes, Richard E. La Motte; Production Manager, William Kerr; Assistant Directors, Ron L. Wright, Michael Green; Sound, Ed Somers; Color; 89 minutes; Rated R; November release. CAST: Parker Stevenson (Bobby Stevens), Geoffrey Lewis (Ralph Rizzo), Brian Tochi (Sam Boon Tong), Robin Dearden (Nancy NcNaughton), Bob Dubac (Al Rosenberg), Tommy Koenig ("Barfer" Bogan), Sydney Lasick (Sheldon Mendlebaum), Eddie Albert (Dean Bradley), Ken Stovitz (Howard Pierce), Russ Marin (Dr. Sidney Berman), Ed McNamara (Osgood Hamilton, Sr.), Susanne Wasson (Judith Bradley), Daniel Greene (Ted Fletcher), Leslie Watson (Cindy), Jenny Neumann (Joan), Tony Longo (Jock) Murl Langston (Ramon The Florist), and Irene Olga Lopez, Antony Ponzini, Frank Annese, Deborah Fallender, Stephanie Faulkner, Marianne Muellerleile, Lucinda Crosby, Rebecca Perle, John Ingle, Leslie Jacob Sumant, Judy Sharp, Jayson Kane, Matthew Tobin, Ellen Crawford, Earl Montgomery, Jr., Barbara Chase, Danna Hansen, Patti Oltremari, Anthony Travalini, Leonard Simon, Marii Mak, Dennis Brown, Tom Rush, Sandy Hackett, Anthony Henderson Ed Karvoski, Susan Woll Sally Champlin, Diana Fredricks, Lisa Figueroa, Peggy Kubena, Le Lucas, Randy Gallion, Florence Sundstrom, Bryant Wheat, John C McLaughlin, Robert Anthony Marcucci

THE TOXIC AVENGER (Troma) Producers, Lloyd Kaufman, Michael Herz; Directors, Michael Herz, Samuel Weil; Screenplay, Joe Ritter; Additional Material, Lloyd Kaufman, Gay Terry, Stuart Struti; Photography, James London, Lloyd Kaufman; Editor, Richard Haine, Alan J. Polyniak; Sound, John Michaels, Mark Pancza; Designer, Barry Shapiro, Alexandra Mazur; Associate Producer, Stuart Struti, Special Effects Make-Up, Jennifer Aspinall, Tom Lauten, Ralph C. Cordero, II; Production Manager, Caroline Baron; Assistant Director, Joe Zubrovich; Songs by various artists; Color; 100 minutes; Rated November release. CAST: Andree Maranda (Sara), Mitchel Cohen (The Toxic Avenger), Jennifer Baptist (Wanda), Cindy Manion (Julie), Robert Prichard (Slub), Gary Schneider (Bozo), Pat Ryan, Jr. (Mayor Belgoody), Mark Torgl (Melvin), Dick Martinsen (O'Clancy), Chris Liano (Walter), David Weiss (Police Chief), Dan Snow (Cigar Face), Doug Isbecque (Knuckles), Charles Lee, Jr. (Nipples), Pat Kilpatri (LeRoy), Larry Sutton (Frank), Mike Russo (Rico), Norma Pratt (M)

Stormy astride Thunder, Rainbow Brite
astride Starlite in "Rainbow Brite
and the Star Stealer" © *Hallmark*

Eddie Albert, Ken Stovitz, Parker
Stevenson in "Stitches"
© *International Film Marketing*

John Byner, Carol Kane
in "Transylvania 6-5000" © *New World*

Steve Guttenberg, Curtis Armstrong, Robert
Romanus, Julie Hagerty, Julie Kavner in
"Bad Medicine" © *20th Century-Fox*

askell), Andrew Craig (Fred), Ryan Sexton (Johnny), Sarabel Levin-on (Mom), Al Pia (Tom), Reuben Guss (Dr. Snodburger), and Ken-eth Kessler, Barbara J. Gurskey, Donna Winter, Mary Ellen David, ennis Souder, Joe Zarro, William Christopher Weiss, Dan Hogan, Myrna Williams, Richard Duggan, Bruce Morton, John Stobaeus, Joe upor, Jr., D. J. Calvitto, Cosmo Wilder, Brigitte Douglaston, Nancy ompansanto, Andrea Suter, Xavier Barquet, Matt Klan, Joey Calder-ne, Sherry Park, Vickie Usher, Barry Shapiro, Andy Stamatin, Betty la, Teddy Copley, Dolly Hall, Alisha Riggs, Vicki Juditz, Roxanne Maranda, Macine Hayt, Teresa Simpson, Don Costello, June De-oung, Jon Curtis, Peter Racini, Martin Scott McMann, Ed Carrion, harles Dicagno, Bruce Zimmerman, Skip Hamra, Eileen Nad Castal-i, Nathan Jon Castaldi, Britt Martinsen, Kristen Martinsen, Lisa Martinsen, Dianna-Jean Flaherty, Donna-Marie Stipo, Mary Cox, Jes-ca Perkins, Giorgio Calderone, William Klan, Margaret Riley

RANSYLVANIA 6-5000 (New World) Producers, Mace Neufeld, Thomas H. Brodek; Director-Screenplay, Rudy DeLuca; Photography, om Pinter; Editor, Harry Keller; Designer, Zeljko Senecic; Costumes, hristine Glazier, Latica Ivanisevic; Executive Producers, Paul Licht-an, Arnie Fishman; Associate Producer, Glenn Neufeld; Assistant irectors, Roger LaPage, Don Heitzer, Zoran Budak; Production Man-er, Milan Stanislic; Special Effects, Marijan Kuroglan; Sound, Pat Mitchell, David Lewis Yewdall; Music, Alfie Kabiljo; Songs by var-us artists; Color; 94 minutes; Rated PG; November release. CAST: ff Goldblum (Jack Harrison), Joseph Bologna (Dr. Malavaqua), Ed egley, Jr. (Gil Turner), Carol Kane (Lupi), Jeffrey Jones (Lepescu), hn Byner (Radu), Geena Davis (Odette), Michael Richards (Fejos), onald Gibb (Wolfman), Norman Fell (Mac Turner), Teresa Ganzel Elizabeth Ellison), Rudy DeLuca (Lawrence Malbot), Inge Apelt Madame Morovia), Bozidar Smiljanic (Insp. Percek), Peter Buntic Munyadi), Dusko Valentic (Twisted Man), Ksenija Prohaska (Mum-y), Sara Grdjan (Laura Ellison), Nada Arbus (Uta), and Visnja onigskneght, Slobodan Milovanovic, Vida Jerman, Venco Kapural, Thomas H. Brodek

CREAMPLAY (Boston Movie Co.) Producer, Dennis M. Piana; irector, Rufus Butler Seder; Screenplay, Mr. Seder, Ed Greenberg; hotography, Dennis M. Piana; Editor, Mr. Seder; Art Director, heryl; Hirschman; Music, George Cordeiro, Basil J. Bova; In black nd white; Not Rated; 90 minutes; November release. CAST: Rufus utler Seder (Edgar Allen), George Kucher (Holly), George Cordeiro gt. Joe Blatz), Basil J. Bova (Tony Cassano), M. Lynda Robinson Mina Ray), Eugene Seder (Al Weiner)

BASIC TRAINING (Movie Store) Producers, Otto Salamon, Gil Adler; Executive Producers, Paul Klein, Lawrence Vanger; Assistant Producer, Allison Rosenfeld; Director, Andrew Sugerman; Screenplay, Bernard M. Kahn; Photography, Steven W. Gray; Editor, Larry Bock; Music, Michael Cruz; Art Director, John Carter; Design, Susan Emshwiller; Costumes, Warden Neil; In DeLuxe Color; Rated R; 88 minutes; November release. CAST: Ann Dusenberry (Melinda), Rhonda Shear (Debbie), Angela Aames (Cheryl), Will Nye (Lt. Cranston), Walter Gotell (Ambassador Gotell)

BAD MEDICINE (20th CENTURY-FOX) Producers, Alex Winitsky, Arlene Sellers; Director-Screenplay-Story, Harvey Miller; Based on novel "Calling Dr. Horowitz" by Steven Horowitz, Neil Offen; Photography, Kelvin Pike; Editors, O. Nicholas Brown, John Jympson; Music, Lalo Schifrin; Designer, Les Dilley; Costumes, Rita Riggs; Co-Producer, Jeffrey Ganz; Co-Executive Producers, Michael Jaffe, Myles Osterneck; Executive Producer-Production Manager-Assistant Director, Sam Manners; Assistant Directors, Michael R. Joyce, Ingo Vallejo-Najera; Sound, Bud Alper; A Lantana Production; Color by DeLuxe; Panavision; 96 minutes; Rated PG-13; November release. CAST: Steve Guttenberg (Jeff Marx), Alan Arkin (Dr. Madera), Julie Hagerty (Liz Parker), Bill Macy (Dr. Gerald Marx), Curtis Armstrong (Dennis Gladstone), Julie Kavner (Cookie Katz), Joe Grafasi (Gomez), Robert Romanus (Carlos), Taylor Negron (Pepe), Candi Milo (Maria Morales), Gilbert Gottfried (Tony Sandoval), Arturo Venegas (Jesus), Arne Gordon (Witch Doctor), Manuel Pereiro Rodriguez (Dr. Cervantes), Eileen Way (Sra. Madera), Alan Corduner (Dr. Diaz), Tresa Hughes (Dr. Elisabeth Marx), Martha Greene (Dr. Helene Marx), Jose Canalejas (Prof. Hugo), Charles Paktell (Cadaver), John Sterland (Dr. Beatty), Maria Del Pilar Garcia Alvarez (Estrellita), Emilia Lopez Isunza (Alms), Angel A. Camarata (Aguilar), Simon Andreu Trobat (Dr. Ortega), Luis E. Hidalgo (Raul Rodriguez), Pedro Luis Lavilla Fonalleras (Pedro), and Luis Bar-Boo, Luis Gaspar, Luis Maluenda, Alfredo Alvarez Perez, Jose Maria Munoz Gambin, Jose Yepes, Joe Ochoa, Anastasio Pozo, Carolina Mata Garcia, Joaquin Solis Del Cerro, Paloma Cela Molinero, Felix Lazaro Ramos

THE BEACH BOYS: AN AMERICAN BAND (High Ridge Productions) Producers, Malcolm Leo, Bonnie Peterson; Director-Screenplay, Malcolm Leo; Editor, David Fairfield; Documentary; Color; 103 minutes; Rated PG-13; November release. CAST: Brian Wilson, Carl Wilson, Mike Love, Al Jardine, Bruce Johnston, Dennis Wilson

"The Toxic Avenger"
© *Troma Team*

Steve Guttenberg, Julie Haggerty
in "Bad Medicine"
© *20th Century-Fox*

THAT WAS THEN . . . THIS IS NOW (Paramount) Producers, Gary R. Lindberg, John M. Ondov; Director, Christopher Cain; Screenplay, Emilio Estevez; Based on novel by S. E. Hinton; Executive Producers, Alan Belkin, Brnadon K. Phillips; Photography, Juan Ruiz Anchia; Editor, Ken Johnson; Music, Keith Olsen, Bill Cuomo; Associate Producers, Jim Geib, Martin M. Weiss; Assistant Directors, Robert Koster, Michael Kennedy; Art Director, Chester Kaczenski; Costumes, Ann Wallace; In Technicolor and Dolby Stereo; Rated R; 103 minutes; November release. CAST: Emilio Estevez (Mark Jennings), Craig Sheffer (Bryon Douglas), Larry B. Scott (Terry Jones), Matthew Dudley (Curly Shepard), Jill Schoelen (Angela Shepard), Kim Delaney (Cathy), Barbara Babcock (Mrs. Douglas), Frank Howard (M & M), Morgan Freeman (Charlie), Frank McCarthy (Carlson), Diane Dorsey (Mrs. Carlson), Ramon Sheen (Mike), David Miller (Punk), Steven Pringle (Dirty Dave), Bob Swan (Smitty), John O'Brien (Snob), Paul Lane (Paul), Brooks Gardner (Tim), Sharon Thomas (Doctor), Tom Walsh, Bill Lane

VLADIMIR HOROWITZ, THE LAST ROMANTIC (Cami Video) Executive Producer, Peter Gelb; Producer, Susan Froemke; Film by David Maysles, Albert Maysles, Susan Froemke, Deborah Dickson, Patricia Jaffe; Editors, Deborah Dickson, Patricia Jaffe; Music Producer, Jack Pfeiffer; In color; Not Rated; 88 minutes; November release. A documentary on the 81 year old pianist.

SANTA CLAUS: THE MOVIE (Tri-Star) Producers, Ilya Salkind, Pierre Spengler; Director, Jeannot Szwarc; Screenplay, David Newman; Story, David and Leslie Newman; Photography, Arthur Ibbetson; Music, Henry Mancini; Designer, Anthony Pratt; Flying and 2nd Unit Director, David Lane; Visual Effects Director, Derek Meddings; Editor, Peter Hollywood; Costumes, Bob Ringwood; Assistant Director, Derek Cracknell; Choreography, Pat Garrett; Sound, Don Sharpe, David Crozier; Songs by various artists; Color; Dolby Stereo; 112 minutes; Rated PG; November release. CAST: Dudley Moore (Patch), John Lithgow (B. Z.), David Huddleston (Claus), Burgess Meredith (Ancient Elf), Judy Cornwell (Anya), Jeffrey Kramer (Towzer), Christian Fitzpatrick (Joe), Carrie Kei Heim (Cornelia), John Barrard (Dooley), Anthony O'Donnell (Puffy), Melvyn Hayes (Goober), Don Estelle (Groot), Tim Stern (Boog), Peter O'Farrell (Honka), Christopher Ryan (Vout), Dickie Arnold (Goobler), Aimee Delamain (Storyteller), Dorothea Phillips (Miss Tucker), John Hallam (Grizzard), Judith Morse (Miss Abruzzi), Jerry Harte (Senate Chairman), and Paul Aspland, Sally Cranfield, Michael Drew, Walter Goodman, John Cassady, Ronald Fernee, Michael Ross

BRING ON THE NIGHT (Samuel Goldwyn) Producer, David Manson; Director, Michael Apted; Photography, Ralf D. Bode; Associate Producer-Editor, Robert K. Lambert; Editor, Melvin Shapiro; Costumes, Colleen Atwood; Designer, Ferdinando Scarfiotti; Music Producers, Pete Smith, Sting; Technical Advisor, Vic Garbarini; Executive Producers, Gil Friesen, Andrew Meyer; An A & M Films Production; Color; Dolby Stereo; 97 minutes; Rated PG-13; November release. CAST: Sting (vocals and guitar), Omar Hakim (drums), Darryl Jones (bass), Kenny Kirkland (keyboards), Branford Marsalis (saxophones), Dolette McDonald, Janice Pendarvis (background vocals)

COCAINE WARS (Concorde/Cinema Group) Producers, Roger Corman, Alex Sessa; Director, Hector Olivera; Screenplay, Steven M. Krauzer; Story, Hector Olivera, David Vinas; Photography, Victor Kaulen; Editor, Edward Lowe; Music, George Brock; Designer, Julie Bertotto; Production Manager, Alex Plowing; Assistant Directors, Americk Von Zaratt, Claude Reitter; Sound, Norman Newcastle; Special Effects, Willy Smith; Color; 83 minutes; Rated R; November release. CAST: John Schneider (Cliff), Kathryn Witt (Janet), Royal Dano (Bailey), Federico Luppi (Gonzalo Reyes), Rodolfo Ranni (Gen. Lwan), Ivan Grey (Klausman), Richard Hamlin (Wilhelm), Edgar

Emilio Estevez, Craig Sheffer, Morgan Freeman
in "That Was Then . . . This Is Now" © *Paramount*

Moore (Rikki), Armand Capo (Oswaldo), Martin Korey (Gomez), Tom Cundom (Driver), Ken Edgar (Kenny), Joe Capanga (Miguel), Mark Woinski (Pugg), Jacques Arndt (Franco), Willy Marcos (Hernando), John Vitaly (Marcelo Villalba), Patricia Davis (Rosita), Heidi Paddl (Lola), Helen Grant (Pia), Ted McNabney, Patricia Schener (Reporters)

THE DIRT BIKE KID (Concorde/Cinema Group) Producer, Julie Corman; Director, Hoite C. Caston; Screenplay, David Brandes, Lewis Colick; Story, J. Halloran; Photography, Daniel LaCambre; Music, Bill Bowersock, Phil Shenale; Editor, Jeff Freeman; Production Manager, Paul Rapp; Assistant Directors, Thomas Herod, Jr., Cara Giallanza; Designers, Becky Block, J. Grey Smith; Costumes, Sawnie R Baldridge; Sound, Daniel Henke; from Trinity Pictures, Inc.; Color; 9 minutes; Rated PG; November release. CAST: Peter Billingsley (Jack Simmons), Stuart Pankin (Mr. Hodgkins), Anne Bloom (Janet Simmons), Patrick Collins (Mike), Sage Parker (Miss Clavell), Cha Sheets (Bo), Gavin Allen (Max), Danny Breen (Flaherty), "Weasel" Forshaw (Big Slime), John William Galt (Chief), Courtney Kraus (Beth), Holly Schenck (Sue), Al Evans (Mr. Zak), and Angie Bolling, Gena Sleete, Betty R. King, Bill Shaw, Barnett Shpritz, Brian Sadlier, Harvey Christiansen, Gary Carter, Dale Kassel, Beth Larson, Elain Williams, Tyress Allen, Emily Rose Kelley

IN HER OWN TIME (Direct Cinema) Producers, Vikram Jayant Lynne Littman; Director, Lynne Littman; Based on field work of D Barbara Myerhoff; Photography, William Moffitt; Editor, Suzann Pettit; Music, James Horner; In color; Not rated; 60 minutes; November release. A Documentary based on the exploration of the diverse Fairfa district Jewish community in Los Angeles.

BARBARIAN QUEEN (Concorde/Cinema Group) Producers Frank Isaac, Alex Sessa; Photography, Rudy Donovan; Editor, Sylvi Roberts, Leslie Rosenthal; Music, Chris Young, Jamie Horner; De signer, Julia Bertram; Production Manager, Alex Plowing; Assistar Directors, Andrew Sargent, Charles Ritter, Alex Sessa, Jr., Paul Asco Sound, Daniel Castle; Special Effects, Willy Smith, Arny Alfieri; Rodeo Production; Color; 82 minutes; Rated R; December release CAST: Lana Clarkson (Amathea), Katt Shea (Estrild), Frank Zagarin (Argon), Dawn Dunlap (Taramis), Susana Traverso (Tiniara), Victo Bo (Strymon), Arman Chapman (Arrakur), Andrea Barbizo (Zoraida), Tony Middleton (Zohar), Andrea Scriven (Dariac), Robe

John Schneider, Kathryn Witt
in "Cocaine Wars" © *Concorde*

Christian Fitzpatrick, David Huddleston
in "Santa Claus: The Movie"
© *Tri-Star*

134

Sage Parker, Patrick Collins, Peter
Billingsley in "Dirt Bike Kid"
© Concorde

Sting in "Bring on the Night"
© Samuel Goldwyn Co.

Carson (Shibdiz), Matilda Muir (Eunuco), Eddie Little (Vendedor),
Patrick Duggan (Shaman), Lucy Tiller (Orellia), Ivan Green (Karax),
Theo McNabney (Cerus), Richard R. Jordan (Vanir), John Head (Alfasa), Daniel Seville (Kantaka), Eva Donnelly (Ciega), and Henry Finn,
Grace Castle, Louis Alday, Norman Friedman, Alexander Essex, Guy
Reed, Alfred Alexander, Arthur Neal

BOGGY CREEK II (Howco) Producer-Director, Charles B. Pierce;
Screenplay, Mr. Pierce; Photography-Editor, Shirah Kojayan; Music,
Frank McKelvey; Narration, Mr. Pierce; Associate Producer, Joy N.
release. CAST: Charles B. Pierce (Prof. Lockhart), Cindy Butler (Leslie Ann Walker), Serene Hedin (Tanya), Chuck Pierce (Tim), Jimmy
Clem (Crenshaw), Rick (Rock) Hildreth (Deputy Williams) Fabus
Griffin (Adult Creature), Victor Williams (Young Creature)

WORD OF HEAVEN (Trans World) Producer, Joseph J. Randazzo; Co-producer, Britt Lomond; Director, Byron Meyers; Screenplay,
James Bruner, Britt Lomond, William P. O'Hagan, Joseph Randazzo;
Photography, Gil Hubbs; Editor, Warren Chadwick; Music, Christopher L. Stone; Associate Producer, Don Wilkerson; Martial Arts Coordinator, Tadashi Yamashita; In DeLuxe Color; Rated R; 85 minutes;
December release. CAST: Tadashi Yamashita (Tadashi), Mel Novak
(Dirk), Gerry Gibson (Patrick), Joe Randazzo (Cain), Mika (Satoko),
Wynston A. Jones (Cal), Bill Superfoot Wallace, Karen Lee Shepherd,
Venus Jones

SCREAM (Cal-Com) formerly "The Outing"; Executive Producer,
Byron Quisenberry; Producers, Clara Huff, Hal Buchanan, Larry
Quisenberry; Direction-Screenplay, Byron Quisenberry; Photography,
Dick Pepin; Editor, B. W. Kestenberg; Music, Joseph Conlan; Assistant Director, Fred Allison; In Cinereel Color; Rated R; 81 minutes;
December release. CAST: Pepper Martin (Bob), Hank Worden (John),
Ivy Moore (Al), John Ethan Wayne (Stan), Julie Marine (Laura),
Gregg Palmer (Ross), Woody Strode (Charlie), Bobby Diamond,
Joseph Alvarado, Anna Bronston, Nancy St. Marie

CLUE (Paramount) Producer, Debra Hill; Director-Screenplay,
Jonathan Lynn; Story, John Landis, Jonathan Lynn; Based on the
Parker Brothers' board game "Clue"; Photography, Victor Kemper;
Editors, David Bretherton, Richard G. Haines; Music, John Morris;
Executive Producers, Jon Peters, Peter Guber, John Landis, George
Folsey, Jr.; Color; 87 minutes; Rated PG; December release. CAST:
Eileen Brennan (Mrs. Peacock), Tim Curry (Wadsworth), Madeline

Kahn (Mrs. White), Christopher Lloyd (Prof. Plum), Michael McKean
(Mr. Green), Martin Mull (Col. Mustard), Lesley Ann Warren (Miss
Scarlet), Coleen Camp (Yvette), Lee Ving (Mr. Boddy), Bill Henderson (Cop), Jeffrey Kramer (Motorist), Kellye Nakahara (Mrs. Ho),
Jane Wiedin (Singing Telegram Girl)

HEAD OFFICE (Tri-Star) Producer, Debra Hill; Director-Screenplay, Ken Finkleman; Photography, Gerald Hirschfeld; Designer,
Elayne Barbara Ceder; Editors, Danford B. Greene, Bob Lederman;
Music, James Newton Howard; Executive Producers, Jon Peters, Peter
Guber; Production Manager, Marilyn Stonehouse; Assistant Directors,
Michael Zenon, Elizabeth Scherberger; Costumes, Judith R. Gellman;
Sound, Peter Shewchuk; Special Effects, Martin Malivoire; Song,
General Public; Metrocolor; Panavision; Dolby Stereo; 86 minutes;
Rated PG-13; December release. CAST: Eddie Albert (Helmes), Merritt Butrick (John Hudson), George Coe (Sen. Issel), Danny DeVito
(Stedman), Lori-Nan Engler (Rachel), Ron Frazier (Nixon), Ron James
(Mark Rabinovich), John Kapelos (Gen. Sepulveda), Don King (Himself), Richard Masur (Max Landsberger), Rick Moranis (Gross), Brian
Doyle Murray (Tolliver), Don Novello (Sal), Michael O'Donoghue
(Dantley), Judge Reinhold (Jack), Diane Robin (Gross' Secretary),
Jane Seymour (Jane), Wallace Shawn (Hoover), Bruce Wagner (Kennedy), Hrant Alianak (Pres. Sanchez), and Lee Broker, Howard Busgang, Tom Butler, Jeremiah Chechick, Richard Comar, Nancy Cser,
Billy Curtis, Dominic Cuzzocrea, William Davis, Louis De Bianco,
Carolyn Dunn, Denis Forest, Elizabeth Irwin, Marvin Karon, Derek
Kuervost, Kathy Lasky, Don McManus, Mike McManus, Robin
Menken, Maxine Miller, Myron Natwick, Laura Press, Elizabeth
Shepherd, Ralph Small, Barry Thomson, Shawn Thompson, Christopher Ward, Gay Claitman, Myra Fried, Megan Smith, Theresa Tova,
Eric Keenleyside, Don Keppy, Tex Konig, Francine Volker, DeVonne
L. Green, Patricia Nember, Eric Young, Annie McAuley, Catherine
McClenahan

IGOR AND THE LUNATICS (Troma Team) Producers-Screenplay, Jocelyn Beard, Billy Parolini; Director, Billy Parolini;
Story, Jocelyn Beard; Photography, John Raugalis; Music, Sonia Rutstein; Editor, Billy Parolini; Special Effects Make-Up, Simon Deitch;
Executive Producers, Lloyd Kaufman, Michael Herz; Horror, Action,
and Suspense Sequences Directors, Tom Doran, Brendan Faulkner;
Demento-Vision; Trauma-Sound; 84 minutes; Rated R; December release. CAST: Joseph Eero, Joe Niola, T. J. Michaels, Mary Ann
Schacht

Lesley Ann Warren, Martin Mull, Madeline Kahn,
Michael McKean, Tim Curry, Christopher Lloyd,
Eileen Brennan in "Clue" © Paramount

Jane Seymour(L), Don King (R)
in "Head Office" © Tri-Star

135

David Maysles, Al Maysles, Vladimir Horowitz
in "The Last Romantic" © *Cami*

Tim Curry, Lesley Ann Warren
in "Clue" © *Paramount*

LENZ (Mirror Films) Producer-Director-Screenplay-Photography, Alexandre Rockwell; Music, First Notated Music, Ambrosian Chants, Humns of South American Shaman; Based on a fragmented novel by George Buchner based on the facts of Jacob Michael Reinhold Lenz' life; Voted one of the Outstanding Films of 1981 by the British Film Institute, 25th London Film Festival; 97 minutes; Not rated; December release. CAST: (Non-professionals) Street People of New York

NAKED VENGEANCE (Westbrook/M. P. Films) Producers, Anthony Maharaj, Cirio Santiago; Director, Cirio Santiago; Story, Anthony Maharaj; Music, Ron Jones; Color; Rated R; December release. CAST: Deborah Tranelli, Kaz Garaz, Bill McLaughlin, Ed Crick.

PRINCE JACK (LMF Productions) Producer, Jim Milio; Director, Screenplay, Bert Lovitt; Photography, Hiro Narita; Designer, Michael Corenblith; Music, Elmer Bernstein; Editor, Janice Hampton; Costumes, Bobbie Mannix; Associate Producers, Alain Silver, Patrick Regan; Metrocolor; 100 minutes; Not rated; December release. CAST: Dana Andrews (The Cardinal), Jim Bakus (Dealy), Theodore Bikel (Georgi), Robert Guillaume (Martin), Robert Hogan (Jack), James F. Kelly (Bobby), Kenneth Mars (Lyndon), Cameron Mitchell (Walker), Lloyed Nolan (Joe), William Windom (Ferguson)

SPIES LIKE US (Warner Bros.) Producers, Brian Grazer, George Folsey, Jr.; Director, John Landis; Screenplay, Dan Aykroyd, Lowell Ganz, Babaloo Mandel; Story, Dan Aykroyd, Dave Thomas; Photography, Robert Paynter; Designer, Peter Murton; Editor, Malcolm Campbell; Music, Elmer Bernstein; Costumes, Deborah Nadoolman; Executive Producer, Bernie Brillstein; Associate Producers, Sam Williams, Leslie Belzberg; Assistant Directors, Dusty Symonds, Gareth Tandy, Nick Heckstall-Smith; Production Manager, Claude Hudson; Special Effects, Brian Johnson; Visual Effects, Derek Meddings; Songs by various artists; Technicolor; 109 minutes; Rated PG; December release. CAST: Chevy Chase (Emmet Fitz-Hume), Dan Aykroyd (Austin Milbarge), Mark Stewart (Courier), Sean Daniel (Driver), Bruce Davison (Mr. Ruby), William Prince (Mr. Keyes), Steve Forrest (Gen. Sline), Tom Hatten (Gen. Miegs), Ronald Reagan (The President of the United States), Jeff Harding (Fitz-Hume's Associate), Heidi Sorenson (Fitz-Hume's Supervisor), Stephen Hoye (Capt. Hefling), Margo Random, Douglas Lambert (Reporters), Frank Oz (Test Monitor), Christopher Malcolm (Jumpmaster), Bernie Casey (Col. Rhombus), Terrance Conder, Matt Frewer (Soldiers), Jim Staahl (Bud Schnelker), James Daughton (Rob Hodges), Tony Cyrus (The Khan), Custi Bogok (Dr. La Fong), Terry Gilliam (Dr. Imhaus), Donna Dixon (Karen Boyer), Derek Meddings (Dr. Stinson), Ray Harryhausen (Dr. Marston), Robert Paynter (Dr. Gill), Gurdial Sira (Khan's Brother), and Jo Coen, Sam Raimi, Michael Apted, B. B. King, Larry Cohen, Martin Brest, Rico Ross, Richard Sharpe, Stuart Milligan, Sally Anlauf, Cos Cavras, Seva Novgorodtsev, John Daveikis, Laurence Bilzerian, Richard Kruk, Sergei Rousakov, Bjarne Thomsen, Garrick Dombro-ski, Svetlana Plotnikova, Vanessa Angel, Heather Henson, Eric Folsey, Bob Swaim

Left Center: James F. Kelly, Robert Hogan,
Kenneth Mars in "Prince Jack"
© *Castle Hill*
Above: Susana Traverso in "Barbarian Queen"
© *Concorde/Cinema Group*

Donna Dixon, Dan Aykroyd, Chevy Chase
in "Spies Like Us" © *Warner Bros.*

PROMISING NEW ACTORS OF 1985

MAXWELL CAULFIELD

CARLIN GLYNN

WHOOPI GOLDBERG

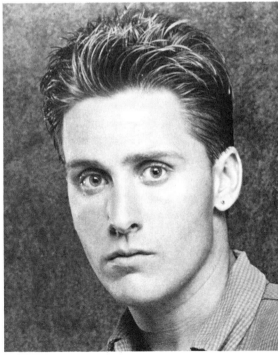

EMILIO ESTEVEZ

MICHAEL J. FOX

JULIE HAGERTY

JUDITH IVEY

STEPHEN GEOFFREYS

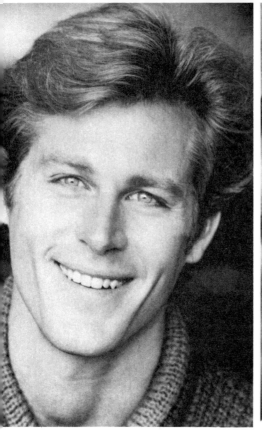

BRIAN KERWIN

DIANNE WIEST

OPRAH WINFREY

JOE MORTON

OUT OF AFRICA

(UNIVERSAL) Producer-Director, Sydney Pollack; Screenplay, Ku
Luedtke; Based on "Out of Africa" and other writings by Isak Dinese
"Isak Dinesen: The Life of a Storyteller" by Judith Thurman, an
"Silence Will Speak" by Errol Trzebinski; Designer, Stephen Grime
Photography, David Watkin; Editors, Fredric Steinkamp, Willia
Steinkamp, Pembroke Herring, Sheldon Kahn; Music, John Barr
Costumes, Milena Canonero; Co-Producer, Terence Clegg; Associa
Producers, Judith Thurman, Anna Cataldi; Executive Producer, Ki
Jorgensen; Assistant Directors, David Tomblin, Roy Button, Produ
tion Manager, Gerry Levy; Sound, Peter Handford; Additional Musi
Wolfgang Amadeus Mozart; Special Visual Effects, Syd Dutton, B
Taylor; A Mirage Enterprises Production; Technicolor; Technovisio
Dolby Stereo; 150 minutes; Rated PG; December release

CAST

Karen	Meryl Stree
Denys	Robert Redfo
Bror	Klaus Maria Brandaue
Berkeley	Michael Kitche
Farah	Malick Bowe
Kamante	Joseph Thaiak
Kinanjui	Stephen Kinyanj
Delamere	Michael Goug
Felicity	Suzanna Hamilt
Lady Belfield	Rachel Kempsc
Lord Belfield	Graham Crowde
Sir Joseph	Leslie Philli
Belknap	Shane Rimm
Juma	Mike Buga
Kanuthia	Job Sec
Ismail	Mohammed Um
Doctor	Donal McCar
Banker	Kenneth Mas
Commissioners	Tristram Jellinek, Stephen Grim
Lady Byrne	Annabel Mau
Minister	Benny You
Beefy Drunk	Sbish Trzebins
Rajiv	Allaudin Qures
Young Officer	Niven Bo
Mariammo	Im
Huge Man	Peter Stro
Esa	Abdullah Suna
Victoria	Amanda Park
Lady Delamere	Muriel Gro
Dowager	Ann Palm
Missionary Teacher	Keith Pears

*1985 Academy Awards for Best Picture, Best Director
Best Screenplay Adaptation, Best Cinematography
Best Original Score, Best Art Direction, Best Sound*

**Left: Meryl Streep
Above: Meryl Streep Top: Meryl Streep,
Robert Redford**

Klaus Maria Brandauer, Meryl Streep

Meryl Streep, Robert Redford

BEST PICTURE OF 1985

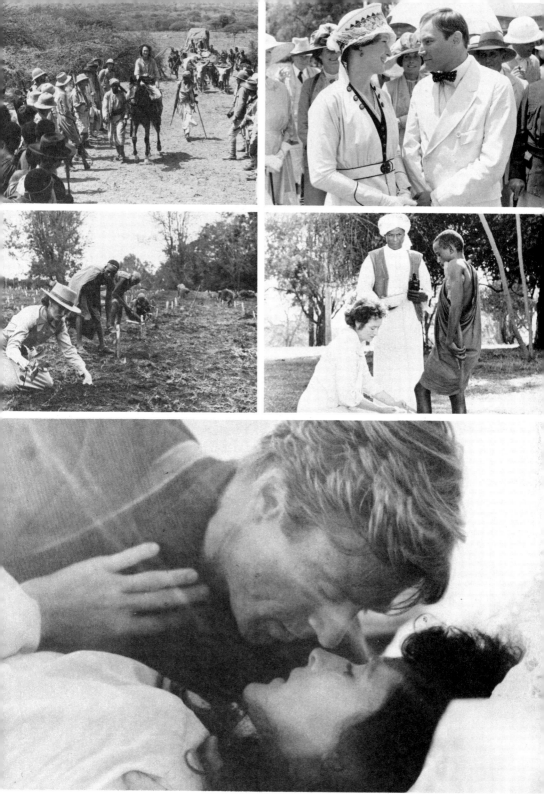

Robert Redford, Meryl Streep Top Left: Meryl Streep Below: Meryl Streep
Top Right: Meryl Streep, Klaus Maria Brandauer Below: Meryl Streep,
Malick Bowens, Joseph Thiaka © *Universal*

WILLIAM HURT
in "Kiss of the Spider Woman"
© *Island Alive*

1985 ACADEMY AWARD FOR BEST ACTOR

GERALDINE PAGE
in "The Trip to Bountiful"
© *Island Pictures*

1985 ACADEMY AWARD FOR BEST ACTRESS

143

DON AMECHE
in "Cocoon"
© *20th Century Fox*

1985 ACADEMY AWARD FOR BEST SUPPORTING ACTOR

ANJELICA HUSTON
in "Prizzi's Honor"
© *20th Century Fox*

1985 ACADEMY AWARD FOR BEST SUPPORTING ACTRESS

BROKEN RAINBOW

(EARTHWORKS) Producers-Writers-Editors, Maria Florio, Victor Mudd; Photography, Michael Anderson, Fred Elmes, Joan Weidman, Tony St. John, Baird Bryant, Victoria Mudd; Songs composed and performed by Laura Nyro; Associate Director, Thom Tyson; Associate Producers, Roslyn Dauber, Tommie Smith; Sound, Sesumu Tukunov, Jim Rossolini, Trevor Black, Clyde Smith, Haline Paul, Johanna D metrakas; Documentary; Color; 70 minutes Not rated; November release. VOICES: Martin Sheen (Narrator), and Burgess Meredith, Buf Sainte-Marie, Semu Huaute

Academy Award for Best Feature Documentary

Mr. Bikadie
Top: Martin Sheen

Mrs. K. Smith
Above: Laura Nyro

1985 ACADEMY AWARD FOR BEST FEATURE DOCUMENTARY

Semu Huaute
Top: Violet Bikadie

Buffy Saint-Marie
Top: Ruby Askie

147

THE OFFICIAL STORY

(ALMI PICTURES INC.) Producers, Historias Cinematograficas Progress Communication Corporation; Director, Luis Puenzo; Screenplay, Luis Puenzo, Aida Bortnik; Photography, Felix Monti; Editor Juan Carlos Macias; Music, Atilio Stampone; Designer, Abel Facello Costumes, Tiky Garcia Estevez; Assistant Director, Raul Outeda Sound, Abelardo Kushnir; Executive Producer, Marcelo Pineyro Spanish with subtitles; Argentina; Color; 112 minutes; Not rated November release.

CAST

Roberto	Hector Alteri
Alicia	Norma Aleandr
Sara	Chela Rui
Ana	Chunchuna Villafan
Enrique	Hugo Aran
Benitez	Patricio Contrera
Jose	Guillermo Battagli
Nata	Maria Luisa Robled
Gaby	Analia Castr
Macci	Jorge Petragli
General	Augusto Larret
Father Ismael	Leal Re

Recipient of Academy Award for Best Foreign-Language Film of 1985

Left: Norma Aleandro
© ALMI Pictures

Analia Castro, Hector Alterio, Norma Aleandro

1985 ACADEMY AWARD FOR BEST FOREIGN-LANGUAGE FILM

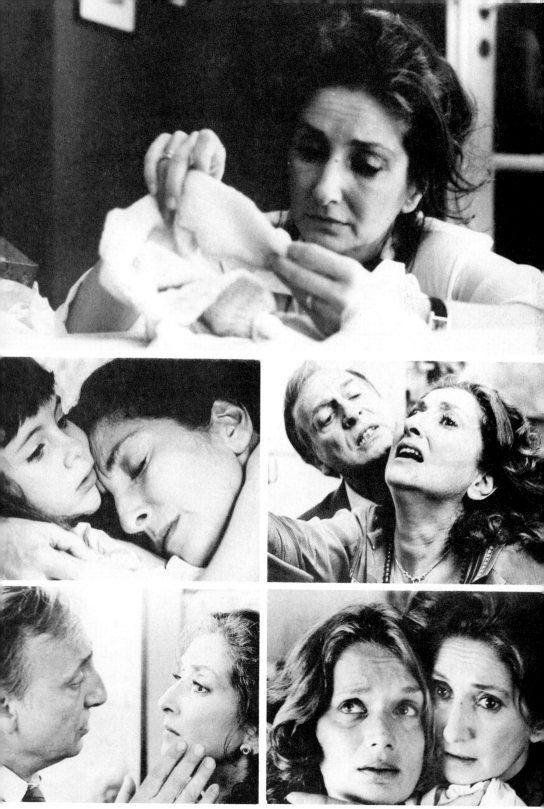

Hector Alterio, Norma Aleandro
Above: Analia Castro, Aleandro
Top: Norma Aleandro

Chunchuna Villafane, Norma Aleandro
Above: Aleandro, Hector Alterio

Dustin Hoffman	Eileen Heckart	Paul Newman	Estelle Parsons	Sidney Poitier	Eva Marie Saint

PREVIOUS ACADEMY AWARD WINNERS

(1) Best Picture, (2) Actor, (3) Actress, (4) Supporting Actor, (5) Supporting Actress, (6) Director, (7) Special Award, (8) Best Foreign Language Film

1927–28: (1) "Wings," (2) Emil Jannings in "The Way of All Flesh," (3) Janet Gaynor in "Seventh Heaven," (6) Frank Borzage for "Seventh Heaven," (7) Charles Chaplin.

1928–29: (1) "Broadway Melody," (2) Warner Baxter in "Old Arizona," (3) Mary Pickford in "Coquette," (6) Frank Lloyd for "The Divine Lady."

1929–30: (1) "All Quiet on the Western Front," (2) George Arliss in "Disraeli," (3) Norma Shearer in "The Divorcee," (6) Lewis Milestone for "All Quiet on the Western Front."

1930–31: (1) "Cimarron," (2) Lionel Barrymore in "A Free Soul," (3) Marie Dressler in "Min and Bill," (6) Norman Taurog for "Skippy."

1931–32: (1) "Grand Hotel," (2) Fredric March in "Dr. Jekyll and Mr. Hyde" tied with Wallace Beery in "The Champ," (3) Helen Hayes in "The Sin of Madelon Claudet," (6) Frank Borzage for "Bad Girl."

1932–33: (1) "Cavalcade," (2) Charles Laughton in "The Private Life of Henry VIII," (3) Katharine Hepburn in "Morning Glory," (6) Frank Lloyd for "Cavalcade."

1934: (1) "It Happened One Night," (2) Clark Gable in "It Happened One Night," (3) Claudette Colbert in "It Happened One Night," (6) Frank Capra for "It Happened One Night," (7) Shirley Temple.

1935: (1) "Mutiny on the Bounty," (2) Victor McLaglen in "The Informer," (3) Bette Davis in "Dangerous," (6) John Ford for "The Informer," (7) D. W. Griffith.

1936: (1) "The Great Ziegfeld," (2) Paul Muni in "The Story of Louis Pasteur," (3) Luise Rainer in "The Great Ziegfeld," (4) Walter Brennan in "Come and Get It," (5) Gale Sondergaard in "Anthony Adverse," (6) Frank Capra for "Mr. Deeds Goes to Town."

1937: (1)"The Life of Emile Zola," (2) Spencer Tracy in "Captains Courageous," (3) Luise Rainer in "The Good Earth," (4) Joseph Schildkraut in "The Life of Emile Zola," (5) Alice Brady in "In Old Chicago," (6) Leo McCarey for "The Awful Truth," (7) Mack Sennett, Edgar Bergen.

1938: (1) "You Can't Take It with You," (2) Spencer Tracy in "Boys' Town," (3) Bette Davis in "Jezebel," (4) Walter Brennan in "Kentucky," (5) Fay Bainter in "Jezebel," (6) Frank Capra for "You Can't Take It with You," (7) Deanna Durbin, Mickey Rooney, Harry M. Warner, Walt Disney.

1939: (1) "Gone with the Wind," (2) Robert Donat in "Goodbye, Mr. Chips," (3) Vivien Leigh in "Gone with the Wind," (4) Thomas Mitchell in "Stagecoach," (5) Hattie McDaniel in "Gone with the Wind," (6) Victor Fleming for "Gone with the Wind," (7) Douglas Fairbanks, Judy Garland.

1940: (1) "Rebecca," (2) James Stewart in "The Philadelphia Story," (3) Ginger Rogers in "Kitty Foyle," (4) Walter Brennan in "The Westerner," (5) Jane Darwell in "The Grapes of Wrath," (6) John Ford for "The Grapes of Wrath," (7) Bob Hope.

1941: (1) "How Green Was My Valley," (2) Gary Cooper in "Sergeant York," (3) Joan Fontaine in "Suspicion," (4) Donald Crisp in "How Green Was My Valley," (5) Mary Astor in "The Great Lie," (6) John Ford for "How Green Was My Valley," (7) Leopold Stokowski, Walt Disney.

1942: (1) "Mrs. Miniver," (2) James Cagney in "Yankee Doodle Dandy," (3) Greer Garson in "Mrs. Miniver," (4) Van Heflin in "Johnny Eager," (5) Teresa Wright in "Mrs. Miniver," (6) William Wyler for "Mrs. Miniver," (7) Charles Boyer, Noel Coward.

1943: (1) "Casablanca," (2) Paul Lukas in "Watch on the Rhine," (3) Jennifer Jones in "The Song of Bernadette," (4) Charles Coburn in "The More the Merrier," (5) Katina Paxinou in "For Whom the Bell Tolls," (6) Michael Curtiz for "Casablanca."

1944: (1) "Going My Way," (2) Bing Crosby in "Going My Way," (3) Ingrid Bergman in "Gaslight," (4) Barry Fitzgerald in "Going My Way," (5) Ethel Barrymore in "None but the Lonely Heart," (6) Leo McCarey for "Going My Way," (7) Margaret O'Brien, Bob Hope.

1945: (1) "The Lost Weekend," (2) Ray Milland in "The Lost Weekend," (3) Joan Crawford in "Mildred Pierce," (4) James Dunn in "A Tree Grows in Brooklyn," (5) Anne Revere in "National Velvet," (6) Billy Wilder for "The Lost Weekend," (7) Walter Wanger, Peggy Ann Garner.

1946: (1) "The Best Years of Our Lives," (2) Fredric March in "The Best Years of Our Lives," (3) Olivia de Havilland in "To Each His Own," (4) Harold Russell in "The Best Years of Our Lives," (5) Anne Baxter in "The Razor's Edge," (6) William Wyler for "The Best Years of Our Lives," (7) Laurence Olivier, Harold Russell, Ernst Lubitsch, Claude Jarman, Jr.

1947: (1) "Gentleman's Agreement," (2) Ronald Colman in "A Double Life," (3) Loretta Young in "The Farmer's Daughter," (4) Edmund Gwenn in "Miracle On 34th Street," (5) Celeste Holm in "Gentleman's Agreement," (6) Elia Kazan for "Gentleman's Agreement," (7) James Baskette, (8) "Shoe Shine."

1948: (1) "Hamlet," (2) Laurence Olivier in "Hamlet," (3) Jane Wyman in "Johnny Belinda," (4) Walter Huston in "The Treasure of the Sierra Madre," (5) Claire Trevor in "Key Largo," (6) John Huston for "The Treasure of the Sierra Madre," (7) Ivan Jandl, Sid Grauman, Adolph Zukor, Walter Wanger, (8) "Monsieur Vincent."

1949: (1) "All the King's Men," (2) Broderick Crawford in "All the King's Men," (3) Olivia de Havilland in "The Heiress," (4) Dean Jagger in "Twelve O'Clock High," (5) Mercedes McCambridge in "All the King's Men," (6) Joseph L. Mankiewicz for "A Letter to Three Wives," (7) Bobby Driscoll, Fred Astaire, Cecil B. DeMille, Jean Hersholt, (8) "The Bicycle Thief."

1950: (1) "All about Eve," (2) Jose Ferrer in "Cyrano de Bergerac," (3) Judy Holliday in "Born Yesterday," (4) George Sanders in "All about Eve," (5) Josephine Hull in "Harvey," (6) Joseph L. Mankiewicz for "All about Eve," (7) George Murphy, Louis B. Mayer, (8) "The Walls of Malapaga."

1951: (1) "An American in Paris," (2) Humphrey Bogart in "The African Queen," (3) Vivien Leigh in "A Streetcar Named Desire," (4) Karl Malden in "A Streetcar Named Desire," (5) Kim Hunter in "A Streetcar Named Desire," (6) George Stevens for "A Place in the Sun," (7) Gene Kelly, (8) "Rashomon."

1952: (1) "The Greatest Show on Earth," (2) Gary Cooper in "High Noon," (3) Shirley Booth in "Come Back, Little Sheba," (4) Anthony Quinn in "Viva Zapata," (5) Gloria Grahame in "The Bad and the Beautiful," (6) John Ford for "The Quiet Man," (7) Joseph M. Schenck, Merian C. Cooper, Harold Lloyd, Bob Hope, George Alfred Mitchell, (8) "Forbidden Games."

1953: (1) "From Here to Eternity," (2) William Holden in "Stalag 17," (3) Audrey Hepburn in "Roman Holiday," (4) Frank Sinatra in "From Here to Eternity," (5) Donna Reed in "From Here to Eternity," (6) Fred Zinnemann for "From Here to Eternity," (7) Pete Smith, Joseph Breen.

1954: (1) "On the Waterfront," (2) Marlon Brando in "On the Waterfront," (3) Grace Kelly in "The Country Girl," (4) Edmond O'Brien in "The Barefoot Contessa," (5) Eva Marie Saint in "On the Waterfront," (6) Elia Kazan for "On the Waterfront," (7) Greta Garbo, Danny Kaye, Jon Whitely, Vincent Winter, (8) "Gate of Hell."

1955: (1) "Marty," (2) Ernest Borgnine in "Marty," (3) Anna Magnani in "The Rose Tattoo," (4) Jack Lemmon in "Mister Roberts," (5) Jo Van Fleet in "East of Eden," (6) Delbert Mann for "Marty," (8) "Samurai."

1956: (1) "Around the World in 80 Days," (2) Yul Brynner in "The King and I," (3) Ingrid Bergman in "Anastasia," (4) Anthony Quinn in "Lust for Life," (5) Dorothy Malone in "Written on the Wind," (6) George Stevens for "Giant," (7) Eddie Cantor, (8) "La Strada."

Jason Robards	**Maureen Stapleton**	**Cliff Robertson**	**Beatrice Straight**	**Jon Voight**	**Elizabeth Taylor**

1957: (1) "The Bridge on the River Kwai," (2) Alec Guinness in "The Bridge on the River Kwai," (3) Joanne Woodward in "The Three Faces of Eve," (4) Red Buttons in "Sayonara," (5) Miyoshi Umeki in "Sayonara," (6) David Lean for "The Bridge on the River Kwai," (7) Charles Brackett, B. B. Kahane, Gilbert M. (Bronco Billy) Anderson, (8) "The Nights of Cabiria."

1958: (1) "Gigi," (2) David Niven in "Separate Tables," (3) Susan Hayward in "I Want to Live," (4) Burl Ives in "The Big Country," (5) Wendy Hiller in "Separate Tables," (6) Vincente Minnelli for "Gigi," (7) Maurice Chevalier, (8) "My Uncle."

1959: (1) "Ben-Hur," (2) Charlton Heston in "Ben-Hur," (3) Simone Signoret in "Room at the Top," (4) Hugh Griffith in "Ben-Hur," (5) Shelley Winters in "The Diary of Anne Frank," (6) William Wyler for "Ben-Hur," (7) Lee de Forest, Buster Keaton, (8) "Black Orpheus."

1960: (1) "The Apartment," (2) Burt Lancaster in "Elmer Gantry," (3) Elizabeth Taylor in "Butterfield 8," (4) Peter Ustinov in "Spartacus," (5) Shirley Jones in "Elmer Gantry," (6) Billy Wilder for "The Apartment," (7) Gary Cooper, Stan Laurel, Hayley Mills, (8) "The Virgin Spring."

1961: (1) "West Side Story," (2) Maximilian Schell in "Judgment at Nuremberg," (3) Sophia Loren in "Two Women," (4) George Chakiris in "West Side Story," (5) Rita Moreno in "West Side Story," (6) Robert Wise for "West Side Story," (7) Jerome Robbins, Fred L. Metzler, (8) "Through a Glass Darkly."

1962: (1) "Lawrence of Arabia," (2) Gregory Peck in "To Kill a Mockingbird," (3) Anne Bancroft in "The Miracle Worker," (4) Ed Begley in "Sweet Bird of Youth," (5) Patty Duke in "The Miracle Worker," (6) David Lean for "Lawrence of Arabia," (8) "Sundays and Cybele."

1963: (1) "Tom Jones," (2) Sidney Poitier in "Lilies of the Field," (3) Patricia Neal in "Hud," (4) Melvyn Douglas in "Hud," (5) Margaret Rutherford in "The V.I.P.'s," (6) Tony Richardson for "Tom Jones," (8) "8½."

1964: (1) "My Fair Lady," (2) Rex Harrison in "My Fair Lady," (3) Julie Andrews in "Mary Poppins," (4) Peter Ustinov in "Topkapi," (5) Lila Kedrova in "Zorba the Greek," (6) George Cukor for "My Fair Lady," (7) William Tuttle, (8) "Yesterday, Today and Tomorrow."

1965: (1) "The Sound of Music," (2) Lee Marvin in "Cat Ballou," (3) Julie Christie in "Darling," (4) Martin Balsam in "A Thousand Clowns," (5) Shelley Winters in "A Patch of Blue," (6) Robert Wise for "The Sound of Music," (7) Bob Hope, (8) "The Shop on Main Street."

1966: (1) "A Man for All Seasons," (2) Paul Scofield in "A Man for All Seasons," (3) Elizabeth Taylor in "Who's Afraid of Virginia Woolf?," (4) Walter Matthau in "The Fortune Cookie," (5) Sandy Dennis in "Who's Afraid of Virginia Woolf?," (6) Fred Zinnemann for "A Man for All Seasons," (8) "A Man and A Woman."

1967: (1) "In the Heat of the Night," (2) Rod Steiger in "In the Heat of the Night," (3) Katharine Hepburn in "Guess Who's Coming to Dinner," (4) George Kennedy in "Cool Hand Luke," (5) Estelle Parsons in "Bonnie and Clyde," (6) Mike Nichols for "The Graduate," (8) "Closely Watched Trains."

1968: (1) "Oliver!," (2) Cliff Robertson in "Charly," (3) Katharine Hepburn in "The Lion in Winter" tied with Barbra Streisand in "Funny Girl," (4) Jack Albertson in "The Subject Was Roses," (5) Ruth Gordon in "Rosemary's Baby," (6) Carol Reed for "Oliver!," (7) Onna White for "Oliver!" choreography, John Chambers for "Planet of the Apes" make-up, (8) "War and Peace."

1969: (1) "Midnight Cowboy," (2) John Wayne in "True Grit," (3) Maggie Smith in "The Prime of Miss Jean Brodie," (4) Gig Young in "They Shoot Horses, Don't They?," (5) Goldie Hawn in "Cactus Flower," (6) John Schlesinger for "Midnight Cowboy," (7) Cary Grant, (8) "Z."

1970: (1) "Patton," (2) George C. Scott in "Patton," (3) Glenda Jackson in "Women in Love," (4) John Mills in "Ryan's Daughter," (5) Helen Hayes in "Airport," (6) Franklin J. Schaffner for "Patton," (7) Lillian Gish, Orson Welles, (8) "Investigation of a Citizen above Suspicion."

1971: (1) "The French Connection," (2) Gene Hackman in "The French Connection," (3) Jane Fonda in "Klute," (4) Ben Johnson in "The Last Picture Show," (5) Cloris Leachman in "The Last Picture Show," (7) William Friedkin for "The French Connection," (7) Charles Chaplin, (8) "The Garden of the Finzi-Continis."

1972: (1) "The Godfather," (2) Marlon Brando in "The Godfather," (3) Liza Minnelli in "Cabaret," (4) Joel Grey in "Cabaret," (5) Eileen Heckart in "Butterflies Are Free," (6) Bob Fosse for "Cabaret," (7) Edward G. Robinson, (8) "The Discreet Charm of the Bourgeoisie."

1973: (1) "The Sting," (2) Jack Lemmon in "Save the Tiger," (3) Glenda Jackson in "A Touch of Class," (4) John Houseman in "The Paper Chase," (5) Tatum O'Neal in "Paper Moon," (6) George Roy Hill for "The Sting," (8) "Day for Night."

1974: (1) "The Godfather Part II," (2) Art Carney in "Harry and Tonto," (3) Ellen Burstyn in "Alice Doesn't Live Here Anymore," (4) Robert DeNiro in "The Godfather Part II," (5) Ingrid Bergman in "Murder on the Orient Express," (6) Francis Ford Coppola for "The Godfather Part II," (7) Howard Hawks, Jean Renoir, (8) "Amarcord."

1975: (1) "One Flew over the Cuckoo's Nest," (2) Jack Nicholson in "One Flew over the Cuckoo's Nest," (3) Louise Fletcher in "One Flew over the Cuckoo's Nest," (4) George Burns in "The Sunshine Boys," (5) Lee Grant in "Shampoo," (6) Milos Forman for "One Flew over the Cuckoo's Nest," (7) Mary Pickford, (8) "Dersu Uzala."

1976: (1) "Rocky," (2) Peter Finch in "Network," (3) Faye Dunaway in "Network," (4) Jason Robards in "All the President's Men," (5) Beatrice Straight in "Network," (6) John G. Avildsen for "Rocky," (8) "Black and White in Color."

1977: (1) "Annie Hall," (2) Richard Dreyfuss in "The Goodbye Girl," (3) Diane Keaton in "Annie Hall," (4) Jason Robards in "Julia," (5) Vanessa Redgrave in "Julia," (6) Woody Allen for "Annie Hall," (7) Maggie Booth (film editor), (8) "Madame Rosa."

1978: (1) "The Deer Hunter," (2) Jon Voight in "Coming Home," (3) Jane Fonda in "Coming Home," (4) Christopher Walken in "The Deer Hunter," (5) Maggie Smith in "California Suite," (6) Michael Cimino for "The Deer Hunter," (7) Laurence Olivier, King Vidor, (8) "Get Out Your Handkerchiefs."

1979: (1) "Kramer vs. Kramer," (2) Dustin Hoffman in "Kramer vs. Kramer," (3) Sally Field in "Norma Rae," (4) Melvyn Douglas in "Being There," (5) Meryl Streep in "Kramer vs. Kramer," (6) Robert Benton for "Kramer vs. Kramer," (7) Robert S. Benjamin, Hal Elias, Alec Guinness, (8) "The Tin Drum."

1980: (1) "Ordinary People," (2) Robert DeNiro in "Raging Bull," (3) Sissy Spacek in "Coal Miner's Daughter," (4) Timothy Hutton in "Ordinary People," (5) Mary Steenburgen in "Melvin and Howard," (6) Robert Redford for "Ordinary People," (7) Henry Fonda, (8) "Moscow Does Not Believe in Tears."

1981: (1) "Chariots of Fire," (2) Henry Fonda in "On Golden Pond," (3) Katharine Hepburn in "On Golden Pond," (4) John Gielgud in "Arthur," (5) Maureen Stapleton in "Reds," (6) Warren Beatty for "Reds," (7) Fuji Photo Film Co., Barbara Stanwyck, (8) "Mephisto."

1982: (1) "Gandhi," (2) Ben Kingsley in "Gandhi," (3) Meryl Streep in "Sophie's Choice," (4) Louis Gossett, Jr. in "An Officer and a Gentleman," (5) Jessica Lange in "Tootsie," (6) Richard Attenborough for "Gandhi," (7) Mickey Rooney, (8) "Volver a Empezar" (To Begin Again).

1983: (1) "Terms of Endearment," (2) Robert Duvall in "Tender Mercies," (3) Shirley MacLaine in "Terms of Endearment," (4) Jack Nicholson in "Terms of Endearment," (5) Linda Hunt in "The Year of Living Dangerously," (6) James L. Brooks for "Terms of Endearment," (7) Hal Roach, (8) "Fanny and Alexander."

1984: (1) "Amadeus," (2) F. Murray Abraham in "Amadeus," (3) Sally Field in "Places in the Heart," (4) Haing S. Ngor in "The Killing Fields," (5) Peggy Ashcroft in "A Passage to India," (6) Milos Forman for "Amadeus," (7) James Stewart, (8) "Dangerous Moves" (Switzerland)

151

FOREIGN FILMS RELEASED IN U. S. IN 1985

1984

(ATLANTIC) Producer, Simon Perry; Director-Screenplay, Michael Radford; based on the novel by George Orwell; Executive Producer, Marvin J. Rose Rosenblum; Co-Producers, Al Clark, Robert Devereux; Photography, Roger Deakins; Editor, Tom Priestley; Designer, Allan Cameron; Music, Dominic Muldowney, Eurythmics; Associate Producer, John Davies; Production Manager, Gladys Pearce; Assistant Director, Chris Rose; Sound, Bruce White; Art Directors, Martin Herbert, Grant Hicks; Costumes, Emma Porteous; Color; British; 111 minutes; Rated R; January release

CAST

Winston Smith	John Hurt
O'Brien	Richard Burton
Julia	Suzanna Hamilton
Carrington	Cyril Cusack
Parsons	Gregor Fisher
Syme	James Walker
Tillotson	Andrew Wilde
Tillotson's Friend	David Trevena
Martin	David Cann
Jones	Anthony Benson
Rutherford	Peter Fry
Waiter	Roger Lloyd Pack
Winston as a boy	Rubert Baderman
Winston's Mother	Corinna Seddon
Winston's Sister	Martha Parsey
Mrs. Parsons	Merelina Kendall
William Parsons	P. J. Nichola
Susan Parsons	Lynne Radford
Inner Party Speaker	Pip Donaghy
Whore	Shirley Stelfox
Instructress	Janey Ke
Artsem Lecturer	Hugh Walters
Telescreen Announcer	Phyllis Logan
The Washerwoman	Pam Gem
Aaronson	Joscik Barbarossa
Goldstein	John Boswall
Big Brother	Bob Flag

Left: Richard Burton, and top with John Hurt
© Atlantic Releasing Corp.

John Hurt

Suzanna Hamilton, John Hurt

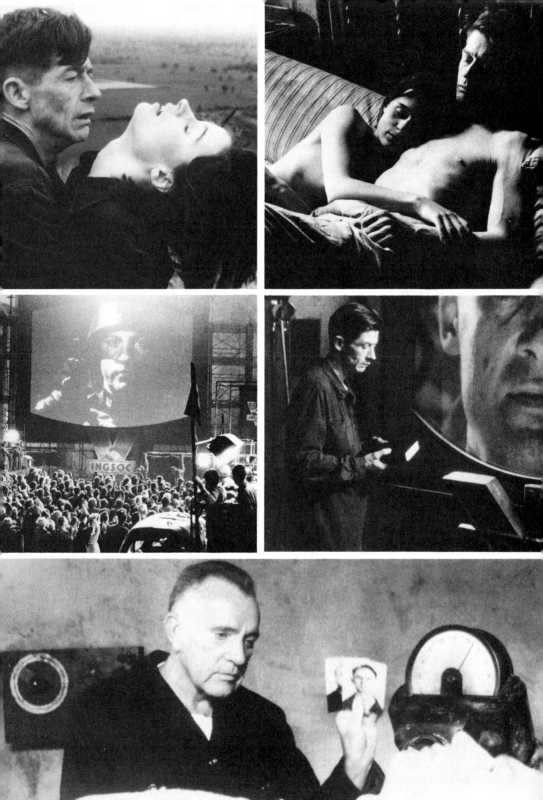

Richard Burton, John Hurt Top: (L & R) John Hurt, Suzanna Hamilton
Center: (R) John Hurt

THE BAY BOY

(ORION) Producers, John Kemeny, Denis Heroux; Director-Screenplay, Daniel Petrie; Photography, Claude Agostini; Executive Producers, Susan Cavan, Frank Jacobs; Co-Producer, Rene Cleitman; Editor, Susan Shanks; Costumes, Renee April; Designer, Wolf Kroeger; Music, Claude Bolling; Associate Producer, Paulo De Oliveira; Production Manager, Stephane Reichel; Assistant Directors, Pierre Magny, Jacques Methe, Judi Kemeny; Special Effects, Martin Malivoire, Michael Kavanaugh; Presented by International Cinema Corporation; Canadian; Bellevue Pathe Color; 104 minutes; Rated R; February release

CAST

Donald Campbell	Keifer Sutherland
Mrs. Campbell	Liv Ullmann
Mr. Campbell	Peter Donat
Sgt. Tom Coldwell	Alan Scarfe
Father Chaisson	Mathieu Carriere
Chief Charlie McInnes	Chris Wiggins
Father McKinnon	Thomas Peacocke
Mary McNeil	Isabelle Mejias
Diana Coldwell	Jane MacKinnon
Saxon Coldwell	Leah Pinsent
Joe Campbell	Peter Spence
Marie Chaisson	Josephine Chaplin
Janine Chaisson	Pauline Laffont
Paul Ratchford	Roy McMullin
Sister Roberta	Kathy McGuire
Frank Carrey	Robbie Gallivan
Danny McIsaac	Robert Rose
Malcolm Broderick	Darren Arsenault
Walt Roach	David Ferrey
Nurse	Betty MacDonald
Mrs. Silver	Fannie Shore
Mr. Silver	Sander Zilbert
Sol Silver	Tom Rack
Paddy O'Neil	Robert Taylor
Rory McInnes	Joe MacPherson
Mr. Rankin	Kevin McKenzie
Mrs. Carrey	Iris Currie
Terry O'Shea	Francis MacNeil
Basil Broderick	Michael Egyes
Aunt Coldwell	Mary MacKinnon

Right: Mathieu Carriere Above: Liv Ullmann, Kiefer Sutherland Top: Peter Donat, Liv Ullmann © *Orion Pictures*

Liv Ullmann

Kiefer Sutherland, Isabelle Mejias

THE HIT

ISLAND ALIVE) Producer, Jeremy Thomas; Director, Stephen Frears; Screenplay, Peter Prince; Photography, Mike Molloy; Editor, Mick Audsley; Music, Paco De Lucia, Eric Clapton; Designer, Andrew Sanders; Assistant Director, Carlos Gill; Production Manager, Jesus Margoles; Costumes, Marit Allen; Sound, Paul Le Mare; Special Effects, Alan Whibley, Reyes Abades; Great Britain, 1984; Color; 100 minutes; Rated R; February release

CAST

Willie Parker	Terence Stamp
Braddock	John Hurt
Myron	Tim Roth
Maggie	Laura Del Sol
Harry	Bill Hunter
Chief Inspector	Fernando Rey
Uniformed officer	Carlos Lucena
First government agent	Freddie Stuart
Second government agent	Ralph Brown
Third government agent	A. J. Clarke
Mr. Corrigan	Lennie Peters
Hopwood	Bernie Searl
Fellows	Brian Royal
Jordan	Albie Woodington
Judge	Willoughby Gray
Barrister	Jim Broadbent
Juan, Willie's bodyguard	Manuel De Benito
Priest	Juan Calot

and Quique San Francisco, Joaquin Alonso, Jose Luis Fernandez, Camilo Vilanova (Kidnappers), Carlos Zabala, Eneko Olazagasti, Pat-Barko, Xavier Aguirre (Young Basques), Mr. Carlos Tristancho (garage attendant)

Right: Terence Stamp
© *Island Alive*

Tim Roth, Laura Del Sol, John Hurt, Terence Stamp Above: Hurt, Del Sol

Laura Del Sol

155

Robert Aldini (C) and top

MAN UNDER SUSPICION

(SPECTRAFILM INC.) Producers, FFAT Munchen, Pro-ject Fil
produktion im Filmverlag der Autoren; Director, Norbert Kuckelma
Screenplay, Norbert Kuckelmann, Thomas Petz, Dagmar Kekule; Ph
tography, Jurgen Jurges, Renato Fortunato; Editor, Sigrun Jager; M
sic, Markus Urchs; Assistant Directors, Renate Leiffer, Peter C
penter; Designers, Winfried Hennig, Franz Bauer, Michael Adlmul
Sound, Hayo Von Zundt; Executive Producer, Inge Richter; Winn
Silver Bear, Berlin Film Festival 1984; German; Colour; 126 minut
No rating; February release

CAST

Landau	Maxmilian Sch
Jessica	Lena Sto
Werner Kranz	Robert Ald
Watergate	Wolfgang Kiel
Magistrate	Kathrin Ackerma
Public prosecutor	Dr. Manfred Re
Holm	Reinhard Ha
Sommer	Jorg H
Presiding magistrate	Klaus Hol
Attorney-general	Robert Atz
Kathrin	Patricia Kuckelma
Kathrin's boyfriend	Markus Ur

Top Left: Maxmilian Schell
© *International Spectrafilm*

Maxmilian Schell, Lena Stolze

THE RETURN OF THE SOLDIER

(EUROPEAN CLASSICS) Producers, Ann Skinner, Simon Relph; Director, Alan Bridges; Screenplay, Hugh Whitemore; Based on novel by Rebecca West; Photography, Stephen Goldblatt; Editor, Laurence Mery Clark; Costumes, Shirley Russell; Designer, Luciana Arrighi; Music, Richard Rodney Bennett; Executive Producers, Edward Simons, John Quested, J. Gordon Arnold; Presented by George Walker; Production Manager, Redmond Morris; Assistant Director, Allan James; Sound, Simon Kaye; Special Effects, Nick Allder; Technicolor; Panavision; 101 minutes; Not rated; British; February release

CAST

Margaret	Glenda Jackson
Kitty	Julie Christie
Jenny	Ann-Margret
Chris	Alan Bates
Doctor Anderson	Ian Holm
William	Frank Finlay
Frank	Jeremy Kemp
Ward	Hilary Mason
Carson	John Sharp
Emery	Elizabeth Edmonds
Beatrice	Valerie Whittington
Mrs. Plummer	Patsy Byrne
Chauffeur	Robert Keegan
Alexandra	Amanda Grinling
Ward	Edward De Souza
Stephen	Michael Cochrane
Jessica	Vickery Turner
Sister	Sheila Keith
Ward Sister	Shirley Caine

Right: Glenda Jackson, Alan Bates
Top: Glenda Jackson, Julie Christie,
Ann-Margret
© European Classics

Ann-Margret

Julie Christie

WARTIME ROMANCE

(INTERNATIONAL FILM EXCHANGE) Producer, Odessa Fi
Studio; Director-Screenplay, Pyotr Todorovsky; Photography, Val
Blinov; Sets, Valentin Konovalov; Score, I. Kantiukov, Pyotr Tod
ovsky; USSR, 1984; In Russian with English subtitles; Color;
minutes; Not rated; February release

CAST

Alexander	Nikolai Burlya
Liuba	Natalia Andreiche
Vera	Inna Churik
Theatre Manager	Z. Ge
His wife	E. Kozelk
Housing official	V. Prosku
Liuba's landlord	V. Shilov
The Major	A. Martyn
Liuba's daughter	Katya Yud

Left: Natalia Andreichenko, A. Martynov
© *International Film Exchange*

Nikolay Bourlyayev, Victor Proskurin

WHERE THE GREEN ANTS DREAM

(ORION CLASSICS) Producer, Lucki Stipetic; Director-Screenplay, Werner Herzog; Photography, Jorg Schmidt-Reitwein; Music, Gabriel Faure, Ernst Block, Klaus-Jochen Wiese, Richard Wagner, Wandjuk Marika; Editor, Beate Mainka-Jellinghaus; Designer, Ulrich Bergfelder; Sound, Peter Rappel; Special Effects, Brian Pearce; Costumes, Frances D. Hogan; Additional Dialogue, Bob Ellis; Australian, 1983; Color; 100 minutes; Rated R; February release

CAST

Hackett	Bruce Spence
Dayipu	Roy Marika
Miliritbi	Wandjuk Marika
Ferguson	Norman Kaye
Cole	Ray Barrett
Miss Strehlow	Colleen Clifford
Fletcher	Ralph Cotterill
Arnold	Nicolas Lathouris
Blackburn	Basil Clarke
Coulthard	Ray Marshall
Walila	Dhungula (1) Marika
Watson	Gary Williams
Fitzsimmons	Tony Llewellyn-Jones
Daisy	Marraru Wunungmurra
Prof. Stanner	Robert Brissenden
Secretary	Susan Greaves
Riot	Michael Glynn
Young Attorney	Michael Edols
Bailiff	Noel Lyon
Police Officer	Max Fairchild
Supermarket Manager	Bob Ellis

and Trevor Orford, Hugh Keays-Byrne, Andrew Mack, Maria Strazd, Michael Mandalis, Anastasios Chatzidimpas, Maria Chatzidimas, Paul Cox, Philip Radke, Ricky & Ronnie, James Ricketson, Christopher Cain, Paul Donazzan, Tim Cartwright

Right Center: Roy Marika, Wandjuk Marika

Roy Marika, Werner Herzog (director)

CAMILA

(EUROPEAN CLASSICS) Producers, GEA Cinematografica, Impala; Director, Maria Luisa Bemberg; Screenplay, Maria Luisa Bemberg, Beda Docampo Feijoo, Juan Bautista Stagnaro; Photography, Fernando Arribas; Designer, Miguel Rodriguez; Costumes, Graciela Galan; Sound, Esmeralda Almonacid; Music, Luis Maria Serra; Executive Producer, Lita Stantic; Associate Producer, Paco Molero; Historical Adviser, Lenor Calvera; Eastmancolor; Argentina; 105 minutes; Not Rated; March release.

CAST

Camila O'Gorman	Susu Pecoraro
Father Ladislao Gutierrez	Imanol Arias
Adolfo O'Gorman	Hector Alterio
Dona Jaoquina O'Gorman	Elena Tasisto
Monsignor Elortondo	Carlos Munoz
Comandant Soto	Hector Pellegrini
Brother Eduardo O'Gorman	Claudio Gallardou
Ignacio	Boris Rubabja
La Perichona	Mona Maris

Right: Susu Pecoraro, Imanol Arias
Below: Susu Pecoraro, Elena Tasisto
© *European Classic*

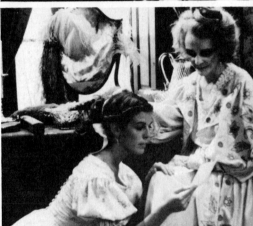

Imanol Arias, Susu Pecoraro
(also above)

Susu Pecoraro, Imanol Arias

FRENCH CANCAN

(NICOLE JOUVE INTERAMA) Director, Jean Renoir; Screenplay, Jean Renoir, Andre Paul Antoine; Photography, Michel Kelber; Editor, Boris Lewin; Designer, Max Douy; Music, Georges Van Parys; Choreography, G. Grandjean; Dound, Antoine Pettijean; Costumes, Rosine Delamore; Production Manager, Louis Wipf; France, 1955; Technicolor; 105 minutes; Not rated; March release

CAST

Danglard	Jean Gabin
Nini	Francoise Armoul
La Belle Abbesse	Maria Felix
Baron Walter	Jean Roger Caussimon
Patron	Max Dalban
La Genisse	Dora Doll
Servant	Gaston Modot
Coudrier	Jean Paredes
Guidon	Jean-Marc Tennberg
Olympe	Valentine Tessier
Paulo	Franco Pastorino
Guibole	Lydia Johnson
Le Prince	Gianni Esposito
Esarlette Vibert	Anna Amendola
Casimir	Philippe Clay
Eleanore	Michele Phillippe

and France Roche, Annik Morice, Jacques Jouaneau, Michele Nadal, Sylvine Delannoy, Anne-Marie Mersen, Albert Remy, Michel Piccoli, Patachou, Andre Claveau, Edith Piaf, Jean Raymond

Right: Francoise Arnoul, Jean Gabin
© *Nicole Jouve Interama*

Francoise Arnoul, Jean Gabin, and above with Maria Felix

Francoise Arnoul

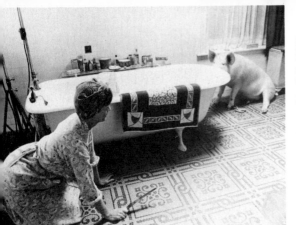

A PRIVATE FUNCTION

(ISLAND ALIVE) Producer, Mark Shivas; Director, Malcolm Mo bray; Screenplay, Alan Bennett; Story, Alan Bennett, Malcolm Mo bray; Photography, Tony Pierce-Roberts; Editor, Barrie Vince; Musi John Du Prez; Executive Producers, George Harrison, Denis O'Brie Designer, Stuart Walker; Assistant Directors, Guy Travers, Ch Thompson, Nick Godden; Costumes, Phyllis Dalton; Production Ma ager, Ann Wingate; Sound, Tony Jackson; Great Britain, 1984; Col 93 minutes; Rated R; March release

CAST

Gilbert Chilvers	Michael Pa
Joyce Chilvers	Maggie Sm
Betty the Pig	Hims
Dr. Swaby	Denholm Elli
Allardyce	Richard Griffi
Sutcliff	Tony Hayga
Lockwood	John Normin
Wormold	Bill Pater
Mother	Liz Sm
Mrs. Allardyce	Alison Steadm
Inspector Noble	Jim Ca
Nuttal	Pete Postlethw
Mrs. Sutcliff	Eileen O'Br
Mrs. Forbes	Rachel Dav
P.C. Penny	Reece Dinsd
Preston	Philip Wilem
Medcalf	Charles McKeo
Mrs. Medcalf	Susan Por
Father	Donald Ecc
Hotel Manager	Denys Hawtho
Barraclough	Don Este
Ernest	Eli Wo
Veronica	Amanda Greg
Mrs. Turnbull	Paula Tilbr
Painter	Bernard Wrig
Painter's Boy	Lee Da
Dorothy	Gilly Co
Woman	Maggie Ollerensh
Mrs. Beavers	Josie L
Mervin	David Mor

Left: Maggie Smith, Denholm Elliott
Top: Maggie Smith, Betty
© *Island Alive*

Michael Palin, Betty, Maggie Smith

Michael Palin, Maggie Smith

THE WILD DUCK

(RKR ENTERTAINMENT) Producer, Phillip Emanuel; Director-
Screenplay, Henri Safran; Adapted from Henrik Ibsen's play of same
name by Tette Lemkow, Dido Merwen, Mr. Safran; Additional Material,
Peter Smalley; Photography, Peter James; Editor, Don Saunders; Co-
Producer, Basil Appleby; Assistant Director, David Munro; Art Director, Igor Nay; Costumes, David Rowe; A Tinzu Pty. Limited Production from Australia; Color; 96 minutes; Rated PG; March release

CAST

...na	Liv Ullman
...rold	Jeremy Irons
...nrietta	Lucinda Jones
...d Ackland	John Meillon
...egory	Arthur Dignam
...ardle	Michael Pate
...ollison	Colin Croft
...Roland	Rhys McConnochie
...s. Summers	Marion Edward
...ers	Peter DeSalis
...nson	Jeff Truman
...ay	Clive Marshall
...bby Gentleman	Robert Bruning
...ding Guest	Desmond Tester
...retaker	Georgie Stirling

Top: (L) Liv Ullmann, Lucinda Jones and
below with Jeremy Irons Right: Lucinda
Jones Top: Irons, Jones
© *RKR Entertainment Group*

Jeremy Irons, Liv Ullmann

163

MY FIRST WIFE

(Spectrafilm) Producers, Jane Ballantyne, Paul Cox; Director, Paul Cox; Screenplay, Paul Cox, Bob Ellis; Photography, Yuri Sokol; Designer, Asher Bilu; Editors, Tim Lewis, Peter McBain; Sound, Ken Hammond; Assistant Director, Erwin Rado; Associate Producer, Tony Llewellyn-Jones; Australia, 1984; 1984 Australian Academy Awards Winner: Best Director/Best Actor/Best Screenplay; Color; 99 minutes; Not Rated; April release

CAST

John	John Hargreaves
Helen	Wendy Hughes
Lucy	Lucy Angwin
Tom	David Cameron
Kristin	Julia Blake
Hilary	Anna Jemison
Helen's Father	Charles Tingwell
Helen's Mother	Betty Lucas
John's Father	Robin Lovejoy
John's Mother	Lucy Uralov
John's Sister	Xenia Groutas
Bernard	Jon Finlayson
Psychiatrist	Ron Falk
Priest	Reg Roddick
Barmaid	Renee Geyer
Barbra	Sabrina Lorenz
Bar Singer	Christopher Holligan

and Tony Llewellyn-Jones, Linden Wilkinson (Doctors), Symonetta Dennis, Jentah Sobott (Nurses), Neela Dey, Marlene Grech (Migrant Teachers), Rex Callahan, Terry Rodman (Radio Station Technicians), Jay Mannering, Ian Mumby (Policemen), Bianca Russell (Girl with dog), Hartley Newnham, Nehama Patkin, Megan Garner, Patrick Nolan (Quartet), The Tudor Choristers, David Carolane

Top Right: Wendy Hughes, John Hargreaves
Below: Hughes, Julia Blake, Lucy Angwin,
John Hargreaves
© Spectrafilm

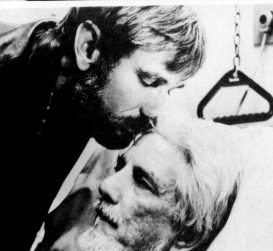

John Hargreaves, Robin Lovejoy
Above: Wendy Hughes, Hargreaves

John Hargreaves, Lucy Angwin,
Wendy Hughes

WHAT HAVE I DONE TO DESERVE THIS!

(Cinevista) Executive Producer, Herve Hachuel; Director-Screenplay,
Pedro Almodovar; Photography, Angel Luis Fernandez; Assistant Di-
rectors, Terry Lennox, Jose Maria De Cossio; Production Director,
Deo Villalba; Spanish with subtitles; Color; 100 minutes; Not Rated;
April release

CAST

Gloria	Carmen Maura
Polo	Luis Hostalot
Bendo Master	Ryo Hiruma
Antonio	Angel De Andres-Lopez
Lucas	Gonzalo Suarez
Cristal	Veronica Forque
Toni	Juan Martinez
Grandmother	Chus Lampreave
Juani	Kiti Manver
Vanessa	Sonia Anabela Holimann
Girl	Cecilia Roth
Boy	Diego Caretti
Neighborhood Pal	Jose Manuel Bello
Play-Back	Almodovar-McNamara
Miguel	Miguel Angel Herranz
Circus Boy	Beni
Porter	Carmen Giralt
Patricia	Amparo Soler Leal
Pedro	Emilio Gutierrez Caba
Mark	Tinin Almodovar

and El Churri, Francisca Caballero, Javier Gurruchaga, Jaime Chavarri, Esteban Aspiazu, Katia Loritz, Maria Del Carmen Rives, Jesus
Ignacio, Luciano Berriatua, Pilar Ortega, Carlos Miguel

Jaime Chavarri, Veronica Forque,
Carmen Maura Top: Carmen Maura,
Lampreave, Veronica Forque
Left: Angel De Andres-Lopez, Carmen Maura
© Cinevista

WHEN THE RAVEN FLIES

(FILM FORUM) Producers, Bo Jonsson for F.I.L.M., Viking Film,
Swedish Film Institute; Director-Screenplay-Editor, Hrafn Gunn-
laugsson; Photography, Tony Forsberg; Music, Hans-Erik Phillip; Ice-
land/Sweden, 1984; Icelandic with subtitles; Color; 109 minutes; Not
Rated; April release.

CAST

Gest	Jacob Thor Einarsson
Gest's Sister	Edda Bjorgvinsdottir
Tor	Helgi Skulason
Tor's Brother	Egill Olafsson
	Flosi Olafsson

"When the Raven Flies"

THE COMPANY OF WOLVES

(CANNON GROUP) Producers, Chris Brown, Stephen Wooley; Director, Neil Jordan; Screenplay, Angela Carter, Neil Jordan; Story, Angela Carter; Photography, Bryan Loftus; Designer, Anton Furst; Music, George Fenton; Editor, Rodney Holland; Special Effects Makeup, Christopher Tucker; Animatronic Wolf, Rodger Shaw; Executive Producers, Stephen Woolley, Nick Powell; Costumes, Elizabeth Waller; Production Manager, Vivien Pottersman; Assistant Directors, Simon Hinkly, Clive Hedges; Color; Dolby Stereo; British; 95 minutes; Rated R; April release

CAST

Granny	Angela Lansbury
Father	David Warner
Old Priest	Graham Crowden
Amorous Boy's Father	Brian Glover
Young Bride	Kathryn Pogson
Young Groom	Stephen Rea
Mother	Tusse Silberg
Huntsman	Micha Bergese
Rosaleen	Sarah Patterson
Alice	Georgia Slowe
Amorous Boy's Mother	Susan Porrett
Amorous Boy	Shane Johnstone
Witch Woman	Dawn Archibald
Wealthy Groom	Richard Morant
Wolfgirl	Danielle Dax
Devil Boy	Vincent McClaren
Dowager	Ruby Buchanan
Ancient	Jimmy Gardner
Eyepatch	Roy Evans
Lame Fiddler	Edward Marks
Blind Fiddler	Jimmy Brown

Top: Angela Lansbury, Sarah Patterson
Below: Wedding Party Guests
© *Cannon*

Angela Lansbury
Top: Sarah Patterson, Micha Bergese

MacARTHUR'S CHILDREN

(ORION CLASSICS) Producers, You-No-Kai, Masato Hara; Director, Masahiro Shinoda; Screenplay, Takeshi Tamura; Based on the novel by Yu Aku; Photography, Kazuo Miyagawa; Designer, Yoshinobu Nishioka; Music, Shinichiro Ikebe; Lighting, Takeharu Sano; Editor, Sachiko Yamaji; Sound, Hideo Nishizaki; Japanese: Color; 115 minutes; Rated PG; May release.

CAST

Ryuta Ashigara	Takaya Yamauchi
Saburo Masaki (Baraketsu)	Yoshiyuki Omori
Mume Hatano	Shiori Sakura
Komako Nakai	Masako Natsume
Tadao Ashigara	Shuji Otaki
Haru Ashigara	Haruko Kato'
Tetsuo Nakai	Ken Watanabe
Kiyo	Naomi Chiaki
ro Masaki	Shinsuke Shimada
nzo Nakai	Taketoshi Naito
etsuko	Miyuki Tanigawa
oko Masaki	Chiharu Shukuri
Lieutenant Anderson	Bill Jensen
	Howard Mohett
terpreter	Takashi Tsumura
eruo Nakai (Debukuni)	Akihiro Hattori
n Nitta (Ninjin)	Osamu Yamazaki
insuke Orihara (Bora)	Munekatsu Mori
aruo Kanda (Gancha)	Takeshi Marutani
akayuki Yoshizawa (Dankichi)	Tsutomu Tatsumi
amoru Takase (Anone)	Kuniyasu Toda
intaro Ikeda	Ryuji Sawa
dmiral Hatano	Jyuzo Itami
asao Nakai	Hiromi Go
ome Anabuki	Shima Iwashita

Right: Shiori Sakura, Yoshiyuki Omori
© *Orion Classics*

Masko Natsume

Yoshiyuki Omori, Takaya Yamauchi

ORDEAL BY INNOCENCE

(CANNON GROUP, INC.) Producer, Jenny Craven; Director, Desmond Davis; Screenplay, Alexander Stuart; Based on the novel by Agatha Christie; Photography, Billy Williams; Editor, Timothy Gee; Music, Dave Brubeck; Designer, Ken Bridgeman; Costumes, Gwenda Evans; Executive Producers, Menahem Golan, Yoram Globus; Associate Producer, Michael Kagan; Production Manager, Jeanne Ferber; Assistant Directors, David Tringham, Michael Stevenson, Ken Shane; Sound, Derek Ball, Robin Gregory; Eastmancolour; Not rated; British; May release

CAST

Arthur Calgary	Donald Sutherland
Rachel Calgary	Faye Dunaway
Leo Argyle	Christopher Plummer
Mary Durrant	Sarah Miles
Philip Durrant	Ian McShane
Gwenda Vaughan	Diana Quick
Kirsten Lindstrom	Annette Crosbie
Inspector Huish	Michael Elphick
Archie Leach	George Innes
Hester Argyle	Valerie Whittington
Tina Argyle	Phoebe Nichols
Micky Argyle	Michael Maloney
Maureen Clegg	Cassie Stuart
Martha Jessup	Anita Carey

and Ron Pember, Kevin Stoney, John Bardon, Brian Glover, Billy McColl, Rex Holdsworth, Martyn Townsend, Doel Luscombe, Alex Porwal, Robert McBain

Right: Michael Maloney, Phoebe Nichols
Top: Diana Quick, Christopher Plummer
© *Cannon*

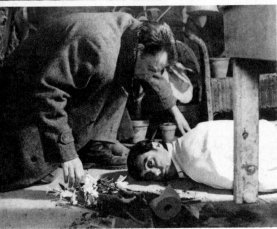

Donald Sutherland, Ian McShane
Above: Sarah Miles, Faye Dunaway

Valerie Whittington, Diana Quick

SECRET PLACES

20th CENTURY-FOX) Producers, Simon Relph, Ann Skinner; Director-Screenplay, Zelda Barron; Composer, Michel LeGrand; Title Song Lyrics, Alan Jay Lerner; Editor, Laurence Mery-Clark; Designer, Eileen Diss; Photography, Peter MacDonald; Assistant Director, Simon Relph; Costumes, Jane Robinson; Art Directors, Bob Cartwright, Judith Lang; Based on novel by Janice Elliott; A British Skreba/Virgin Production in color; Rated PG-13; 96 minutes; May release

CAST

Laura Meister	Marie-Theres Relin
Patience MacKenzie	Tara MacGowran
Sophie Meister	Claudine Auger
Miss Lowrie	Jenny Agutter
Nina	Cassie Stuart
Rose	Ann-Marie Gwatkin
Barbara	Pippa Hinchley
Dr. Wolfgang Meister	Klaus Barner
Miss Trott	Sylvia Coleridge
Mrs. McKenzie	Rosemary Martin
Miss Winterton	Amanda Grinling
Miss Mallard	Veronica Clifford
Stephen	Adam Richardson
Jack	John Henson
Gerald	Robert Kenly
David	Paul Ambrose
Hannah the Boots	Rosamund Greenwood
Valerie	Erika Spotswood
Mr. Watts	Bill Ward
Mrs. Burgess	Margaret Lacey
Police Sergeant	Maurice O'Connell
Junior	Zoe Caryl
Soldiers on train	Mike Haywood, John Blundell
Woman on train	Lesley Nightingale
Scots Soldier	Andrew Byatt
Cockney Soldier	Tony London
Cordelia	Georgia Slowe
Alfredo	Stewart Guidotti
Dino	Mark Lewis
Girls in art room	Jessica Walker, Sian Dunlop
Dr. Parrish	Alan Barry
Al	John Segal

Top Right: Tara MacGowran, Marie-Theres
Relin, Jenny Agutter
© 20th Century-Fox

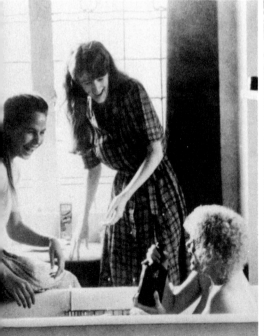

Marie-Theres Relin, Tara MacGowran,
Cassie Stuart

Tara MacGowran, Marie-Theres Relin

THE SHOOTING PARTY

(EUROPEAN CLASSICS) Producer, Geoffrey Reeve; Director, Alar Bridges; Screenplay, Julian Bond; Based on the novel by Isabel Cole gate; Photography, Fred Tammes; Editor, Peter Davies; Designer Morley Smith; Costumes, Tom Rand; Music, John Scott; Executive Producer, Jeremy Saunders; Associate Producer, Peter Dolman; Assis tant Directors, Richard Hoult, Fraser Copp, Terence Fitch; Sound, Bol Allen, Gerry Humphries, Alan Paley; British; Technicolor; 108 minutes; Not rated; May release

CAST

Sir Randolph Nettleby	James Mason
Lady Minnie Nettleby	Dorothy Tutin
Lord Gilbert Hartlip	Edward Fox
Lady Aline Hartlip	Cheryl Campbell
Cornelius Cardew	John Gielgud
Tom Harker	Gordon Jackson
Sir Reuben Hergesheimer	Aharon Ipale
Lionel Stephens	Rupert Frazer
Lord Bob Lilburn	Robert Hardy
Lady Olivia Lilburn	Judi Bowker
Ida Nettleby	Sarah Bade
Cicely Nettleby	Rebecca Saire
Count Tibor Rakassyi	Joris Stuyck
Glass	Frank Windsor
Jarvis	John J. Carney
Mildred Stamp	Ann Castle
John	Daniel Chatto
Violet	Mia Fothergill
Ogden	Thomas Heathcote
Weir	Barry Jackson
Dan Glass	Jonathan Lacey
Doctor West	Richard Leech
Harry Stamp	Jack May
Ellen	Deborah Miles
Maidment	Daniel Moynihan
Charlie Lyne	Patrick O'Connell
Osbert	Nicholas Pietrek
Marcus	Warren Saire
Rogers	Lockwood West

Left: James Mason, John Gielgud
Top: Cheryl Campbell, Edward Fox
© European Classics

Cheryl Campbell, Dorothy Tutin

Edward Fox, Cheryl Campbell

SILVER CITY

(SAMUEL GOLDWYN) Producer, Joan Long; Director, Sophia Tur-
kiewicz; Screenplay, Sophia Turkiewicz, Thomas Keaneally; Photog-
raphy, John Seale; Music, William Motzing; Editor, Don Saunders;
Designer, Igor Nay; Costumes, Jan Hurley; Production Manager, Sue
Wild; Limelight Productions Pty Ltd.; Australian; Color Widescreen;
Dolby Stereo; 110 minutes; Rated PG; May release.

CAST

Nina	Gosia Dobrowolska
Julian	Ivar Kants
Anna	Anna Jemison
Viktor	Steve Bisley
Helena	Debra Lawrance
Mrs. Bronowska	Ewa Brok
Young Daniel	Joel Cohen
Mr. Roy	Tim McKenzie
Max	Dennis Miller
Dorothy	Annie Byron
Stefan	Steve Jacobs
Ella	Halina Abramowicz
Priest	Joseph Drewniak
Arthur Calwell	Ron Blanchard

Top: Joel Cohen (on shoulders), Ivar
Kants, Anna Jemison, Gosia Dobrowolska
© Samuel Goldwyn Co.

Anna Jemison, Gosia Dobrowolska

TOKYO MELODY, A FILM ABOUT RYUICHI SAKAMOTO

Produced by National Audiovisual Institute France and Yoroshita; Director, Elizabeth Lennard; Photography, Jacques Pamart; Editor, Makiko Suzuki; 62 minutes; Not Rated

No photos available

Nigel Terry, Eleanor David, Tom Wilkinson Above: Eleanor David

SYLVIA

(MGM/UA CLASSICS) Producers, Don Reynolds, Michael Firth; Director, Michael Firth; Screenplay, Michael Quill, F. Fairfax, Michael Firth; Based on the books "Teacher" and "I Passed This Way" by Sylvia Ashton-Warner; Photography, Ian Paul; Editor, Michael Horton; Costumes, Anne McKay; Designer, Gary Hansen; Music, Leonard Rosenman; Production Manager, Jane Gilbert; Assistant Directors, Deuel Drodgan, Tony Forster, Paul Grinder; Sound, Graham Morris; New Zealand; Color; 98 minutes; Rated PG; May release

CAST

Sylvia Henderson	Eleanor David
Aden Morris	Nigel Terry
Keith Henderson	Tom Wilkinson
Opal Saunders	Mary Regan
Seven	Joseph George
Lilac	Eileen Glover
Ashton	Graham Glover
Jasmine	Tessa Well
Elliot	Jonathan Porteou
Pearly	Cherie Nepi
Ihaka	Robert Nepi
Olga	Erica Edwards-Brown
Tiny	Paul Kin
Wai	Frank Natha
Moana	Awhina Soloma
Hauwiti	Kristofer Haurak
Manu	Aaron Pak
Tweenie	Norma Taylo
Caroline	Waione Te Pa
Rewi	Naomi Ru
Kata	Carol Henr
Jacob	Andrew Glove

and Martyn Sanderson, Terence Cooper, David Letch, Sarah Peirse, James Cross, Peter Thorpe, Roy Pearce, Ian Harrop, Te Whatanu Skipwith, Norman Forsey, Margaret Murray, Millie Bradfield, Brian Flegg, Arthur Wright, Ron McKitterick, Sheila Summers, Ngair Horton, Deborah Cuzens, Ingrid Wahlberg, Mavis Tuoro, Nigel Har brow, Joanna Paul, Debbie Dorday, Norman Fletcher

Top: Eleanor David, and left with
Nigel Terry, Tom Wilkinson, Mary Regan
© MGM/UA Entertainment Co.

A VIEW TO A KILL

(MGM/UA) Producers, Albert R. Broccoli, Michael G. Wilson; Director, John Glen; Screenplay, Richard Maibaum, Michael G. Wilson; Photography, Alan Hume; Music, John Barry; Title Song, Duran Duran, John Barry; Designer, Peter Lamont; Costumes, Emma Porteous; Editor, Peter Davies; Special Effects, John Richardson; Production Managers, Philip Kohler, Serge Touboul, Leonard Gmur, Ned Kopp & Co., John Thor Hannesson; Assistant Director, Gerry Gavigan; Sound, Derek Ball; British; Panavision Widescreen; Metrocolor; Dolby Stereo; 131 minutes; Rated PG; May release

CAST

James Bond	Roger Moore
Max Zorin	Christopher Walken
Stacey Sutton	Tanya Roberts
May Day	Grace Jones
Tibbett	Patrick MacNee
Scarpine	Patrick Bauchau
Chuck Lee	David Yip
Pola Ivanova	Fiona Fullerton
Bob Conley	Manning Redwood
Jenny Flex	Alison Doody
Dr. Carl Mortner	Willoughby Gray
Q	Desmond Llewelyn
M	Robert Brown
Miss Moneypenny	Lois Maxwell
General Gogol	Walter Gotell
Minister of Defense	Geoffrey Keen
Aubergine	Jean Rougerie
Howe	Daniel Benzali
Klotkoff	Bogdan Kominowski
Pan Ho	Papillon Soo Soo
Kimberley Jones	Mary Stavin

and Dominique Risbourg, Carole Ashby, Anthony Chin, Lucien Jerome, Joe Flood, Gerard Buhr, Dolph Lundgren, Tony Sibbald, Bill Ackridge, Ron Tarr, Taylor McAuley, Peter Ensor, Seva Novgorodtsev

Right: Christopher Walken, Grace Jones, Tanya Roberts, Roger Moore Top: Roger Moore, Grace Jones
© *MGM/UA Entertainment Co.*

Roger Moore

Roger Moore, Tanya Roberts

A MAN LIKE EVA

(Promovision) Producer, Horst Schier, Laurens Straub; Director, Radu Gabrea; Screenplay, Radu Gabrea, Laurens Straub; Based on an idea by Horst Schier, Laurens Straub; Photography, Horst Schier; Music, La Traviata by Guiseppe Verdi, Sung by Maria Callas; Lighting, Heinz Kowalczyk, Michael Ostermann; Costumes, Tina Stockl; Editor, Dragos-Emmanuel Witkowski; Choreographer, Heino Hallhuber; West German; German with subtitles; Color; 92 minutes; Not rated; June release.

CAST

Eva	Eva Mattes
Gudrun	Lisa Kreuzer
Yvonne	Charles Regnier
Walter	Werner Stocker
Ali	Charley Muhamed Huber
Else	Carola Regnier
Max	Albert Kitzl
Producer	Towje Kleiner
Administrator	Lothar Borowsky
Dancer	Maria Mettke
Walter's Wife	Sybelle Rauch
Walter's Child	Frederike Wilde

**Right: Eva Mattes Top: Eva Mattes,
Lisa Kreuzer Left: Stocker, Mattes**
© *Promovision*

Reiko Ohara, Kiyoshi Atsumi

TORA-SAN'S FORBIDDEN LOVE

(SHOCHIKU CO., LTD.) Producers, Kiyoshi Simazu/Shigehiro Nakagawa; Director-Story, Yoji Yamada; Screenplay, Yoji Yamada, Yoshitaka Asame; Photography, Tetsuo Takaba; Designer, Mitsu Dekawa; Music, Naozumi Yamamoto; Planned by Shunichi Kobayashi; Color; 107 minutes; Japanese; Rated PG-13; June release.

CAST

Tora-san	Kiyoshi Atsum
Sakura	Chieko Baish
Fujiko	Reiko Ohar
Kojima	Masakane Yonekur
Uncle	Masami Shimoj
Aunt	Chieko Misak
Hiroshi	Gin Maed
Printer	Hisao Daza
His daughter	Jun Mih
Priest	Chishu Ry

© *Shochiku Co.*

THE COCA-COLA KID

(CINECOM) Producer, David Roe; Director, Dusan Makevejev; Screenplay, Frank Moorhouse; Based on the Books "The Americans, Baby" and "The Electrical Experience" by Frank Moorhouse; Designer, Graham (Grace) Walker; Photography, Dean Semler; Costumes, Terry Ryan; Editor, John Scott; Music, William Motzing; Songs, Tim Finn; Sound, Mark Lewis; Executive Producer, Les Lithgow; Co-Producer, Syvlie Le Clezio; Australian; Eastmancolor; Panavision; Dolby Stereo; 94 minutes; Not rated; July release

CAST

Becker	Eric Roberts
Terri	Greta Scacchi
T. George McDowell	Bill Kerr
Kim	Chris Haywood
Juliana	Kris McQuade
Frank	Max Gilles
Bushman	Tony Barry
Fred	Paul Chubb
Waiter	David Slingsby
Philip	Tim Finn
Mrs. Haversham	Colleen Clifford
DMZ	Rebecca Smart
Country Hotel Manager	Esben Storm
Mr. Joe	Steve Dodd
Margorie	Ian Gilmour
Newspaper Vendor	David A'gue
Rock Musicians	Ricky Fataar, Mark Moffatt, Paul Hester, Rex Goh

Right: Eric Roberts
© Cinecom

**Greta Scacchi, Eric Roberts
Above: Bill Kerr, Eric Roberts**

Greta Scacchi

KISS OF THE SPIDER WOMAN

(ISLAND ALIVE) Producer, David Weisman; Director, Hecto
Babenco; Screenplay, Leonard Schrader; Based on a novel by Manue
Puig; Photography, Rodolfo Sanchez; Music, John Neschling, Nand
Carneiro, Wally Badarou; Editor, Mauro Alice; Designer, Felipe Cres
centi; Costumes, Patricio Bisso; Executive Producer, Francisco Rama
ho, Jr.; Associate Producers, Jane Holzer, Michael Maiello, Studi
Artes Visuals, Jayme Sverner, Cena Filmes, Gustavo Halbreich, Alta
miro Boscoli, Paulo Francini; An H. B. Filmes Production In Associa
tion with Sugarloaf Films; MGM Color; 119 minutes; Rated R; Brazi
lian; July release

CAST

Luis Molina	William Hu
Valentin Arregui	Raul Juli
Leni Lamaison/Marta/Spider Woman	Sonia Brag
Warden	Jose Lewgo
Pedro	Milton Goncalve
Mother	Miriam Pire
Gabriel	Nuno Leal Ma
Americo	Fernando Torre
Greta	Patricio Biss
Werner	Herson Cap
Michele	Denise Dummo
Leader of Resistance	Nildo Paren
Clubfoot	Antonio Petri
Flunky	Wilson Gre
Lieutenant	Miguel Falabel
Prison Doctor	Luis Ser
Lidia	Ana Maria Brag

and Walter Breda, Luis Guilherme, Waldmir Barros, Benjamin Cattan
Oswaldo Barreto, Sergio Bright, Claudio Curi, Lineu Dias, Joe Kanto
Luis Roberto Galizia, Pericles Campos, Edmilson Santos, Walter Vi
ca, Kenichi Kaneko, Georges Schlesinger, Carlos Fariello, Frederic
Botelho, Sylvio Band, Paulo Ludmer, Elvira Bisso

***William Hurt received an Academy Award for Best
Actor of 1985***

**Left: Sonia Braga, Raul Julia
Top: Raul Julia, William Hurt**
© Island Alive

Sonia Braga, Herson Capri

William Hurt

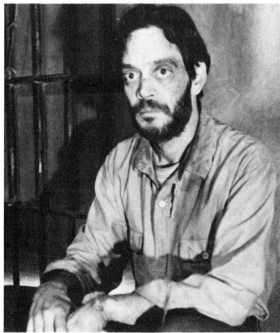

Sonia Braga
Top: Raul Julia, William Hurt

Raul Julia

LETTERS FROM MARUSIA

(FILM FORUM) Producers, Conacine, Arturo Feliu; Director-Screenplay, Miguel Littin; Story, Patricio Manz; Photography, Jorge Stahl, Jr.; Music, Mikis Theodorakis; Mexico; Spanish with subtitles; 110 minutes; Not rated; July release

CAST

Gregorio	Gian Maria Volonte
Luisa	Diana Brancho

Right: Gian Maria Volonte

Pierre Richard, Gerard Depardieu

LA CHEVRE

(EUROPEAN CLASSICS) Producer, Alain Poire; Director-Story Screenplay, Francis Veber; Music, Vladimir Cosma; Photography Alex Phillips; Designer, Jacques Bufnoir; Editor, Albert Jurgenso; Sound, Bernard Rochut; Assistant Directors, Patrice Poire, Davi Kodsi; A Gaumont International/Fideline Films Co-Production France; Color; 91 minutes; Not rated; July release

CAST

Francois Perrin	Pierre Richa
Campana	Gerard Depardie
Marie Bens	Corynne Charb
Mr. Bens	Michel Rob
Meyer	Andre Valarc
Custao	Pedro Armendariz,

**Above: Gerard Depardieu also left
with Pierre Richard
© European Classics**

MAD MAX BEYOND THUNDERDOME

(WARNER BROS.) Producer, George Miller; Directors, George Miller, George Ogilvie; Screenplay, Terry Hayes, George Miller; Music, Maurice Jarre; Editor, Richard Francis-Bruce; Photography, Dean Semler; Visual Design Consultant, Ed Verreaux; Costumes, Norma Moriceau; Designer, Graham "Grace" Walker; Co-Producers, Doug Mitchell, Terry Hayes; Production Manager, Antonia Barnard; Associate Producers, Steve Amezdroz, Marcus D'Arcy; Sound, Roger Savage, Bruce Lamshed; Assistant Directors, Steve Andrews, Stuart Freeman, Chris Webb, Ian Kenny, Murray Robertson, Ian Freeman; Special Effects, Mike Wood, Steve Courtley, Brian Cox; Color; Panavision; Widescreen; Dolby Stereo; Australian; 108 minutes; Rated PG-13; July release

CAST

Mad Max	Mel Gibson
Jedediah	Bruce Spence
Jedediah Jr.	Adam Cockburn
Aunty Entity	Tina Turner
The Collector	Frank Thring
The Master	Angelo Rossitto
The Blaster	Paul Larsson
Ironbar	Angry Anderson
Pigkiller	Robert Grubb
Blackfinger	George Spartels
Dr. Dealgood	Edwin Hodgeman
Waterseller	Bob Hornery
Ton Ton Tattoo	Andrew Oh
Savannah Nix	Helen Buday
Mr. Skyfish	Mark Spain
Gekko	Mark Kounnas
Scrooloose	Rod Zuanic
Anna Goanna	Justine Clarke
Eddie	Shane Tickner
Tusha	Toni Allaylis
Gubba Tintye	James Wingrove
Finn McCoo	Adam Scougall
Slake	Tom Jennings
Mr. Scratch	Adam Willits

and Ollie Hall, Susan Leonard, Ray Turnbull, Lee Rice, Robert Simper, Brian Ellison, Gerard Armstrong, Max Worrall, Virginia Wark, Keeling, Gerry D'Angelo, Travis Latter, Miguel Lopez, Paul Daniel, Tushka Hose, Emily Sbocker, Sandie Lillingston, Ben Chesterman, Liam Nikkinen, Dan Chesterman, Christopher Norton, Katharine Cullen, Heilan Robertson, Gabriel Dilworth, Hugh Sands, Rebekah Elmaglou, Marion Sands, Shari Flood, Kate Tatar, Rachael Graham, Pega Williams, Emma Howard, Tarah Williams, Joanna McCarroll, Daniel Willits, Toby Messiter, Tonya Wright, Charlie Kenney, Amanda Nikkinen, Flynn Kenney, Luke Panic, William Manning, James Robertson, Adan McCreadie, Sally Morton

**Right: Tina Turner, and top with
Mel Gibson**
© *Warner Bros.*

Tina Turner

Mel Gibson

TOSCA'S KISS

(FILM FORUM) Producers, Hans-Ulrich Jordi, Marcel Hoehn; Director, Daniel Schmid; Photography, Renato Berta; Music, Giuseppe Verdi, Giacomo Puccini, Gaetano Donizetti; Documentary; Switzerland; Italian with subtitles; 87 minutes; Not rated; July release.

CAST

Sara Scuderi, Giovanni Puligheddu, Leonida Bellon, Salvatore Locapo, Giuseppe Manacchini

Right: Sara Scuderi

WETHERBY

(MGM/UA CLASSICS) Producer, Simon Relph; Director-Screenplay, David Hare; Photography, Stuart Harris; Editor, Chris Wimb. Music, Nick Bicat; Designer, Hayden Griffin; Costumes, Jane Gree wood, Lindy Hemming; Sound, Clive Winter; Associate Produc Patsy Pollock; Production Manager, Linda Bruce; Assistant Direct Ian Madden; Color; British; 102 minutes; Rated R; July release

CAST

Jean Travers	Vanessa Redgra
Stanley Pilborough	Ian Ho
Marcia Pilborough	Judi Den
Verity Braithwaite	Marjorie Ya
Roger Braithwaite	Tom Wilkins
John Morgan	Tim McInner
Karen Creasy	Suzanna Hamilt
Mike Langdon	Stuart Wils

and Diane Whitley, Mike Kelly, Howard Crossley, Matthew Guinne Ted Beyer, Joely Richardson, Robert Hines, Katy Behean, Bert Kir Paula Tilbrook, Christopher Fulford, David Foreman, Stephanie Nc lett, Richard Marris, Jonathan Lazenby, Nigel Rooke, John Robe Norman Mills, Vanessa Rosenthal, Trevor Lunn, Guy Nicholls, Bleasdale, Peter Martin

Above: Vanessa Redgrave
Left: Tim McInnerny
© *MGM/UA Classics*

Ian Holm, Vanessa Redgrave

DANCE WITH A STRANGER

(SAMUEL GOLDWYN) Producer, Roger Randall-Cutler; Director, Mike Newell; Screenplay, Shelagh Delaney; Photography, Peter Hannan; Editor, Mick Audsley; Designer, Andrew Mollo; Music, Richard Hartley; Costumes, Pip Newbery; Associate Producer, Paul Cowan; A Goldcrest Production; Best Foreign Film 1985 Cannes Film Festival; United Kingdom, 1984; Color; 101 minutes; Rated R; August release

CAST

Ruth Ellis	Miranda Richardson
David Blakely	Rupert Everett
Desmond Cussen	Ian Holm
Andy	Matthew Carroll
Anthony Findlater	Tom Chadbon
Carole Findlater	Jane Bertish
Cliff Davis	David Troughton
Clive Gunnell	Paul Mooney
Morrie Conley	Stratford Johns
Christine	Joanne Whalley
Barbara	Susan Kyd
Maryanne	Lesley Manville
Claudette	Sallie-Anne Field

and David Beale, Martin Murphy, Tracy-Louise Ward, Michael Jenn, Alan Thompson, Nicholas McArdle, Miki Iveria, Lizzie McKenzie, Ian Hurley, Charles Cork, Patrick Field, Colin Rix, Tony Mathews, Sharon Bourke, Elizabeth Newell

Right: Miranda Richardson
© Samuel Goldwyn Co.

Rupert Everett, Miranda Richardson

Miranda Richardson, Ian Holm

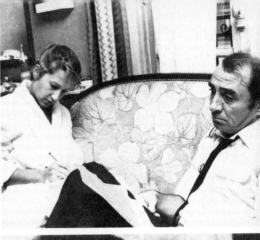

DETECTIVE

(SPECTRAFILM) Executive Producer, Alain Sarde; Director, Jean-Luc Godard; Scenario, Alain Sarde, Philippe Stebon; Adaptation, Anne-Marie Mieville, Jean-Luc Godard; Dialogue, Jean-Luc Godard; Assistant Director, Renald Calcagni; Photography, Bruno Nuytten; Sound, Pierre Gamet, Francois Musy; Music, Schubert, Wagner, Chopin, Listz, Honegger, Chabrier, Ornette Colemann, Jean Schwarz; A Sara Films/Jean-Luc Godard Films Co-Production; Switzerland, 1983; Eastman Color; Subtitles; 98 minutes; Dolby Stereo; Not rated; August release

CAST

Francoise Chenal	Nathalie Baye
Emile Chenal	Claude Brasseur
Jim Fox Warner Impressario	Johnny Hallyday
Tiger Jones	Stephane Ferrara
Eugene	Eugene Berthier
Grace Kelly	Emmanuelle Seigner
The Punk	Cyril Autin
The Wise Young Girl	Julie Delpy
Uncle William Prospero	Laurent Terzieff
Inspector Neveu	Jean-Pierre Leaud
My Sister Anne	Anne Gisele Glass
Ariel	Aurele Doazan
Old Maffioso	Alain Cuny
Young Son	Pierre Bertin
Young Daughter	Alexandra Garijo
Accountant	Xavier Saint Macary

Top: Johnny Hallyday, Nathalie Baye
Right: Nathalie Baye, Claude Brasseur
© *International Spectrafilm*

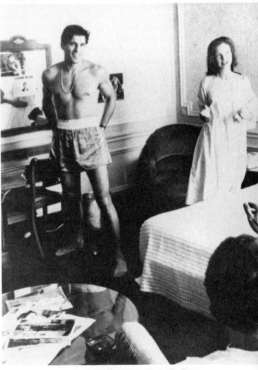

Johnny Hallyday, Nathalie Baye
also above

THE FLAXFIELD

(FILM FORUM) Producers, Jan van Raemdonck, Gerrit Visscher; Director-Screenplay, Jan Gruyaert; Based on the novel by Stijn Streuvels; Photography, Ben Tenniglo; Belgium-The Netherlands, 1983; Flemish with subtitles; M. D. Wax/Courier Films release; Color; 90 minutes; Not rated; August release

CAST

Farmer Vermeulen	Vic Moeremans
Barbele	Dora van der Groen
Schellebelle	Gusta Gerritsen
Louis	Rene van Sambeek

Right Top: Gusta Gerritsen, Rene van Sambeek

MY OTHER "HUSBAND"

(TRIUMPH FILMS) Producer, Alain Poire; Director, Georges Lautner; Screenplay, Jean-Loup Dabadie; Editor, Michelle David; Photography, Henri Decae; Music, Philippe Sarde; French with subtitles; Color; 110 minutes; Rated PG13; August release

CAST

Alice	Miou-Miou
Philippe	Roger Hanin
Vincent	Eddy Mitchell
Solange	Dominique Lavanant
Cynthia	Charlotte de Turckheim
Simon	Rachid Ferrache
Pauline	Ingrid Lurienne
Jean	Vincent Barazzoni
Nino	Venantino Venantini
Surgeon	Francois Perrot
Conductor	Lionel Rocheman
Translator	Andre Valardy
Madam Le Boucau	Renee Saint-Cyr
Truck Driver	Patrick Floersheim
Zelda	Florence Giorgetti
Raphael	Philippe Khorsand
Jeff	Roland Giraud
Maitre d'	Robert Dalban
Mr. Santaluccia	Jean Rougerie

Above: Miou-Miou and Right
with Eddy Mitchell and children
© *Columbia Pictures*

Miou-Miou, Roger Hanin

RAN

(ORION CLASSICS) Producers, Serge Silberman, Masato Hara; Director, Akira Kurosawa; Screenplay, Mr. Kurosawa, Hideo Oguni, Masato Ide; Photography, Takao Saito, Masaharu Ueda, with the collaboration of Asakazu Nakai; Designers, Yoshiro Muraki, Shinobu Muraki; Costumes, Emi Wada; Music, Toru Takemitsu; Performed by Sapporo Symphony; Executive Producer, Katsumi Furukawa; A French and Japanese Co-production; Editor, Akira Kurosawa; Rated R. In color; 160 minutes; September release

CAST

Hidetora Ichimonji	Tatsuya Nakadai
Taro	Akira Terao
Jiro	Jimpachi Nezu
Saburo	Daisuke Ryu
Lady Kaede	Mieko Harada
Lady Sue	Yoshiko Miyazaki
Ikoma	Kazuo Kato
Tango	Masayuki Yui
Kyoami	Peter
Fujimaki	Hitoshi Ueki
Kurogane	Hisashi Ikawa
Tsurumaru	Takeshi Nomura

Recipient of 1985 Academy Award for Best Costume Design

Left: Tatsuya Nakadai
© *Orion Classics*

Akira Terao, Jinpachi Nezu, Daisuke Ryu, Kazuo Kato, Masayuki Yui

Peter, Tatsuya Nakadai Top: (L) Jinpachi Nezu (R) Kazuo Kato (R)
Center: (L) Mieko Harada (R) Daisuke Ryu

LAS MADRES DE PLAZA DE MAYO

(FIRST RUN) Producers-Directors-Screenplay, Susan Munoz, Lourdes Portillo; Photography, Michael Anderson; Music, Inti-Illimani, Astor Piazzola; Narration, Carmen Zapata; Documentary; Spanish with subtitles; Color; 64 minutes; Not rated; September release

Right: Pope John Paul II

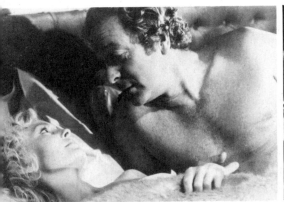

THE HOLCROFT COVENANT

(UNIVERSAL) Producers, Edie and Ely Landau; Director, John Frankenheimer; Screenplay, George Axelrod, Edward Anhalt, John Hopkins; Based on novel by Robert Ludlum; Executive Producer, Mo Abrahams; Music, Stanislas; Co-producer, Otto Plaschkes; Associa Producer, Tom Sachs; Assistant Director, Don French; Editor, Ralp Sheldon; Designer, Peter Mullins; Photographer, Gerry Fisher; Co tumes, Derek Hyde; In Technicolor; British; Rated R; 112 minute September release

CAST

Noel Holcroft	Michael Cair
Johann Tennyson von Tiebolt	Anthony Andrev
Helden Tennyson von Tiebolt	Victoria Tenna
Althene Holcroft	Lilli Palm
Jurgen Maas (Erich Kessler)	Mario Adc
Manfredi	Michael Lonsda
Leighton	Bernard Hept
Oberst	Richard Mun
Beaumont	Carl Ri
Leger	Andre Penve
Hartman	Andrew Bradfo
Lt. Miles	Shane Rimm
Gen. Clausen	Alexander Ke
Gen. Kessler	Michael Wc
Gen. von Tiebolt	Hugo Bow
Hard Hat	Michael Balfo
Assassin	Tharita Olivera De Se
Fritzl	Guntbert War
Oberst's Guard	Paul Humpole
Concierge	Tom Deining
Policeman	Keith Edwar
Switchboard Operator	Andrea Brow
Executive Secretary	Shelley Thomps
Manfredi's Secretary	Eve Ada
Carnival Director	Jorge Tre
Rescuer	Tim Condr

Michael Caine Above: Anthony Andrews, Victoria Tennant

Above: Anthony Andrews, Victoria Tennant, Michael Caine Left: Tennant, Caine
© *Universal*

THE ASSISI UNDERGROUND

(CANNON) Producers, Menahem Golan, Yoram Globus; Director-screenplay, Alexander Ramati, based on his documentary novel "The Assisi Underground"; Photography, Giuseppe Rotunno; Editor, Michael Duthie; Designer, Luciano Spadoni; Costumes, Adriana Spasaro; Music, Dov Seltzer; Associate Producer, John Thompson; Production Manager, Attilio Viti; Assistant Directors, Albino Cocco, Joseph Rochlitz; Sound, Gaetano Testa; Special Effects, Giovanni Corridori; Technicolor; British; 178 minutes; Rated PG; September release

CAST

Padre Rufino	Ben Cross
Bishop Nicolini	James Mason
Mother Giuseppina	Irene Papas
Col. Mueller	Maximilian Schell
Capt. von Velden	Karl-Heinz Hackl
Luigi Brizzi	Riccardo Cucciolla
Giorgio Kropf	Angelo Infanti
Paolo Josza	Paolo Malco
Gen. Bremer	Tom Felleghy
Countess Cristina	Delia Boccardo
Cardinal Della Costa	Edmund Purdom
Prof. Rieti	Roberto Bisacco
Mrs. Eva Rieti	Didi Ramati
Police Chief Bertolucci	Geoffrey Copleestone
Pietro "The Smuggler"	Venantino Venantini
Tito "The Smuggler"	Maurice Poli
Gino Bartali	Alfredo Pea
The Rabbi	Marne Maitland
Carlo Maionica	Samuel Goldzader
Lt. Podda	Paolo Giusti
Franca Covarelli	Eurilla Del Bono
Col. Gay	Giancarlo Prete
Don Brunacci	Sergio Nicolai
Sister Beata	Alessandra Mussolini
Sister Amata	Gabriella D'Olive
Gino Maionica	Gianni Williams
Otto Maionica	Riccardo Salvino
Lita Maionica	Greta Vaillant
Little Maionica	Lucia Mollaioli
The Ovra Man	Tom Johnson
Ima	Pee Bee De La Cruz
Mario	Pierfrancesco Aiello
Jacob Baruch	Mark Malicz
The Forester	Francesco Carnelutti
Nella Gelb	Roberta Manfredi
Deborah Gelb	Stefani Maccari
Edward Gelb	Jorge Krimer
Mrs. Gelb	Margherita Sala
Hanna Gelb	Maya Ramati
Monsignore	Alfredo Varelli
Sister Alfonsina	Rita Guerrieri
Don Paolo	Massimo Sarchielli
Brother Euralio	Matteo Corvino
Brother Felice	Renato Miracco

and Carlo Monni (SS Sergeant), Fabio Meyer (SS Man), Luigi Marturano (Interpreter), Max Turilli (Prison Guard), Lionello Pio De Savoia (Col. Kruger), Helmut Hagen (Capt. Knabbe), Carlos De Carvalho, David Haughton (English Officers), Neil Hansen (Lt. Philip Garrigue), Mike Knevels (Gestapo Man), Al Ramati (Refugee), Claudia Costa (Girl in cafe), Franco Trevisi (Don Giovanni)

Top Right: Ben Cross
Below: James Mason, Maximilian Schell
© *Cannon*

James Mason
Above: Irene Papas

187

7 UP/28 UP

(GRANADA) Two documentaries from England; "7 Up" (1963, 40 minutes) prepared by Paul Almond with Michael Apted; "28 Up" (1984, 136 minutes) was directed by Michael Apted; Executive Producer, Steve Morrison; Photography, George Jesse Turner; Editors, Oral Norrie Ottey, Kim Horton; Researcher, Claire Lewis; Not rated; October release. A documentary on the "growing up" of 14 children from 1963 to 1984 with interviews at 7, 14, 21, and 28 years of age.

Right: one of the documented children

SHOAH

(NEW YORKER) Director, Claude Lanzmann; Co-producer, L Films Aleph Historia Films with the participation of the French Minist of Culture; Assistants to director, Corinna Coulmas, Irene Steinfel Levi; Photography, Dominique Chapuis, Jimmy Glasberg, Willia Lubchansky; Editors, Ziva Postec, Anna Ruiz; In many languages wi subtitles; In color, black and white; Made in France; Not rated; 9 hou and 23 minutes; October release. An epic documentary on the Na concentration camps. The title (in Hebrew) means "annihilation." Th major witnesses (all survivors) who appear are Simon Srebnik, Abr ham Bomba, Dr. Rudolf Vrba, Richard Glazar, Filip Muller, Fra Suchomel, Dr. Franz Grassler, Jan Karski

Above: Filip Muller (Auschwitz survivor)
Left: Simon Srebnik (Chelmno survivor)
Top Left: Dr. Frank Grassler (Nazi Commissioner)
© *New Yorker Films*

A YEAR OF THE QUIET SUN

(SANDSTAR) Director-Screenplay, Krzysztof Zanussi; Photography, Slawomir Idziak; Designer, Janusz Sosnowski; Sound, Wieslawa Deminska; Music, Wojciech Kilar; Editor, Marek Denys; Production, Film Polski/Teleculture Inc./Regina Ziegler/Filmproduction; Executive Producers, Michal Sczerbic, Michael Boehme; A Polish-American-German Co-Production; Golden Lion Award, Venice Film Festival 1984; Color; 106 minutes; Not rated; October release

CAST

Norman	Scott Wilson
Emilia	Maja Komorowska
Mother	Hanna Skarzanka
Stella	Ewa Dalkowska
Hermann	Vadim Glowna
David	Daniel Webb
Czary	Zbigniew Zapasiewicz
Translator	Tadeusz Bradecki
Doctor	Jerzy Nowak
Adzio	Jerzy Stuhr

Right: Maja Komorowska, Scott Wilson
Below: Maja Komorowska Left: Hanna Skarzanka
© Sandstar

Jerzy Stuhr, Maja Komorowska

Maja Komorowska

WHEN FATHER WAS AWAY
ON BUSINESS

(ANNON**)** Producer, "Forum" Sarajevo; Director, Emir Kusturica; reenplay, Abdulah Sidran; Photography, Vilko Filac; Editor, Andrija franovic; Music, Zoran Simjanovic; Costumes, Divna Jovanovic; ecutive Producer, Mirza Pasic; Production Manager, Vera Mihiclic; Sound, Ljubomir Petek, Hasan Vejzagic; Yugoslav with subes; WS Colour; 135 minutes; Rated R; October release

CAST

alik	Moreno D'E Bartolli
esha	Miki Manojlovic
nija	Mirjana Karanovic
jo	Mustafa Nadarevic
nkica	Mira Furlan
irza	Davor Dujmovic
anjo	Predrag Lakovic
uzamer	Pavle Vujisic
kic	Slobodan Aligrudic
vka	Eva Ras
. Ljahaov	Aleksandar Dorcev
icle Fahro	Emir Hadzihafisbegovic
ko	Zoran Radmilovic
tasha	Jelena Covic
jidza	Tomislav

No Captions Available
© *Cannon*

COLONEL REDL

(ORION CLASSICS) Executive Producer, Manfred Durniok; Director, Istvan Szabo; Screenplay, Istvan Szabo, Peter Dobai; Addition Dialogue, Gabriella Prekop, Heinz Freitag; Photography, Lajos Kolt Editor, Zsuzsa Csakany; Designer, Jozsef Romvari; Sound, Gyor Fek; Costumes, Peter Pabst; Music, Schumann/Chopin/Liszt/Pen Strauss; Musical Director, Zdenko Tamassy; Assistant Director, Ma Luttor; Lighting, Antal Torok; Production Manager, Lajos Ovari; A Hungarian/West German/Austrian Co-Production of Mafilm-Objek Studio/Manfred Durniok Produktion/ORF/ZDF; German with su titles; Eastmancolor; 144 minutes; Rated R; November release

CAST

Alfred Redl	Klaus Maria Brandau
The Crown Prince	Armin Mueller-Sta
Katalin Kubinyi	Gudrun Landgre
Kristof Kubinyi	Jan Nik
Colonel von Roden	Hans-Christian Ble
Colonel Ruzitska	Laszlo Mensar
Dr. Gustav Sonnenschein	Andras Bal
Lt. Jaromil Schorm	Karoly Eperj
Clarissa	Dorottya Udvar
Alfredo Velocchio	Laszlo Ga
Baron Ullmann	Robert Rator
Alfred as a Child	Gabor Svidro
Redl's Mother	Eva Sza
Kristof as a child	Gyorgy Ra
Katalin as a child	Dora Lend
Grandfather Kubinyi	Tamas Ma
Grandmother Kubinyi	Maria Majl
Redl's Sister	Flora Kac
Wilhelmina	Agnes T. Kato
Adjutant to Crown Prince	Gyorgy Ban
Female Singer	Athina Papadimit
Auctioneer	Istvan Vereb

Gudrun Landgrebe, Klaus Maria Brandauer (also top left)

Klaus Maria Brandauer, Gudrun Landgrebe
Top: Gyorgy Banffy, Armin Mueller-Stahl

JOSHUA THEN AND NOW

(20th CENTURY-FOX) Producers, Robert Lantos, Stephen J. Roth; Director, Ted Kotcheff; Screenplay, Mordecai Richler from his novel; Music, Philippe Sarde; Associate Producer, Julian Marks; Editor, Ron Wisman; Designer, Anne Pritchard; Photography, Francois Protat; Assistant Directors, Craig Huston, Pedro Gandol, David Bailey; Costumes, Louise Jobin; Art Director, Harold Thrasher; Choreographer, Brian Foley; Canadian production in Bellevue Pathe Colour; Rated R; 127 minutes; October release

CAST

Joshua Shapiro	James Wood
Pauline Shapiro	Gabrielle Lazure
Reuben Shapiro	Alan Arkin
Kevin Hornby	Michael Sarrazin
Esther Shapiro	Linda Sorensen
Jack Trimble	Alan Scarfe
Sidney Murdoch	Ken Campbell
Jane Trimble	Kate Trotter
Senator Hornby	Alexander Knox
Young Joshua Shapiro	Eric Kimmel
Seymour Kaplan	Chuck Shamata
Young Seymour Kaplan	Yuval Kernerman
Colin Fraser	Robert Joy
Dr. Jonathan Cole	Harvey Atkin
Eli Seligson	Paul Hecht
Ralph Murdoch	Andrew Powell
Dr. Danziger	Jack Rider
Susy Shapiro	Talya Rubin
Alex Shapiro	Robert Howard
Teddy Shapiro	Gordon Woolvet
Ryan	Michael Donaghue
Mr. Abbot	Rob Roy
Mrs. Abbot	Catherine Colvey
Mr. Hickey	Christopher Eisenhardt
Mrs. Hickey	Linda Smith
Mr. Friar	Philip Pretten
Mrs. Friar	Bronwen Mantel
Bulgarian Poet	Kliment Denchev
Bulgarian Translator	Nuvit Ozdogru
Joanna	Alexandra Innes
Woman on telephone	Harriet Stein
R.C.C. Boy	David Shaffer
Doorman	Sonny Lewis

Right: Alan Scarfe, James Woods, Michael Sarrazin Above: Woods, Gabrielle Lazure, Alan Arkin Top: Eric Kimmel (L), Linda Sorensen © *20th Century-Fox*

Alan Arkin, Eric Kimmel

Kate Trotter, Gabrielle Lazure

FLOWING

(EAST-WEST CLASSICS) Producer, Toho Company Ltd; Director, Mikio Naruse; Screenplay, Sumie Tanaka, Toshiro Ide; Based on the novel by Aya Koda; Photography, Masao Tamai; Designer, Satoshi Chuko; Music, Ichiro Saito; Executive Producer, Sanezumi Fujimoto; Japan 1956; Japanese with subtitles; Black and White; 116 minutes; Not Rated; November release

CAST

Rika Yamanaka (Oharu)	Kinuyo Tanaka
Tsutayakko	Isuzu Yamada
Katsuyo	Hideko Takamine
Nanako	Mariko Okada
Someka	Haruko Sugimura
Madame Mizuno	Sumiko Kurishima
Yoneko	Chieko Nakakita
Otoyo	Natsuko Kahara
Nokogiriyama	Seiji Miyaguchi
Takagi	Daisuke Kato
Saeki	Noboru Nakaya
Fujiko	Natsuko Matsuyama

No Photos Available

CAMORRA

(CANNON) Producers, Menahem Golan, Yoram Globus; Director-screenplay, Lina Wertmuller; Screenplay Consultant, Elvio Porta; Photography, Giuseppe Lanci; Editor, Luigi Zita; Designer, Enrico Job; Costumes, Benito Persico; Music, Tony Esposito; Choreography, Daniel Ezralow; Executive Producer, Fulvio Lucisano; Associate Producer, John Thompson; Assistant Directors, Antonio Gabrielli, Bruno Nappi; Sound, Fabio Ancillai; Special Effects, Giovanni Corridori; Songs, Paolo Conte; Cinecitta Color; Dolby Stereo; Italian; 107 minutes; Rated R: November release

CAST

Annunziata	Angela Molina
Guaglione	Francisco Rabal
Frankie	Harvey Keitel
Noto	Daniel Ezralow
Tony	Vittorio Squillante
Tango	Paolo Bonacelli
Baba	Tommaso Bianco
Cummarurella	Raffaele Verita
Commissario	Elvio Porta
Rosa	Mario Scarpetta
Terremoto	Franco Angrisano
Carmela	Isa Danieli
Nicolino Cammel	Roberto Marafante
Elena	Annie Papa
'O Dimonio	Pino Amendola
Io Conte	Sebastiano Nardone
Rotunno	Gino Carcione
Rammarano	Rosario Campese
Police Clerk	Riccardo Perrotti
Gangster	P. L. Cuomo
Lawyer	Lucio Amelio
Annunziata's Brother	Nuccio Pianese
Assunta	Anna Maria Porta
Mauriello	Mario Porfito
Tango's Wife	Mietta Albertini
Emergency Room Doctor	Alberto De Stasio
Gangster Cammel	Elio Steiner
Policeman	Claudio Ciocca

Top Right: Angela Molina (C)
Below: Daniel Ezralow, Angela Molina
© *Cannon*

Angela Molina, Harvey Keitel
Above: (C) Angela Molina

195

SUGARBABY

(KINO INTERNATIONAL) Producer-Director, Johanna Heer; Editor, Jean-Claude Piroue; Sound, Rainer Wiehr; Music, Dreieier; Designers, Johanna Heer, Matthias Heller; Theme Song, Peter Kraus; Executive Producer, Eleonore Adlon; Production Company, Pelemele Film GmbH; German with subtitles; Color; 86 minutes; Not rated; November release

CAST

Marianne	Marianne Sagebrecht
Huber 133	Eisi Gulp
Old Subway Driver	Toni Berger
Huber's Wife	Manuela Denz
Funeral Director	Will Spindler
Dance Hall Band	The Paul Wurges Combo

Top: Eisi Gulp, Marianne Sagerbrecht
© *Kino International*

Eisi Gulp, Marianne Sagerbrecht

LATE CHRYSANTHEMUMS

(FILM FORUM) Producer, Toho Company; Director, Mikio Naruse; Screenplay, Sumie Tanaka, Toshiro Ide; Based on three stories by Fumiko Hayashi; Photography, Masao Tami; Japan 1954; Japanese with subtitles; Black and White; 101 minutes; Not rated; November release

CAST

Kin	Haruko Sugimura
Nobu	Sadako Sawamura
Tamae	Chikako Hosokawa
Tomi	Yuko Mochizuki
Tabe	Ken Uehara
Sachiko	Ineko Arima
Kiyoshi	Hiroshi Suzuki
Seki	Bontaro Miake

Top Right: Haruko Sugimura, Ken Uehara

Enrico Montesano, Veronica Lario

SOTTO . . . SOTTO

(TRIUMPH FILMS) Producers, Mario & Vittorio Cecchi Gori; Director-Story, Lina Wertmuller; Screenplay, Enrico Oldoini, Lina Wertmuller; Designer, Enrico Job; Photography, Dante Spinotti; Editor, Luigi Zita; Music, Paolo Conte; Set, Gianni Giovagnoni; Costumes, Christiana La Fayette; Production Manager, Vivien Boden; An Intercapital Production; Italian with subtitles; Color; 105 minutes; Rated R; November release

CAST

Oscar	Enrico Montesano
Ester	Veronica Lario
Adele	Luisa De Santis
Ginetto	Massimo Wertmuller
Amilcare	Mario Scarpetta
Rosa	Isa Danieli
Sora Ines	Elena Fabrizi
Bellissima	Antonia Dell'Atte
Mario	Renato D'Amore
Priest	Alfredo Bianchini

**Above: Veronica Lario, Isa Danieli,
Luisa De Santis Left: Enrico
Montesano, Veronica Lario**
© Columbia

197

EL DIPUTADO
(The Deputy)

(AWARD FILMS) Director, Eloy de la Iglesia; Screenplay, Gonzalo Goicoechea, Eloy de la Iglesia; Photography, Antonio Cuevas; Editor, Julio Pena; Design, Gumer; A Figaro Films/Zeta/UFESA Production; Released by David Whitten Promotions; In Eastman Color; Not rated; 111 minutes; November release

CAST

Roberto Orbea .... Jose Sacristan
Carmen Orbea .... Maria Luisa San Jose
Juanito .... Jose L. Alonso
Nes .... Angel Pardo
Carres .... Agustin Gonzales
Moreno Pastrana .... Enrique Vivo
Juanito's Mother .... Queta Claver
with special appearance by Juan Antonio Bardem

Right: Jose Sacristan, Maria Luisa San Jose
Below: Jose L. Alonso, Jose Sacristan
© *Award Films*

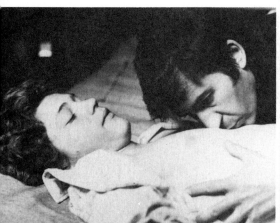

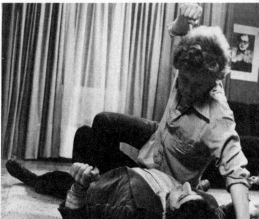

Maria Luisa San Jose, Jose Sacristan, Jose L. Alonso
Left Center: Jose L. Alonso, Jose Sacristan

YOUNG SHERLOCK HOLMES

(PARAMOUNT) Producer, Mark Johnson; Director, Barry Levinson; Screenplay, Chris Columbus; Suggested by characters created by Sir Arthur Conan Doyle, with the permission of Dame Jean Conan Doyle; Photography, Stephen Goldblatt; Designer, Norman Reynolds; Editor, Stu Linder; Music, Bruce Broughton; Costumes, Raymond Hughes; Executive Producers, Steven Spielberg, Frank Marshall, Kathleen Kennedy; Associate Producer, Harry Benn; Special Effects, Kit West; Animatronics, Stephen Norrington; Production Manager, Donald Toms; Assistant Directors, Michael Murray, Ian Hickinbotham; Visual Effects, Dennis Muren; Sound, Paul Bruce Richardson; An Amblin Entertainment Production in Association with Henry Winkler/Roger Birnbaum; Technicolor; Panavision; Dolby Stereo; British; 110 minutes; Rated PG-13; December release

CAST

Sherlock Holmes	Nicholas Rowe
John Watson	Alan Cox
Elizabeth	Sophie Ward
Rathe	Anthony Higgins
Mrs. Dribb	Susan Fleetwood
Bragwitch	Freddie Jones
Waxflatter	Nigel Stock
Lestrade	Roger Ashton-Griffiths
Dudley	Earl Rhodes
Master Snelgrove	Brian Oulton
Mobster	Patrick Newell
Reverend Nesbitt	Donald Eccles
Dudley's Friends	Matthew Ryan, Matthew Blakstad, Jonathan Lacey
Ethan Engel	Walter Sparrow
Egyptian Tavern Owner	Nadim Sawalha
Mr. Holmes	Roger Brierley
Mrs. Holmes	Vivienne Chandler
Curio Shop Owner	Lockwood West
Cemetery Caretaker	John Scott Martin
School Porter	George Malpas
School Reverend	Willoughby Goddard
Policemen	Michael Cule, Ralph Tabakin
Hotel Receptionist	Nancy Nevinson
Voice of Older Watson	Michael Hordern

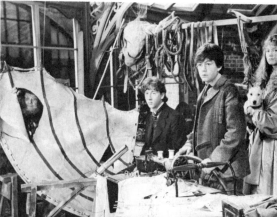

Right: Nigel Stock, Nicholas Rowe, Alan Cox, Sophie Ward Top: Anthony Higgins, Nicholas Rowe © Paramount

Nicholas Rowe, Alan Cox

Sophie Ward, Alan Cox

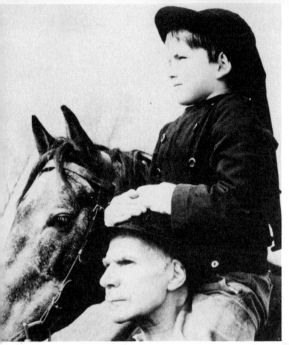

THE HORSE OF PRIDE

(FILM FORUM) Producer, Bela Productions/TFI; Director, Claude Chabrol; Screenplay, Daniel Boulanger; Based on the novel by Pierre Jakez Helias; Adaptation, Daniel Boulanger, Claude Chabrol; Photography, Jean Rabier; Music, Pierre Jansen; Distributor, Nicole Jouve Interama; France 1980; French with subtitles; 118 minutes; Not rated; December release

CAST

Grandpa	Jacques Dufilho
Pierre-Alain	Francois Cluzet
Anne Marie	Bernadette Le Sach

Left: Jacques Dufilho, Francois Cluzet

PATAKIN

(CINEMA GUILD) Director, Manuel Octavio Gomez; Screenplay, Manuel Octavio Gomez, Eugenio H. Espinosa; Photography, Luis Garcia Mesa; Story, Eugenio H. Espinosa; Editor, Justo Vega; Producer, Santiago Llapur; Music, Rembert Egues; Lyrics, Manuel Octavio Gomez; Choreography, Victor Cuellar; Costumes, Gabriel Hierrezuelo; Design, Manuel O. Gomez, Luis Lacosta; Cuba 1982; Spanish with English subtitles; In color; Not rated; 108 minutes; December release

CAST

Shango Valdes	Miguel Benavides
Candelaria	Assenah Rodriquez
Ogun Fernandez	Enrique Arredondo
Elegua	Litico Rodriguez
Caridad	Alina Sanchez
Nico	Carlos Moctezuma
Mercedes, Shango's Mother	Hilda Oates
Icu (Death)	Jorge Losada

and dancers from Danza Nacional de Cuba and Teatro Musical de la Habana, and musical groups Guaycan and Campo Alegre

Right Center: Miguel Benavides (center)
© Cinema Guild

Miguel Benavides, Assenah Rodriguez

Roger Moore, Anne Archer
in "The Naked Face" © *Cannon*

Nikolas Vogel, Roger Schauer
in "The Inheritors" © *Island Alive*

THE NAKED FACE (CANNON GROUP) Producers, Menahem Golan, Yoram Globus; Screenplay-Direction, Bryan Forbes; Based on the novel by Sidney Sheldon; Associate Producer, Rony Yacov; Music, Michael J. Lewis; Editor, Philip Shaw; Photography, David Gurfinkel; Designer, William Fosser; Production Manager; Assistant Directors, Richard Luke Rothschild, James Giovanetti, Jr.; Sound, Glen Williams; Costumes, J. Hurley, Sandra Davidson; Set, Ken Turek; Special Effects, Robert Shelley, Jr.; Metrocolor; Not rated; British; 105 minutes; January release. CAST: Roger Moore (Dr. Judd Stevens), Rod Steiger (Lt. McGreavy), Elliott Gould (Angeli), Art Carney (Morgens), Anne Archer (Ann Blake), David Hedison (Dr. Hadley), Deanna Dunagan (Mr. Hadley), Ron Parady (Cortini), Dick Sollenberger (Captain Martelli), James Spinks (Prison Supervisor), John Kapelos (Frank), Cynthia Baker Schuyler (Teri Goldman), Virginia Smith (Rose Graham), Joe D. Lauck (Boyd), Jimmie F. Skaggs (Fallon), Mary Demas (Policewoman), Frankie Hill (Carol), Nancy Serlin (Betty), Sarah Partridge (Waitress), Richard Burton Brown (Bartender), Sheila Keenan (Flower Seller), Roslyn Alexander (Lady in Elevator), Ron Hattie (Man in Elevator), Cyndi Maxey (Nurse), Rosemary Schoeninger (Prison Wardress), Jerry Tullos (Eddie), Edward L. Burba (Charley), Will Zahrn (Nick), and Paul Ilmer, Michael E. Meyers, Ann Bernadette Coyle, Rob Maxey, Les Podewell, John T. Stibich, Carmela Melendez, Richard Henael, Mark Houston, Jeffrey Feathergill, Jeff Jenkins, Corney Morgan, Martin Grace, Hank Baumert, Ed Fernandez, Jon Maldonado

THE PERILS OF GWENDOLINE IN THE LAND OF THE YIK YAK (Samuel Goldwyn) Producers, Jean-Claude Eleury, Serge Laski; Director-Screenplay, Just Jaeckin; Photography, Andre Domage; Music, Pierre Bachelet; Editor, Michele Boehm; Designer, Francoise Deleu; Art Director, Andrew Guerin; Costumes, Daniel Elis; Sound, Rene Levert, Michele Amsellem; Production Manager, Pierre Gauchet; Makeup, Reiko Kurk, Dominique Colladant; Dolby Stereo; France, 1984; Color; 88 minutes; Rated R; January release. CAST: Tawny Kitaen (Gwendoline), Brent Huff (Willard), Zabou (Beth), Bernadette Lafont (The Queen), Jean Rougerie (D'Arcy), and Roland Amstutz, Jean Stanislas Capoul, Chen Chang Ching, Vernon Dobtcheff, Andre Julien, Takashi Kawahara, Kristopher Kum, Loi Lam Duc, Maurice Lamy, Jim Adhi Limas, Georges Lycan, Dominique Marcas, Roger Paschy, Hua Quach

FALASHA: EXILE OF THE BLACK JEWS (Pan-Canadian) Producers, Matari Film, Simcha Jacobovici, Jamie Boyd; Associate Producer, Susan Price; Director-Writer, Simcha Jacobovici; Photography, Martin Duckworth, Peter Raymount; Editor, Roger Pyke; Music, Sara Jacobovici; Canadian; Documentary; Color; 72 minutes; January release

THE INHERITORS (Island Alive) Producer-Director, Walter Bannert; Screenplay, Walter Bannert, Eric A. Richter; Photography, Hanua Polak; Editor, Walter Bannert; Music, Gustav Mahler; Design, German Pizzini, Rudolf Czettel; Costumes, Regina Amon; Sound, Ekkehard Baumung; Special Effects, Willy Neuner; Production Manager, Gottfried A. Roeblreiter; Austria, 1983; German/English subtitles; 89 minutes; Not rated; January release. CAST: Nikolar Vogel (Thomas Feigl), Roger Schauer (Charly), Anneliese Stoeckl-Eberhard (Tomas' Mother), Jaromir Borek (Tomas' Father), Klaus Novak (Ernst), Johanna Tomek (Charly's Mother), Frank Dietrich (Charley's Father), Edd Stavjanik (Schweiger), Gabriele Bolen (Charley's Girlfriend), Titanila Kraus (Anna), Michael Janisch (Gunther), Wolfgang Gasser (Norbert Furst), Helmust Kahn (Speaker at Rally), Ottwald John (Camp Trainer), and Rudi Schippel, Gerlad Distl, Sascha Stein, Evelyn Faber, Guenter Treptow, Bernhard Werner, Alexander Wussow, Kurt Jaggberg, Gerhard Swoboda, Alexander Berg

THE SUN'S BURIAL (New Yorker) Producer, Shochiku; Director, Nagisa Oshima; Screenplay, Nagiza Oshima, Toshiro Ishido; Photography, Takashi Kawamata; Music, Riichiro Manabe; Japan, 1960; Color; 87 minutes; Not rated; January release. CAST: Kayoko Honoo (Hanako), Junzaburo Ban (Hanako's father), Jun Hamamura (The old soldier), Kei Sato (The doctor), Masahiko Tsugawa (Shin, the gang leader), Isao Sasaki (Takeshi), Yusuke Kawazu (Yasu), and Mutsuhiro Toura, Fumio Watanabe, Kamatari Fujiwara, Tanie Kitabayashi, Koji Nakahira

TRANSES (Jouve Interama) Producers, Izza Genini, Souhel Ben Barka; Director-Screenplay-Photography, Ahmed el-Maanouni; Editors, Jean-Clause Bonfanti, Atika Tahiri; Music, Nass el Ghiwane; Documentary; Arabic/English subtitles; 87 minutes; Not rated; January release. CAST: Boujema Hgour (Percussion), Omar Sayed (Percussions-Bendir), Allal Yaala (Banjo), Aberrahman Paco (Basse-Sentir), Larbi Batma (Percussion-Tbilat)

(center) Brent Huff, Tawny Kitaen
in "Perils of Gwendoline"
© *Samuel Goldwyn*

Masahiko Tsugawa, Mutsuhiro Toura, Isao
Sasaki, Kayoko Honoo in "The Sun's Burial"
© *New Yorker Films*

Donald Pleasence, Barry Crocker
in "Barry McKenzie Holds His Own"
© *Satori Entertainment*

Mia Nygren
in "Emmanuelle 4" © *Cannon*

BARRY McKENZIE HOLDS HIS OWN (Satori) Producer-Director-Writer, Bruce Beresford; Co-writer, Barry Humphries; Photography, Don McAlpine; Editor, William Anderson; Music, Peter Best; Design, John Stoddart; Australian; Not rated; 93 minutes; January release. CAST: Barry Crocker (Barry McKenzie/Kevin McKenzie), Barry Humphries (Edna Everage), Donald Pleasence (Count Plasma), Dick Bently (Col the Frog), Louis Negin (Hugo Cretin), Paul Humpoletz (Imbecile)

CAMMINACAMMINA (Grange Communications Inc./IFEX) Producer - Director - Screenplay - Photography - Editor - Designer - Costumes, Ermanno Olmi; Producer, RAI-Radiotelevisione Italiana-Scenario s.r.l.; Producer, Bruno Nicolai; Music, Bruno Nicolai; Executive Producer, Giancarlo Santi; RAI Executive Producer, Ludovica Alessandrini; Assistant Director, Marcello Siena; Sound, Amedeo Casati; Italy, 1983; Italian with subtitles; Color; 150 minutes; January release. CAST: (all actors are non-professional) Alberto Fumagalli (The priest Mel), Antonio Cucciarre (Rupo), Eligio Martellacci (Kaipaco), and Renzo Samminiatesi, Marco Bartolini, Lucia Peccianti, Guido Del Testa, Tersilio Cheilardini, Aldo Fanucci, Fernando Guarguaglini, Anna Vanni, Giulio Paradisi, Rosanna Cuffaro, Simone Migliorini, Stefano Ghelardini, Adelmo Mugnaini, Licurgo Londoni, Bruno Benini, Dina Bianchi, Nicola Pineschi, Marco Bertini, Vezio Gabellieri, Ivan Kioroglian, Alessandro Mazzupappa, Pietro Costantini, Alberto Nanni, Margherita Nanni, Mila Dell'Olmo, Viviana Baldeschi, Roberto Bartolini, Duilio Milianti, Giovanni Benassai, Italo Tertulliani, Rosario Bianchi, Cristina Morganti, Renato Bulleri, Alfredo Millo, Vasco Scali, Primo Giustarini, Giovanni Beccuzzi, Alvaro Carpietlli, Angelo Giani, Stefano Tonelli, Lodovico Viterbo, Gualtiero Varroni, Fabrizio Zucchelli, Michele Petternella, Giovanni Spinelli, Lucia Giannetti, Roberta Guazzini, Massimo Nencioni, Luigi Bulleri, Giancarlo Santi, Antonio Rocca, Vittorio Trinciarelli, Cianpaolo Lombardini, Gino Tempesti, Daniela Dell'Olmo, Caterina Zizi, Claudio Camerini

DEAR SUMMER SISTER (New Yorker Films) Producer, Sozosha/ATG Film; Director, Nagisa Oshima; Screenplay, Nagisa Oshima, Tsutomu Tamura, Mamoru Sasaki; Photography, Yasuhiro Yoshioka; Music, Toru Takemitsu; Japan, 1972; Color; 96 minutes; Not rated; January release. CAST: Hiromi Kurita (Sunaoko), Lily (Momoko) Hosei Komatsu (Kosuke Kikuchi), Akiko Koyama (Tsuru Omura), Shoji Ishibashi (Tsuruo), Kei Sato (Shinka Kuniyoshi), Taiji Tonoyama (Takuzo Sakurada), Mutsuhiro Toura (Rintoku Teruya)

EMMANUELLA 4 (CANNON GROUP) Producer, Alain Siritzky; Director, Francis Giacobetti; Screenplay, Francis Leroy, Iris Letans; Based on the Novel by Emmanuella Arsan; Music, Michel Magne; Production Manager, Christine Gozlan; Photography, Jean-Francis Gondre; Editor, Helene Plemianikov; Sound, Claude Gazeau; Make-up, Josee De Luca; Art Director, Jean Baptiste Poirot; Costumes, Laurence Heller; Color; French; Not rated; January release. CAST: Sylvia Kristel (Sylvia), Mia Nygren (Emmanuelle), Patrick Bauchau (Marc), Deborah Power (Donna), Sophie Berger (Maria), Sonia Martin (Suzanna), Dominique Troyes (Nadine), Gerard Dimiglio (Rodrigo), Gerard Antoine Huart (Nelson), Gilbert Grosso (Alfredo), Christopher Young (Miguel), Fabrice Luchini (Oswald), Stephens Trevor (Raul), Xavier Fultot (Rapist), David Jalil (Handsome Man), Isabelle Estelle (Marc's Secretary)

ESCAPE FROM THE BRONX (New Line Cinema) Producers, Fulvia Film S.r.l., Fabrizio De Angelis; Director, Enzo G. Castellari; Screenplay, Tito Carpi, Castellari; Story by Capri; Photography, Blasco Giurato; Editor, Gianfranco Amicucci; Music, Francesco De Masi; Design/Costumes, Giuseppe Giglietti; Special Effects, Corridori; Italian; Telecolor; 89 minutes; No rating; January release. CAST: Mark Gregory (Trash), Henry Silva (Wangler), Valeria D'Obici (Moon), Timothy Brent (Strike), and Paolo Malco, Thomas Moore, Antonio Sabato, Alessandro Prete, Massimo Vanni, Andrea Coppola, Eva Czemerys

THE EXTERMINATORS OF THE YEAR 3000 (New Line Cinema) Producers, 2T Produzione Film S.r.l (Rome)/Globe Film (Madrid), Ugo Tucci, Camillo Teti; Director, Jules Harrison; Screenplay, Elisa Briganti, Dardano Sacchetti, Jose Truchado Reyes; Photography, Alejandro Ulloa; Editor, Adriano Tagliavia; Music, Detto Mariano; Assistant Director, Geffredo Unger; Design, Enrico Fiorentini; Special Effects, Gino De Rossi, Edmondo Natali; Costumes, Luciana Marinucci; Italian-Spanish; Luciano Vittori color; 91 minutes; Rated R; January release. CAST: Robert Jannucci (Alien), Alicia Moro (Trash), Alan Collins (Papillion), Luca Ventantini (Tommy), Venantino Venantini (John), and Eduardo Fajardo, Fred Harris, Beryl Cunningham, Anna Orso, Sergio Mioni

Hiromi Kurita, Lily
in "Dear Summer Sister"
© *New Yorker Films*

"Cammina Cammina"
© *IFEX*

Jean-Hughes Anglade, Vittorio Mezzogiorno
in "L'Homme Blesse" © *Promovision*

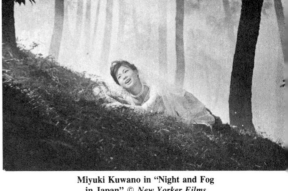

Miyuki Kuwano in "Night and Fog
in Japan" © *New Yorker Films*

'HOMME BLESSE (Promovision International) Presented by aumont, Ajo; Producers, a Partner's Production, Renn Productions, liane Productions Azor Films, FR 3 Production; Director, Patrice néreau; Screenplay, Herve Guilbert, Patrice Chereau; Photography, enato Berta; Designer, Richard Peduzzi; Producers, Marie-Laure eyre, Claude Berri, Ariel Zeitoun; French with subtitles; 89 minutes; o rating; January release. CAST: Jean-Huges Anglade (Henri), Vitrio Mezzogiorno (Jean), Roland Bertin (Bosmans), Lisa Kreuzer Elizabeth), Armin Müller-Stahl (The Father), Claude Berri (The lient), Gérard Desarthe (Man who cries), Annik Alane (The Mother), ammou Graîa (Young Man in the Station), Sophie Edmond (The ster), and Maria Verdi, Laurent De Berward, Suzanne Chavance, oland Chalosse, Charly Chemouni, Eddy Roos, Daniel Geiger, Rond Vargoz, Philippe Allaire, Franck Coquet, Francoise Maimone, se Gagnol, Patrice Finet, Denis Lavant

IOVING OUT (Satori) Producers, Jane Ballantyne, Michael Patnson; Director, Michael Pattinson; Screenplay, Jan Sardi; Associate roducer, Julie Monton; Editor, Robert Martin; Songs, Umberto Tozzi, iancarlo Bigazzi; Music, Danny Beckerman; Designer, Neil Angwin; notography, Vincent Monton; Color; Australian; No rating; 91 inutes; January release. CAST: Vince Colosimo (Gino), Maurice evincentis (Renato), Tibor Gyapjas (Allan), Sally Cooper (Sandy), esiree Smith (Helen), Nicole Miranda (Maria), Santina Failla (Fran), Julia Dalleore (Pippo), Peter Sardi (Gino's father), Kate Jason Gino's mother), Brian James (Mr. Aitkens), Sandy Gore (Miss Stanis-us), Ivar Kants (Mr. Clarke)

HE MYSTERY OF ALEXINA (European Classics) Producerirector, Rene Feret; Screenplay, Jean Gruault, Rene Feret; Photograny, Bernard Zittermann; Sound, Michel Brethez; Editor, Ariane oeglin; Sets, Georges Stoll, Isabelle Manescau; Costumes, Isabelle lanescau; Music, Anne-Marie Deschamps; Assistant Director, Henri rimault; Associate Producer, Marc Thiebault; French with subtitles; olor; 86 minutes; Not rated; January release. CAST: Vuillemin (Alexa/Camille), Valerie Stroh (Sara), Veronique Silver (Madame Avril), ernard Freyd (Armand), Marianne Basler (Marie Avril), Pierre Vial riest), Philippe Clevenot (Dr. Chesnet), Isabelle Gruault (Josephine), ucienne Hamon, Michel Amphoux (Hotel Managers), Claude Bouchry (Inspector), Olivier Sabran (Doctor), Anne Cornaly (Mother), and e Children of Brou sur Chantereine

NIGHT AND FOG IN JAPAN (New Yorker) Producer, Shochiku Studios; Director, Nagisa Oshima; Screenplay, Nagisa Oshima, Toshiro Ishido; Photography, Takashi Kawamuta; Music, Riichiro Manabe; Japan, 1960; Color; 107 minutes; Not rated; January release. CAST: Miyuki Kuwano (Reiko), Fumio Watanabe (Heruaki), Masahiko Tsugawa (Ota), Hiroshi Akutagawa (Udagawa), Akiko Koyama (Misako), Mutsuhiro Toura (Toura), Kei Sato (Sakamaki)

THE CLAW AND THE TOOTH (Nicole Jouve Interama) Producer, Les Cineastes Animaliers Associes; Directors-Photography, Francois Bel, Gerard Vienne; Sound Composer, Michel Fano; Editor, Jacqueline LeCompte; Sound, Francois Bel, Pierre Ley; Production Manager, Walter Spohr; Assistant Director, Bruno Vienne; Assistant Editor, Catherine Mauchain; Wildlife Documentary; France; Color; Stereo; 98 minutes; Not rated; January release.

WATER (Rank) Producer, Ian LaFrenais; Co-producer, David Wimbury; Executive Producers, George Harrison, Denis O'Brien; Director, Dick Clement; Screenplay, Dick Clement, Ian LaFrenais, Bill Persky; Photography, Douglas Slocombe; Design, Norman Garwood; Costumes, Jim Acheson; Editor, John Victor Smith; Music, Mike Moran; British in color; Not rated; 95 minutes; February release. CAST: Michael Caine (Baxter), Valerie Perrine (Pamela), Brenda Vaccaro (Bianca), Billy Connolly (Delgado), Leonard Rossiter (Sir Malcom), Maureen Lipman (Prime Minister), Dennis Dugan (Rob), Fulton Mackay (Eric), Chris Tummings (Garfield), Trevor Laird (Pepto), Kevin Olmaro (Nado), Oscar James (Miguel), Stefan Kalipha (Angola), Alan Ibgon (Jesus), Fred Gwynne (Industrialist)

NO HARVEST BUT A THORN (Kay) Producers, Kamarul Ariffin, Sarimah; Direction-Screenplay, Jamil Sulong; Photography, Johan Ibraham; Editor, Johari Ibrahim; Music, Ooi Eow Jin; In color and widescreen; Malaysian; Not rated; 101 minutes; February release. CAST: Ahmad Mahmood (Lahuma), Sarimah (Jeha), Puteri Salbiah (Sanah), Noraishas (Milah), Rohayatie (Jenab), Marlia (Semek), Malissa (Liah), Rosmawaite (Lebar/Kiah)

ALLONSANFAN Directors, Paolo, Vittorio Taviani; Italian with subtitles; 115 minutes; Not rated; CAST: Marcello Mastroianni, Laura Betti

Vuillemin, Valerie Stroh
in "The Mystery of Alexina"
© *European Classics*

Maurice DeVincentis, Tibor Gyapjas, Vince
Colosimi in "Moving Out"
© *Satori Entertainment*

Jon Blake in "Freedom"
© *Satori Entertainment*

Corin Redgrave (R) in "Between Wars"
© *Satori Entertainment*

BETWEEN WARS (Satori) Producer-Director, Michael Thornhill; Screenplay, Frank Moorhouse; Photography, Russell Boyd; Editor, Max Lemon; Designer, Bill Hutchinson; Music, Bill Hasler, Romola Constantina, Adrian Ford; Costumes, Marilyn Kippax; Sound, Ken Hammond; Associate Producer, Hal McElroy; Australian; Color; 97 minutes; Not rated; February release. CAST: Corin Redgrave (Dr. Edward Trenbow), Arthur Dignam (Dr. Peter Avante), Judy Morris (Deborah Trenbow), Patricia Leehy (Marguerite Saunders), Gunter Meisner (Dr. Karl Schneider), Brian James (Father), Jan Winchester (Mother), Reg Gillam (Trenbow Sr.), Betty Lucas (Mrs. Trenbow), Peter Cummins (Steele), John Morris (Superintendent), Martin Harris (Hook)

THE CLINIC (Satori) Producers, Robert Le Tet, Bob Weis; Director, David Stevens; Screenplay, Greg Millin; Photography, Ian Baker; Designer, Tracy Watt; Editor, Edward McQueen-Mason; Australian; 93 minutes; Not rated; February release. CAST: Chris Haywood (Eric Linden), Simon Burke (Paul Armstrong), Gerda Nicolson (Linda), Rona McLeod (Carol), Suzanne Royland (Pattie), Veronica Lang (Nancy), Pat Evison (Aldo), Max Bruch (Hassad), Gabrielle Hartley (Gillian), Jane Clifton (Sharon)

THE DEATH OF MARIO RICCI (New Line) Producers, Daniel Messere, Norbert Chalon; Director-Screenplay, Claude Goretta; Associate Producers, Herbert Kloibert, Yves Gasser; Photography, Hans Liechti; Designer, Yanko Hodjis; Editor, Joele Van Effenterre; Sound, Daniel Ollivier; Music, Arie Dzierlatka, Orchestre Osmose, Christian Bonneau; A French-Swiss co-production; 100 minutes; Not rated; February release. CAST: Gian-Maria Volonte (Bernard Fontana), Magali Noel (Solange), Heinz Bennet (Henri), Mimsy Farmer (Cathy), Jean-Michel Dupuis (Didier), Michel Robin (Fernand), Lucas Belvaux (Tephane), Claudio Caramaschi (Giuseppe), Michel Cassagne (Armand), Michael Hinz (Otto), Marblum Jequier (Odette), Jean-Claude Perrin (Edgar), Andre Schmidt (Maurice), Bernard Soufflet (Gerard), Roger Jendly (Francis), Bernard Pierre Donnadieu (Jacky), Claude Inga Barbey (Sylvia), Francois Berthet (The Cameraman), Edmee Crozet (Suzanna), Gerard Despierre (Angelo), Neige Dolsky (Mathilde), Anne Lise Fritsch (Gisele), Michelle Gleizer (Jeanine), Alfredo Gnasso (Pietro), Jean-Pierre Gos (Ficelle), Arthur Grosjean (Alexis)

FAVORITES OF THE MOON (Spectrafilm) Producers, Philippe Dussart Productions, the French Minister of Culture, RAI-TVI; Director, Otar Ioseliani; Screenplay, Ioseliani, Gerard Brach; Photography, Philippe Theaudiere; Sound, Alix Comte, Claude Bertrand, Jacque Maumont; Music, Nicolas Zourabichvil; Artistic Collaboration, Catherine Foulon, Dimitri Eristavi, Leila Naskidachvil; Editor, Dominique Bellfort; Production Manager, Michel Choquet; Associate Producer, Pierre Andre Boutang; French, 1984; Color; 101 minutes; Not rated; February release. CAST: Alix de Montaigu (Delphine Laplace), Pascal Aubier (Monsieur Laplace), Gaspard Flori (Christian Laplace), Emilie Aubry (Lucie Laplace), Hans Peter Cloos (Monsieur Duphour-Paquet), Maite Nahyr (Madeline Duphour-Paquet), Baptiste Blanche (Marc Duphour-Paquet), Jean-Pierre Beauviala (Colas), Mathieu Amalric (Julien), Christiane Bailly (Agnes), Rene Vo Van Mind (Jean), Katja Rupe (Claire), Bernard Eisenschitz (Gustave), Francoi Michel (Philippe), Fanny Dupin (Riviere), Vincent Blanchet (Pluton), Gabriella Scheer (Nicole), Marie-Claude Povesle (Christine), Mari Parra Aledo (Blanche)

FREEDOM (Satori) Producer, Matt Carrol; Director, Scott Hicks; Screenplay, John Emery; Script Editor, Graeme Koetsveld; Photography, Ron Johanson; Production Manager, Valerie Hardy; Designer, Herbert Pinter; Music, Cold Chisel; Executive Producer, Jim George; Australian; 100 minutes; Not rated; February release. CAST: Jon Blake (Ron), Candy Raymond (Annie), Jad Capelja (Sally), Charles "Bud" Tingwell (Cassidy), Chris Haywood (Phil), Reg Lye (Old Farmer)

HOUSE ON THE EDGE OF THE PARK (Bedford Entertainment Trio Entertainment) Producers, F. D. Cinematografica, Franco Palaggi, Franco Di Nunzio; Director, Ruggero Deodato; Screenplay, Gianfranco Clerici, Vincenzo Mannini; Photography, Sergio D'Offizi; Editor, Vincenzo Tomassi; Music, Riz Ortolani; Designer-Costumes, M. A. Geleng; Lúciano Vittori color; 91 minutes; Not rated; February release. CAST: David Hess (Alex), Annie-Belle (Lisa), John Morghe (Ricky), Lorraine De Selle (Gloria), and Christian Borromeo, Mari Claude Joseph

LADIES ON THE ROCKS (New Yorker) Producer, The Danish Film Institute; Director, Christian Braad Thomsen; Screenplay, Helle Ryslinge, Anne Marie Helger, Mr. Thomsen; Photography, Dirk Bruel, Fritz Schroder; Music, Helle Ryslinge, Parvion; In Danish with subtitles; 100 minutes; Not rated; February release. CAST: Helle Ryslinge (Micha), Anne Marie Helger (Laura), Flemming Quist Moller (Lennart), Hans Herik Clemmensen (Hans-Henrik)

"Favorites of the Moon"
© *International Spectrafilm*

Helle Ryslinge, Anne Marie Helger
in "Ladies on the Rocks"

Keiko Kishi, Koji Ishizaka, Yoshiko Sakuma,
Yuko Kotegawa, Sayuri Yoshinaga in "The
Makioka Sisters" © *Michael Jeck*

Tomasz Hudziec in "Shivers"
© *New Yorker Films*

THE MAKIOKA SISTERS (Michael Jeck) Producers, Tomoyuki Tanaka, Kon Ichikawa; Director, Kon Ichikawa; Screenplay, Shinya Hidaka, Kon Ichikawa; From the novel by Junichiro Tanizaki; Photography, Kiyoshi Hasegawa; Music, Sinnosuke Okawa; Designer, Shinou Muraki; Sound, Tetsuya Ohashi; Lighting, Kojiro Sato; Editor, Chizuko Nagata; Costumes, Hiroshi Saito; An R5/S8 Presentation; Japanese with subtitles; Color; 140 minutes; Not rated; February release. CAST: Keiko Kishi (Tsuruko), Yoshiko Sakuma (Sachiko), Sayuri Yoshinaga (Yukiko), Yuko Kotegawa (Taeko), Koji Ishizaka (Teinosuke), Juzo Itami (Tatsuo), Ittoku Kishibe (Itakura), Kobaicho Katsura (Okubata), Motoshi Egi (Higashidani), Shoji Kobayashi (Mr. Imba), Kazunga Tsuji (Miyoshi), Fujio Tsuneda (Igarashi), Jun Hamamura (Otokichi), Kazuyo Kozaka (Nomura), Michiyo Yokoyama (Itani), Kuniko Miyake (Aunt Tominaga), Akemi Negishi (Mrs. Shimozuna), Toshiyuki Hosokawa (Hashidera)

SHIVERS (New Yorker) Producers, The Polish Corp. for Film Production "Zespoly Filmowe"; Director-Screenplay, Woiciech Marcewski; Photography, Jerzy Zielinski; Music, Andrzei Trzaskowski; Polish with subtitles; Poland, 1981; Awarded a Silver Bear at the Berlin Film Festival, 1982; 106 minutes; Not rated; February release. CAST: Tomasz Hudziec, Teresa Marczewska, Merek Kondrat, Zdzislaw Warlein, Teresa Sawicka, Jerzy Binnczycki, Bogdan Koca, Zygmunt Bielawski

SURE DEATH (Shochiku Co., Ltd.) Producers, Hisashi Yamaouchi, Yozo Sakura, Yoshiki Nomura; Director, Masahisa Sadanaga; Screenplay, Tatsuo Nogami, Go Yoshida; Photography, Ko Ishihara; Music, Masaaki Hirao; Designer, Nobutaka Yoshino; Color; 124 minutes; Rated R; February release. CAST: Makoto Fujita (Mondo Nakamura), Isuzu Yamada (Oriku), Kunihiko Mitamura (Hide), Izumi Iyukawa (Kayo), Kiyoshi Nakajo (Yuji), Gannousuke Ashiya (Masa), Naoko Ken (Oyone), Yukiji Asaoka (Oko), Toshiro Ishido (Shobei), Kie Nakai (Oyo), Takao Kataoka (Asanosuke), Kin Sugai (Sen), Mari Shiraki (Ritsu)

CHAO PANTIN (European Classics) Producer, Renn productions; Director, Claude Berri; Screenplay, Alain Page, Claude Berri; Photography, Bruno Nuytten; Editor, Herve De Luze; Music, Charlelie Couture; French; 100 minutes; Not rated. CAST: Coluche (Lambert), Richard Anconina (Bensoussan), Agnes Sorai (Lola), Philippe Leotard (Bauer)

ARTIE SHAW: TIME IS ALL YOU'VE GOT (Telefilm Canada) Producer-Director-Screenplay, Brigitte Berman; Associate Producer, Don Haig; Photography, Mark Irwin, Jim Aquila; Editors, Brigitte Berman, Barry Backus; Music, Artie Shaw and others; In color, black and white; Not rated; 114 minutes; March release. A documentary cataloging the life and music of the band leader and clarinettist.

AN UNSUITABLE JOB FOR A WOMAN (Castle Hill) Producers, Michael Relph, Peter McKay; Director, Christopher Petit; Screenplay, Elizabeth McKay, Brian Scobie, Mr. Petit; based on the novel by P. D. James; Photography, Martin Schafer; Music, Chas Jankel, Philip Bagenal, Peter VanHooke; Executive Producer, Don Boyd; 90 minutes; Not Rated; March release. CAST: Billie Whitelaw (Elizabeth Leaming), Paul Freeman (James Callender), Pippa Guard (Cordelia Gray), Dominic Guard (Andrew Lunn), Elizabeth Spriggs (Miss Markland), David Horovitch (Sergeant Maskell), Dawn Archibald (Isobel)

THE HOMEFRONT (Homefront) Produced-Directed-Written by Steven Schechter; Coproducer, Mark Jonathan Harris; Executive Producer, Jack Kaufman; Editor, Ron Brody; Associate Producer-Historian, Franklin D. Mitchell; In color, black and white; Not rated; 89 minutes; March release. CAST: Leslie Nielsen (Narrator)

MY NEW PARTNER (Orion) Producer, Films 7; Director, Claude Zidi; Screenplay-Adaption, Mr. Zidi; Photography, Jean-Jacques Tarbes; Editor, Nicole Saunier; French with subtitles; 107 minutes; Rated R; March release. CAST: Philippe Noiret (Rene), Thierry Lhermitte (Francois), Regine (Simone), Grace D. Capitani (Natacha), Julien Guiomar (Commissaire Bioret), Claude Brosset (Inspecteur Vidal), Albert Simono (Inspecteur Leblanc), Bernard Bijaoui (Camoun), Pierre Frag (Pierrot), Jacques Santi (Inspecteur de l'I.G.S.)

THE CARE BEARS MOVIE (Samuel Goldwyn) Producers, Michael Hirsh, Patrick Loubert, Clive Smith; Director, Arna Selznick; Screenplay, Peter Sauder; Music, John Sebastian, Carole King, Walt Woodward; a Nelvana Production; Animated; Color; 75 minutes; Canadian; Rated G; March release. VOICES: Mickey Rooney (Mr. Cherrywood), Georgia Engel (Love-a-Lot Bear), Harry Dean Stanton (Brave Heart Lion)

Coluche, Agnes Soral
in "Tchao Pantin"
© *European Classics*

Kim and Jason and the Care Bears
in "The Care Bears Movie"
© *Samuel Goldwyn Co.*

205

Lenore Zann, Tim Choate, Maury Chaykin
in "Def-Con 4" © *New World Pictures*

"In the Name of the People"
© *Icarus Films*

DEF-CON 4 (New World) formerly "Ground Zero"; Producers, B. A. Gillian, Maura O'Connell, Paul Donovan; Director-Screenplay, Paul Donovan; Designers, J. W. Walch, Emanuel Jannasch; Photography, Doug Connell, Les Krizan; Editors, Michael Spence, Todd Ramsay; Music, Chris Young; 90 minutes; Canadian; Rated R; March release. CAST: Jeff Pustil (Lacey), Donna King (Alice), Allan MacBillivray (Boomer), Florence Paterson (Mrs. Boyd), Karen Kenedy (WWN Newscaster), and Ken Ryan, Geoff Harrington, Al Foster, Hugh Orr, Bruce Piercy, Peter Falconer

IMPERATIVE (Teleculture) Producer, Telefilm Saar; Director-Screenplay, Krzystof Zanussi; Photography, Slavomir Idaziak; Editor, Liesgret Schmitt-Kink; Music, Wojciech Kilar; West German, 1982; Venice Special Jury Prize; Black and white and color; 96 minutes; Not rated; March release. CAST: Robert Powell (Augustin), Brigitte Fossey (Yvonne), Sigfrit Steiner (Professor), Matthias Habich (Theologist), Leslie Caron (Mother)

IN THE NAME OF THE PEOPLE (Icarus Films) Producers, Alex W. Drehsler, Frank Christopher; Director-Editor, Frank Christopher; Associate Producer, Isaac Artenstein; Written by Alex W. Drehsler; Photography, John Chapman; Sound, Doug Bruce; Music, El Grupo Insurecto de Guazapa; Documentary from El Salvador; 73 minutes; Not rated; March release. Narrator, Martin Sheen

MAKE-UP (Shochiku) "Kesho"; Executive Producer, Masatake Wakita; Director, Kazuo Ikehiro; Screenplay, Yozo Tanaka, Keiji Nagao; Based on a novel by Junichi Watanabe; Photography, Noritaka Sakamoto; Designers, Yoshinobu Nishioka, Shigemori Shigeta; Music, Shigeru Ikeno; CAST: Keiko Matsuzaka (Yoriko), Kimiko Ikegami, Yuuko Kazu (Makiko), Machiko Kyo (Tsune), Akira Emoto (Kikuo), Kiichi Nakai (Kusaka), Juzo Itami (Kumakura), Muga Takewaki (Shiina), Akira Nakao (Akiyama)

UP TO A CERTAIN POINT (New Yorker) "Hasta Cierto Punto"; Producer, Humberto Hernandez; Director, Tomas Gutierrez Alea; Screenplay, Juan Carlos Tabio, Serafin Quinones, Tomas Gutierrez Alea; Photography, Mario Garcia Joya; Designer, Jose Manuel Villa; Editor, Mirian Talavera; Music, Leo Brouwer; Orquesta Sinfonica Nacional under the direction of Manuel Duchesne Cuzan; Cuban, 1983;

Spanish with subtitles; Color; 88 minutes; Not rated. CAST: Osca: Alvarez (Oscar), Mirta Ibarra (Lina), Omar Valdes (Arturo), Corali Veloz (Marian), Rogelio Blain (Diego), Ana Vina (Flora), Claudio A Tamayo (Claudio), Luis Celeiro (Quinones), Elsa Medina (Vecina Marisela Justiz (Obrera)

WEST INDIES (Mypheduh Films Inc.) Producers, Les Films Sole O, in association with Yanek Services Ltd., Societe Interafricaine d Production Cinemagraphique, Radiodiffusion Television Algerienne Office National de Cinema Mauritanien; Director-Screenplay, Me Hondo; Based on the book "Les Negriers" by Daniel Boukman; Photog raphy, Francois Cartonne; Editor, Youcef Tobni; Music, George Rabol; French with subtitles; French, 1979, 125 minutes; Not rated CAST: Jenny Alpha, Roland Bertin, Gerlad Bloncourt, Philipp Clovernot, Jean Paul Denizon, Gabriel Glissant, Georges Hilarion Kassimo Sterling, Theo Legitimus, Robert Liensol, Elliot Roy, T Emile, Helene Vincent

TELL THEM NOT TO KILL ME (University of Andes) Executiv Producer, Maria Saldvia; Direction-Screenplay, Edited by Fredd Sosp; Based on story by Juan Rulfo; Photography, Mario Robles; 〡 color; Venezuelan; Not rated; 98 minutes; March release. No othe credits.

MISSISSIPPI BLUES (Film Forum) Produced by William Ferris; A film by Bertrand Tavernier and Robert Parrish; Photography, Pierre William Glenn; Editor, Ariane Boeglin; Presented by Tavernier a Yannick Bernard, Les Films A2, the University of Mississipp Documentary; French with subtitles; 96 minutes; Not Rated; Marc release.

MY BROTHER'S WEDDING presented by the Film Society o Lincoln Center and the Department of Film of the Museum of Moder Art; Producers, Charles Burnett, Gaye Shannon-Burnett; Director Screenplay-Photography, Charles Burnett; Editor, Tom Pennick; Mu sic, Johnny Ace, John Briggs; 120 minutes; Not Rated; March release CAST: Everett Silas (Pierce Mundy), Jessie-Holmes (Mrs. Mundy Gaye Shannon-Burnett (Sonia), Ronnie Bell (Soldier Richards), Den nis Kemper (Wendell Muncy), Sy Richardson (Father), Frances Nea (Mother)

Oscar Alvarez, Mirta Ibarra
in "Up to a Certain Point"
© *New Yorker Films*

"Make-Up"
© *Scochiku*

Arnon Zadok, Muhamad Bakri
in "Beyond the Walls" © *Warner Bros.*

"All My Good Countrymen"

THE LITTLE SISTER (American Playhouse) Producer, Steve Wax; Direction-Screenplay, Jan Egleson; Photography, Ed Lachman; Editor, Tanya Polonsky; Music, Pat Metheny; In DuArt Color; Not rated; 103 minutes; March release. CAST: John Savage (Tim Donovan), Tracy Pollan (Nicki Davis), Roxanne Hart (Sarah), Jack Kehoe, Henry Tomaszewski, Richard Jenkins

LA SEGUA (Cinematograficia Costarricense) Producer, Oscar Castillo; Executive Producer, Alvaro Sancho; Director, Antonio Yglesias; Screenplay, Alberto Canas, Antonio Yglesias, Sidney Field; Based on play by Alberto Canas; Photography, Mario Cardona; Editor, Rafael Ceballos; Design, Jean Moulaert; Music, Benjamin Gutierrez, Orlando Garcia; In color; Not rated; Costa Rican; 102 minutes; March release. CAST: Isabel Hidalgo (Encarnacion Sancho), Blanca Guerra (Petronial, Oscar Castillo, Ana Poltronieri, Fresia Astica, Rafa Rojas, Alfredo Catania, Fernando del Castillo, Ana Maria Barrlonucevo, Luis A. Chocano, Carlos Catania, Orlando Garcia, William Ziniga, Marcelo Johnson

BLUE MONEY (London Weekend Blue Money) Producer, Juen Roberts, Jo Apted; Executive Producer, Nick Elliott; Director, Colin Bucksey; Screenplay, Stewart Parker; Photography, Peter Jessop; Editor, Ron Costelloe; Music, Richard Hartley; Design, Mike Oxley; Costumes, Brenda Fox; In Rank Color; Not rated; British; 85 minutes; March release. CAST: Tim Curry (Larry Gormley), Debby Bishop (Pam Hodge), Billy Connolly (Des), Dermot Crowley (Brogan), Frances Tomelty (Fidelma)

THE WHEEL Producer, Chung Wung-ki; Director, Lee Doo-yong; Screenplay, Lim Chung; Photography, Lee Sung-choon; Editor, Lee Kyung-ja; Music, Chung Yun-ji; Korean with subtitles; 100 minutes; Not Rated; April release. CAST: Won Mi-kyung (Gil-rye), Shin Il-yong (Yun-po), Ch'oe Song-kwan (Mun Chong-suk Wife), Pak Min-ho (Ho'oe Chin-sa), Ch'oe Song-ho (Yun Pa-sa), Mun Mi-pong (Wife), Hyon Kil-su (Man-sang), Chong Kyu-yong (Salt Trader)

WHERE'S PICONE? (Italtoons) Producer, Gianni Minervini; Director, Nanni Loy; Screenplay, Elvio Porta, Mr. Loy; Based on an idea by Mr. Loy; Photography, Claudio Cirillo; Music, Tullio de Piscopo; Editor, Franco Fraticelli; Italian with subtitles; Color; 112 minutes; Not rated; April release. CAST: Giancarlo Giannini (Salvatore), Lina Sastri (Luciella), Clelia Rondinella (Teresa), Carlo Croccolo (Baron Armato), Marzio C. Honorato (Micone), Armando Marra (Troncone), Mario Santella (Severino), Carlo Taranto (Gallina), Gerardo Scala (Gennaro), Nicola di Pinto (Cametta), Leo Gullotta (Sgueglia), Aldo Giuffre (Coco)

ALL MY GOOD COUNTRYMEN (Film Forum) Director-Screenplay, Vojtech Jasny; Photography, Jaroslav Kucera; Music, Svatopluk Havelka; Czech, 1968, Banned in its native country; Color; 126 minutes; Not rated; April release. CAST: Rodoslav Brozobohaty, Vladimir Mensik, Vlastermil Brodsky

BEYOND THE WALLS (Warner Bros.) Producer, Rudy Cohen; Director, Uri Barbash; Screenplay, Benny Barbash, Eran Pries, Uri Barbash; Photography, Amnon Salomon; Editor, Tova Asher; Music, Ilan Virtzberg; Hebrew with subtitles; Israeli; 103 minutes; Rated R; April release. CAST: Arnon Zadok (Uri), Muhamed Bakri (Issam), Assi Dayan (Assaf), Rami Danon (Fittusi), Boaz Sharaabi (The Nightingale), Adib Jahashan (Walid), Roberto Polak (Yechiel), Haim Shinar (Hoffman), Naffi Salach (Sanji), Loueteof Noussir (Fatchi)

BREAKING ALL THE RULES (New World) Executive Producer, Robert Cooper; Director, James Orr; Screenplay, James Orr, James Cruickshank; Story, Rafal Zielinski, Edith Rey; Production Manager, Lyse LaFontaine; Co-Producers, Pierre David, Pieter Kroonenburg, David J. Patterson; Assistant Directors, David McLeod, Frank Ruszczynski, Val Stefoff; Photography, Rene Verzier; Costumes, Laurie Drew; Editors, Nick Rotundo, Janet Lazare; Color; Canadian; 90 minutes; Rated R; April release. CAST: Carl Marotte (Jack), Thor Bishopric (David), Carolyn Dunn (Debbie), Rachel Hayward (Angie), Michael Rudder (Harry), Papusha Demitro (Patty), Pierre Andre Larocoque (Babyface), Walter Massey (Charlie), Vlasta Vrana (Detective), Eve Napier (Emma), Michele Scarabelli (Rachel), Jerome Tigerghien (Frank), Bob Pierson (Tony), Tiffany Silverman (Sister), Lilian Horowitz (Mother), Daniel Nalbach (Father), Susanne De Laurentis (Cindy), Donny Silverman (Nerd), and Brigitte Boulet, Allan Katz, Judy Gault, Derek McKinnon, Babs Gadbois, Aaron Rand, David Sisak, Jaine Marzan, Martine Mayer, Winston Wood, Arthur Grosser, Ceil Bruessing, Lionel-Nicolas Etienne, Rebecca Dewey

HOLI, a Film Unit Production; Director, Ketan Mehta; Screenplay, Mahesh Elkunchwar; Photography, Jehangir Chaudhary; Editor, Subhash Sehgai; Music, Rajat Dholakia; Hindi with subtitles; 120 minutes; Not Rated; April release. CAST: Sanjeev Gandhi, Rahul Ranade, Asutosh Gowarikar, Amol Gupte, Naseeruddin Shah, Om Puri, Deepti Naval, Dr. Shreeram Lagoo

Rachel Hayward, Carolyn Dunn
in "Breaking All the Rules"
© *New World*

Thor Bishopric, Carl Marotte
in "Breaking all the Rules"
© *New World*

"The Illusionist"
© Castle Hill

Oleg Yankovsky, Yevgenia Clushenko
"In Love at His Own Choice"
© IFEX

HOMECOMING (Floreal Company) Producers, Bluebird Movie Enterprises Ltd., Target Film Company Ltd.; Director, Yim Ho; Screenplay, Kong Liang; Photography, Poon Hang Sang; Editor, Kin Kin; Music, Kitaro; Chinese with subtitles; Color; 96 minutes; Not Rated; April release. CAST: Si Qin Gao Wa (Shan Shan), Josephine Koo (Ah Zhen), Xie Wei Xiong (Tsong), Zhou Yun (Zhong), Zhang Ju Goa (Tiao), Ye Wai Zheng (Qiong), Ceng Yu (Beannie)

THE ILLUSIONIST (Film Forum) Producers, Big Boy Productions, Stanley Hillebrandt; Director, Jos Stelling; Screenplay, Freek De Jong, Jos Stelling; Photography, Theo Van De Sande; Music, Willem Breuker; Dutch; Awarded The Golden Calf for Best Feature, Utrecht Film Festival, 1984; Color; Widescreen; 90 minutes; Not Rated; April release. CAST: Freek De Jonge, Jim Van Der Woude, Catrien Wolthuizen, Gerard Thoolen

IN LOVE AT HIS OWN CHOICE (International Film Exchange) Producer, Lenfilm; Director, Sergei Mikaelyan; Screenplay, Sergei Mikaelyan, Alexander Vasinsky; Photography, Sergei Astakhov; Designer, Alexei Rudyakov; Music, Igor Tsvetkov; a Sovexportfilm; Russian with subtitles; Color; 88 minutes; Not Rated; April release. CAST: Oleg Yankovsky, Yevgenia Glushenko, Vsevolod Shilovsky, Irina Reznikova

ORNETTE: MADE IN AMERICA (Caravan of Dreams) Producer, Kathelin Hoffman; Directed and Edited by Shirley Clarke; Photography, Ed Lachman; Music, Ornette Coleman; In color; Not rated; April release. A documentary about Ornette Coleman and his hometown.

MANCHURIAN AVENGER (Facet) Executive Producer, Timothy Stephenson; Producer, Robyn Bensinger; Director, Ed Warnick; Screenplay, Pat Hamilton; From story by Richard Kim; Photography, Rich Lerner; Editor, Hal Freeman; Music, Paul Conly; Assistant Director, Don Rase; Art Director, Sarah Liles; Associate Producer, M. J. Studer; In Western Cine Color; Rated R; 81 minutes; April release. CAST: Bobby Kim (Joe), Bill Superfoot Wallace (Kamikaze), Michael Stuart (Diego), Leila Hee (Booyong), Jose Payo (Kilo), Bob Coulson (Harry), Barbara Minardi (Maria), Y. Tsuchimoto, Steven Harp, Larry Shephard, Song Padulla, Rich Occhuzzio, Karl Niccoletti, Jerry Witt, Sy Meheen

OUR MARRIAGE Producer, Les Films du Passage; Director, Valeria Sarimento; Screenplay, Valeria Sarimento, Raoul Ruiz; From the novel "Mi Bodo Contigo" by Corin Tellado; Photography, Acacio de Almeda; Editor, Claudio Martinez, Martine Bouquin; Music, Jorge Arriada; French with subtitles; 90 minutes; Not Rated; April release. CAST Nicolas Silberg, Nadege Clair, Jean-Pierre Teilhade, Maude Raye Aurelie Chazelie

PETIT CON (Samuel Goldwyn) Producer, Marcel Dassault; Director, Gerard Lauzier; Screenplay, Gerard Lauzier, based on his Book "Souvenirs d'un Jeune Homme"; Photography, Jean-Paul Schwart Editor, Georges Klotz; Music, Vladimir Cosma; French with subtitle Color; 90 minutes; Rated R; April release. CAST: Bernard Brie (Michel), Buy Marchand (Bob), Caroline Cellier (Annie), Eric Carl (Alain), Claudine Delvaux (Maryse), Pierre Fayet (Rene), Josia Balasko (Rolande)

SELF DEFENSE (New Line Cinema) Producers, Paul Donova Michael Donovan, John Walsch, Maura O'Connell; Directors, Pa Donovan, Maura O'Connell; Screenplay, Paul Donovan; Canadia Color; 85 minutes; Rated R; April release. CAST: Tom Nardini (Hor tio), Brenda Bazinet (Barbara), Doug Lennox (Cabe), Darel Haer (Chester), Terry Despres (Daniel), Jeff Pustil (Goose)

THE STREET OF DESIRES (Shochiku Co., Ltd.) Producer Yoshitaro Nomura, Nobutoshi Masumoto; Director, Haruhiko Mimura; Screenplay, Haruhiko Mimura, Shigero Nakakura, Tai Kato, Yosh taro Nomura; Story, Seicho Matsumoto; Photography, Mitsus Hanada; Designer, Yutaka Yokoyama; Music, Hajima Kaburag Japanese; Color 135 minutes; Rated R; April release. CAST: Hiroyu Sanada (George), Yuko Natori (Fumi), Mikijiro Hira (Shojiro), Sak toshi Yonekura (Shirota), Isao Natsuki (Hideo), Makoto Sa (Kyosuke), Kazuko Yoshiyuki (Kasuko), Tsunehiko Watase (Sada chi), Rentaro Mikuni (Tadao)

TOKYO-GA (Gray City) Producer, Chris Sievernich; Directo Screenplay, Wim Wenders; Photography, Ed Lachman; Editors, Jo Neuburger, Mr. Wenders, Solveig Dommartin; Music, "Dick Tracy Loorie Petitgand, Meche Mamecier, Chico Rogo Ortega; Japanes 1983; Color; 92 minutes; Not Rated; April release. CAST: Chishu Ry Yuharu Atsuta, Werner Herzog

Brenda Bazinet, Tom Nardini
in "Self Defense" © New Line Cinema

Chishu Ryu in "Tokyo-Ga"
© Gray City

"The Street of Desires"
© *Shochiku Co.*

Julie Hagerty (L) in "Goodbye,
New York" © *Castle Hill*

GAZA GHETTO (Film Forum) Producer-Director-Screenplay, PeA Holmquist, Joan Mandell, Pierre Bjorklund; Photography, Holmquist, Koram Millo; An HB Holmquist Film Production; Sweden, 1984; In Arabic, Hebrew, and English with subtitles; Banned in Israel and the occupied territories; 82 minutes; Not rated; May release. CAST: Abu l-Adel (Grandfather), Itidhal (Daughter), Mustafa (Husband), and Ra'ida, Ariel Sharon, Ben Eliezar, Reuven Rosenblatt, Yitzhak Rabin (Children)

GOODBYE, NEW YORK (Castle Hill) Producer, Jett Monroe; Director-Screenplay, Amos Kollek; Photography, Amnon Salomon; Editor, Alan Heim; Music, Michael Abene; Associate Producer, Mary Jane Cahill; A Koke-Hill Production; Israeli; Color; 90 minutes; Not rated; May release. CAST: Julie Hagerty (Nancy Callaghan), Amos Kollek (David), David Topaz (Albert), Aviva Ger (Illana), Samuel Shiloh (Moishe), Jennifer Babtist (Lisa), Christopher Goutman (Jack)

REMBETIKO (Athos Entertainment) Producer, George Zervoulakos; Director, Costas Ferris; Screenplay, Sotiria Leonardou, Mr. Ferris; Photography, Takis Zervoulakos; Music, Stavros Xarchakos; Greek with subtitles; 101 minutes; Not rated. May release. CAST: Sotiria Leonardou (Marika), Nikos Kalogeropoulos (Bobbis), Themis Bazaka (Adrianna), Michalis Maniatis (Giorgakis), Nikos Dimitratos (Panagis), Giorgos Zorbas (Thomas), Konstantinos Tzumas (Juan), Vicky Vanita (Rosa)

THE EIGHTIES (World Artists) Producer, Paradise Films; Director, Chantal Akerman; Screenplay, Jean Gruault, Chantal Akerman; Photography, Michel Houssiau; Costumes, Michele Blondeel, Cecile Pecher; Music, Marc Herouet; Lyrics, Chantal Akerman; Executive Producer, Marilyn Watelet; Assistant Director, Jean-Philippe Laroche; Sound, Daniel Deshays, Marc Mallinus, Henri Morelle; Editors, Nadine Keseman, Francine Sandberg, Chantal Hymans, Marie-Catherine Miqueau; French with subtitles; 85 minutes; Not rated; May release. CAST: (First Part: "Audition", Second Part: "Project") Aischa Benteboche, Francisca Best, Kath Best, Francois Beukelaers, Daniela Bisconti, Warre Borgmans, Anne-Marie Cappeliez, Cathy Carrera, Amid Chakir, Eric Chale, Aurore Clement, Harry Cleven, Nicole Debarre, Patrick Dehene, Goel Derrick, Jo Deseur, Annick Detollenaere, Patricia Frans, Herman Gillis, Ioanna Gkizas, Lucy Grauman, Catherine Jauniaux, Michel Karchevksy, Martine Kivits, Fabienne Lambert, Francine

Landrain, Helene Lapiower, Dominique Laprique, Susanna Lastreto, Marie-Line Lefevre, Lio, Carmela Locantore, Daniela Luca, Xavier Lukomsky, Florence Madec, Cecile Marcandela, Estelle Marion, Rachel Michael, Blase Mills, Agnes Muckensturm, Anne Nelissen, Claire Nelissen, Magali Noel, Yvette Poirier, Christine Pouquet, Isabelle Pousseur, Christiane Ramseyer, Marie-Rose Roland, Nel Rosiers, Pascale Salkin, Marc Schreiber, Francois Sikivie, Guy Swinnen, Samy Szlingerbaum, Nora Tilly, Hilde Van Mieghem, Nicole Valberg, Johann Van Assche, Florence Vercheval, Yvon Vromman, Gabrielle Weilbach, Michel Weinstadt, Nathalie Williame, Jean-Claude Wouters, Bernard Yerles, Simon Zaleski, Chantal Akerman

TERMINAL CHOICE (Almi Pictures, Inc.) formerly "Deathbed"; Producer, Gary Magder; Director, Sheldon Larry; Screenplay, Neal Bell; Story, Peter Lawrence; Photography, Zale Magder; Editor, Murray Magder; Music, Brian Bennett; Designer, David Jaquest; Executive Producers, Jean Ubaud, Maqbool Hameed; Associate Producer, Keith Cavele; Costumes, Patti Unger; Canadian; Color; 95 minutes; Rated R; May release. CAST: Joe Spano (Frank Holt), Diane Venora (Anna), David McCallum (Dr. Dodson), Robert Joy (Dr. Rimmer), Don Francks (Chauncey Rand), Nicholas Campbell (Henderson), Ellen Barkin (Mary O'Connor), Chapelle Jaffe (Mrs. Dodson), Clare Coulter (Nurse Barton), James Kidnie (Dr. Kline), Les Rubie (Miles Kingsley), and Martha Gibson, Chas Lawther, Terry Austin, Tom Harvey, Sandra Warren, Lynda Mason Green, Gaye McDonald, Eric Fink, Clarke Johnson, Gilles Sayard, Marilyn Boyle, Cheryl Wilson, Heidi Palleske, Monica Parker, Bob Sher, Ingrid Izzard, Caroline Yeager, Fred Lee, Kurt Schiegl, Monique Savarin, Fred Toshoff, Richard Parker, Sharon Lackie

THE HOLY INNOCENTS (Samuel Goldwyn) Producer, Julian Mateos; Director, Mario Camus; Screenplay, Antonio Larreta, Manuel Matji, Mr. Camus; Based on the novel by Miguel Delibes; Photography, Hans Burmann; Editor, Jose Maria Biurrun; Music, Anton Garcia Abril; Spanish with subtitles; 108 minutes; Rated PG; May release. CAST: Alfredo Landa (Paco), Francisco Rabal (Azarias), Terele Paves (Regula), Belén Ballesteros (Nieves), Juan Sanchez (Quirce), Susana Sanchez (The Little One), Agata Lys (Dona Purita), Agustin Gonzalez (Don Pedro), Juan Diego (Master Ivan), Mary Carillo (Marchioness) Maribel Martin (Miriam), Jose Guardiola (Senorito de la Jara), Manuel Zarzo (Physician)

Diane Venora, David McCallum
in "Terminal Choice"
© *Almi Pictures*

Agata Lys, Augustin Gonzalez, Mary Carillo,
Maribel Martin in "The Holy Innocents"
© *Samuel Goldwyn Co.*

209

Jaclyn Smith, Nigel Terry
in "Deja Vu" © *Cannon Group*

"Return to Waterloo"
© *New Line Cinema*

DÉJÀVU (Cannon Group, Inc.) Producers, Menahem Golan, Yoram Globus; Director, Anthony Richmond; Screenplay, Ezra D. Rappaport, Anthony Richmond, Arnold Schmidt; Adaptation, Joane A. Gil; Based on the novel "Always" by Trevor Meldal-Johnsen; Music, Pino Donaggio; Photography, David Holmes; Editor, Richard Trevor; Designer, Tony Wollard; Associate Producer, Michael Kagan; Costumes, Marit Allen; Production Manager, Clive Challis; Assistant Directors, Gerry Gavigan, Terence Madden; Sound, Colin Charles; Produced in association with Dixons Films; British; Color; 90 minutes; Rated R; May release. CAST: Jaclyn Smith (Brooke Ashley/Maggie Rogers), Nigel Terry (Michael Richardson/Gregory Thomas), Shelley Winters (Olga Nabakov), Claire Bloom (Eleanor Harvey), Richard Kay (William Tanner-1935), Frank Gatliff (William Tanner-1984), Michael Ladkin (Willmer), David Lewin (Reporter), Marianne Stone (Mabel), and Virginia Guy, David Adams, Josephine Buchan, Richard Graydon, Claire Bayliss, Elizabeth Cantillon, Robin James, Philippa Luce, Wendy Roe, Gillian Winn

SMORGASBORD (Warner Bros.) Producers, Arnold Orgolini, Peter Nelson; Director, Jerry Lewis; Screenplay, Mr. Lewis, Bill Richmond; Photography, Gerald Perry Finnerman; Editor, Gene Fowler Jr.; Music, Morton Stevens; Color; 90 minutes; Rated PG; May release. CAST: Jerry Lewis (Warren Nefron), Herb Edelman (The Psychiatrist), Zane Busby (The Waitress), and Dick Butkus, Francine York, John Abbott, Steve Franken, Bill Richmond, Milton Berle

LES ANNEES 80 (World Artists) Producer, Paradise Films; Director, Chantal Akerman; Executive Producer, Marilyn Watelet; Screenplay, Jean Gruault, Chantal Akerman; Photography, Michel Houssiau; Editors, Nadine Keseman, Francine Sandberg; Music, Marc Herouet; Lyrics, Chantal Akerman; Costumes, Michele Blondeel; Designer, Michel Boermans; In French with subtitles; Belgium 1983; In color; 80 minutes; May release.

VENGEANCE IS MINE (Kino) Producers, Kazuo Inoue for the Shochiku Company; Director, Shohei Imamura; Screenplay, Ataru Baba; Based on a novel by Ryuzo Saki; Photography, Shinsaku Himeda; Editor, Keiichi Uraoka; Music, Shinichiro Ikebe; 1979 Japanese with subtitles; Color; 125 minutes; Not rated; June release. CAST: Ken Ogata, Mayumi Ogawa, Mitsuko Baisha, Rentaro Mikuni, Nijiko Kiyokawa, Chocha Miyako

RETURN TO WATERLOO (New Line Cinema) Producer, Dennis Woolf; Director-Screenplay-Songs, Ray Davies; Photography, Roger Deakins; Editor, David Mingay; Designer, Terry Pritchard; Choreographer, James Cameron; Production Manager, Paul Sparrow; Sound, Bruce White; British; 80 minutes; Rated PG-13; June release. CAST: Ken Colley, Valerie Holliman, Dominique Barnes, Hywel Williams Ellis, Aaron Probyn, Gretchen Franklin, Betty Romaine, Michael Cule, Christopher Godwin, Wanda Rokicki, Alan Mitchell, Claire Parker, Timothy Davies, Joan Blackham, Tim Roth, Mike Smart, Sally Anne, Lizzie McKenzie, Sheila Collings, Myrtle Devenish, Nat Jackley, Wally Thomas, Roy Evans, Sue Vanner, Claire Rayner, Michael Fish, Neil Landor, Theresa Pattison, Ray Davies, Mick Avory, Jim Rodford, Ian Gibbons

WARRIORS OF THE WIND (New World) Producer, Isao Takahata; Director, Kazuo Komatsubara; Screenplay, Kazunori Ito; Editor, Tomoko Kida; Designer, Mitsuki Nakamura; Music, Shigeharu Shiba; Assistant Directors, Takashi Tanzawa, Kazuyoshi Katayama; Production Manager, Noboru Sakai; Japanese; Animated; Color; 95 minutes; Rated PG; June release

WHITE ELEPHANT Producer-Director-Story, Werner Grusch; Screenplay, Mr. Grusch, Ashley Pharoah; Photography, Tom D. Hurwitz; Editor, Tomas Schwalm; England; 99 minutes; Not rated; June release. CAST: Peter Firth

HENRY IV (Orion Classics) Producer, Enzo Porcelli; Director-Screenplay, Marco Bellocchio; With the collaboration of Tonino Guerra; Freely adapted from the play "Henry IV" by Luigi Pirandello; Photography, Guiseppe Lanci; Sets, Giancarlo Basili, Leonardo Scarpa; Costumes, Lina Nerli Taviani; Music, Astor Piazzolla; Editor, Mirco Garrone; Sound, Remo Ugolinelli; Associate Producer, Roberta Carlotto; Assistant Director, Lisa Caracciolo; Production Manager, Angelo Barbagallo; A Rai Radiotelevisione Italiana Tete 2TV-Odyssia production; Presented by Sacis; Italian with subtitles; Color; 95 minutes; Rated PG-13; June release. CAST: Marcello Mastroianni (Henry IV), Claudia Cardinale (Matilda), Leopoldo Trieste (Psychiatrist), Paolo Bonacelli (Belcredi), Gianfelice Imparato (Di Nolli), Claudio Spadaro (Lolo), Giuseppe Cederna (Fino Pagliuca), Giacomo Bertozzi (Giacomo), Frabrizio Macciantelli (Fabrizio), Luciano Bartoli (Young Henry IV), Latou Chardons (Frida)

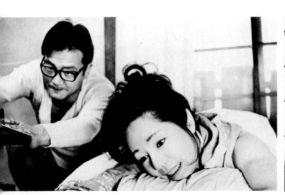

"Vengeance Is Mine"
© *Kino International*

Marcello Mastroianni as "Henry IV"
© *Orion Classics*

Swatilekha Chatterjee in "The Home
and the World" © *European Classic*

Michael Sopkiw, Valentine Monnier
in "After the Fall of New York" © *Almi*

THE HOME AND THE WORLD (European Classics) Producer, The National Film Development Corporation of India; Director-Screenplay, Satyajit Ray; Based on the novel by Rabindranath Tagore; Photography, Soumendu Roy; Editor, Bulal Dutt; Music, Mr. Ray; Bengali with subtitles; Color; 130 minutes; Not rated; June release. CAST: Soumitra Chatterjee (Sandip), Victor Banerjee (Nikhil), Swatilekha Chatterjee (Bimala), Copa Aich (Sister-in-law), Jennifer Kapoor (Miss Gilby), Manoj Mitra (Headmaster), Indrapramit Roy (Amulya), Bimai Chatterjee (Kulada)

AFTER THE FALL OF NEW YORK (Almi Pictures, Inc.) Producer, Luciano Martino; Director, Martin Dolman; Screenplay, Julian Berry, Martin Dolman, Gabriel Rossini; Based on a story by Julian Berry, Martin Dolman; Photography, Giancarlo Ferrando; Music, Oliver Onions; Designer, Antonello Geleng; Editor, Eugenio Alabiso; Special Effects, Paulo Ricci; Costumes, Adriana Spadaro; An Italo-French Co-Production; Eastmancolor; Telecolor; 95 minutes; Rated R; July release. CAST: Michael Sopkiw (Parsifal), Valentine Monnier (Giaiada), Anna Kanankis (Ania), Roman Geer (Rachet), Vincent Scalondro (Bronx), George Eastman (Big Ape), Edmund Purdum (President), Louis Ecclesia (Shorty)

CEMETERY OF TERROR Producer, Raul Galindo; Director-Screenplay, Ruben Galindo Jr.; Adaptation, Carlos Valdemar; Photography, Rosalio Solano, Luis Besina; Editor, Carlos Savage; Music, Chucho Sarsoza; Sound, Daniel Lopez; A Dynamic Films/Prods. Torrente S.A. presentation; Mexico; Color; 88 minutes; Not rated; July release. CAST: Hugo Stiglitz (Dr. Cardan), Usi Velasco, Erika Buenfil, Edna Bolkan, Maria Rebeca, Eduardo Capetillo, Cesar Velasco, Servando Manzetti, Andres Garcia Jr., Rene Cardona 3rd., Jacqueline Castro

THE LIFT (Island Alive) Producer, Matthijs Van Heijningen; Director-Screenplay, Dick Maas; Photography, Andre Sjouerman; Editor, Hans Van Dongen; Lights, Cor Roodhart, Franc Van Zutphen; Sound, Georges Bossaers; Special Effects, Rene Stouthamer, Leo Cahn; Designer, Harry Ammerlaan; Costumes, Jany Van Hellenberg Hubar, Yvonne De Boer; Assistant Director, Myrna Van Gilst; Production Manager, Jos Van Der Linden; Holland, 1984; Dutch with subtitles; Color; 90 minutes; Rated R; July release. CAST: Huub Stapel (Felix Adelaar), Willeke Van Ammelrooy (Mieke), Josine Van Dalsum

(Saskia), Hans Veerman (Kroon), Ab Abspoel (Chief of Maintenance), Hans Dagelet (Spiekerman), Frederik De Groot (Makelaar), Bertus Botterman (Blind Man), Henri Serge Valcke (Kraayvanger), Siem Vroom (Bolhuis), Aad Ceelen (Smit), and Gerard Thoolen, Peter Romer, Luk Van Mello, Cor Witschge, Paul Gieske, Adrian Brine, Arnica Elsendoorn, Guus Hoes, Sidney Kuyer, Emma Onrust, Pieter Lutz, Liz Snoyink, Wiske Sterringa

A THOUSAND LITTLE KISSES (Cinecom International) Producers, Zvi Spielmann, Shlomo Mograbi; Director-Screenplay, Mira Recanati; Photography, David Gurfinkel; Editor, Jacquot Ehrlich; Music, Schlomo Gronich, Benjamin Britten; an Israfilm presentation; Israeli; 110 minutes; Not rated; July release. CAST: Dina Doronne (Ruta), Rivka Neuman (Alma), Gad Roll (Mika), Rina Orchitel (Mara), Doron Tavori (Uri), Nissim Zohar (Eli), Nirit Gronich (Nili), Daphna Recanati (Daphna)

ANIMALS ARE BEAUTIFUL PEOPLE (Warner Bros. Classics) carried in Volume 26 as "Beautiful People"

PERIL (Triumph) Producer, Emmanuel Schlumberger; Adaptation-Dialogue-Direction, Michel Deville; From novel "Sur La Terre comme au Ciel" by Rene Belletto; Executive Producer-Assistant Director-Co-writer, Rosalinde Damamme; Photography, Martial Thury; Music, Brahms, Granados, Schubert; Editor, Raymonde Guyot; Costumes, Cecile Balme; French with subtitles; In Eastmancolor; Rated R; 110 minutes; August release. CAST: Christophe Malavoy (David), Nicole Garcia (Julia), Michel Piccoli (Graham), Richard Bohringer (Daniel), Anemone (Edwige), Anais Jeanneret (Vivianne), Jean-Claude Jay (Father), Helene Roussel (Mother), Elisabeth Vital; (Waitress), Frank Lapersonne (Guitar Salesman), Daniel Verite (Assailant)

JUNGLE RAIDERS (Cannon) Producer, Luciano Appignani for L'Immagine S.R.L.; Director, Anthony M. Dawson; Screenplay, Giovanni Simonelli; Photography, Gugliello Nancori; Music, Cal Taornina; Italian; Color; 98 minutes; Rated R; August release. CAST: Christopher Connelly, Marina Costa, Lee Van Cleef

Huub Stapel in "The Lift"
© *Island Alive*

Nicole Garcia, Michel Piccoli,
Christophe Malavoy in "Peril"
© *Columbia Pictures*

Alan Shearman, Bryan Pringle, Diz White
in "Bullshot" © *Island Alive*

Donald Pleasence (L) in "Creepers"
© *New Line Cinema*

THE BAR ESPERANZA (Quartet Films) Producer, Producao Ltda; Director, Hugo Carvana; Screenplay, Armando Costa, Denise Bandeira, Euclides Marinho, Hugo Carvana, Martha Alencar; Music, Tomaz Improta; Photography, Edgar Moura; Brazil, 1983; Color; 126 minutes; Not rated; August release. CAST: Marilia Pera (Ana), Hugo Carvana (Zeca), Silvio Bandeira (Cotinha), and Wilson Grey, Anselmo Vasconcellos, Nelson Dantas, Julio Braga, Louise Cardosa, Paulo Cesar Pereio, Telma Reston, Antonio Pedro, Luis F. Guimaraes

BULLSHOT (Island Alive) Producer, Ian La Frenais; Director, Dick Clement; Photography, Alex Thomson; Music, John Du Prez, Ray Cooper; Designer, Norman Garwood; Costumes, Jim Acheson; Editor, Alan Jones; Executive Producers, George Harrison, Denis O'Brien; Associate Producer, David Wimbury; Assistant Directors, Gary White, Adrian Rawle, Derek Harrington; Special Effects, Jon Bunker; Sound, Jim Roddan; British; Color; 95 minutes; Rated PG; August release. CAST: Alan Shearman (Capt. Hugh "Bullshot" Crummond), Diz White (Rosemary Fenton), Ron House (Count Otto von Bruno), Frances Tomelty (Lenya von Bruno), Michael Aldridge (Prof. Rupert Fenton), Ron Pember (Dobbs), Christopher Good (Lord "Binky" Brancaster), Mel Smith ("Crouch"), Billy Connolly ("Hawkeye" McGillicuddy), Geoffrey Bayldon (Col. Hinchcliff), and Christopher Godwin, Bryan Pringle, Angela Thorne, Peter Bayliss, John Wells, Nicholas Lydhurst, Ray Cooper, Derek Deadman, "Legs" Larry Smith, John Du Prez, GB "Zoot" Money, Paul Herzberg, Rupert Frazer, Christina Greatrex, Francesca Brill, Lucy Hornak, Ted Moult, Hilary Mason Ann Way, Ballard Berkeley, Diana Van Proosdy, Albert Evansky, Anthony Milner

INSIGNIFICANCE (Island Alive) Producer, Jeremy Thomas; Director, Nicolas Roeg; Screenplay, Terry Johnson; Photography, Peter Hannan; Designer, David Brockhurst; Costumes, Shuna Harwood; Sound, Paul Le Mare; Editor, Tony Lawson; Executive Producer, Alexander Stuart; Associate Producer, Joyce Herlihy; Assistant Director; Michael Zimbrich; A Zenith Production in association with The Recorded Picture Company; British; Color; 110 minutes; Rated R; August release. CAST: Gary Busey (The Ballplayer), Tony Curtis (The Senator), Michael Emil (The Professor), Theresa Russell (The Actress), Will Sampson (The Elevator Attendant)

CREEPERS (New Line Cinema) formerly "Phenomena"; Producer-Director, Dario Argento; Screenplay, Dario Argento, Franco Ferrini; Costumes; Giorgio Armani; Music, Bill Wyman, Iron Maiden, Motorhead, Simon Boswell, Goblin; A Dacfilm Production in Panavision Widescreen; Italian; 83 minutes; Rated R; August release. CAST: Jennifer Connelly, Daria Nicolodi, Dalila Di Lazzaro, Patrick Bauchau, Donald Pleasence

GODZILLA 1985 (New World) Producers, Tomoyuki Tanaka, Anthony Randel; Directors, Kohji Hashimoto, R. J. Kizer; Screenplay, Shuichi Nagahara, Lisa Tomei; Story, Tomoyuki Tanaka; Special Effects, Teruyoshi Nakano; Photography, Kazutami Hara; Designer, Akira Sakuragi; Sound, Nobuyuki Tanaka; Lighting, Shinji Kojima; Production Manager, Takahide Morichi; Associate Producers, Fumio Tanaka, Andrea Stern; Music, Reijiro Koroku; Song by various artists; Assistant Director, Takao Ohgawara; Color; widescreen; 91 minutes; Rated PG; Japanese; August release. CAST: Raymond Burr (Steve Martin), Keiju Kobayashi (Prime Minister Mitamura), Ken Tanaka (Goro Maki), Yasuko Sawaguchi (Naoko Okumura), Shin Takuma (Hiroshi Okumura), Eitaro Ozawa (Kanzaki), Taketoshi Naito (Takegami), Nobuo Kaneko (Isomura), Takeshi Katoh (Kasaoka), Mizuho Suzuki (Kanzaki), Junkichi Orimoto (Mohri), Shinsuke Mikimoto (Kakurai), Mikita Mori (Ohkochi), Yoshifumi Tajime (Hidaka), Kiyoshi Tamamoto (Kajita), Hiroshi Koizumi (Minami), Kunio Murai (Henmi), Kei Sato (Gondo), Takenori Emoto (Kitagawa), Shinpei Hayashiya (Kamijo), Yosuke Natsuki (Hayashida), and Takeo Morimoto, Koji Ishizaka, Tetsuya Takeda

STEAMING (Losey) Director, Joseph Losey; Producer, Paul Mills; Screenplay, Patricia Losey; Photography, Christopher Challis; Editor, Reginald Beck; Music, Richard Harvey; British film in color; Not rated; 95 minutes; September release. CAST: Vanessa Redgrave (Nancy), Sarah Miles (Sarah), Diana Dors (Violet), Patti Love (Josie), Brenda Bruce (Mrs. Meadows), Felicity Dean (Dawn), Sally Sagoe (Celia)

Tony Curtis, Theresa Russell
in "Insignificance"
© *Island Alive*

Godzilla in "Godzilla 1985"
© *New World Pictures*

Stellan Skarsgard, Maria Johansson
in "Simple-Minded Murderer" © *Roxie*

Richard Berry, Victoria Abril
in "L'Addition" © *New World*

THE SIMPLE-MINDED MURDERER (Roxie) Director-Screenplay, Hans Alfredson; Photography, Jorgen Persson, Rolf Lindstrom; Editor, Jan Persson; Assistant Director, Niklas Radstrom; Music, Verdi; Fujicolor; Swedish; 105 minutes; Not rated; September release; CAST: Stellan Skarsgard (The Idiot), Hans Alfredson (Hoglund), Maria Johansson (Anna), Per Myrberg (Anderson), Lena Pia Bernardsson (Mrs. Anderson), Tomas Alfredson (Axel), Cecilia Walton (Vera), Nils Ahlroth (Mansson), Lars Amble (Bengt), Wallis Grahn (Mrs. Hoglund), Lena Nyman (Legless Lady), Gosta Ekman (New Driver), Else Marie Brandt (Idiot's Mother), Carl-Ake Erikson (Wallin), Carl Billquist (Flodin), Anders Granstrom (Berghald), Anna-Carin Krokstade (Marit), Bjorn Andresen, Daniel Alfredson, Erik Spangenberg (Angels), Georg Arlin (Commissioner)

WARRIOR OF THE LOST WORLD (Visto International) Producers, Roberto Bessi, Frank E. Hildebrand; Director-Screenplay, David Worth; Photography, Giancarlo Ferrando; Editor, Cesare D'Amico; Music, Daniele Patucchi; Production Manager, Franco Cucco; Assistant Director, Tony Brandt; Designer, Antonello Geleng; Special Effects, Roberto Arcangeli; An A.D.I. Production; Presented by Eduard Sarlui; Luciano Vittori Color; Italy; 86 minutes; Rated R; September release. CAST: Robert Ginty (Warrior), Persis Khambatta (Nastasia), Donald Pleasence (Prosser), Fred Williamson (Henchman), Harrison Muller (McWayne), and Janna Ryan, Consuelo Marcaccini, Harrison Muller Jr., Russel Case

SHEER MADNESS (R5/S8) Producer, Eberhard Junkersdorf; Direction-Screenplay, Margarethe von Trotta; Photography, Michael Ballhaus; Editor, Dagmar Hirtz; Music, Nicolas Economou; Art Director, Jurgen Henze; Costumes, Monika Hasse; A German-French Co-production with subtitles; In color, black and white; Not rated; 105 minutes; September release. CAST: Hanna Schygulla (Olga), Angela Winkler (Ruth), Peter Striebeck (Franz), Franz Buchrieser (Dieter), Vladimir Yordanoff (Alexej), Felix Moeller (Christof), Agnes Fink (Ruth's Mother), Christine Fersen (Erika), Jochen Striebeck (Bruno), Therese Affolter (Renate), Werner Eichhorn (Schlesinger), Helga Ballaus (Gallery Owner), Peter Aust (Hansen), Carla Egerer (Mrs. Hansen), Karl Striebeck (Father), Selda Bondy (Doctor), Alexander Volz (Child), Wieland Wittig (Egon), Dorte Volz (Gisela), Peter Wagenreth (Judge), Luca Winkler, Tamo Winkler (Children), Basbousa (Palmist), Mervat Kamal (Egyptian)

THE TOKYO TRIAL (Film Forum) Producers, Hiroshi Suto, Masaya Araki, Ryu Yasutake; Director, Masaki Kobayashi; Screenplay, Kobayashi, Kiyoshi Ogasawara; Editor, Keiichi Uraoka; Narrators, Stuart Atkin, Frank Rogers (in English); Japan 1983; Not rated 270 minutes; September release. A documentary on the International Military Tribunal for the Far East, Japan's version of the Nuremberg Trials.

WAR AND LOVE (Cannon) formerly "The Children's War"; Producer, Jack Eisner; Director, Moshe Mizrahi; Screenplay, Abby Mann; Based on book "The Survivor" by Jack P. Eisner; Editor, Peter Zinner; Music, Mahler; Performed by Israeli Philharmonic with Zubin Mehta conducting; In color; Rated PG13; 112 minutes; September release. CAST: Sebastian Keneas (Jacek), Kyra Sedgwick (Halina), David Spielberg (Aron), Cheryl Gianini (Zlatka), Eda Reiss-Merin (Masha), Brita Youngblood (Hela), Reuel Schiller (Lutek), Eric Faber (Yankele), Stephen Mailer (Sevek)

L'ADDITION (New World) Executive Producers, Norbert Chalon, Pierre Tati; Producer, Norbert Saada; Director, Denis Amar; Screenplay, Jean Curtelin; Story, Denis Amar, Jean Pierre Bastid, Jean Curtelin; Music, Jean-Claude Petit; Photography, Robert Fraisse; Editor, Jacques Witta; Assistant Directors, Bernard Bolzinger, Frederic Blum; Costumes, Elisabeth Tavernier; In color; French with subtitles; 93 minutes; Not rated; September release. CAST: Richard Berry (Bruno), Richard Bohringer (Lorca), Victoria Abril (Patty), Farid Chopel (Jose), Fabrice Eberhard (Minet), Daniel Sarky (Constantini), Simon Reggiani (Lenuzza), Jacques Sereys (Guard), Riton Liebman (Jeannot), Luc Florian (Supermarket Security), Daniel Verite (Stuntman)

LIFE IS A BED OF ROSES (International Spectrafilm) Producer, Philippe Dussart; Director, Alain Resnais; Screenplay, Jean Gruault; Photography, Bruno Nuytten; Music, M. Philippe-Gerard; Art Director, Jacques Saulnier; Editors, Albert Jurgenson, Jean-Pierre Besnard; Costumes, Catherine Leterrier; In color; Rated PG; 111 minutes; September release. CAST: Vittorio Gassman (Walter), Ruggero Raimondi (Michel Forbek), Geraldine Chaplin (Nora), Fanny Ardant (Livia), Pierre Arditi (Robert), Sabine Azema (Elizabeth), Robert Manuel (Georges), Martine Kelly (Claudine), Samson Fainsilber (Zoltan), Nathalie Holberg (Veronique), Raoul Vandamme (Andre)

Franz Buchrieser, Hanna Schygulla
in "Sheer Madness"
© R5/S8

Vittorio Gassman, Geraldine Chaplin
in "Life Is a Bed of Roses"
© *Spectrafilm*

Derek de Lint in "Bastille"
© East-West Classics

Ken Ogata in Mishima"
© Warner Bros.

MORONS FROM OUTER SPACE (Universal) Producer, Barry Hanson; Director, Mike Hodges; Screenplay, Mel Smith, Griff Rhys Jones; Executive Producer, Verity Lambert; Music, Peter Brewis; Editor, Peter Boyle; Designer, Brian Eatwell; Photography, Phil Meheux; Art Directors, Terry Gough, Bert Davey; A Thorn EMI Screen Entertainment Production color; Dolby Stereo; Rated PG; 87 minutes; September release. CAST: Jimmy Nail (Desmond), Mel Smith (Bernard), Paul Bown (Julian), Joanne Pearce (Sandra), Griff Rhys Jones (Graham), Robert Austin (Newscaster), John Barcroft (McKenzie), Bill Stewart (Walters), R. J. Bell (Klutz), Peter Whitman (Friborg), Olivier Pierre (Jabowlski), Billy J. Mitchell (Commander), Deredk Deadman, Angela Crow, Jimmy Mulville, Lesley Grantham, Joanna Dickens, Leonard Fenton, James Taylor, Christopher Northey, Dinsdale Landen, George Innes, Jo Ross, John Joyce, Mark Jones, James B. Sikking, Joss Buckley, Roger Hammond, Karen Lancaster, Tristram Jellinek, Andre Maranne, Edward Wiley, Barbara Hicks, Tim Barker, Shane Rimmer

BASTILLE (East-West Classics) Producers, George Sluizer, Ann Lordon; Director, Rudolf van den Berg; Screenplay, Annemarie van de Putte, Rudolf van den berg, Leon de Winter; Based on story by Leon de Winter; Photography, Toni Kuhn; In Dutch and French with subtitles; Netherlands 1984; In color; Not rated 100 minutes; September release. CAST: Derek de Lint (Paul de Wit), Geert de Jong (Mieke), Evelyne Dress (Nadine), Loudi Nijhoff (Midwife), Ischa Meijer (Prof. Polak), Dora Doll (Mrs. Friedlander)

THE HORIZON (Shochiku) Producer, Genshiro Kawamoto; Direction-Screenplay, Kaneto Shindo; Planned by Akihisa Kanai; Music, Hikaru Hayashi; Art Director, Kazumasa Yamato, Photography, Keiji Maruyama; A Marugen production; Japanese with subtitles; In color; Rated R; 133 minutes; September release. CAST: Nobuko Otowa (Hideyo after 40), Miwako Fujitani (Hideyo after 20), Toshiyuki Nagashima (Yoshio Fujiki), Saburo Tokito (Taro), Kumiko Akiyoshi (Sakura), Misako Tanaka (Momoko), Maiko Kawakami (Ayame)

THE SICILIAN CONNECTION (Cannon) Director, Damiano Damiani; Photography, Nino Celeste; Rated R; No other credits; September release. CAST: Michele Placido, Mark Case.

MISHIMA: A LIFE IN FOUR CHAPTERS (Warner Bros.) Producers, Mata Yamamoto, Tom Luddy; Director, Paul Schrader; Written by Paul Schrader, Leonard Schrader; In Japanese with English subtitles; Photography, John Bailey; Editor, Michael Chandler Tomaya Oshima; Music, Philip Glass; In color, black and white; Rated R; 122 minutes; September release. CAST: Ken Ogata (Mishima) Mashayuki Shionoya (Morita), Junkichi Orimoto (Gen. Mashita) Naoko Otani (Mother), Go Riju (Mishima 18–19), Masato Aizawa (Mishima 9–14), Yuki Nagahara (Mishima 5), Kyuzo Kobayash (Literary Friend), Haruko Kato (Grandmother), Yuki Kitazume (Dancing Friend)

RUTHLESS ROMANCE (International Film Exchange) Director Screenplay, Eldar Ryazanov; Photography, Vadim Alisov; Art Director, Alexander Borisov; Music, Andrei Petrov; A 1984 Mosfilm Studios production in color; Russian with English subtitles; Not rated; 14 minutes; September release. CAST: Nikita Mikhalkov (Sergei Paratov), Larisa Guseeva (Larisa), Alisa Friendlikh (Mme. Ogudalova) Andrei Myagkov (Yuli Karandyshev), Alexei Petrenko (Knurov), Victor Proskurin (Vasya Vozhevatov)

RAZORBACK (Warner Bros.) Producer, Hal McElroy; Director Russell Mulcahy; Screenplay, Everette DeRoche; Based on novel b Peter Brennan; Photography, Dean Semler; Editor, William Anderson Music, Iva Davies; Australian; In Dolby Stereo and color; Rated R; 9 minutes; September release. CAST: Gregory Harrison (Carl), Arki Whiteley (Sarah), Bill Kerr (Jake), Chris Haywood (Benny), Davi Argue (Dicko), John Howard (Danny), John Ewart (Turner), Jud Morris (Beth), Don Smith (Wallace), Mervyn Drake (Andy)

PINK NIGHTS Producers-Editors, Phillip Koch, Sally Marschall Director-Screenplay, Phillip Koch; Photography, Charlie Lieberman Set, Gail Specht; Costumes, Rachel Herbener; Music, Jim Tullic Jeffery Vanston; Sound, Hans Roland; Choreography, Shaun Allen Don Franklin; Color; 84 minutes; Not rated; October release. CAST Shaun Allen (Terry), Kevin Anderson (Danny), Peri Kaczmare (Esme), Larry King (Jeff), Jonathan Jancovic Michaels (Zero), Jessic Vitkus (Marcy), Mike Bacarella (Bruno), Ron Dean (Pop), Tor Towles (Ralph the Lounge Lizard), Denyse Leahy (Mother)

"The Horizon"
© Shochiku Co.

Larisa Guseeva, Nikita Mikhalkov
in "Ruthless Romance"
© International Film Exchange

Kevin McNally, Mio Takaki, Gudrun Landgrebe
in "Berlin Affair" © *Cannon Group*

Carlo Verdone, Natasha Hovey
in "Acqua E Sapone" © *Triumph Films*

THE BERLIN AFFAIR (CANNON) Producers, Menahem Golan, Yoram Globus; Director, Liliana Cavani; Screenplay, Liliana Cavani, Roberta Mazzoni; Based on "The Buddhist Cross" by Junichiro Tanizaki; Photography, Dante Spinotti; Editor, Ruggero Mastroianni; Costumes, Jusoburo Tsujimura, Alberto Verso; Music, Pino Donaggio; Designers, Luciano Ricceri, Verde Visconte Di Modrone; Associate Producer, John Thompson; Assistant Directors, Paola Tallarigo, Carlo Carlotto, Olivier Gerard; Production Manager, Gino Santarelli; Sound, Mario Bramonte; Luciano Vittori Color; Italian; 119 minutes; Rated R; October release. CAST: Gudrun Landgrebe (Louise Von Hollendorf), Kevin McNally (Heinz Von Hollendorf), Mio Takaki (Mitsuko Matsurae), Hanns Zischler (Wolf Von Hollendorf), Massimo Girotti (Werner Von Heiden), Phillipe LeRoy (Herbert Gessler), William Berger (Professor), Andrea Prodan (Joseph Benno), Tomoko Tanaka (Ume), Claudio Lorimer (Otto), Edward Farrelly (Bernhard), John Steiner (Oskar), Enrica Maria Scrivano (Lotte), Clara Algranti (Ilse), Benedetta Fantoli (Concierge), Pieter Daniel (Edmund), James Crompton (Dr. Lipp), Sarah Blum (Cook), Silke Meyer (Model), Jusaburo Tsujimura (Spiritual Guide)

THE DOCTOR AND THE DEVILS (20th Century-Fox) Producer, Jonathan Sanger; Director, Freddie Francis; Screenplay, Ronald Harwood; Based on an original screenplay by Dylan Thomas; Photography, Gerry Turpin, Norman Warwick; Editor, Laurence Mery-Clark; Designer, Robert Laing; Costumes, Imogen Richardson; Music, John Morris; Sound, Ken Weston; Executive Producer, Mel Brooks; Associate Producer, Geoffrey Helman; Associate Producer, Jo Lustig; Assistant Directors, Peter Bennett, Andrew Warren, Simon Haveland; Special Effects, Alan Bryce; A Brooksfilms Production in Association with Dr. Barrington Cooper, Burton Gintell; British; J-D-C Widescreen; Dolby Stereo; 93 minutes; Rated R; October release. CAST: Timothy Dalton (Dr. Thomas Rock), Jonathan Pryce (Robert Fallon), Twiggy (Jenny Bailey), Julian Sands (Dr. Murray), Stephen Rea (Timothy Broom), Phyllis Logan (Elizabeth Rock), Lewis Fiander (Dr. Thornton), Beryl Reid (Mrs. Flynn), T. P. McKenna (O'Connor), Patrick Stewart (Prof. Macklin), Sian Phillips (Anabella Rock), Philip Davis (Billy Bedlam), Philip Jackson (Andrew Merry-Lees), Danny Schiller (Praying Howard), Bruce Green (Mole), Toni Palmer (Rosie), David Bamber (Cronin), Nichola McAuliffe (Alice), Deidre Costello (Nelly), Terry Neason (Kate), Paul Curran (Tom), Merelina Kendall

(Mrs. Webb), Dermot Crowley (Mr. Webb), Sarah Melia (Nora), Stephen Yardley (Joseph), John Horsley (Dr. Mackendrick), Jack May (Dr. Stevens), Rachel Herbert (Mrs. Stevens), Simon Shepherd (Harding), David Parfitt (Billings), Simon Adams (Green), Morgan Sheppard (Lambert), and Jennifer Jayne, Moira Brooker, P. G. Stevens, Roy Evans, Peter Burton, Leonard Maguire, Hedger Wallace, Ray Dunbobbin, Martin Herring, Shaun Curry, David Grahame, Kevin Duffield, Ray Armstrong, Sam Bartlett

ACQUA E SAPONE (Triumph) Director, Carlo Verdone; Story and Screenplay, Enrico Oldoini, Franco Ferrini, Carlo Verdone; Photography, Danilo Desideri; Editor, Antonio Siciliano; Music, Fabio Liberatori; Producers, Mario and Vittorio Ceochi Gori; Italian with English subtitles; In Color; Rated PG; 105 minutes; October release. CAST: Carlo Verdone (Rolando), Natasha Hovey (Sandy), Florinda Bolkan (Sandy's Mother), Fabrizio Bracconeri (Aunt Ines/Enzo)

DREAMCHILD (Universal) Producers, Rick McCallum, Kenith Trodd; Director, Gavin Millar; Executive Producers, Dennis Potter, Verity Lambert; Screenplay, Dennis Potter; Alice in Wonderland Characters designed and performed by Jim Henson's Creature Shop; Music, Stanley Myers; Photography, Billy Williams; Designer, Roger Hall; Editor, Angus Newton; Costumes, Jane Robinson; Assistant Director, Guy Travers; Additional Music, Max Harris; Art Directors, Len Huntingford, Marianne Ford; In color; British; Rated PG; 100 minutes; October release. CAST: Coral Browne (Mrs. Hargreaves), Ian Holm (Rev. Dodgson), Peter Gallagher (Jack Dolan), Caris Corfman (Sally), Nicola Cowper (Lucy), Jane Asher (Mrs. Liddell), Amelia Shankley (Little Alice), Imogen Boorman (Lorina), Emma King (Edith), Rupert Wainwright (Hargreaves), Roger Ashton-Griffiths (Rev. Duckworth), James Wilby (Baker), Shane Rimmer (Marl), Peter Whitman, Ken Campbell, William Hootkins, Jeffrey Chiswick, Pat Starr, Johnny M, Alan Sherman, Danny Brainin, Sam Douglas, Peter Banks, Derek Hoxby, Ron Berglas, Ron Travis, Thomasine Heiner, Olivier Pierre, Tony Mansell

Timothy Dalton, Unidentified, Stephen Rea,
Jonathan Pryce in "The Doctor and the Devils"
© *20th Century-Fox*

Julian Sands, Twiggy
in "The Doctor and the Devils"
© *20th Century-Fox*

Peter Smith, Alison Routledge, Bruno Lawrence
in "The Quiet Earth" © *Skouras Pictures*

Robert Parada, Oscar Castro
in "With Burning Patience"
© *Horizon*

ONIMASA (Filmtribe) Director, Hideo Gosha; Screenplay, Koji Takada; Japanese with subtitles; Editor, Isamu Ichida; Producer, Shigeru Okada; In color; Not rated; 142 minutes; October release. CAST: Tatsuya Nakadai (Onimasa), Masako Natsume (Matsue), Noriko Sendo (Young Matsue), Shima Awashita (Ute), Kaori Takasugi (Hanako), Akiko Kane (Tsuru), Tetsuro Taba (Suenaga), Kei Yamamoto (Tanabe)

THE QUIET EARTH (Skouras) Director, Geoff Murphy; Co-Producers, Don Reynolds, Sam Pillsbury; Screenplay, Bill Baer, Bruno Lawrence, Sam Pillsbury; Photography, James Bartle; Editor, Michael Horton; Art Director, Rick Kofoed; Music, John Charles; New Zealand; In color and Dolby Stereo; Rated R; 91 minutes; October release. CAST: Bruno Lawrence (Zac Hobson), Alison Routledge (Joanne), Peter Smith (Api)

A SENSE OF FREEDOM (Island Pictures) Producer, Jeremy Isaacs; Director, John Mackenzie; Screenplay, Peter McDougall; Photography, Chris Menges; Associate Producer, Raymond Day; Music, Frankie Miller, Rory Gallagher; Designer, Geoff Nixon; Costumes, Tudor George; In color; Not rated; 85 minutes; October release. CAST: David Hayman (Jimmy), Jake D'Arcy (Robbie), Sean Scanlon (Jackie), Alex Norton (Malkie), John Murtagh (Piper), Roy Hanlon (Chief Officer), Martin Black (Bobbie), Fulton Mackay (Inspector Davidson)

CAME A HOT FRIDAY (Orion Classics) Producer, Larry Parr; Director, Ian Mune; Screenplay, Dean Parker, Ian Mune; From novel by Ronald Hugh Morrieson; Photography, Alun Bollinger; Editor, Ken Zemke; Music, Stephen McCurdy; Designer, Ron Highfield; Art Director, John Miles; Costumes, Barbara Darragh; Choreographer, Catherine Cardiff; In Eastman Color and Dolby Stereo; New Zealand; Rated PG; 100 minutes; October release. CAST: Peter Bland (Wesley), Philip Gordon (Cyril), Billy T. James (Tainuia), Michael Lawrence (Don), Marshall Napier (Sel), Don Selwyn (Norm), Marise Wipani (Esmeralda), Erna Larsen (Dinah), Phillip Holder (Dick), Patricia Phillips (Claire), Bruce Allpress (Don's Dad), Michael Morrissey (Morrie), Roy Billing (Darkie), Francis Ullenberg (Pop Simon), Hemi Ropata (Kohi), Bridgett Armstrong (Aunt Agg), Stephen Tozer (Policeman)

WITH BURNING PATIENCE (Horizon) Direction-Screenplay, Antonio Skarmeta; Photography, Joao Abel Aboim; Music, Roberto Lecaros; Editor, Agape Dorstewitz; Art Director, Nene Paraiso; West Germany and Portugal production in color; Spanish with subtitles; Not rated; 79 minutes; October release. CAST: Oscar Castro (Mario), Roberto Parada (Pablo Neruda), Marcela Osorio (Beatriz), Naldy Hernandez (Rosa), Antonio Skarmeta (Postal Clerk), Miguel Viqueira (Labbe)

HIMATSURI (Kino International) Producers, Gunro/Seibu Group, Cine Saison; Director, Mitsuo Yanagimachi; Screenplay, Kenji Nakagami; Designer, Takeo Kimura; Photography, Masaki Tamura; Sound, Yukio Kubota; Music, Toru Takemitsu; Editor, Sachiko Yamaji; Executive Producer, Kazuo Shimizu; Japan; Eastmancolor; 120 minutes; Not rated; October release. CAST: Kinya Kitaoji (Tatsuo), Kiowako Taichi (Kimiko), Ryota Nakamoto (Ryota), Norihei Miki (Yamakawa), Rikiya Yasuoka (Toshio), Junko Miyashita (Sachiko), Kin Suga (Mother), Sachiko Matsushita, Masako Yagi (Sisters), Jukei Fujioka, Nenji Kobayashi, Ippei Sooda (Lumbermen), Aoi Nakajima (Sister), Kenzo Kaneko (Husband), Ban Kojika (Smith), Masato Ibu (Baker), Kosanji Yanagiya (Boatman), Aiko Morishita (Teacher), Eiichi Kudo (Driver), Seiji Kurasaki (Koji), Maiko Kawakami (Miiko), and Yosuke Naka, Gozo Sooma, Koji Miemachi, Yuzuko Kinoshita, Mitsuyo Inomata, Reiko Nanao, Shiro Shimomoto, Yuhei Kurachi, Remon Hori, Baiken Jukkanji, Akira Sakai, Atsushi Imaizumi

HOT TARGET (Crown International) Producers, John Barnett, Brian Cook; Director-Screenplay, Denis Lewiston; Based on a story by Gerry O'Hara; Photography, Alec Mills; Editor, Michael Horton; Music, Gil Melle; Designer, Jo Ford; Costumes, Patrick Steel; Assistant Director, Terry Needham; Set, Paul Radford; An Endeavour Productions Ltd. film; New Zealand; Colorfilm (N.Z.) Color; 93 minutes; Rated R; October release. CAST: Simone Griffeth (Christine Webber), Steve Marchuk (Greg Sandford), Brian Marshall (Clive Webber), Peter McCauley (Det. Nolan), Elizabeth Hawthorne (Suanne Maxwell), Ray Henwood (Douglas Maxwell), John Watson (Benjamin)

Peter Bland, Philip Gordon
in "Came a Hot Friday"
© *Orion Classics*

David Hayman
in "A Sense of Freedom"
© *Island Alive*

Myriem Roussel, Thierry Lacoste
in "Hail Mary" © *Gaumont/New Yorker*

"Himatsuri"
© *Kino International*

AIL MARY (New Yorker) Director, Jean-Luc Godard; Photogra-
ay, Jean-Bernard Menoud, Jacques Firmann; Producers, Philippe
Malignon, Francois Pelissier; Music, Back-Dvorak-Coltrane; French
ith subtitles in English; In color; Not rated; 95 minutes; October
lease. CAST: Part I—"The Book of Mary" directed by Anne-Marie
Mieville: Rebecca Hampton (Mary), Aurore Clement (Her Mother),
uno Cremer (Her Father), Copi (Traveller), Valentine Mercier (1st
irl), Clea Redalier (2nd Girl). Part II—"Hail Mary" with screenplay
y Jean-Luc Godard: Myriem Roussel (Mary), Thierry Lacoste
oseph), Philippe Lacoste (The Angel), Manon Anderson (Little Girl),
liette Binoche (Juliette), Malachi Jara Kohan (Jesus), Dick (Arthur),
hann Leysen (Professor), Anne Gauthier (Eva)

IVING AT RISK (New Yorker) Produced, directed and edited by
lfred Guzzetti, Susan Meiselas, Richard Rogers; Spanish and English
ith subtitles; Not rated; 59 minutes; Documentary on Sandinista
icaragua. Shown with WITNESS TO WAR (First Run Features)
irected and Edited by Deborah Shaffer; Producer, David Goodman;
hotography, Tom Sigel, Sandi Sissel; 29 minutes; a documentary on a
ne-time Vietnam pilot who became a volunteer doctor among the
easants of El Salvador.

**WIZARDS OF THE LOST KINGDOM (Concorde/Cinema
roup)** Producers, Frank Isaac, Alex Sessa; Director, Hector Olivera;
creenplay, Tom Edwards; Photography, Leonard Solis; Music, James
orner, Chris Young; Editor, Silvia Roberts; Designer, Mary Bertram;
ostumes, Gloria Hartwell, Beatrice Rowe; Production Manager, Alex
lowing; Assistant Directors, Andrew Sargent, Charles Ritter, Nick
alter; Special Effects Make-Up, Mike Jones; Sound, George
tevenson; Special Effects, Richard Lennox; U.S./Argentina; Color;
5 minutes; Rated PG; October release. CAST: Bo Svenson (Kor),
idal Peterson (Simon), Thom Christopher (Shurka), Barbara Stock
Udea), Maria Socas (Acrasia), Dolores Michaels (Aura), Edward
Morrow (Wulfrick), August Laretta (King Tylor), Michael Fontaine
Hurla), Mark Welles (Rongar), Mary Gale (Linnea), Norton Freeman
Sipra), Edward Morrow (Old Simon), Arch Gallo (Bobino), Mark
eters (Timmon), Rick Gallo (Malkon), Patrick Duggan (Adviser), Art
ass, Carl Fountain (Warriors), Ernie Smith (Friar), Edward Morrow
Gulfax), Nick Cord (Bat Creature), Carl Garcia (Lizardtaur), and
Helen Grant, J. C. Topper, Richard Paley, Guy Reed

TIME AND TIDE 2 (Shochiku) Producers, Yoshitoshi Masumoto,
Shigehiro Nakagawa; Director, Hiroshi Nagao; Photography, Yoshi-
masa Hanekata; Screenplay, Hiroshi Nagao, Toshio Suzuki; Art Direc-
tor, Nobutaka Yoshino; Music, Teizo Matsumura; Japanese with sub-
titles; In color; Rated R; 97 minutes; October release. CAST: Ikko
Furuya (Yasu), Yuko Natori (Mayumi), Ken'ichi Kato (Tanimura),
Naoki Sugiura (Proprietor), Jun Miho (Yuki), Hideji Ootaki (Imai),
Kotoe Hatsui (Mrs. Imai), Yu Fujiki (Proprietor of Tonkichi), Yumiko
Fujita (His Wife), Kazumi Sawata (Apple), Mariko Kaga (Kaoru),
Kinzo Shin (Fortune Teller)

LES PLOUFFE (International Cinema Corporation) Producer, Jus-
tine Heroux; Director, Gilles Carles; Screenplay, Roger Lemelin, Mr.
Carles; Based on book by Mr. Lemelin; Music, Stephane Venne,
Claude Denjean; French with subtitles; 180 minutes; Not rated; Novem-
ber release. CAST: Emile Genest (Theophile), Juliette Huot
(Josephine), Denise Filiatrault (Cecile), Gabriel Arcand (Ovide), Pierre
Curzi (Napoleon), Serge Dupire (Guillaume), Stephane Audran (Mme.
Boucher), Daniel Ceccaldi (Father Alphonse), Paul Berval (Onesime
Menard), Louise Lapare (Jeanne Duplessis), Remi Laurent (Denis
Boucher)

OUT OF ORDER (Sandstar Releasing Company) Producers, Thomas Schuhly, Matthias Deyle; Director-Screenplay, Carl Schenkel;
Additional Dialogue, Frank Gohre; Photography, Jacques Steyn; Editor, Norbert Herzner; Music, Jacques Zwart; German with subtitles; 90
minutes; Rated PG; November release. CAST: Renee Soutendijk (Marion), Gotz George (Jorg) Wolfgang Kieling (Gossman), Hannes
Jaenicke (Pit), Kurt Raab (Elevator Mechanic), Jan Groth (Doorman),
Claus Wennermann (Heinz), Ralph Richter (Otto), Ekmekyemez Fir-
devs (Cleaning Lady)

RASPUTIN (International Film Exchange) Producer, Mosfilm Stu-
dios; Director, Elem Klimov; Screenplay, Semyon Lunghin, Ilya
Nusinov; Photography, Leonid Kalashnikov; Designer, Sergei Voron-
kov; Music, Alfred Shnitke; U.S.S.R.; Russian with subtitles; Color;
Cinemascope; 104 minutes; Not rated; November release. CAST:
Alexei Petrenko (Rasputin), Anatoly Romashin (Czar Nicholas), Velta
Linne (Alexandra), Alice Freindlikh (Anna Vyrubova)

Alexei Petrenko as "Rasputin"
© *International Film Exchange*

Anatoly Romashin, Alice Freindlikh
in "Rasputin" © *IFEX*

217

Isabelle Adjani, Christopher Lambert
in "Subway" © *Island Alive*

SUBWAY (Island Alive) Producers, Luc Besson, Francois Ruggieri; Director, Luc Besson; Scenario, Luc Besson, Pierre Jolivet, Alain Le Henry, Marc Perrier, Sophie Schmit; Dialogue, Luc Besson, Marc Perrier; Photography, Carlo Varini; Music, Eric Serra, Rickie Lee Jones; Designer, Alexandre Trauner; Editor, Sophie Schmit; Sound, Harald Maury, Harrick Maury; Production Director, Edith Colnel; Executive Producer, Louis Duchesne; A Les Films Loup/TFS Production/Gaumont/TF1 Films Production; France, 1985; CinemaScope; Dolby Stereo; 108 minutes; Rated R; November release. CAST: Isabelle Adjani (Helena), Christopher Lambert (Fred), Richard Bohringer (The Florist), Michel Galabru (Inspector Gesberg), Jean-Hugues Anglade (Roller-Skater), Jean-Pierre Bacri (Batman), Jean Bouise (Station Master), Pierre-Ange Le Pogam (Jean), Jean Reno (Drummer), Arthur Simms (Singer), Constantin Alexandrov (Husband), Jean-Claude Lecas (Robin), Eric Serra (Bassist), Benoit Regent (Salesman), Alain Guillard (Saxophonist), Christian Gomba (Big Bill), Jean-Michel Castanie (Minder)

AMADA (Cinema Guild) Producer, Jose Ramon Perez; Director, Humberto Solas; Screenplay, Nelson Rodriguez, Humberto Solas; Based on novel "La Esfinge" by Miguel de Carrion; Photography, Livio Delgado; Editor/Assistant Director, Nelson Rodriguez; Music, Leo Brouwer; Designer, Pedro Garcia Espinosa; Costumes, Derubin Jacome; Cuba 1983; Spanish with subtitles; In color; Not rated; 95 minutes; December release. CAST: Eslinda Nunez (Amada), Cesar Evora (Marcial), Silvia Planas (Dona Herminia), Andres Hernandez (Dionisio), Oneida Hernandez (Joaquina), Gerardo Riveron (Alberto), Monica Guffanti (Violeta), Georgina Almanza (Tomasa), Elio Mesa (Priest), Fela Jar (Cristina)

HOUSE FOR SWAP (Se Permuta) (Cinema Guild) Director, Juan Carlos Tabio; Story, Juan Carlos Tabio, Jesus Gregorio, Tomas Gutierrez Alea; Screenplay, Juan Carlos Tabio, Raul Garcia; Editor, Roberto Bravo; Photography, Julio Valdes; Cuba 1983; Spanish with subtitles; In color; 103 minutes; December release. CAST: Rosita Fornes (Gloria), Isabel Santos (Yolanda), Mario Balmaseda (Pepe), Ramoncito Veloz, Jr. (Guillermito), Silvia Planas (Angelina), Manuel Porto (Orlando)

HABANERA (Cinema Guild) Producer, Jose Ramon Perez; Director, Pastor Vega; Story, Pastor Vega, Ambrosio Fornet; Screenplay, Ambrosio Fornet; Photography, Livio Delgado; Editor, Nelson Rodriguez; Music, Carlos Farinas; Cuba 1984; Spanish with subtitles; In color; 108 minutes; December release. CAST: Daisy Granados (Laura), Ely Menz (Isabel), Marcia Barreto (Leonor), Adolfo Llaurado (Carlos), Miguel Benavides (Mario), Cesar Evora (Jose Luiz)

THE TABLES TURNED (Cinema Guild) "Los Parajos Tirandole a la Escopeta"; Producer, Evelio Delgado; Director, Rolando Diaz; Screenplay, Miriam Lexcano; Photography, Pablo Martinez; Editor, Jorge Abello; Music, Juan Formell; Cuba 1984; Spanish with subtitles; In color; 90 minutes; December release. CAST: Reinaldo Miravalles (Felo), Consuelo Vidal (Hilda), Alberto Pujol (Emilito), Beatriz Valdes (Magadalena), Silvia Planas (Grandmother), Nestor Jimenez (Braulio), Filiberto Romero (Portero)

AMIGOS (Manicato) Producer, Camilo Vila; Executive Producer, Marcelino Miyares; Director, Ivan Acosta; Screenplay, Ivan Acosta; Photography, Henry Vargas; Editor Gloria Pineyro; Music, Sergio Garcia-Marruz; Art Director, Siro Del Castillo; Assistant Director, Oscar Costo; In Spanish with English subtitles; Not rated; In color; 108 minutes; December release. CAST: Ruben Rabasa (Ramon), Reynaldo Medina (Pablo), Lucy Pereda (Magaly), Juan Granda (Olmedo), Armando Naser (Gavilan), Blanca de Abril (Cecilia), Lilian Hurst (Mirta), Luisa Gil (Consuelo), Juan Troya (Pellon), Dania Victor, Uva Clavijo, George Prince, Mercedes Enriquez, Celia DeMunio, Manuel Estanillo, Ellen Cody, Carlos Bermudez, Tony Calbino

GUARDIAN OF HELL (Film Concept Group) Presented by John L. Chambliss, Michael Franzese; Director, Stefan Oblowsky; No other credits available; In CFI Color; Italian; Rated R; 85 minutes; December release. CAST: Sandy Samuel, Frank Garfeeld

JE TU IL ELLE (World Artists) Producer, Paradise Films; Director-Screenplay, Chantal Akerman; Photography, Benedicte Delesalle; Editor, Luc Freche; Sound, Samy Szlingerbaum, Gerard Rousseau; Sound Effects, Marc Lobet; Assistant Director, Charlotte Szlovak; France, 1974; French with subtitles; Black and white; 90 minutes; Not rated; December release. CAST: Chantal Akerman (Je:Julie), Niels Arestrup (Il:The Truck Driver); Claire Wauthion (Elle:The Girlfriend)

ONLY EMPTINESS REMAINS (Cinema Guild) Producer, Luis Megino; Director, Rodolfo Kuhn; Screenplay, Osvaldo Bayer; Photography, Angel Luis Fernandez; Editor, Jose Salcedo; Spanish with subtitles; Music, Victor Manuel; Documentary; 114 minutes; Not rated; December release

REVOLUTION (Warner Bros.) Producer, Irwin Winkler; Director, Hugh Hudson; Photography, Bernard Lutic; Editor, Stuart Baird; Music, John Corigliano; Designer, Assheton Gorton; Costumes, John Mollo; Executive Producer, Chris Burt; Production Manager, David Barron; Assistant Director, Derek Cracknell, Melvin Lind; Sound, David Crozier; Special Effects, Alan Whibley; Presented by Warner Bros./Goldcrest/Viking; Technicolor; System 35 Widescreen; Dolby Stereo; British/Norwegian; 125 minutes; Rated PG; December release. CAST: Al Pacino (Tom Dobb), Donald Sutherland (Sgt. Major Peasy), Nastassja Kinski (Daisy), Joan Plowright (Mrs. McConnahay), Dave King (Mr. McConnahay), Steven Berkoff (Sgt. Jones), John Wells (Corty), Annie Lennox (Liberty Woman), Dexter Fletcher (Ned), Sid Owen (Young Ned), Richard O'Brien (Lord Hampton), Paul Brooke (Lord Darling), Eric Milota (Merle), Felicity Dean (Betsy), Jo Anna Lee (Amy), Cheryl Miller (Cuffy), Harry Ditson (Israel), Rebecca Calder (Bella), Theresa Boden (Abby), Jesse Birdsall (Corp.), Cameron Johann (Ben), Danny Potts (Ahab), William Marlowe (Sgt. Marley), Stefan Gryff (Capt. Lacy), Frank Windsor (Gen. Washington), Skeeter Vaughan (Tonti), Larry Sellers (Honehwah), Graham Greene (Ongwata), and Denis Lacroix, Joseph Runningfox, Harold Pacheco, John Patrick, Malcolm Terris, Steve Kligerman, Adrian Rawlins, Manning Redwood, Kate Hardie, Richard Hicks, Tristram Jellinek, Lex Van Delden, Matthew Sim, Jonathan Adams, Robbie Coltrane, Brendan Conrow, Paul Humpoletz

Consuelo Vidal, Alberto Pujol, Beatriz Valdes
in "The Tables Turned"
© *Cinema Guild*

Al Pacino, Sid Owen
in "Revolution"
© *Warner Bros.*

Willie
Aames

Brooke
Adams

Wesley
Addy

Jane
Alexander

Anthony
Andrews

Ann-Margret

BIOGRAPHICAL DATA

(Name, real name, place and date of birth, school attended)

AAMES, WILLIE (William Upton): 1961.

ABBOTT, DIAHNNE: NYC, 1945.

ABBOTT, JOHN: London, June 5, 1905.

ABEL, WALTER: St. Paul, MN, June 6, 1898. AADA.

ABRAHAM, F. MURRAY: Pittsburgh, PA, Oct. 24, 1939. UTx.

ADAMS, BROOKE: NYC, 1949. Dalton.

ADAMS, DON: NYC, 1927.

ADAMS, EDIE (Elizabeth Edith Enke): Kingston, PA, Apr. 16, 1929. Juilliard, Columbia.

ADAMS, JULIE (Betty May): Waterloo, Iowa, Oct. 17, 1928. Little Rock Jr. College.

ADAMS, MAUD (Maud Wikstrom): Lulea, Sweden.

ADDY, WESLEY: Omaha, NB, Aug. 4, 1913. UCLA.

ADJANI, ISABELLE: Paris, 1955.

ADRIAN, IRIS (Iris Adrian Hostetter): Los Angeles, May 29, 1913.

AGAR, JOHN: Chicago, Jan. 31, 1921.

AGUTTER, JENNY: London, 1953.

AIELLO, DANNY: June 20, 1935, NYC.

AIMEE, ANOUK: Paris, Apr. 27, 1934. Bauer-Therond.

AKINS, CLAUDE: Nelson, GA, May 25, 1936. Northwestern U.

ALBERGHETTI, ANNA MARIA: Pesaro, Italy, May 15, 1936.

ALBERT, EDDIE (Eddie Albert Heimberger): Rock Island, IL, Apr. 22, 1908. U. of Minn.

ALBERT, EDWARD: Los Angeles, Feb. 20, 1951. UCLA.

ALBRIGHT, LOLA: Akron, OH, July 20, 1925.

ALDA, ALAN: NYC, Jan. 28, 1936. Fordham.

ALDA, ROBERT (Alphonso D'Abruzzo): NYC, Feb. 26, 1914. NYU.

ALDERSON, BROOKE: Dallas, Tx.

ALEJANDRO, MIGUEL: NYC, Feb. 21, 1958.

ALEXANDER, JANE (Quigley): Boston, MA, Oct. 28, 1939. Sarah Lawrence.

ALLEN, KAREN: Carrollton, IL. Oct. 5, 1951. UMd.

ALLEN, NANCY: NYC 1950.

ALLEN, REX: Wilcox, AZ, Dec. 31, 1922.

ALLEN, STEVE: New York City, Dec. 26, 1921.

ALLEN, WOODY (Allen Stewart Konigsberg): Brooklyn, Dec. 1, 1935.

ALLYSON, JUNE (Ella Geisman): Westchester, NY, Oct. 7, 1917.

ALONSO, MARIA CONCHITA: Cuba 1957.

ALVARADO, TRINI: NYC, 1967.

AMECHE, DON (Dominic Amichi): Kenosha, WI, May 31, 1908.

AMES, ED: Boston July 9, 1929.

AMES, LEON (Leon Wycoff): Portland, IN, Jan. 20, 1903.

AMIS, SUZY: Oklahoma City, Ok., 1958. Actors Studio.

AMOS, JOHN: Newark, NJ, Dec. 27, 1940. Colo. U.

ANDERSON, JUDITH: Adelaide, Australia, Feb. 10, 1898.

ANDERSON, LONI: St. Paul, Mn., Aug. 5, 1946.

ANDERSON, LYNN: Grand Forkes, ND; Sept. 26, 1947. UCLA.

ANDERSON, MELODY: Canada 1955, Carlton U.

ANDERSON, MICHAEL, JR.: London, Eng., 1943.

ANDERSSON, BIBI: Stockholm, Nov. 11, 1935. Royal Dramatic Sch.

ANDES, KEITH: Ocean City, NJ, July 12, 1920. Temple U., Oxford.

ANDRESS, URSULA: Switz., Mar. 19, 1936.

ANDREWS, ANTHONY: London, 1948.

ANDREWS, DANA: Collins, MS, Jan. 1, 1909. Sam Houston Col.

ANDREWS, HARRY: Tonbridge, Kent, Eng., Nov. 10, 1911.

ANDREWS, JULIE (Julia Elizabeth Wells): Surrey, Eng., Oct. 1, 1935.

ANGEL, HEATHER: Oxford, Eng., Feb. 9, 1909. Wycombe Abbey.

ANNABELLA (Suzanne Georgette Charpentier): Paris, France, July 14, 1912/1909.

ANN-MARGRET (Olsson): Valsjobyn, Sweden, Apr. 28, 1941. Northwestern U.

ANSARA, MICHAEL: Lowell, MA, Apr. 15, 1922. Pasadena Playhouse.

ANTHONY, TONY: Clarksburg, WV, Oct. 16, 1937. Carnegie Tech.

ANTON, SUSAN: Yucaipa, CA. Oct. 12, 1950. Bernardino Col.

ANTONELLI, LAURA: Pola, Italy.

ARCHER, JOHN (Ralph Bowman): Osceola, NB, May 8, 1915. USC.

ARDEN, EVE (Eunice Quedens): Mill Valley, CA, Apr. 30, 1912.

ARKIN, ALAN: NYC, Mar. 26, 1934. LACC.

ARNAZ, DESI: Santiago, Cuba, Mar. 2, 1915. Colegio de Dolores.

ARNAZ, DESI, JR.: Los Angeles, Jan. 19, 1953.

ARNAZ, LUCIE: Hollywood, July 17, 1951.

ARNESS, JAMES (Aurness): Minneapolis, MN, May 26, 1923. Beloit College.

ARTHUR, BEATRICE (Frankel): NYC, May 13, 1926. New School.

ARTHUR, JEAN: NYC, Oct. 17, 1905.

ARTHUR, ROBERT (Robert Arthaud): Aberdeen, WA, June 18, 1925. U. Wash.

ASHLEY, ELIZABETH (Elizabeth Ann Cole): Ocala, FL, Aug. 30, 1939.

ASSANTE, ARMAND: NYC, Oct. 4, 1949. AADA.

ASTAIRE, FRED (Fred Austerlitz): Omaha, NB, May 10, 1899.

ASTIN, JOHN: Baltimore, MD, Mar. 30, 1930. U. Minn.

ASTIN, PATTY DUKE: (see Patty Duke)

ASTOR, MARY (Lucile V. Langhanke): Quincy, IL, May 3, 1906. Kenwood-Loring School.

ATHERTON, WILLIAM: Orange, CT, July 30, 1947. Carnegie Tech.

ATKINS, CHRISTOPHER: Rye, NY, Feb. 21, 1961.

ATTENBOROUGH, RICHARD: Cambridge, Eng., Aug. 29, 1923. RADA.

AUBERJONOIS, RENE: NYC, June 1, 1940. Carnegie Tech.

AUDRAN, STEPHANE: Versailles, Fr., 1933.

AUGER, CLAUDINE: Paris, Apr. 26, 1942. Dramatic Cons.

AULIN, EWA: Stockholm, Sweden, Feb. 14, 1950.

AUMONT, JEAN PIERRE: Paris, Jan. 5, 1909. French Nat'l School of Drama.

AUTRY, GENE: Tioga, TX, Sept. 29, 1907.

AVALON, FRANKIE (Francis Thomas Avallone): Philadelphia, Sept. 18, 1939.

| Lauren Bacall | Kevin Bacon | Ellen Barkin | Steven Bauer | Senta Berger | David Birney |

AYKROYD, DAN: Ottawa, Can., 1952.
AYRES, LEW: Minneapolis, MN, Dec. 28, 1908.
AZNAVOUR, CHARLES (Varenagh Aznourian): Paris, May 22, 1924.
BACALL, LAUREN (Betty Perske): NYC, Sept. 16, 1924. AADA.
BACH, BARBARA: Aug. 27, 1946.
BACKUS, JIM: Cleveland, Ohio, Feb. 25, 1913. AADA.
BACON, KEVIN: Philadelphia, PA., July 8, 1958.
BADDELEY, HERMIONE: Shropshire, Eng., Nov. 13, 1906 Margaret Morris School.
BAILEY, PEARL: Newport News, VA, March 29, 1918.
BAIN, BARBARA: Chicago, Sept. 13, 1934. U. ILL.
BAIO, SCOTT: Brooklyn, NY, Sept. 22, 1961.
BAKER, BLANCHE: NYC, Dec. 20, 1956.
BAKER, CARROLL: Johnstown, PA, May 28, 1931. St. Petersburg Jr. College.
BAKER, DIANE: Hollywood, CA, Feb. 25, 1938. USC.
BAKER, KATHY WHITTON: Midland, TX., June 8, 1950. UCBerkley.
BALABAN, ROBERT (Bob); Chicago, Aug. 16, 1945. Colgate.
BALDWIN, ADAM: Chicago, IL. 1962.
BALIN, INA: Brooklyn, Nov. 12, 1937. NYU.
BALL, LUCILLE: Celaron, NY, Aug. 6, 1910. Chatauqua Musical Inst.
BALSAM, MARTIN: NYC, Nov. 4, 1919. Actors Studio.
BANCROFT, ANNE (Anna Maria Italiano): Bronx, NY, Sept. 17, 1931. AADA.
BANNEN, IAN: Airdrie, Scot., June 29, 1928.
BARBEAU, ADRIENNE: Sacramento, CA. June 11, 1945. Foothill Col.
BARDOT, BRIGITTE: Paris, Sept. 28, 1934.
BARKIN, ELLEN: Bronx, NY, 1959. Hunter Col.
BARNES, BINNIE (Gitelle Enoyce Barnes): London, Mar. 25, 1906
BARRAULT, MARIE-CHRISTINE: Paris, 1946.
BARRETT, MAJEL (Hudec): Columbus, OH, Feb. 23. Western Reserve U.
BARRON, KEITH: Mexborough, Eng., Aug. 8, 1936. Sheffield Playhouse.

BARRY, GENE (Eugene Klass): NYC, June 14, 1921.
BARRY, NEILL: NYC, Nov. 29, 1965.
BARRYMORE, DREW: Los Angeles, Feb. 22, 1975.
BARRYMORE, JOHN BLYTH: Beverly Hills, CA, June 4, 1932. St. John's Military Academy.
BARTHOLOMEW, FREDDIE: London, Mar. 28, 1924.
BARYSHNIKOV, MIKHAIL: Riga, Latvia, Jan. 27, 1948.
BASINGER, KIM: Athens, GA. 1954. Neighborhood Playhouse.
BATEMAN, JUSTINE: Woodland Hills, Ca., 1966.
BATES, ALAN: Allestree, Derbyshire, Eng., Feb. 17, 1934. RADA.
BAUER, STEVEN: (Steven Rocky Echevarria): Havana, Cuba, Dec. 2, 1956. UMiami.
BAXTER, KEITH: South Wales, Apr. 29, 1933. RADA.
BEAL, JOHN (J. Alexander Bliedung): Joplin, MO, Aug. 13, 1909. PA. U.
BEATTY, NED: Louisville, KY. 1937.
BEATTY, ROBERT: Hamilton, Ont., Can., Oct. 19, 1909. U. of Toronto.
BEATTY, WARREN: Richmond, VA, March 30, 1937.
BECK, MICHAEL: Horseshoe Lake, AR, 1948.
BEDELIA, BONNIE: NYC, Mar. 25, 1948. Hunter Col.
BEDI, KABIR: India, 1945.
BEERY, NOAH, JR.: NYC, Aug. 10, 1916. Harvard Military Academy.
BEGLEY, ED, JR.: NYC, Sept. 16.
BELAFONTE, HARRY: NYC, Mar. 1, 1927.
BELASCO, LEON: Odessa, Russia, Oct. 11, 1902.
BEL GEDDES, BARBARA: NYC, Oct. 31, 1922.
BELL, TOM: Liverpool, Eng., 1932.
BELLAMY, RALPH: Chicago, June 17, 1904.
BELLER, KATHLEEN: NYC, 1957.
BELLWOOD, PAMELA (King): Scarsdale, NY
BELMONDO, JEAN PAUL: Paris, Apr. 9, 1933.
BENEDICT, DIRK (Niewoehner): White Sulphur Springs, MT. March 1, 1945. Whitman Col.
BENJAMIN, RICHARD: NYC, May 22, 1938. Northwestern U.
BENNENT, DAVID: Lausanne, Sept. 9, 1966.

BENNETT, BRUCE (Herman Brix): Tacoma, WA, May 19, 1909. U. Wash.
BENNETT, JILL: Penang, Malay, Dec. 24, 1931.
BENNETT, JOAN: Palisades, NJ, Feb. 27, 1910. St. Margaret's School.
BENSON, ROBBY: Dallas, TX, Jan 21, 1957.
BERENSON, MARISSA: NYC, Feb. 15, 1947.
BERGEN, CANDICE: Los Angeles, May 9, 1946. U. PA.
BERGEN, POLLY: Knoxville, TN, July 14, 1930. Compton Jr. College.
BERGER, HELMUT: Salzburg, Aus., 1945.
BERGER, SENTA: Vienna, May 13, 1941. Vienna Sch. of Acting.
BERGER, WILLIAM: Austria, Jan. 20, 1928. Columbia.
BERGERAC, JACQUES: Biarritz, France, May 26, 1927. Paris U.
BERLE, MILTON (Berlinger): NYC, July 12, 1908.
BERLIN, JEANNIE: Los Angeles, Nov. 1, 1949.
BERLINGER, WARREN: Brooklyn, Aug. 31, 1937. Columbia.
BERNARDI, HERSCHEL: NYC, 1923.
BERNHARD, SANDRA: Arizona 1956.
BERRI, CLAUDE (Langmann): Paris, July 1, 1934.
BERRIDGE, ELIZABETH: Westchester, NY, May 2, 1962. Strasberg Inst.
BERTO, JULIET: Grenoble, France, Jan. 1947.
BEST, JAMES: Corydon, IN, July 26, 1926.
BETTGER, LYLE: Philadelphia, Feb. 13, 1915. AADA.
BEYMER, RICHARD: Avoca, IA, Feb. 21, 1939.
BIEHN, MICHAEL: Ariz. 1957.
BIKEL, THEODORE: Vienna, May 2, 1924. RADA.
BIRNEY, DAVID: Washington, DC, Apr. 23, 1939. Dartmouth, UCLA.
BIRNEY, REED: Alexandria, VA., Sept. 11, 1954. Boston U.
BISHOP, JOEY (Joseph Abraham Gottlieb): Bronx, NY, Feb. 3, 1918.
BISHOP, JULIE (formerly Jacqueline Wells): Denver, CO, Aug. 30, 1917. Westlake School.
BISSET, JACQUELINE: Waybridge, Eng., Sept. 13, 1944.
BIXBY, BILL: San Francisco, Jan. 22, 1934. U. CAL.

| Karen Black | Robert Blake | Betsy Brantley | Tony Britton | Blair Brown | LeVar Burton |

BLACK, KAREN (Ziegler): Park Ridge, IL, July 1, 1942. Northwestern.

BLADES, RUBEN: Panama 1948, Harvard.

BLAINE, VIVIAN (Vivian Stapleton): Newark, NJ, Nov. 21, 1923.

BLAIR, BETSY (Betsy Boger): NYC, Dec. 11, 1923.

BLAIR, JANET (Martha Jane Lafferty): Blair, PA, Apr. 23, 1921.

BLAIR, LINDA: Westport, CT, Jan. 22, 1959.

BLAKE, AMANDA (Beverly Louise Neill): Buffalo, NY, Feb. 20, 1921.

BLAKE, ROBERT (Michael Gubitosi): Nutley, NJ, Sept. 18, 1933.

BLAKELY, SUSAN: Frankfurt, Germany 1950. U. TEX.

BLAKLEY, RONEE: Stanley, ID, 1946. Stanford U.

BLOOM, CLAIRE: London, Feb. 15, 1931. Badminton School.

BLYTH, ANN: Mt. Kisco, NY, Aug. 16, 1928. New Wayburn Dramatic School.

BOCHNER, HART: Toronto, 1956. U. San Diego.

BOGARDE, DIRK: London, Mar. 28, 1918. Glasgow & Univ. College.

BOLGER, RAY: Dorchester, MA, Jan. 10, 1903.

BOLKAN, FLORINDA (Florinda Soares Bulcao): Ceara, Brazil, Feb. 15, 1941.

BOND, DEREK: Glasgow, Scot., Jan. 26, 1920. Askes School.

BONO, SONNY (Salvatore): Feb. 16, 1935.

BOONE, PAT: Jacksonville, FL, June 1, 1934. Columbia U.

BOOTH, SHIRLEY (Thelma Ford): NYC, Aug. 30, 1907.

BORGNINE, ERNEST (Borgnino): Hamden, CT, Jan. 24, 1918. Randall School.

BOSTWICK, BARRY: San Mateo, CA., Feb. 24, 1945. NYU.

BOTTOMS, JOSEPH: Santa Barbara, CA, Aug. 30, 1954.

BOTTOMS, TIMOTHY: Santa Barbara, CA, Aug. 30, 1951.

BOULTING, INGRID: Transvaal, So. Africa, 1947.

BOVEE, LESLIE: Bend, OR, 1952.

BOWIE, DAVID: (David Robert Jones) Brixton, South London, Eng. Jan. 8, 1947.

BOWKER, JUDI: Shawford, Eng., Apr. 6, 1954.

BOXLEITNER, BRUCE: Elgin, IL., 1950.

BOYLE, PETER: Philadelphia, PA, 1937. LaSalle Col.

BRACKEN, EDDIE: NYC, Feb. 7, 1920.

BRADY, SCOTT (Jerry Tierney): Brooklyn, Sept. 13, 1924. Bliss-Hayden Dramatic School.

BRAGA, SONIA: Maringa, Brazil, 1951.

BRAND, NEVILLE: Kewanee, IL, Aug. 13, 1920.

BRANDO, JOCELYN: San Francisco, Nov. 18, 1919. Lake Forest College, AADA.

BRANDO, MARLON: Omaha, NB, Apr. 3, 1924. New School.

BRANDON, CLARK: NYC 1959.

BRANDON, HENRY: Berlin, Ger., June 18, 1912. Stanford.

BRANDON, MICHAEL (Feldman): Brooklyn, NY.

BRANTLEY, BETSY: Rutherfordton, NC, 1955. London Central Sch. of Drama.

BRAZZI, ROSSANO: Bologna, Italy, Sept. 18, 1916. U. Florence.

BRENNAN, EILEEN: Los Angeles, CA., Sept. 3, 1935. AADA.

BRIAN, DAVID: NYC, Aug. 5, 1914. CCNY.

BRIDGES, BEAU: Los Angeles, Dec. 9, 1941. UCLA.

BRIDGES, JEFF: Los Angeles, Dec. 4, 1949.

BRIDGES, LLOYD: San Leandro, CA, Jan. 15, 1913.

BRINKLEY, CHRISTIE: Malibu, CA., Feb. 2, 1954.

BRISEBOIS, DANIELLE: Brooklyn, June 28, 1969.

BRITT, MAY (Maybritt Wilkins): Sweden, Mar. 22, 1936.

BRITTANY, MORGAN: (Suzanne Caputo): Los Angeles, 1950.

BRITTON, TONY: Birmingham, Eng., June 9, 1924.

BRODIE, STEVE (Johnny Stevens): Eldorado, KS, Nov. 25, 1919.

BROLIN, JAMES: Los Angeles, July 18, 1940. UCLA.

BROMFIELD, JOHN (Farron Bromfield): South Bend, IN, June 11, 1922. St. Mary's College.

BRONSON, CHARLES (Buchinsky): Ehrenfeld, PA, Nov. 3, 1920.

BROSNAN, PIERCE: Ireland, 1952.

BROWN, BLAIR: Washington, DC, 1948; Pine Manor.

BROWN, BRYAN: Panania, Aust., 1947.

BROWN, GARY (Christian Brando): Hollywood, Ca., 1958.

BROWN, GEORG STANFORD: Havana, Cuba, June 24, 1943. AMDA.

BROWN, JAMES: Desdemona, TX, Mar. 22, 1920. Baylor U.

BROWN, JIM: St. Simons Island, NY, Feb. 17, 1935. Syracuse U.

BROWN, TOM: NYC, Jan. 6, 1913.

BROWNE, CORAL: Melbourne, Aust., July 23, 1913.

BROWNE, LESLIE: NYC, 1958.

BUCHHOLZ, HORST: Berlin, Ger., Dec. 4, 1933. Ludwig Dramatic School.

BUCKLEY, BETTY: Big Spring, Tx., July 3, 1947. TxCU.

BUETEL, JACK: Dallas, TX, Sept. 5, 1917.

BUJOLD, GENEVIEVE: Montreal, Can., July 1, 1942.

BURKE, PAUL: New Orleans, July 21, 1926. Pasadena Playhouse.

BURNETT, CAROL: San Antonio, TX, Apr. 26, 1933. UCLA.

BURNS, CATHERINE: NYC, Sept. 25, 1945. AADA.

BURNS, GEORGE (Nathan Birnbaum): NYC, Jan. 20, 1896.

BURR, RAYMOND: New Westminster, B.C., Can., May 21, 1917. Stanford, U. CAL., Columbia.

BURSTYN, ELLEN (Edna Rae Gillooly): Detroit, MI, Dec. 7, 1932.

BURTON, LeVAR: Los Angeles, CA. Feb. 16, 1958. UCLA.

BUSEY, GARY: Tulsa, OK, 1944.

BUTTONS, RED (Aaron Chwatt): NYC, Feb. 5, 1919.

BUZZI, RUTH: Wequetequock, RI, July 24, 1936. Pasadena Playhouse.

BYGRAVES, MAX: London, Oct. 16, 1922. St. Joseph's School.

BYRNES, EDD: NYC, July 30, 1933. Haaren High.

CAAN, JAMES: Bronx, NY, Mar. 26, 1939.

CABOT, SUSAN: Boston, July 6, 1927.

CAESAR, SID: Yonkers, NY, Sept. 8, 1922.

CAINE, MICHAEL (Maurice Michelwhite): London, Mar. 14, 1933.

CAINE, SHAKIRA (Baksh): Guyana, Feb. 23, 1947. Indian Trust Col.

CALHOUN, RORY (Francis Timothy Durgin): Los Angeles, Aug. 8, 1922.

CALLAN, MICHAEL (Martin Calinieff): Philadelphia, Nov. 22, 1935.

Colleen Camp	Glen Campbell	Irene Cara	Art Carney	Rosalind Cash	John Cassavet

CALVERT, PHYLLIS: London, Feb. 18, 1917. Margaret Morris School.

CALVET, CORRINE (Corrine Dibos): Paris, Apr. 30, 1925. U. Paris.

CAMP, COLLEEN: San Francisco, 1953.

CAMPBELL, BILL: Virginia 1960.

CAMPBELL, GLEN: Delight, AR, Apr. 22, 1935.

CANALE, GIANNA MARIA: Reggio Calabria, Italy, Sept. 12.

CANNON, DYAN (Samille Diane Friesen): Tacoma, WA, Jan. 4, 1935.

CANTU, DOLORES: 1957, San Antonio, TX.

CAPERS, VIRGINIA: Sumter, SC, 1925. Juilliard.

CAPSHAW, KATE: Ft. Worth, TX. 1953. UMo.

CAPUCINE (Germaine Lefebvre): Toulon, France, Jan. 6, 1935.

CARA, IRENE: NYC, Mar. 18, 1958.

CARDINALE, CLAUDIA: Tunis, N. Africa, Apr. 15, 1939. College Paul Cambon.

CAREY, HARRY, JR.: Saugus, CA, May 16, 1921. Black Fox Military Academy.

CAREY, MACDONALD: Sioux City, IA, Mar. 15, 1913. U. of Wisc., U. Iowa.

CAREY, PHILIP: Hackensack, NJ, July 15, 1925. U. Miami.

CARMEN, JULIE: Mt. Vernon, NY, Apr. 4, 1954.

CARMICHAEL, IAN: Hull, Eng., June 18, 1920. Scarborough Col.

CARNE, JUDY (Joyce Botterill): Northampton, Eng., 1939. Bush-Davis Theatre School.

CARNEY, ART: Mt. Vernon, NY, Nov. 4, 1918.

CARON, LESLIE: Paris, July 1, 1931. Nat'l Conservatory, Paris.

CARPENTER, CARLETON: Bennington, VT, July 10, 1926. Northwestern.

CARR, VIKKI (Florence Cardona): July 19, 1942. San Fernando Col.

CARRADINE, DAVID: Hollywood, Dec. 8, 1936. San Francisco State.

CARRADINE, JOHN: NYC, Feb. 5, 1906.

CARRADINE, KEITH: San Mateo, CA, Aug. 8, 1951. Colo. State U.

CARRADINE, ROBERT: San Mateo, CA, 1954.

CARREL, DANY: Tourane, Indochina, Sept. 20, 1936. Marseilles Cons.

CARRIERE, MATHIEU: West Germany 1950.

CARROLL, DIAHANN (Johnson): NYC, July 17, 1935. NYU.

CARROLL, MADELEINE: West Bromwich, Eng., Feb. 26, 1902. Birmingham U.

CARROLL, PAT: Shreveport, LA, May 5, 1927. Catholic U.

CARSON, JOHN DAVID: 1951, Calif. Valley Col.

CARSON, JOHNNY: Corning, IA, Oct. 23, 1925. U. of Neb.

CARSTEN, PETER (Ransenthaler): Weissenberg, Bavaria, Apr. 30, 1929. Munich Akademie.

CARTER, NELL: Birmingham, AL., Dec. 13.

CASH, ROSALIND: Atlantic City, NJ, Dec. 31, 1938. CCNY.

CASON, BARBARA: Memphis, TN, Nov. 15, 1933. U. Iowa.

CASS, PEGGY (Mary Margaret): Boston, May 21, 1925.

CASSAVETES, JOHN: NYC, Dec. 9, 1929. Colgate College, AADA.

CASSEL, JEAN-PIERRE: Paris, Oct. 27, 1932.

CASSIDY, DAVID: NYC, Apr. 12, 1950.

CASSIDY, JOANNA: Camden, NJ, 1944. Syracuse U.

CASSIDY, SHAUN: Los Angeles, CA., Sept. 27, 1958.

CASTELLANO, RICHARD: Bronx, NY, Sept. 3, 1934.

CAULFIELD, JOAN: Orange, NJ, June 1, 1922. Columbia U.

CAULFIELD, MAXWELL: Glasgow, Scot., Nov. 23, 1959.

CAVANI, LILIANA: Bologna, Italy, Jan. 12, 1937. U. Bologna.

CHAKIRIS, GEORGE: Norwood, OH, Sept. 16, 1933.

CHAMBERLAIN, RICHARD: Beverly Hills, CA, March 31, 1935. Pomona.

CHAMPION, MARGE: Los Angeles, Sept. 2, 1925.

CHANNING, CAROL: Seattle, Jan. 21, 1921. Bennington.

CHANNING, STOCKARD (Susan Stockard): NYC, 1944. Radcliffe.

CHAPIN, MILES: NYC, Dec. 6, 1954. HB Studio.

CHAPLIN, GERALDINE: Santa Monica, CA, July 31, 1944. Royal Ballet.

CHAPLIN, SYDNEY: Los Angeles, Mar. 31, 1926. Lawrenceville.

CHARISSE, CYD (Tula Ellice Finklea): Amarillo, TX, Mar. 3, 1922. Hollywood Professional School.

CHASE, CHEVY (Cornelius Crane Chase): NYC, Oct. 8, 1943.

CHER (Cherlin Sarkesian): May 20 1946, El Centro, CA.

CHIARI, WALTER: Verona, Italy 1930.

CHONG, RAE DAWN: Vancouver, Can., 1962.

Jean-Pierre Cassel	Joanna Cassidy	Maxwell Caulfield	Carol Channing	Miles Chapin	Rae Da Chong

Diane Cilento	James Coburn	Adrienne Corri	Bill Cosby	Lindsay Crouse	Keene Curtis

CHRISTIAN, LINDA (Blanca Rosa Welter): Tampico, Mex., Nov. 13, 1923.

CHRISTIE, JULIE: Chukua, Assam, India, Apr. 14, 1941.

CHRISTOPHER, DENNIS (Carelli): Philadelphia, PA, 1955. Temple U.

CHRISTOPHER, JORDAN: Youngstown, OH, Oct. 23, 1940. Kent State.

CILENTO, DIANE: Queensland, Australia, Oct. 5, 1933. AADA.

CLAPTON, ERIC: London, Mar. 30, 1945.

CLARK, DANE: NYC, Feb. 18, 1915. Cornell, Johns Hopkins U.

CLARK, DICK: Mt. Vernon, NY, Nov. 30, 1929. Syracuse U.

CLARK, MAE: Philadelphia, Aug. 16, 1910.

CLARK, PETULA: Epsom, England, Nov. 15, 1932.

CLARK, SUSAN: Sarnid, Ont., Can., Mar. 8, 1940. RADA.

CLAYBURGH, JILL: NYC, Apr. 30, 1944. Sarah Lawrence.

CLERY, CORRINNE: Italy, 1950.

CLOONEY, ROSEMARY: Maysville, KY, May 23, 1928.

CLOSE, GLENN: Greenwich, CT., Mar. 19, 1947. William & Mary Col.

COBURN, JAMES: Laurel, NB, Aug. 31, 1928. LACC.

COCA, IMOGENE: Philadelphia, Nov. 18, 1908.

COCO, JAMES: NYC, Mar. 21, 1929.

CODY, KATHLEEN: Bronx, NY, Oct. 30, 1953.

COLBERT, CLAUDETTE (Lily Chauchoin): Paris, Sept. 15, 1903. Art Students League.

COLE, GEORGE: London, Apr. 22, 1925.

COLEMAN, GARY: Zion, IL., 1968.

COLEMAN, JACK: Easton, PA., 1958. Duke U.

COLLETT, CHRISTOPHER: NYC, Mar. 13, 1968. Strasberg Inst.

COLLINS, JOAN: London, May 21, 1933. Francis Holland School.

COLLINS, STEPHEN: Des Moines, IA, Oct. 1, 1947. Amherst.

COLON, MIRIAM: Ponce, PR., 1945. UPR.

COMER, ANJANETTE: Dawson, TX, Aug. 7, 1942. Baylor, Tex. U.

CONANT, OLIVER: NYC, Nov. 15, 1955. Dalton.

CONAWAY, JEFF: NYC, Oct. 5, 1950. NYC.

CONDE, RITA (Elizabeth Eleanor): Cuba.

CONNERY, SEAN: Edinburgh, Scot., Aug. 25, 1930.

CONNERY, JASON: London 1962.

CONNORS, CHUCK (Kevin Joseph Connors): Brooklyn, Apr. 10, 1921. Seton Hall College.

CONNORS, MIKE (Krekor Ohanian): Fresno, CA, Aug. 15, 1925. UCLA.

CONRAD, WILLIAM: Louisville, KY, Sept. 27, 1920.

CONVERSE, FRANK: St. Louis, MO, May 22, 1938. Carnegie Tech.

CONVY, BERT: St. Louis, MO, July 23, 1935. UCLA.

CONWAY, KEVIN: NYC, May 29, 1942.

CONWAY, TIM (Thomas Daniel): Willoughby, OH, Dec. 15, 1933. Bowling Green State.

COOK, ELISHA, JR.: San Francisco, Dec. 26, 1907. St. Albans.

COOPER, BEN: Hartford, CT, Sept. 30, 1932. Columbia U.

COOPER, JACKIE: Los Angeles, Sept. 15, 1921.

CORBETT, GRETCHEN: Portland, OR, Aug. 13, 1947. Carnegie Tech.

CORBY, ELLEN (Hansen): Racine, WI, June 13, 1913.

CORCORAN, DONNA: Quincy, MA, Sept. 29, 1942.

CORD, ALEX (Viespi): Floral Park, NY, Aug. 3, 1931. NYU, Actors Studio.

CORDAY, MARA (Marilyn Watts): Santa Monica, CA, Jan. 3, 1932.

COREY, JEFF: NYC, Aug. 10, 1914. Fagin School.

CORLAN, ANTHONY: Cork City, Ire., May 9, 1947. Birmingham School of Dramatic Arts.

CORLEY, AL: Missouri, 1956. Actors Studio.

CORNTHWAITE, ROBERT: St. Helens, OR. Apr. 28, 1917. USC.

CORRI, ADRIENNE: Glasgow, Scot., Nov. 13, 1933. RADA.

CORTESA, VALENTINA: Milan, Italy, Jan. 1, 1925.

COSBY, BILL: Philadelphia, July 12, 1937. Temple U.

COSTER, NICOLAS: London, Dec. 3, 1934. Neighborhood Playhouse.

COTTEN, JOSEPH: Petersburg, VA, May 13, 1905.

COURTENAY, TOM: Hull, Eng., Feb. 25, 1937. RADA.

COURTLAND, JEROME: Knoxville, TN, Dec. 27, 1926.

CRAIG, MICHAEL: India, Jan. 27, 1929.

CRAIN, JEANNE: Barstow, CA, May 25, 1925.

CREMER, BRUNO: Paris, 1929.

CRENNA, RICHARD: Los Angeles, Nov. 30, 1926. USC.

CRISTAL, LINDA (Victoria Moya): Buenos Aires, Feb. 25, 1934.

CROSBY, HARRY: Los Angeles, CA, Aug. 8, 1958.

CROSBY, KATHRYN GRANT: (see Kathryn Grant)

CROSBY, MARY FRANCES: Calif., Sept. 14, 1959.

CROSS, BEN: London, 1948. RADA.

CROSS, MURPHY (Mary Jane): Laurelton, MD, June 22, 1950.

CROUSE, LINDSAY ANN: NYC, May 12, 1948. Radcliffe.

CROWLEY, PAT: Olyphant, PA, Sept. 17, 1932.

CRUISE, TOM: Syracuse, NY, 1962.

CRYSTAL, BILLY: NYC 1948.

CULLUM, JOHN: Knoxville, TN, Mar. 2, 1930. U. Tenn.

CULP, ROBERT: Oakland, CA., Aug. 16, 1930. U. Wash.

CULVER, CALVIN: Canandaigua, NY, 1943.

CUMMINGS, CONSTANCE: Seattle, WA, May 15, 1910.

CUMMINGS, QUINN: Hollywood, Aug. 13, 1967.

CUMMINGS, ROBERT: Joplin, MO, June 9, 1910. Carnegie Tech.

CUMMINS, PEGGY: Prestatyn, N. Wales, Dec. 18, 1926. Alexandra School.

CURTIN, JANE: Cambridge, MA; Sept. 6, 1947.

CURTIS, JAMIE LEE: Los Angeles, CA., Nov. 21, 1958.

CURTIS, KEENE: Salt Lake City, UT, Feb. 15, 1925. U. Utah.

CURTIS, TONY (Bernard Schwartz): NYC, June 3, 1924.

CUSACK, CYRIL: Durban, S. Africa, Nov. 26, 1910. Univ. Col.

CUSHING, PETER: Kenley, Surrey, Eng., May 26, 1913.

DAHL, ARLENE: Minneapolis, Aug. 11, 1928. U. Minn.

DALLESANDRO, JOE: Pensacola, FL, Dec. 31, 1948.

DALTON, TIMOTHY: Wales, 1945. RADA.

DALTREY, ROGER: London, Mar. 1, 1945.

DALY, TYNE: NYC, 1946. AMDA.

DAMONE, VIC (Vito Farinola): Brooklyn, June 12, 1928.

DANCE, CHARLES: Plymouth, Eng., 1946.

D'ANGELO, BEVERLY: Columbus, OH., 1954.

DANIELS, JEFF: Georgia, 1955. EastMichState.

DANIELS, WILLIAM: Bklyn, Mar. 31, 1927. Northwestern.

DANNER, BLYTHE: Philadelphia, PA. Bard Col.

DANO, ROYAL: NYC, Nov. 16, 1922. NYU.

DANSON, TED: Flagstaff, AZ, 1949. Stanford, Carnegie Tech.

DANTE, MICHAEL (Ralph Vitti): Stamford, CT, 1935. U. Miami.

DANTON, RAY: NYC, Sept. 19, 1931. Carnegie Tech.

DANZA, TONY: Brooklyn, NY., 1951. UDubuque.

DARBY, KIM: (Deborah Zerby): North Hollywood, CA, July 8, 1948.

DARCEL, DENISE (Denise Billecard): Paris, Sept. 8, 1925. U. Dijon.

DARREN, JAMES: Philadelphia, June 8, 1936. Stella Adler School.

DARRIEUX, DANIELLE: Bordeaux, France, May 1, 1917. Lycee LaTour.

DAVIDSON, JOHN: Pittsburgh, Dec. 13, 1941. Denison U.

DAVIS, BETTE: Lowell, MA, Apr. 5, 1908. John Murray Anderson Dramatic School.

DAVIS, BRAD: Fla., 1950. AADA.

DAVIS, MAC: Lubbock, TX, 1942.

DAVIS, NANCY (Anne Frances Robbins): NYC July 8, 1921, Smith Col.

DAVIS, OSSIE: Cogdell, GA, Dec. 18, 1917. Howard U.

DAVIS, SAMMY, JR.: NYC, Dec. 8, 1925.

DAVIS, SKEETER (Mary Frances Penick): Dry Ridge, KY. Dec. 30, 1931.

DAY, DENNIS (Eugene Dennis McNulty): NYC, May 21, 1917. Manhattan College.

DAY, DORIS (Doris Kappelhoff): Cincinnati, Apr. 3, 1924.

DAY, LARAINE (Johnson): Roosevelt, UT, Oct. 13, 1917.

DAYAN, ASSEF: Israel, 1945. U. Jerusalem.

DEAN, JIMMY: Plainview, TX, Aug. 10, 1928.

DeCARLO, YVONNE (Peggy Yvonne Middleton): Vancouver, B.C., Can., Sept. 1, 1922. Vancouver School of Drama.

DEE, FRANCES: Los Angeles, Nov. 26, 1907. Chicago U.

DEE, JOEY (Joseph Di Nicola): Passaic, NJ, June 11, 1940. Patterson State College.

DEE, RUBY: Cleveland, OH, Oct. 27, 1924. Hunter Col.

DEE, SANDRA (Alexandra Zuck): Bayonne, NJ, Apr. 23, 1942.

DeFORE, DON: Cedar Rapids, IA, Aug. 25, 1917. U. Iowa.

DeHAVEN, GLORIA: Los Angeles, July 23, 1923.

DeHAVILLAND, OLIVIA: Tokyo, Japan, July 1, 1916. Notre Dame Convent School.

DELL, GABRIEL: Barbados, BWI, Oct. 7, 1930.

DELON, ALAIN: Sceaux, Fr., Nov. 8, 1935.

DELORME, DANIELE: Paris, Oct. 9, 1927. Sorbonne.

DeLUISE, DOM: Brooklyn, Aug. 1, 1933. Tufts Col.

DEMONGEOT, MYLENE: Nice, France, Sept. 29, 1938.

DeMORNAY, REBECCA: Los Angeles, Ca., 1962. Strasberg Inst.

DENEUVE, CATHERINE: Paris, Oct. 22, 1943.

DeNIRO, ROBERT: NYC, Aug. 17, 1943, Stella Adler.

DENISON, MICHAEL: Doncaster, York, Eng., Nov. 1, 1915. Oxford.

DENNER, CHARLES: Tarnow, Poland, May 29, 1926.

DENNIS, SANDY: Hastings, NB, Apr. 27, 1937. Actors Studio.

DEPARDIEU, GERARD: Chateauroux, Fr., Dec. 27, 1948.

DEREK, BO (Mary Cathleen Collins): Long Beach, CA, Oct. 1956.

DEREK, JOHN: Hollywood, Aug. 12, 1926.

DERN, BRUCE: Chicago, June 4, 1936. U PA.

DERN, LAURA: California, 1966.

DeSALVO, ANNE: Philadelphia, PA., Apr. 3.

DEVINE, COLLEEN: San Gabriel, CA, June 22, 1960.

DEWHURST, COLLEEN: Montreal June 3, 1926. Lawrence U.

DEXTER, ANTHONY (Walter Reinhold Alfred Fleischmann): Talmadge, NB, Jan. 19, 1919. U. Iowa.

DeYOUNG, CLIFF: Los Angeles, CA, Feb. 12, 1945. Cal State.

DHIEGH, KHIGH: New Jersey, 1910.

DIAMOND, NEIL: NYC, Jan. 24, 1941. NYU.

DICKINSON, ANGIE: Kulm, ND, Sept. 30, 1932. Glendale College.

DIETRICH, MARLENE (Maria Magdalene von Losch): Berlin, Ger., Dec. 27, 1901. Berlin Music Academy.

DILLER, PHYLLIS (Driver): Lima, OH, July 17, 1917. Bluffton College.

DILLMAN, BRADFORD: San Francisco, Apr. 14, 1930. Yale.

DILLON, MATT: Larchmont, NY., Feb. 18, 1964. AADA.

DILLON, MELINDA: Hope, AR, Oct. 13, 1939. Goodman Theatre School.

DIVINE (Glenn) Baltimore, MD, 1945.

DOBSON, TAMARA: Baltimore, MD, 1947. MD. Inst. of Art.

DOMERGUE, FAITH: New Orleans, June 16, 1925.

DONAHUE, TROY (Merle Johnson): NYC, Jan. 27, 1937. Columbia U.

DONAT, PETER: Nova Scotia, Jan. 20, 1928. Yale.

DONNELL, JEFF (Jean Donnell): South Windham, ME, July 10, 1921. Yale Drama School.

DOOHAN, JAMES: Vancouver, BC, Mar. 3, Neighborhood Playhouse.

DOOLEY, PAUL: Parkersburg, WV, Feb. 22, 1928. U. WV.

DOUGLAS, DONNA (Dorothy Bourgeois): Baton Rouge, LA, 1935.

DOUGLAS, KIRK (Issur Danielovitch): Amsterdam, NY, Dec. 9, 1916. St. Lawrence U.

DOUGLAS, MICHAEL: New Brunswick, NJ, Sept. 25, 1944. U. Cal.

DOUGLASS, ROBYN: Sendai, Japan; June 21, 1953. UCDavis.

DOURIF, BRAD: Huntington, WV, Mar. 18, 1950. Marshall U.

DOVE, BILLIE: NYC, May 14, 1904.

DOWN, LESLEY-ANN: London, Mar. 17, 1954.

DRAKE, BETSY: Paris, Sept. 11, 1923.

DRAKE, CHARLES (Charles Rupert): NYC, Oct. 2, 1914. Nichols College.

DREW, ELLEN (formerly Terry Ray): Kansas City, MO, Nov. 23, 1915.

DREYFUSS, RICHARD: Brooklyn, NY, Oct. 19, 1947.

DRIVAS, ROBERT: Chicago, Oct. 7, 1938. U. Chi.

DRU, JOANNE (Joanne LaCock): Logan, WV, Jan. 31, 1923. John Robert Powers School.

DUBBINS, DON: Brooklyn, NY, June 28.

DUFF, HOWARD: Bremerton, WA, Nov. 24, 1917.

DUFFY, PATRICK: Montana, 1949. U. Wash.

DUKE, PATTY (Anna Marie): NYC, Dec. 14, 1946.

DULLEA, KEIR: Cleveland, NJ, May 30, 1936. Neighborhood Playhouse, SF State Col.

DUNAWAY, FAYE: Bascom, FL, Jan. 14, 1941, Fla. U.

DUNCAN, SANDY: Henderson, TX, Feb. 20, 1946. Len Morris Col.

DUNNE, Griffin: NYC 1956. Neighborhood Playhouse.

DUNNE, IRENE: Louisville, KY, Dec. 20, 1898. Chicago College of Music.

DUNNOCK, MILDRED: Baltimore, Jan. 25, 1900. Johns Hopkins and Columbia U.

DUPEREY, ANNY: Paris, 1947.

DURBIN, DEANNA (Edna): Winnipeg, Can., Dec. 4, 1921.

DURNING, CHARLES: Highland Falls, NY, Feb. 28, 1933. NYU.

DUSSOLLIER, ANDRE: Annecy, France, Feb. 17, 1946.

DUVALL, ROBERT: San Diego, CA, 1930. Principia Col.

DUVALL, SHELLEY: Houston, TX, July 7, 1949.

EASTON, ROBERT: Milwaukee, Nov. 23, 1930. U. Texas.

EASTWOOD, CLINT: San Francisco, May 31, 1930. LACC.

EATON, SHIRLEY: London, 1937. Aida Foster School.

EBSEN, BUDDY (Christian, Jr.): Belleville, IL, Apr. 2, 1910. U. Fla.

ECKEMYR, AGNETA: Karlsborg, Swed., July 2. Actors Studio.

EDEN, BARBARA (Moorhead): Tucson, AZ, Aug. 23, 1934.

EDWARDS, VINCE: NYC, July 9, 1928. AADA.

EGAN, RICHARD: San Francisco, July 29, 1923. Stanford U.

EGGAR, SAMANTHA: London, Mar. 5, 1939.

EICHHORN, LISA: Reading, PA, 1952. Queens Ont. U. RADA.

EILBER, JANET: Detroit, MI, July 27, 1951. Juilliard.

EKBERG, ANITA: Malmo, Sweden, Sept. 29, 1931.

EKLAND, BRITT: Stockholm, Swed., 1942.

ELIZONDO, HECTOR: NYC, Dec. 22, 1936.

ELLIOTT, DENHOLM: London, May 31, 1922. Malvern College.

ELLIOTT, SAM: Sacramento, CA, 1944. U. Ore.

ELY, RON (Ronald Pierce): Hereford, TX, June 21, 1938.

Rebecca
eMornay

Cliff
DeYoung

Lisa
Eichhorn

Rupert
Everett

Morgan
Fairchild

Peter
Firth

ERDMAN, RICHARD: Enid, OK, June 1, 1925.

ERICSON, JOHN: Dusseldorf, Ger., Sept. 25, 1926. AADA.

ESMOND, CARL: Vienna, June 14, 1906. U. Vienna.

ESTEVEZ, EMILIO: NYC 1962.

ESTRADA, ERIK: NYC, Mar. 16, 1949.

EVANS, DALE (Francis Smith): Uvalde, TX, Oct. 31, 1912.

EVANS, GENE: Holbrook, AZ, July 11, 1922.

EVANS, LINDA (Evanstad): Hartford, CT., Nov. 18, 1942.

EVANS, MAURICE: Dorchester, Eng., June 3, 1901.

EVERETT, CHAD (Ray Cramton): South Bend, IN, June 11, 1936.

EVERETT, RUPERT: Norfolk, Eng., 1959.

EWELL, TOM (Yewell Tompkins): Owensboro, KY, Apr. 29, 1909. U. Wisc.

FABARES, SHELLEY: Los Angeles, Jan. 19, 1944.

FABIAN (Fabian Forte): Philadelphia, Feb. 6, 1940.

FABRAY, NANETTE (Ruby Nanette Fabares): San Diego, Oct. 27, 1920.

FAIRBANKS, DOUGLAS JR.: NYC, Dec. 9, 1907. Collegiate School.

FAIRCHILD, MORGAN: (Patsy McClenny) Dallas, TX., 1950. UCLA.

FALK, PETER: NYC, Sept. 16, 1927. New School.

FARENTINO, JAMES: Brooklyn, Feb. 24, 1938. AADA.

FARINA, SANDY (Sandra Feldman): Newark, NJ, 1955.

FARR, DEREK: London, Feb. 7, 1912.

FARR, FELICIA: Westchester, NY, Oct. 4, 1932. Penn State Col.

FARRELL, CHARLES: Onset Bay, MA, Aug. 9, 1901. Boston U.

FARROW, MIA: Los Angeles, Feb. 9, 1945.

FAULKNER, GRAHAM: London, Sept. 26, 1947. Webber-Douglas.

FAWCETT, FARRAH: Corpus Christie, TX. Feb. 2, 1947. TexU.

FAYE, ALICE (Ann Leppert): NYC, May 5, 1912.

FEINSTEIN, ALAN: NYC, Sept. 8, 1941.

FELDON, BARBARA (Hall): Pittsburgh, Mar. 12, 1941. Carnegie Tech.

FELLOWS, EDITH: Boston, May 20, 1923.

FERRELL, CONCHATA: Charleston, WV, Mar. 28, 1943. Marshall U.

FERRER, JOSE: Santurce, P.R., Jan. 8, 1909. Princeton U.

FERRER, MEL: Elberon, NJ, Aug. 25, 1917. Princeton U.

FERRIS, BARBARA: London, 1943.

FERZETTI, GABRIELE: Italy, 1927. Rome Acad. of Drama.

FIELD, SALLY: Pasadena, CA, Nov. 6, 1946.

FIGUEROA, RUBEN: NYC 1958.

FINNEY, ALBERT: Salford, Lancashire, Eng., May 9, 1936. RADA.

FIRESTONE, ROCHELLE: Kansas City, MO., June 14, 1949. NYU.

FIRTH, PETER: Bradford, Eng., Oct. 27, 1953.

FISHER, CARRIE: Los Angeles, CA, Oct. 21, 1956. London Central School of Drama.

FISHER, EDDIE: Philadelphia, Aug. 10, 1928.

FITZGERALD, GERALDINE: Dublin, Ire., Nov. 24, 1914. Dublin Art School.

FLANNERY, SUSAN: Jersey City, NJ, July 31, 1943.

FLEMING, RHONDA (Marilyn Louis): Los Angeles, Aug. 10, 1922.

FLEMYNG, ROBERT: Liverpool, Eng., Jan. 3, 1912. Haileybury Col.

FLETCHER, LOUISE: Birmingham, AL, July 1934.

FOCH, NINA: Leyden, Holland, Apr. 20, 1924.

FOLDI, ERZSEBET: Queens, NY, 1967.

FONDA, JANE: NYC, Dec. 21, 1937. Vassar.

FONDA, PETER: NYC, Feb. 23, 1939. U. Omaha.

FONTAINE, JOAN: Tokyo, Japan, Oct. 22, 1917.

FOOTE, HALLIE: NYC 1953. UNH.

FORD, GLENN (Gwyllyn Samuel Newton Ford): Quebec, Can., May 1, 1916.

FORD, HARRISON: Chicago, IL, July 13, 1942. Ripon Col.

FOREST, MARK (Lou Degni): Brooklyn, Jan. 1933.

FORREST, STEVE: Huntsville, TX, Sept. 29, 1924. UCLA.

FORSLUND, CONNIE: San Diego, CA, June 19, 1950. NYU.

FORSTER, ROBERT (Foster, Jr.): Rochester, NY, July 13, 1941. Rochester U.

FORSYTHE, JOHN (Freund): Penn's Grove, NJ, Jan. 29, 1918.

FOSTER, JODIE (Ariane Munker): Bronx, NY, Nov. 19, 1962. Yale.

FOX, EDWARD: London, 1937, RADA.

FOX, MICHAEL J.: Vancouver, BC, 1961.

FOX, JAMES: London, 1939.

FOXWORTH, ROBERT: Houston, TX, Nov. 1, 1941. Carnegie Tech.

FOXX, REDD: St. Louis, MO, Dec. 9, 1922.

FRANCIOSA, ANTHONY (Papaleo): NYC, Oct. 25, 1928.

FRANCIS, ANNE: Ossining, NY, Sept. 16, 1932.

FRANCIS, ARLENE (Arlene Kazanjian): Boston, Oct. 20, 1908. Finch School.

FRANCIS, CONNIE (Constance Franconero): Newark, NJ, Dec. 12, 1938.

FRANCISCUS, JAMES: Clayton, MO, Jan. 31, 1934. Yale.

FRANCKS, DON: Vancouver, Can., Feb. 28, 1932.

FRANK, JEFFREY: Jackson Heights, NY, 1965.

FRANKLIN, PAMELA: Tokyo, Feb. 4, 1950.

FRANZ, ARTHUR: Perth Amboy, NJ, Feb. 29, 1920. Blue Ridge College.

FRAZIER, SHEILA: NYC, 1949.

FREEMAN, AL, JR.: San Antonio, TX, 1934. CCLA.

FREEMAN, MONA: Baltimore, MD, June 9, 1926.

FREY, LEONARD: Brooklyn, Sept. 4, 1938. Neighborhood Playhouse.

FULLER, PENNY: Durham, NC, 1940. Northwestern U.

FURNEAUX, YVONNE: Lille, France, 1928. Oxford U.

FYODOROVA, VICTORIA: Russia 1946.

GABOR, EVA: Budapest, Hungary, Feb. 11, 1920.

GABOR, ZSA ZSA (Sari Gabor): Budapest, Hungary, Feb. 6, 1918.

GAINES, BOYD: Atlanta, GA., May 11, 1953. Juilliard.

GALLAGHER, PETER: Armonk, NY, 1956, Tufts U.

GALLIGAN, ZACH: NYC, 1963. ColumbiaU.

GAM, RITA: Pittsburgh, PA, Apr. 2, 1928.

GARBER, VICTOR: Montreal, Can., Mar. 16, 1949.

GARBO, GRETA (Greta Gustafson): Stockholm, Sweden, Sept. 18, 1905.

GARDENIA, VINCENT: Naples, Italy, Jan. 7, 1922.

GARDNER, AVA: Smithfield, NC, Dec. 24, 1922. Atlantic Christian College.

GARFIELD, ALLEN: Newark, NJ, Nov. 22, 1939. Actors Studio.

GARLAND, BEVERLY: Santa Cruz, CA, Oct. 17, 1930. Glendale Col.

GARNER, JAMES (James Baumgarner): Norman, OK, Apr. 7, 1928. Okla. U.

GARR, TERI: Lakewood, OH, 1952.

GARRETT, BETTY: St. Joseph, MO, May 23, 1919. Annie Wright Seminary.

GARRISON, SEAN: NYC, Oct. 19, 1937.

GARSON, GREER: Ireland, Sept. 29, 1906.

GASSMAN, VITTORIO: Genoa, Italy, Sept. 1, 1922. Rome Academy of Dramatic Art.

GAVIN, JOHN: Los Angeles, Apr. 8, 1935. Stanford U.

GAYNOR, MITZI (Francesca Marlene Von Gerber): Chicago, Sept. 4, 1930.

GAZZARA, BEN: NYC, Aug. 28, 1930. Actors Studio.

GEARY, ANTHONY: Utah, 1948.

GEESON, JUDY: Arundel, Eng., Sept. 10, 1948. Corona.

GEOFFREYS, STEPHEN: Cincinnati, Oh., Nov. 22, 1964. NYU.

GEORGE, BOY (George O'Dowd): London 1962.

GEORGE, SUSAN: West London, Eng. July 26, 1950.

GERARD, GIL: Little Rock, AR, 1940.

GERE, RICHARD: Philadelphia, PA, Aug. 29, 1949. U. Mass.

GERROLL, DANIEL: London, Oct. 16, 1951. Central.

GHOLSON, JULIE: Birmingham, AL, June 4, 1958.

GHOSTLEY, ALICE: Eve, MO, Aug. 14, 1926. Okla U.

GIANNINI, CHERYL: Monessen, PA., June 15.

GIANNINI, GIANCARLO: Spezia, Italy, Aug. 1, 1942. Rome Acad. of Drama.

GIBSON, MEL: Oneonta, NY., Jan. 1951. NIDA.

GIELGUD, JOHN: London, Apr. 14, 1904. RADA.

GILFORD, JACK: NYC, July 25, 1907.

GILLIS, ANNE (Alma O'Connor): Little Rock, AR, Feb. 12, 1927.

GILLMORE, MARGALO: London, May 31, 1897. AADA.

GINGOLD, HERMIONE: London, Dec. 9, 1897.

GIROLAMI, STEFANIA: Rome, Italy, 1963.

GISH, LILLIAN: Springfield, OH, Oct. 14, 1896.

GLASER, PAUL MICHAEL: Boston, MA, 1943. Boston U.

GLASS, RON: Evansville, IN, 1946.

GLEASON, JACKIE: Brooklyn, Feb. 26, 1916.

GLENN, SCOTT: Pittsburgh, PA, Jan. 26, 1942; William and Mary Col.

GLOVER, JOHN: Kingston, NY, Aug. 7, 1944.

GODDARD, PAULETTE (Levy): Great Neck, NY, June 3, 1911.

GOLDBERG, WHOOPI (Caryn Johnson): NYC, Nov. 13, 1949.

GOLDBLUM, JEFF: Pittsburgh, PA, Oct. 22, 1952. Neighborhood Playhouse.

GOLDEN, ANNIE: NYC, 1952.

GONZALES-GONZALEZ, PEDRO: Aguilares, TX, Dec. 21, 1926.

GOODMAN, DODY: Columbus, OH, Oct. 28, 1915.

GORDON, GALE (Aldrich): NYC, Feb. 2, 1906.

GORDON, KEITH: NYC, Feb. 3, 1961.

GORING, MARIUS: Newport Isle of Wight, 1912. Cambridge, Old Vic.

GORMAN, CLIFF: Jamaica, NY, Oct. 13, 1936. NYU.

GORSHIN, FRANK: Apr. 5, 1933.

GORTNER, MARJOE: Long Beach, CA, 1944.

GOSSETT, LOUIS: Brooklyn, May 27, 1936. NYU.

GOULD, ELLIOTT (Goldstein): Brooklyn, Aug. 29, 1938. Columbia U.

GOULD, HAROLD: Schenectady, NY, Dec. 10, 1923. Cornell.

GOULET, ROBERT: Lawrence, MA, Nov. 26, 1933. Edmonton.

GRANGER, FARLEY: San Jose, CA, July 1, 1925.

GRANGER, STEWART (James Stewart): London, May 6, 1913. Webber-Douglas School of Acting.

GRANT, CARY (Archibald Alexander Leach): Bristol, Eng., Jan. 18, 1904.

GRANT, DAVID MARSHALL: Westport, CT, 1955. Yale.

GRANT, KATHRYN (Olive Grandstaff): Houston, TX, Nov. 25, 1933. UCLA.

GRANT, LEE: NYC, Oct. 31, 1930. Juilliard.

GRANVILLE, BONITA: NYC, Feb. 2, 1923.

GRAVES, PETER (Aurness): Minneapolis, Mar. 18, 1926. U. Minn.

GRAY, CHARLES: Bournemouth, Eng., 1928.

GRAY, COLEEN (Doris Jensen): Staplehurst, NB, Oct. 23, 1922. Hamline U.

GRAY, LINDA: Santa Monica, CA; Sept. 12, 1940.

GRAYSON, KATHRYN (Zelma Hedrick): Winston-Salem, NC, Feb. 9, 1922.

GREEN, KERRI: Fort Lee, NJ, 1967. Vassar.

GREENE, ELLEN: NYC, Feb. 22, Ryder Col.

GREENE, LORNE: Ottawa, CAN., Feb. 12, 1915. Queens U.

GREENWOOD, JOAN: London, Mar. 4, 1919. RADA.

GREER, JANE: Washington, DC, Sept. 9, 1924.

GREER, MICHAEL: Galesburg, IL, Apr. 20, 1943.

GREGORY, MARK: Rome, Italy. 1965.

GREY, JENNIFER: NYC 1960.

GREY, JOEL (Katz): Cleveland, OH, Apr. 11, 1932.

GREY, VIRGINIA: Los Angeles, Mar. 22, 1917.

GRIEM, HELMUT: Hamburg, Ger. U. Hamburg.

GRIFFITH, ANDY: Mt. Airy, NC, June 1, 1926. UNC.

GRIFFITH, MELANIE: NYC, Aug. 9, 1957 Pierce Col.

GRIMES, GARY: San Francisco, June 2, 1955.

GRIMES, TAMMY: Lynn, MA, Jan. 30, 1934. Stephens Col.

GRIZZARD, GEORGE: Roanoke Rapids, NC, Apr. 1, 1928. UNC.

GRODIN, CHARLES: Pittsburgh, PA, Apr. 21, 1935.

GROH, DAVID: NYC, May 21, 1939. Brown U., LAMDA.

GUARDINO, HARRY: Brooklyn, Dec. 23, 1925. Haaren High.

GUINNESS, ALEX: London, Apr. 2, 1914. Pembroke Lodge School.

GUNN, MOSES: St. Louis, MO, Oct. 2, 1929. Tenn. State U.

GUTTENBERG, STEVEN: Brooklyn, NY, Aug. 1958. UCLA.

GWILLIM, DAVID: Plymouth, Eng., Dec. 15, 1948. RADA.

HACKETT, BUDDY (Leonard Hacker): Brooklyn, Aug. 31, 1924.

HACKMAN, GENE: San Bernardino, CA, Jan. 30, 1931.

HADDON, DALE: Montreal, CAN., May 26, 1949. Neighborhood Playhouse.

HAGMAN, LARRY: (Hageman): Weatherford, TX., Sept. 21, 1931. Bard.

HAIM, COREY: Toronto, Can, 1972.

HALE, BARBARA: DeKalb, IL, Apr. 18, 1922. Chicago Academy of Fine Arts.

HALEY, JACKIE EARLE: Northridge, CA, 1963.

HALL, ALBERT: Boothton, AL, Nov. 10, 1937. Columbia.

HALL, ANTHONY MICHAEL: NYC, 1968.

HAMILL, MARK: Oakland, CA, Sept. 25, 1952. LACC.

HAMILTON, GEORGE: Memphis, TN, Aug. 12, 1939. Hackley.

HAMLIN, HARRY: Pasadena, CA, Oct. 30, 1951. Yale.

HAMPSHIRE, SUSAN: London, May 12, 1941.

HANKS, TOM: Oakland, CA., 1957. CalStateU.

HANNAH, DARYL: Chicago, IL., 1960, UCLA.

HANNAH, PAGE: Chicago, IL., 1964.

HARDIN, TY (Orison Whipple Hungerford II): NYC, June 1, 1930.

HAREWOOD, DORIAN: Dayton, OH, Aug. 6. U. Cinn.

HARMON, MARK: Los Angeles, CA, 1951; UCLA.

HARPER, VALERIE: Suffern, NY, Aug. 22, 1940.

HARRINGTON, PAT: NYC, Aug. 13, 1929. Fordham U.

HARRIS, BARBARA (Sandra Markowitz): Evanston, IL, 1937.

HARRIS, ED: Tenafly, NJ, Nov. 28, 1950. Columbia.

HARRIS, JULIE: Grosse Point, MI, Dec. 2, 1925. Yale Drama School.

HARRIS, RICHARD: Limerick, Ire., Oct. 1, 1930. London Acad.

HARRIS, ROSEMARY: Ashby, Eng., Sept. 19, 1930. RADA.

HARRISON, GREG: Catalina Island, CA, 1950; Actors Studio.

HARRISON, NOEL: London, Jan. 29, 1936.

HARRISON, REX: Huyton, Cheshire, Eng., Mar. 5, 1908.

HARROLD, KATHRYN: Tazewell, VA. 1950. Mills Col.

HARTMAN, DAVID: Pawtucket, RI, May 19, 1935. Duke U.

HARTMAN, ELIZABETH: Youngstown, OH, Dec. 23, 1941. Carnegie Tech.

HASSETT, MARILYN: Los Angeles, CA, 1949.

HAUER, RUTGER: Amsterdam, Hol. 1944.

| Teri Garr | Keith Gordon | Melanie Griffith | Rutger Hauer | Katharine Houghton | Zeljko Ivanek |

HAVER, JUNE: Rock Island, IL, June 10, 1926.

HAWN, GOLDIE: Washington, DC, Nov. 21, 1945.

HAYDEN, LINDA: Stanmore, Eng. Aida Foster School.

HAYES, HELEN: (Helen Brown): Washington, DC, Oct. 10, 1900. Sacred Heart Convent.

HAYS, ROBERT: Bethesda, MD., 1948; SD State Col.

HAYWORTH, RITA: (Margarita Cansino): NYC, Oct. 17, 1918.

HEARD, JOHN: Washington, DC, Mar. 7, 1946. Clark U.

HEATHERTON, JOEY: NYC, Sept. 14, 1944.

HECKART, EILEEN: Columbus, OH, Mar. 29, 1919. Ohio State U.

HEDISON, DAVID: Providence, RI, May 20, 1929. Brown U.

HEGYES, ROBERT: NJ, May 7, 1951.

HEMINGWAY, MARIEL: Nov. 22, 1961.

HEMMINGS, DAVID: Guilford, Eng. Nov. 18, 1938.

HENDERSON, MARCIA: Andover, MA, July 22, 1932. AADA.

HENDRY, GLORIA: Jacksonville, FL. 1949.

HENNER, MARILU: Chicago, IL. Apr. 4, 1952.

HENREID, PAUL: Trieste, Jan. 10, 1908.

HENRY, BUCK (Zuckerman): NYC, 1931. Dartmouth.

HENRY, JUSTIN: Rye, NY, 1971.

HEPBURN, AUDREY: Brussels, Belgium, May 4, 1929.

HEPBURN, KATHARINE: Hartford, CT, Nov. 8, 1907. Bryn Mawr.

HERRMANN, EDWARD: Washington, DC, July 21, 1943. Bucknell, LAMDA.

HERSHEY, BARBARA: see Seagull, Barbara Hershey.

HESTON, CHARLTON: Evanston, IL, Oct. 4, 1922. Northwestern U.

HEWITT, MARTIN: Claremont, CA, 1960; AADA.

HEYWOOD, ANNE (Violet Pretty): Birmingham, Eng., Dec. 11, 1932.

HICKMAN, DARRYL: Hollywood, CA, July 28, 1930. Loyola U.

HICKMAN, DWAYNE: Los Angeles, May 18, 1934. Loyola U.

HILL, ARTHUR: Saskatchewan, CAN., Aug. 1, 1922. U. Brit. Col.

HILL, STEVEN: Seattle, WA, Feb. 24, 1922. U. Wash.

HILL, TERENCE (Mario Girotti): Venice, Italy, Mar. 29, 1941. U. Rome.

HILLER, WENDY: Bramhall, Cheshire, Eng., Aug. 15, 1912. Winceby House School.

HILLIARD, HARRIET: (See Harriet Hilliard Nelson)

HINGLE, PAT: Denver, CO, July 19, 1923. Tex. U.

HIRSCH, JUDD: NYC, Mar. 15, 1935. AADA.

HODGE, PATRICIA: Lincolnshire, Eng., 1946. LAMDA.

HOFFMAN, DUSTIN: Los Angeles, Aug. 8, 1937. Pasadena Playhouse.

HOLBROOK, HAL (Harold): Cleveland, OH, Feb. 17, 1925. Denison.

HOLLIMAN, EARL: Tennesas Swamp, Delhi, LA, Sept. 11, 1928. UCLA.

HOLM, CELESTE: NYC, Apr. 29, 1919.

HOMEIER, SKIP (George Vincent Homeier): Chicago, Oct. 5, 1930. UCLA.

HOOKS, ROBERT: Washington, DC, Apr. 18, 1937. Temple.

HOPE, BOB (Leslie Townes Hope): London, May 26, 1903.

HOPPER, DENNIS: Dodge City, KS, May 17, 1936.

HORNADAY, JEFFREY: San Jose, Ca., 1956.

HORNE, LENA: Brooklyn, June 30, 1917.

HORSLEY, LEE: May 15, 1955.

HORTON, ROBERT: Los Angeles, July 29, 1924. UCLA.

HOUGHTON, KATHARINE: Hartford, CT, Mar. 10, 1945. Sarah Lawrence.

HOUSEMAN, JOHN: Bucharest, Sept. 22, 1902.

HOUSER, JERRY: Los Angeles, July 14, 1952. Valley Jr. Col.

HOUSTON, DONALD: Tonypandy, Wales, 1924.

HOVEY, TIM: Los Angeles, June 19, 1945.

HOWARD, KEN: El Centro, CA, Mar. 28, 1944. Yale.

HOWARD, RON: Duncan, OK, Mar. 1, 1954. USC.

HOWARD, RONALD: Norwood, Eng., Apr. 7, 1918. Jesus College.

HOWARD, TREVOR: Kent, Eng., Sept. 29, 1916. RADA.

HOWELLS, URSULA: London, Sept. 17, 1922.

HOWES, SALLY ANN: London, July 20, 1930.

HUDDLESTON, MICHAEL: Roanoke, VA., AADA.

HUGHES, BARNARD: Bedford Hills, NY, July 16, 1915. Manhattan Col.

HUGHES, KATHLEEN (Betty von Gerkan): Hollywood, CA, Nov. 14, 1928. UCLA.

HULCE, THOMAS: Plymouth, MI, Dec. 6, 1953. N.C.Sch. of Arts.

HUNNICUT, GAYLE: Ft. Worth, TX, Feb. 6, 1943. UCLA.

HUNT, LINDA: Morristown, NJ, Apr. 2, 1945. Goodman Theatre.

HUNT, MARSHA: Chicago, Oct. 17, 1917.

HUNTER, KIM (Janet Cole): Detroit, Nov. 12, 1922.

HUNTER, TAB (Arthur Gelien) NYC, July 11, 1931.

HUPPERT, ISABELLE: Paris, Fr., Mar. 16, 1955.

HURT, MARY BETH (Supinger): Marshalltown, IA., 1948. NYU.

HURT, WILLIAM: Washington, D.C., Mar. 20, 1950. Tufts, Juilliard.

HUSSEY, RUTH: Providence, RI, Oct. 30, 1917. U. Mich.

HUSTON, JOHN: Nevada, MO, Aug. 5, 1906.

HUTTON, BETTY (Betty Thornberg): Battle Creek, MI, Feb. 26, 1921.

HUTTON, LAUREN (Mary): Charleston, SC, Nov. 17, 1943. Newcomb Col.

HUTTON, ROBERT (Winne): Kingston, NY, June 11, 1920. Blair Academy.

HUTTON, TIMOTHY: Malibu, CA, Aug. 16, 1960.

HYDE-WHITE, WILFRID: Gloucestershire, Eng., May 13, 1903. RADA.

HYER, MARTHA: Fort Worth, TX, Aug. 10, 1924. Northwestern U.

IGLESIAS, JULIO: Madrid, Spain, Sept. 23, 1943.

INGELS, MARTY: Brooklyn, NY, Mar. 9, 1936.

IRELAND, JOHN: Vancouver, B.C., CAN., Jan. 30, 1914.

IRONS, JEREMY: Cowes, Eng. Sept. 19, 1948. Old Vic.

IVANEK, ZELJKO: Lujubljana, Yugo., Aug. 15, 1957. Yale. LAMDA.

IVES, BURL: Hunt Township, IL, June 14, 1909. Charleston ILL. Teachers College.

JACKSON, ANNE: Alleghany, PA, Sept. 3, 1926. Neighborhood Playhouse.

JACKSON, GLENDA: Hoylake, Cheshire, Eng., May 9, 1936. RADA.

JACKSON, KATE: Birmingham, AL. Oct. 29, 1948. AADA.

JACKSON, MICHAEL: Gary, Ind., Aug. 29, 1958.

JACOBI, DEREK: Leytonstone, London, Eng. Oct. 22, 1938. Cambridge.

JACOBI, LOU: Toronto, CAN., Dec. 28, 1913.

JACOBS, LAWRENCE-HILTON: Virgin Islands, 1954.

JACOBY, SCOTT: Chicago, Nov. 19, 1956.

JAECKEL, RICHARD: Long Beach, NY, Oct. 10, 1926.

JAGGER, DEAN: Lima, OH, Nov. 7, 1903. Wabash College.

JAGGER, MICK: July 26, 1943.

JAMES, CLIFTON: NYC, May 29, 1921. Ore. U.

JAMES, JOHN (Anderson): Apr. 1956, New Canaan, Ct., AADA.

JARMAN, CLAUDE, JR.: Nashville, TN, Sept. 27, 1934.

JASON, RICK: NYC, May 21, 1926. AADA.

JEAN, GLORIA (Gloria Jean Schoonover): Buffalo, NY, Apr. 14, 1927.

JEFFREYS, ANNE (Carmichael): Goldsboro, NC, Jan. 26, 1923. Anderson College.

JEFFRIES, LIONEL: London, 1927, RADA.

JERGENS, ADELE: Brooklyn, Nov. 26, 1922.

JETT, ROGER (Baker): Cumberland, MD., Oct. 2, 1946. AADA.

JILLIAN, ANN (Nauseda): Massachusetts, Jan. 29, 1951.

JOHN, ELTON: (Reginald Dwight) Middlesex, Eng., Mar. 25, 1947. RAM.

JOHNS, GLYNIS: Durban, S. Africa, Oct. 5, 1923.

JOHNSON, DON: Galena, Mo., Dec. 15, 1950. UKan.

JOHNSON, PAGE: Welch, WV, Aug. 25, 1930. Ithaca.

JOHNSON, RAFER: Hillsboro, TX, Aug. 18, 1935. UCLA.

JOHNSON, RICHARD: Essex, Eng., 1927. RADA.

JOHNSON, ROBIN: Brooklyn, NY: May 29, 1964.

JOHNSON, VAN: Newport, RI, Aug. 28, 1916.

JONES, CHRISTOPHER: Jackson, TN, Aug. 18, 1941. Actors Studio.

JONES, DEAN: Morgan County, AL, Jan. 25, 1936. Actors Studio.

JONES, JACK: Bel-Air, CA, Jan. 14, 1938.

JONES, JAMES EARL: Arkabutla, MS, Jan. 17, 1931. U. Mich.

JONES, JENNIFER (Phyllis Isley): Tulsa, OK, Mar. 2, 1919. AADA.

JONES, SAM J.: Chicago, IL, 1954.

JONES, SHIRLEY: Smithton, PA, March 31, 1934.

JONES, TOM (Thomas Jones Woodward): Pontypridd, Wales, June 7, 1940.

JONES, TOMMY LEE: San Saba, TX, Sept. 15, 1946. Harvard.

JORDAN, RICHARD: NYC, July 19, 1938. Harvard.

JOURDAN, LOUIS: Marseilles, France, June 18, 1920.

JULIA, RAUL: San Juan, PR, Mar. 9, 1940. U PR.

JURADO, KATY (Maria Christina Jurado Garcia): Guadalajara, Mex., 1927.

KAHN, MADELINE: Boston, MA, Sept. 29, 1942. Hofstra U.

KANE, CAROL: Cleveland, OH, 1952.

KAPLAN, JONATHAN: Paris, Nov. 25, 1947. NYU.

KAPOOR, SHASHI: Bombay 1940.

KAPRISKY, VALERIE: Paris, 1963.

KATT, WILLIAM: Los Angeles, CA, 1955.

KAUFMANN, CHRISTINE: Lansdorf, Graz, Austria, Jan. 11, 1945.

KAYE, DANNY: (David Daniel Kominski): Brooklyn, Jan. 18, 1913.

KAYE, STUBBY: NYC, Nov. 11, 1918.

KEACH, STACY: Savannah, GA, June 2, 1941. U. Cal., Yale.

KEATON, MICHAEL: Coraopolis, Pa., 1951. KentStateU.

KEATON, DIANE (Hall): Los Angeles, CA, Jan. 5, 1946. Neighborhood Playhouse.

KEATS, STEVEN: Bronx, NY, 1945.

KEDROVA, LILA: Greece, 1918.

KEEL, HOWARD (Harold Keel): Gillespie, IL, Apr. 13, 1919.

KEELER, RUBY (Ethel): Halifax, N.S., Aug. 25, 1909.

KEITH, BRIAN: Bayonne, NJ, Nov. 15, 1921.

KEITH, DAVID: Knoxville, Tn., 1954. UTN.

KELLER, MARTHE: Basel, Switz., 1945. Munich Stanislavsky Sch.

KELLERMAN, SALLY: Long Beach, CA, June 2, 1938. Actors Studio West.

KELLEY, DeFOREST: Atlanta, GA, Jan. 20, 1920.

KELLY, GENE: Pittsburgh, Aug. 23, 1912. U. Pittsburgh.

KELLY, JACK: Astoria, NY, Sept. 16, 1927. UCLA.

KELLY, NANCY: Lowell, MA, Mar. 25, 1921. Bentley School.

KEMP, JEREMY: Chesterfield, Eng., 1935, Central Sch.

KENNEDY, ARTHUR: Worcester, MA, Feb. 17, 1914. Carnegie Tech.

KENNEDY, GEORGE: NYC, Feb. 18, 1925.

KENNEDY, LEON ISAAC: Cleveland, OH., 1949.

KERR, DEBORAH: Helensburg, Scot., Sept. 30, 1921. Smale Ballet School.

KERR, JOHN: NYC, Nov. 15, 1931. Harvard, Columbia.

KHAMBATTA, PERSIS: Bombay, Oct. 2, 1950.

KIDDER, MARGOT: Yellow Knife, CAN., Oct. 17, 1948. UBC.

KIER, UDO: Germany, Oct. 14, 1944.

KILEY, RICHARD: Chicago, Mar. 31, 1922. Loyola.

KINCAID, ARON (Norman Neale Williams III): Los Angeles, June 15, 1943. UCLA.

KING, ALAN (Irwin Kniberg): Brooklyn, Dec. 26, 1927.

KING, PERRY: Alliance, OH, Apr. 30, 1948. Yale.

KINGSLEY, BEN (Krishna Bhanji): Snaiton, Yorkshire, Eng., Dec. 31, 1943.

KINSKI, NASTASSJA: Germany, Jan. 24, 1960.

KITT, EARTHA: North, SC, Jan. 26, 1928.

KLEMPERER, WERNER: Cologne, Mar. 22, 1920,

KLUGMAN, JACK: Philadelphia, PA, Apr. 27, 1925. Carnegie Tech.

KNIGHT, ESMOND: East Sheen, Eng., May 4, 1906.

KNIGHT, SHIRLEY: Goessel, KS, July 5, 1937. Wichita U.

KNOWLES, PATRIC (Reginald Lawrence Knowles): Horsforth, Eng., Nov. 11, 1911.

KNOX, ALEXANDER: Strathroy, Ont., CAN., Jan. 16, 1907.

KNOX, ELYSE: Hartford, CT, Dec. 14, 1917. Traphagen School.

KOENIG, WALTER: Chicago, IL, Sept. 14. UCLA.

KOHNER, SUSAN: Los Angeles, Nov. 11, 1936. U. Calif.

KORMAN, HARVEY: Chicago, IL, Feb. 15, 1927. Goodman.

KORVIN, CHARLES (Geza Korvin Karpathi): Czechoslovakia, Nov. 21. Sorbonne.

KOSLECK, MARTIN: Barkotzen, Ger., Mar. 24, 1907. Max Reinhardt School.

KOTTO, YAPHET: NYC, Nov. 15, 1937.

KREUGER, KURT: St. Moritz, Switz., July 23, 1917. U. London.

KRISTEL, SYLVIA: Amsterdam, Hol., Sept. 28, 1952.

KRISTOFFERSON, KRIS: Brownsville, TX, June 22, 1936, Pomona Col.

KRUGER, HARDY: Berlin Ger., April 12, 1928.

KULP, NANCY: Harrisburg, PA, 1921.

KUNTSMANN, DORIS: Hamburg, 1944.

KWAN, NANCY: Hong Kong, May 19, 1939. Royal Ballet.

LACY, JERRY: Sioux City, IA, Mar. 27, 1936. LACC.

LADD, CHERYL: (Stoppelmoor): Huron, SD, July 12, 1951.

LADD, DIANE: (Ladnier): Meridian, MS, Nov. 29, 1932. Tulane U.

LaGRECA, PAUL: Bronx, NY, June 23, 1962. AADA.

LAHTI, CHRISTINE: Detroit, MI, Apr. 4, 1950; U. Mich.

LAMARR, HEDY (Hedwig Kiesler): Vienna, Sept. 11, 1913.

LAMAS, LORENZO: Los Angeles, Jan. 1958.

LAMB, GIL: Minneapolis, June 14, 1906. U. Minn.

LAMBERT, CHRISTOPHER: NYC, 1958.

LAMOUR, DOROTHY (Mary Dorothy Slaton): New Orleans, LA.; Dec. 10, 1914. Spence School.

LANCASTER, BURT: NYC, Nov. 2, 1913. NYU.

LANCHESTER, ELSA (Elsa Sullivan): London, Oct. 28, 1902.

LANDAU, MARTIN: Brooklyn, NY, 1931. Actors Studio.

LANDON, MICHAEL (Eugene Orowitz): Collingswood, NJ, Oct. 31, 1936. USC.

LANDRUM, TERI: Enid, OK., 1960.

LANE, ABBE: Brooklyn, Dec. 14, 1935.

LANE, DIANE: NYC, Jan. 1963.

LANGAN, GLENN: Denver, CO, July 8, 1917.

LANGE, HOPE: Redding Ridge, CT, Nov. 28, 1933. Reed Col.

LANGE, JESSICA: Minnesota, Apr. 20, 1949. U. Minn.

LANSBURY, ANGELA: London, Oct. 16, 1925. London Academy of Music.

Page Johnson	Madeline Kahn	Aron Kincaid	Paul LaGreca	Janet Leigh	Calvin Levels

LANSING, ROBERT (Brown): San Diego, CA, June 5, 1929.
LAUPER, CYNTHIA: Astoria, Queens, NYC. June 20, 1953.
LAURE, CAROLE: Montreal, Can., 1951.
LAURIE, PIPER (Rosetta Jacobs): Detroit, MI, Jan. 22, 1932.
LAW, JOHN PHILLIP: Hollywood, Sept. 7, 1937. Neighborhood Playhouse, U. Hawaii.
LAWRENCE, BARBARA: Carnegie, OK, Feb. 24, 1930. UCLA.
LAWRENCE, CAROL (Laraia): Melrose Park, IL, Sept. 5, 1935.
LAWRENCE, VICKI: Inglewood, CA, 1949.
LAWSON, LEIGH: Atherston, Eng., July 21, 1945. RADA.
LEACHMAN, CLORIS: Des Moines, IA, Apr. 30, 1930. Northwestern U.
LEAUD, JEAN-PIERRE: Paris, 1944.
LEDERER, FRANCIS: Karlin, Prague, Czech., Nov. 6, 1906.
LEE, BRANDON: Feb. 1, 1965. Emerson Col.
LEE, CHRISTOPHER: London, May 27, 1922. Wellington College.
LEE, PEGGY (Norma Delores Egstrom): Jamestown, ND, 1920.
LEE, MARK: Australia, 1958.
LEE, MICHELE (Dusiak): Los Angeles, June 24, 1942. LACC.
LEIBMAN, RON: NYC, Oct. 11, 1937. Ohio Wesleyan.
LEIGH, JANET (Jeanette Helen Morrison): Merced, CA, July 6, 1926. College of Pacific.
LEMMON, JACK: Boston, Feb. 8, 1925. Harvard.
LENZ, RICK: Springfield, IL, Nov. 21, 1939. U. Mich.
LEONARD, SHELDON (Bershad): NYC, Feb. 22, 1907. Syracuse U.
LEROY, PHILIPPE: Paris, Oct. 15, 1930. U. Paris.
LESLIE, BETHEL: NYC, Aug. 3, 1929. Brearley School.
LESLIE, JOAN (Joan Brodell): Detroit, Jan. 26, 1925. St. Benedict's.
LESTER, MARK: Oxford, Eng., July 11, 1958.
LEVELS, CALVIN: Cleveland, OH., Sept. 30, 1954. CCC.
LEWIS, DANIEL DAY: London, 1958, Bristol Old Vic.
LEWIS, EMANUEL: Brooklyn, NY, 1971.
LEWIS, JERRY: Newark, NJ, Mar. 16, 1926.
LIGON, TOM: New Orleans, LA, Sept. 10, 1945.

LILLIE, BEATRICE: Toronto, Can., May 29, 1898.
LINCOLN, ABBEY (Anna Marie Woolridge): Chicago, Aug. 6, 1930.
LINDFORS, VIVECA: Uppsala, Sweden, Dec. 29, 1920. Stockholm Royal Dramatic School.
LISI, VIRNA: Rome, 1938.
LITHGOW, JOHN: Rochester, NY, Oct. 19, 1945. Harvard.
LITTLE, CLEAVON: Chickasha, OK, June 1, 1939. San Diego State.
LOCKE, SONDRA: Shelbyville, TN, 1947.
LOCKHART, JUNE: NYC, June 25, 1925. Westlake School.
LOCKWOOD, GARY: Van Nuys, CA, Feb. 21, 1937.
LOCKWOOD, MARGARET: Karachi, Pakistan, Sept. 15, 1916. RADA.
LOGGIA, ROBERT: Staten Island, NY., Jan. 3, 1930. UMo.
LOLLOBRIGIDA, GINA: Subiaco, Italy, July 4, 1927. Rome Academy of Fine Arts.
LOM, HERBERT: Prague, Czechoslovakia, 1917. Prague U.
LOMEZ, CELINE: Montreal, Can., 1953.
LONDON, JULIE (Julie Peck): Santa Rosa, CA, Sept. 26, 1926.
LONG, SHELLEY: Indiana, 1950. Northwestern U.
LONOW, MARK: Brooklyn, NY.
LOPEZ, PERRY: NYC, July 22, 1931. NYU.
LORD, JACK (John Joseph Ryan): NYC, Dec. 30, 1928. NYU.
LOREN, SOPHIA (Sofia Scicolone): Rome, Italy, Sept. 20, 1934.
LOUISE, TINA (Blacker): NYC, Feb. 11, 1934, Miami U.
LOVELACE, LINDA: Bryan, TX, 1952.
LOWE, CHAD: NYC, Jan, 15, 1968.
LOWE, ROB: Ohio, 1964.
LOWITSCH, KLAUS: Berlin, Apr. 8, 1936. Vienna Academy.
LOY, MYRNA (Myrna Williams): Helena, MT, Aug. 2, 1905. Westlake School.
LUCAS, LISA: Arizona, 1961.
LULU: Glasglow, Scot., 1948.
LUNA, BARBARA: NYC, Mar. 2, 1939.
LUND, JOHN: Rochester, NY, Feb. 6, 1913.
LUNDGREN, DOLPH: Stockholm, Sw., 1959. Royal Inst.
LUPINO, IDA: London, Feb. 4, 1916. RADA.
LYDON, JAMES: Harrington Park, NJ, May 30, 1923.
LYNLEY, CAROL (Jones): NYC, Feb. 13, 1942.

LYNN, JEFFREY: Auburn, MA, 1909. Bates College.
LYON, SUE: Davenport, IA, July 10, 1946.
LYONS, ROBERT F.: Albany, NY. AADA.
MacARTHUR, JAMES: Los Angeles, Dec. 8, 1937. Harvard.
MACCHIO, RALPH: Huntington, NY., 1962.
MacGINNIS, NIALL: Dublin, Ire., Mar. 29, 1913. Dublin U.
MacGRAW, ALI: NYC, Apr. 1, 1938. Wellesley.
MacLAINE, SHIRLEY (Beatty): Richmond, VA, Apr. 24, 1934.
MacMAHON, ALINE: McKeesport, PA, May 3, 1899. Barnard College.
MacMURRAY, FRED: Kankakee, IL, Aug. 30, 1908. Carroll Col.
MACNAUGHTON, ROBERT: NYC, Dec. 19, 1966.
MACNEE, PATRICK: London, Feb. 1922.
MacNICOL, PETER: Dallas, TX, Apr. 10, UMN.
MADISON, GUY (Robert Moseley): Bakersfield, CA, Jan. 19, 1922. Bakersfield Jr. College.
MADONNA (Madonna Louise Veronica Cicone): Pontiac, Mi., 1961 UMi.
MAHARIS, GEORGE: Astoria, NY, Sept. 1, 1928. Actors Studio.
MAHONEY, JOCK (Jacques O'Mahoney): Chicago, Feb. 7, 1919. U. of Iowa.
MAJORS, LEE: Wyandotte, MI, Apr. 23, 1940. E. Ky. State Col.
MAKEPEACE, CHRIS: Toronto, Can., 1964.
MALDEN, KARL. (Mladen Sekulovich): Gary, IN, Mar. 22, 1914.
MALET, PIERRE: St. Tropez, Fr., 1955.
MALONE, DOROTHY: Chicago, Jan. 30, 1925. S. Methodist U.
MANN, KURT: Roslyn, NY, July 18, 1947.
MANOFF, DINAH: NYC, Jan. 25, 1958. CalArts.
MANZ, LINDA: NYC, 1961.
MARAIS, JEAN: Cherbourg, France, Dec. 11, 1913. St. Germain.
MARGOLIN, JANET: NYC, July 25, 1943. Walden School.
MARIN, JACQUES: Paris, Sept. 9, 1919. Conservatoire National.
MARINARO, ED: NYC, 1951. Cornell.
MARSHALL, BRENDA (Ardis Anderson Gaines): Isle of Negros, P.I., Sept. 29, 1915. Texas State College.
MARSHALL, E. G.: Owatonna, MN, June 18, 1910. U. Minn.

MARSHALL, KEN: NYC, 1953. Ju-
illiard.
MARSHALL, PENNY: Bronx, NY,
Oct. 15, 1942. U. N. Mex.
MARSHALL, WILLIAM: Gary, IN,
Aug. 19, 1924. NYU.
MARTIN, DEAN (Dino Crocetti):
Steubenville, OH, June 17, 1917.
MARTIN, DEAN PAUL: Los An-
geles, CA, 1952. UCLA.
MARTIN, MARY: Weatherford,
TX, Dec. 1, 1914. Ward-Belmont
School.
MARTIN, STEVE: Waco, TX, 1946.
UCLA.
MARTIN, TONY (Alfred Norris):
Oakland, CA, Dec. 25, 1913. St.
Mary's College.
MARVIN, LEE: NYC, Feb. 19,
1924.
MASON, MARSHA: St. Louis, MO,
Apr. 3, 1942. Webster Col.
MASON, PAMELA (Pamela Kelli-
no): Westgate, Eng., Mar. 10, 1918.
MASSEN, OSA: Copenhagen, Den.,
Jan. 13, 1916.
MASSEY, DANIEL: London, Oct.
10, 1933. Eton and King's Col.
MASTERSON, PETER: Angleton,
TX, June 1, 1934. Rice U.
MASTRANTONIO, MARY ELIZ-
ABETH: Chicago, Il., Nov. 17,
1958. UIll.
MASTROIANNI, MARCELLO:
Fontana Liri, Italy, Sept. 28, 1924.
MATHESON, TIM: Glendale, CA,
Dec. 31, 1947. CalState.
MATHIS, JOHNNY: San Francisco,
Ca., Sept. 30, 1935. SanFran-
StateCol.
MATTHAU, WALTER (Matus-
chanskayasky): NYC, Oct. 1, 1920.
MATTHEWS, BRIAN: Phil-
adelphia, PA, Jan. 24, 1953. St.
Olaf.
MATURE, VICTOR: Louisville,
KY, Jan. 29, 1915.
MAY, ELAINE (Berlin): Phil-
adelphia, Apr. 21, 1932.
MAYEHOFF, EDDIE: Baltimore,
July 7. Yale.
MAYO, VIRGINIA (Virginia Clara
Jones): St. Louis, MO, Nov. 30,
1920.
McCALLUM, DAVID: Scotland,
Sept. 19, 1933. Chapman Col.
McCAMBRIDGE, MERCEDES:
Jolliet, IL, Mar. 17, 1918. Munde-
lein College.
McCARTHY, ANDREW: NYC,
1963, NYU.
McCARTHY, KEVIN: Seattle, WA,
Feb. 15, 1914. Minn. U.
McCLORY, SEAN: Dublin, Ire.,
Mar. 8, 1924. U. Galway.
McCLURE, DOUG: Glendale, CA,
May 11, 1935. UCLA.
McCOWEN, ALEC: Tunbridge
Wells, Eng., May 26, 1925. RADA.
McCREA, JOEL: Los Angeles, Nov.
5, 1905. Pomona College.
McDOWALL, RODDY: London,
Sept. 17, 1928. St. Joseph's.
McDOWELL, MALCOLM
(Taylor): Leeds, Eng., June 15,
1943. LAMDA.
McENERY, PETER: Walsall, Eng.,
Feb. 21, 1940.
McFARLAND, SPANKY: Dallas,
TX, 1936.
McGAVIN, DARREN: Spokane,
WA, May 7, 1922. College of Pacif-
ic.
McGILLIS, KELLY: Newport
Beach, CA, 1958. Juilliard.

McGOVERN, ELIZABETH: Evans-
ton, IL, July 18, 1961. Juilliard.
McGUIRE, BIFF: New Haven, CT,
Oct. 25, 1926. Mass. State Col.
McGUIRE, DOROTHY: Omaha,
NE, June 14, 1918.
McHATTIE, STEPHEN: Anti-
gonish, NS, Feb. 3. AcadiaU,
AADA.
McKAY, GARDNER: NYC, June
10, 1932. Cornell.
McKEE, LONETTE: Detroit, MI,
1954.
McKELLEN, IAN: Burnley, Eng.,
May 25, 1939.
McKENNA, VIRGINIA: London,
June 7, 1931.
McKEON, DOUG: New Jersey,
1966.
McKUEN, ROD: Oakland, CA, Apr.
29, 1933.
McLERIE, ALLYN ANN: Grand
Mere, Can., Dec. 1, 1926.
McNAIR, BARBARA: Chicago,
Mar. 4, 1939. UCLA.
McNALLY, STEPHEN (Horace
McNally): NYC, July 29, 1913.
Fordham U.
McNICHOL, KRISTY: Los An-
geles, CA, Sept. 11, 1962.
McQUEEN, ARMELIA: North
Carolina, Jan. 6, 1952. Bklyn
Consv.
McQUEEN, BUTTERFLY: Tampa,
FL, Jan. 8, 1911. UCLA.
McQUEEN, CHAD: Los Angeles,
CA, 1961. Actors Studio.
MEADOWS, AUDREY: Wuchang,
China, 1919. St. Margaret's.
MEADOWS, JAYNE (formerly,
Jayne Cotter): Wuchang, China,
Sept. 27, 1920. St. Margaret's.
MEARA, ANNE: Brooklyn, NY,
Sept. 20, 1929.
MEDWIN, MICHAEL: London,
1925. Instut Fischer.
MEEKER, RALPH (Ralph Rathge-
ber): Minneapolis, Nov. 21, 1920.
Northwestern U.
MEISNER, GUNTER: Bremen,
Ger., Apr. 18, 1926. Municipal
Drama School.
MEKKA, EDDIE: Worcester, MA,
1932. Boston Cons.
MELATO, MARIANGELA: Milan,
Italy, 1941. Milan Theatre Acad.
MELL, MARISA: Vienna, Austria,
Feb. 25, 1939.
MERCADO, HECTOR JAIME:
NYC, 1949. HB Studio.
MERCOURI, MELINA: Athens,
Greece, Oct. 18, 1915.
MEREDITH, BURGESS: Cleve-
land, OH, Nov. 16, 1908. Amherst.
MEREDITH, LEE (Judi Lee Sauls):
Oct., 1947. AADA.
MERRILL, DINA (Nedinia Hutton):
NYC, Dec. 9, 1925. AADA.
MERRILL, GARY: Hartford, CT,
Aug. 2, 1915. Bowdoin, Trinity.
METZLER, JIM: Oneonda, NY.
Dartmouth Col.
MICHELL, KEITH: Adelaide,
Aus., Dec. 1, 1926.
MIDLER, BETTE: Honolulu, HI.,
Dec. 1, 1945.
MIFUNE, TOSHIRO: Tsingtao,
China, Apr. 1, 1920.
MILES, SARAH: Ingatestone, Eng.,
Dec. 31, 1941. RADA.
MILES, SYLVIA: NYC, Sept. 9,
1932.
MILES, VERA (Ralston): Boise City,
OK, Aug. 23, 1929. UCLA.
MILFORD, PENELOPE: Winnetka,
IL.

MILLER, ANN (Lucille Ann Col-
lier): Chireno, TX, Apr. 12, 1919.
Lawler Professional School.
MILLER, BARRY: Los Angeles,
Ca., Feb. 6, 1958
MILLER, JASON: Long Island City,
NY, Apr. 22, 1939. Catholic U.
MILLER, LINDA: NYC, Sept. 16,
1942. Catholic U.
MILLS, HAYLEY: London, Apr.
18, 1946. Elmhurst School.
MILLS, JOHN: Suffolk, Eng., Feb.
22, 1908.
MILNER, MARTIN: Detroit, MI,
Dec. 28, 1931.
MIMIEUX, YVETTE: Los Angeles,
Jan. 8, 1941. Hollywood High.
MINNELLI, LIZA: Los Angeles,
Mar. 12, 1946.
MIOU-MIOU: Paris, Feb. 22, 1950.
MITCHELL, CAMERON: Dallas-
town, PA, Nov. 4, 1918. N.Y.
Theatre School.
MITCHELL, JAMES: Sacramento,
CA, Feb. 29, 1920. LACC.
MITCHUM, JAMES: Los Angeles,
CA, May 8, 1941.
MITCHUM, ROBERT: Bridgeport,
CT, Aug. 6, 1917.
MONTALBAN, RICARDO: Mexico
City, Nov. 25, 1920.
MONTAND, YVES (Yves Montand
Livi): Mansummano, Tuscany, Oct.
13, 1921.
MONTGOMERY, BELINDA: Win-
nipeg, Can., July 23, 1950.
MONTGOMERY, ELIZABETH:
Los Angeles, Apr. 15, 1933.
AADA.
MONTGOMERY, GEORGE
(George Letz): Brady, MT, Aug.
29, 1916. U. Mont.
MOOR, BILL: Toledo, OH, July 13,
1931. Northwestern.
MOORE, CONSTANCE: Sioux
City, IA, Jan. 18, 1919.
MOORE, DEMI (Guines): Roswell,
NMx, Nov. 11, 1962.
MOORE, DICK: Los Angeles, Sept.
12, 1925.
MOORE, DUDLEY: London, Apr.
19, 1935.
MOORE, FRANK: Bay-de-Verde,
Newfoundland, 1946.
MOORE, KIERON: County Cork,
Ire., 1925. St. Mary's College.
MOORE, MARY TYLER: Brook-
lyn, Dec. 29, 1936.
MOORE, ROGER: London, Oct. 14,
1927. RADA.
MOORE, TERRY (Helen Koford):
Los Angeles, Jan. 7, 1929.
MOREAU, JEANNE: Paris, Jan. 23,
1928.
MORENO, RITA (Rosita Alverio):
Humacao, P.R., Dec. 11, 1931.
MORGAN, DENNIS (Stanley Mor-
ner): Prentice, WI, Dec. 10, 1910.
Carroll College.
MORGAN, HARRY (HENRY)
(Harry Bratsburg): Detroit, Apr. 10,
1915. U. Chicago.
MORGAN, MICHELE (Simone
Roussel): Paris, Feb. 29, 1920. Paris
Dramatic School.
MORIARTY, CATHY: Bronx, NY,
1961.
MORIARTY, MICHAEL: Detroit,
MI, Apr. 5, 1941. Dartmouth.
MORISON, PATRICIA: NYC,
1915.
MORLEY, ROBERT: Wiltshire,
Eng., May 26, 1908. RADA.
MORRIS, ANITA: Durham, NC,
1932.

Lee
Marvin

Armelia
McQueen

Martin
Mull

Patricia
Neal

Don
Nute

Tatum
O'Neal

MORRIS, GREG: Cleveland, OH, Sept. 27, 1934. Ohio State.

MORRIS, HOWARD: NYC, Sept. 4, 1919. NYU.

MORSE, DAVID: Hamilton, MA, 1953.

MORSE, ROBERT: Newton, MA, May 18, 1931.

MOSS, ARNOLD: NYC, Jan. 28, 1910. CCNY.

MOYA, EDDY: El Paso, TX, Apr. 11, 1963. LACC.

MULL, MARTIN: N. Ridgefield, Oh., 1941. RISch. of Design.

MULLIGAN, RICHARD: NYC, Nov. 13, 1932.

MURPHY, EDDIE: Brooklyn, NY, Apr. 3, 1961.

MURPHY, GEORGE: New Haven, CT, July 4, 1902. Yale.

MURPHY, MICHAEL: Los Angeles, CA, 1949.

MURRAY, BILL: Evanston, IL, Sept. 21, 1950. Regis Col.

MURRAY, DON: Hollywood, July 31, 1929. AADA.

MURRAY, KEN (Don Court): NYC, July 14, 1903.

MUSANTE, TONY: Bridgeport, CT, June 30, 1936. Oberlin Col.

NABORS, JIM: Sylacauga, GA, June 12, 1932.

NADER, GEORGE: Pasadena, CA, Oct. 19, 1921. Occidental College.

NADER, MICHAEL: Los Angeles, CA, 1945.

NAPIER, ALAN: Birmingham, Eng., Jan. 7, 1903. Birmingham University.

NATWICK, MILDRED: Baltimore, June 19, 1908. Bryn Mawr.

NAUGHTON, DAVID: 1955

NAUGHTON, JAMES: Middletown, CT, Dec. 6, 1945. Yale.

NAVIN, JOHN P., JR.: Philadelphia, PA, 1968.

NEAL, PATRICIA: Packard, KY, Jan. 20, 1926. Northwestern U.

NEFF, HILDEGARDE (Hildegard Knef): Ulm, Ger., Dec. 28, 1925. Berlin Art Academy.

NELL, NATHALIE: Paris, Oct. 1950.

NELLIGAN, KATE: London, Ont., Can., 1951. U Toronto.

NELSON, BARRY (Robert Nielsen): Oakland, CA, 1920.

NELSON, DAVID: NYC, Oct. 24, 1936. USC.

NELSON, GENE (Gene Berg): Seattle, WA, Mar. 24, 1920.

NELSON, HARRIET HILLIARD (Peggy Lou Snyder): Des Moines, IA, July 18, 1914.

NELSON, LORI (Dixie Kay Nelson): Santa Fe, NM, Aug. 15, 1933.

NELSON, WILLIE: Texas, Apr. 30, 1933.

NETTLETON, LOIS: Oak Park, IL. Actors Studio.

NEWHART, BOB: Chicago, IL, Sept. 5, 1929. Loyola U.

NEWLEY, ANTHONY: Hackney, London, Sept. 21, 1931.

NEWMAN, BARRY: Boston, MA, Mar. 26, 1938. Brandeis U.

NEWMAN, PAUL: Cleveland, OH, Jan. 26, 1925. Yale.

NEWMAR, JULIE (Newmeyer): Los Angeles, Aug. 16, 1935.

NEWTON-JOHN, OLIVIA: Cambridge, Eng., Sept. 26, 1948.

NICHOLAS, PAUL: London, 1945.

NICHOLS, MIKE (Michael Igor Peschkowsky): Berlin, Nov. 6, 1931. U. Chicago.

NICHOLSON, JACK: Neptune, NJ, Apr. 22, 1937.

NICKERSON, DENISE: NYC, 1959.

NICOL, ALEX: Ossining, NY, Jan. 20, 1919. Actors Studio.

NIELSEN, LESLIE: Regina, Saskatchewan, Can., Feb. 11, 1926. Neighborhood Playhouse.

NIMOY, LEONARD: Boston, MA, Mar. 26, 1931. Boston Col., Antioch Col.

NOLAN, KATHLEEN: St. Louis, MO, Sept. 27, 1933. Neighborhood Playhouse.

NOLTE, NICK: Omaha, NE, 1941. Pasadena City Col.

NORRIS, CHRISTOPHER: NYC, Oct. 7, 1943. Lincoln Square Acad.

NORRIS, CHUCK (Carlos Ray): Ryan, OK, 1939.

NORTH, HEATHER: Pasadena, CA, Dec. 13, 1950. Actors Workshop.

NORTH, SHEREE (Dawn Bethel): Los Angeles, Jan. 17, 1933. Hollywood High.

NORTON, KEN: Aug. 9, 1945.

NOURI, MICHAEL: Washington, DC, Dec. 9, 1945.

NOVAK, KIM (Marilyn Novak): Chicago, Feb. 18, 1933. LACC.

NUREYEV, RUDOLF: Russia, Mar. 17, 1938.

NUTE, DON: Connellsville, PA, Mar. 13, Denver U.

NUYEN, FRANCE (Vannga): Marseilles, France, July 31, 1939. Beaux Arts School.

O'BRIAN, HUGH (Hugh J. Krampe): Rochester, NY, Apr. 19, 1928. Cincinnati U.

O'BRIEN, CLAY: Ray, AZ, May 6, 1961.

O'BRIEN, MARGARET (Angela Maxine O'Brien): Los Angeles, Jan. 15, 1937.

O'CONNOR, CARROLL: Bronx, NY, Aug. 2, 1925. Dublin National Univ.

O'CONNOR, DONALD: Chicago, Aug. 28, 1925.

O'CONNOR, GLYNNIS: NYC, Nov. 19, 1956. NYSU.

O'CONNOR, KEVIN: Honolulu, HI, May 7, U. Hi.

O'HANLON, GEORGE: Brooklyn, NY, Nov. 23, 1917.

O'HARA, MAUREEN (Maureen FitzSimons): Dublin, Ire., Aug. 17, 1920. Abbey School.

O'HERLIHY, DAN: Wexford, Ire., May 1, 1919. National U.

O'KEEFE, MICHAEL: Paulland, NJ, 1955, NYU, AADA.

OLIVIER, LAURENCE: Dorking, Eng., May 22, 1907. Oxford.

O'LOUGHLIN, GERALD S.: NYC, Dec. 23, 1921. U. Rochester.

OLSON, NANCY: Milwaukee, WI, July 14, 1928. UCLA.

O'NEAL, GRIFFIN: Los Angeles, 1965.

O'NEAL, PATRICK: Ocala, FL, Sept. 26, 1927. U. Fla.

O'NEAL, RON: Utica, NY, Sept. 1, 1937. Ohio State.

O'NEAL, RYAN: Los Angeles, Apr. 20, 1941.

O'NEAL, TATUM: Los Angeles, Nov. 5, 1963.

O'NEIL, TRICIA: Shreveport, LA, Mar. 11, 1945. Baylor U.

O'NEILL, JENNIFER: Rio de Janeiro, Feb. 20, 1949. Neighborhood Playhouse.

O'SULLIVAN, MAUREEN: Byle, Ire., May 17, 1911. Sacred Heart Convent.

O'TOOLE, ANNETTE: Houston, TX, 1953. UCLA.

O'TOOLE, PETER: Connemara, Ire., Aug. 2, 1932. RADA.

PACINO, AL: NYC, Apr. 25, 1940.

PAGE, GERALDINE: Kirksville, MO, Nov. 22, 1924. Goodman School.

PAGE, TONY (Anthony Vitiello): Bronx, NY, 1940.

PAGET, DEBRA (Debralee Griffin): Denver, Aug. 19, 1933.

PAIGE, JANIS (Donna Mae Jaden): Tacoma, WA, Sept. 16, 1922.

PALANCE, JACK (Walter Palanuik): Lattimer, PA, Feb. 18, 1920. UNC.

PALMER, BETSY: East Chicago, IN, Nov. 1, 1929. DePaul U.

PALMER, GREGG (Palmer Lee): San Francisco, Jan. 25, 1927. U. Utah.

PAMPANINI, SILVANA: Rome, Sept. 25, 1925.

PANTALIANO, JOEY: Hoboken, NJ. 1952.

PAPAS, IRENE: Chiliomodion, Greece, Mar. 9, 1929.

PARE, MICHAEL: Brooklyn, NY, 1959.

PARKER, ELEANOR: Cedarville, OH, June 26, 1922. Pasadena Playhouse.

PARKER, FESS: Fort Worth, TX, Aug. 16, 1927. USC.

PARKER, JAMESON: 1947. Beloit Col.

PARKER, JEAN (Mae Green): Deer Lodge, MT, Aug. 11, 1912.

PARKER, SUZY (Cecelia Parker): San Antonio, TX, Oct. 28, 1933.

PARKER, WILLARD (Worster Van Eps): NYC, Feb. 5, 1912.

PARKINS, BARBARA: Vancouver, Can., May 22, 1943.

PARSONS, ESTELLE: Lynn, MA, Nov. 20, 1927. Boston U.

PARTON, DOLLY: Sevierville, TN, Jan. 19, 1946.

PATINKIN, MANDY: Chicago, IL, 1954. Juilliard.

PATRICK, DENNIS: Philadelphia, Mar. 14, 1918.

PATTERSON, LEE: Vancouver, Can., Mar. 31, 1929. Ontario Col.

PATTON, WILL: Charleston, SC, June 14, 1954.

PAVAN, MARISA (Marisa Pierangeli): Cagliari, Sardinia, June 19, 1932. Torquado Tasso College.

PAYNE, JOHN: Roanoke, Va., March 23, 1912.

PEACH, MARY: Durban, S. Africa, 1934.

PEARL, MINNIE (Sarah Cannon): Centerville, TN, Oct. 25, 1912.

PEARSON, BEATRICE: Denison, TX, July 27, 1920.

PECK, GREGORY: La Jolla, CA, Apr. 5, 1916. U. Calif.

PELIKAN, LISA: Paris, July 12. Juilliard.

PENHALL, BRUCE: Balboa, CA, 1958.

PENN, SEAN: California, Aug. 17, 1960.

PEPPARD, GEORGE: Detroit, Oct. 1, 1928. Carnegie Tech.

PEREZ, JOSE: NYC 1940.

PERKINS, ANTHONY: NYC, Apr. 14, 1932. Rollins College.

PERREAU, GIGI (Ghislaine): Los Angeles, Feb. 6, 1941.

PERRINE, VALERIE: Galveston, TX, Sept. 3, 1944. U. Ariz.

PESCOW, DONNA: Brooklyn, NY, 1954.

PETERS, BERNADETTE (Lazzara): Jamaica, NY, Feb. 28, 1948.

PETERS, BROCK: NYC, July 2, 1927. CCNY.

PETERS, JEAN (Elizabeth): Canton, OH, Oct. 15, 1926. Ohio State U.

PETERS, MICHAEL: Brooklyn, NY, 1948.

PETTET, JOANNA: London, Nov. 16, 1944. Neighborhood Playhouse.

PFEIFFER, MICHELLE: Santa Ana, CA, 1957.

PHILLIPS, MacKENZIE: Hollywood, CA, 1960.

PHILLIPS, MICHELLE (Holly Gilliam): NJ, June 4, 1944.

PICERNI, PAUL: NYC, Dec. 1, 1922. Loyola U.

PINCHOT, BRONSON: 1959, Yale.

PINE, PHILLIP: Hanford, CA, July 16, 1925. Actors' Lab.

PISIER, MARIE-FRANCE: Vietnam, May 10, 1944. U. Paris.

PLACE, MARY KAY: Port Arthur, TX, Sept., 1947. U. Tulsa.

PLAYTEN, ALICE: NYC, Aug. 28, 1947. NYU.

PLEASENCE, DONALD: Workshop, Eng., Oct. 5, 1919. Sheffield School.

PLESHETTE, SUZANNE: NYC, Jan. 31, 1937. Syracuse U.

PLOWRIGHT, JOAN: Scunthorpe, Brigg, Lincolnshire, Eng., Oct. 28, 1929. Old Vic.

PLUMMER, AMANDA: NYC, Mar. 23, 1957. Middlebury Col.

PLUMMER, CHRISTOPHER: Toronto, Can., Dec. 13, 1927.

PODESTA, ROSSANA: Tripoli, June 20, 1934.

POITIER, SIDNEY: Miami, FL, Feb. 27, 1924.

POLITO, LINA: Naples, Italy, Aug. 11, 1954.

POLLARD, MICHAEL J.: Pacific, NJ, May 30, 1939.

PORTER, ERIC: London, Apr. 8, 1928. Wimbledon Col.

POWELL, JANE (Suzanne Burce): Portland, OR, Apr. 1, 1928.

POWELL, ROBERT: Salford, Eng., June 1, 1944. Manchester U.

POWER, TARYN: Los Angeles, CA, 1954.

POWER, TYRONE IV: Los Angeles, CA, Jan. 1959.

POWERS, MALA (Mary Ellen): San Francisco, Dec. 29, 1921. UCLA.

POWERS, STEFANIE (Federkiewicz): Hollywood, CA, Oct. 12, 1942.

PRENTISS, PAULA (Paula Ragusa): San Antonio, TX, Mar. 4, 1939. Northwestern U.

PRESLE, MICHELINE (Micheline Chassagne): Paris, Aug. 22, 1922. Rouleau Drama School.

PRESNELL, HARVE: Modesto, CA, Sept. 14, 1933. USC.

PRESTON, ROBERT (Robert Preston Meservey): Newton Highlands, MA, June 8, 1913. Pasadena Playhouse.

PRESTON, WILLIAM: Columbia, Pa., Aug. 26, 1921. PaStateU.

PRICE, VINCENT: St. Louis, May 27, 1911. Yale.

PRIMUS, BARRY: NYC, Feb. 16, 1938. CCNY.

PRINCE (Rogers Nelson): Minneapolis, MN, 1960.

PRINCE, WILLIAM: Nicholas, NY, Jan. 26, 1913. Cornell U.

PRINCIPAL, VICTORIA: Fukuoka, Japan, Mar. 3, 1945. Dade Jr. Col.

PROCHNOW, JURGEN: Germany, 1941.

PROVAL, DAVID: Brooklyn, NY, 1943.

PROVINE, DOROTHY: Deadwood, SD, Jan. 20, 1937. U. Wash.

PROWSE, JULIET: Bombay, India, Sept. 25, 1936.

PRYOR, RICHARD: Peoria, IL, Dec. 1, 1940.

PURCELL, LEE: Cherry Point, NC, June 15, 1947. Stephens.

PURDOM, EDMUND: Welwyn Garden City, Eng., Dec. 19, 1924. St. Ignatius College.

PYLE, DENVER: Bethune, CO, 1920.

QUAID, DENNIS: Houston, TX, Apr. 9, 1954.

QUAYLE, ANTHONY: Lancashire, Eng., Sept. 7, 1913. Old Vic School.

QUINE, RICHARD: Detroit, MI, Nov. 12, 1920.

QUINLAN, KATHLEEN: Mill Valley, CA, Nov. 19, 1954.

QUINN, AIDAN: Chicago, IL, Mar. 8, 1959.

QUINN, ANTHONY: Chihuahua, Mex., Apr. 21, 1915.

RADNER, GILDA: Detroit, MI, June 28, 1946.

RAFFERTY, FRANCES: Sioux City, IA, June 16, 1922. UCLA.

RAFFIN, DEBORAH: Los Angeles, Mar. 13, 1953. Valley Col.

RAINER, LUISE: Vienna, Aust., 1912.

RAINES, ELLA (Ella Wallace): Snoqualmie Falls, WA, Aug. 6, 1921. U. Wash.

RAMPLING, CHARLOTTE: Surmer, Eng., Feb. 5, 1946. U. Madrid.

RAMSEY, LOGAN: Long Beach, CA, Mar. 21, 1921. St. Joseph.

RANDALL, TONY (Leonard Rosenberg): Tulsa, OK, Feb. 26, 1920. Northwestern U.

RANDELL, RON: Sydney, Australia, Oct. 8, 1920. St. Mary's Col.

RASULALA, THALMUS (Jack Crowder): Miami, FL, Nov. 15, 1939. U. Redlands.

RAY, ALDO (Aldo DeRe): Pen Argyl, PA, Sept. 25, 1926. UCLA.

RAYE, MARTHA (Margie Yvonne Reed): Butte, MT, Aug. 27, 1916.

RAYMOND, GENE (Raymond Guion): NYC, Aug. 13, 1908.

REAGAN, RONALD: Tampico, IL, Feb. 6, 1911. Eureka College.

REASON, REX: Berlin, Ger., Nov. 30, 1928. Pasadena Playhouse.

REDDY, HELEN: Australia, Oct. 25, 1942.

REDFORD, ROBERT: Santa Monica, CA, Aug. 18, 1937. AADA.

REDGRAVE, CORIN: London, July 16, 1939.

REDGRAVE, LYNN: London, Mar. 8, 1943.

REDGRAVE, VANESSA: London, Jan. 30, 1937.

REDMAN, JOYCE: County Mayo, Ire., 1919. RADA.

REED, OLIVER: Wimbledon, Eng., Feb. 13, 1938.

REED, REX: Ft. Worth, TX, Oct. 2, 1939. LSU.

REEMS, HARRY (Herbert Streicher): Bronx, NY, 1947. U. Pittsburgh.

REEVE, CHRISTOPHER: NJ, Sept. 25, 1952. Cornell, Juilliard.

REEVES, STEVE: Glasgow, MT, Jan. 21, 1926.

REGEHR, DUNCAN: Lethbridge, Can., 1954.

REID, ELLIOTT: NYC, Jan. 16, 1920.

REINER, CARL: NYC, Mar. 20, 1922. Georgetown.

REINER, ROBERT: NYC, 1945. UCLA.

REMAR, JAMES: Boston, Ma., Dec. 31, 1953. Neighborhood Playhouse.

REMICK, LEE: Quincy, MA. Dec. 14, 1935. Barnard College.

RETTIG, TOMMY: Jackson Heights, NY, Dec. 10, 1941.

REVILL, CLIVE: Wellington, NZ, Apr. 18, 1930.

REY, FERNANDO: La Coruna, Spain, 1917.

REYNOLDS, BURT: Waycross, GA, Feb. 11, 1935. Fla. State U.

REYNOLDS, DEBBIE (Mary Frances Reynolds): El Paso, TX, Apr. 1, 1932.

Dolly Parton   **Robert Preston**   **Deborah Raffin**   **Kurt Russell**   **Susan Saint James**   **Tom Selleck**

REYNOLDS, MARJORIE: Buhl, ID, Aug. 12, 1921.

RHOADES, BARBARA: Poughkeepsie, NY, 1947.

RICH, IRENE: Buffalo, NY, Oct. 13, 1891. St. Margaret's School.

RICHARDS, JEFF (Richard Mansfield Taylor): Portland, OR, Nov. 1. USC.

RICKLES, DON: NYC, May 8, 1926. AADA.

RIEGERT, PETER: NYC, Apr. 11, 1947. U Buffalo.

RIGG, DIANA: Doncaster, Eng., July 20, 1938. RADA.

RINGWALD, MOLLY: Sacramento, CA, 1968.

RITTER, JOHN: Burbank, CA, Sept. 17, 1948. U.S. Cal.

ROBARDS, JASON: Chicago, July 26, 1922. AADA.

ROBERTS, ERIC: Biloxi, MS, 1956. RADA.

ROBERTS, RALPH: Salisbury, NC, Aug. 17, 1922. UNC.

ROBERTS, TANYA (Leigh): NYC, 1955.

ROBERTS, TONY: NYC, Oct. 22, 1939. Northwestern U.

ROBERTSON, CLIFF: La Jolla, CA, Sept. 9, 1925. Antioch Col.

ROBERTSON, DALE: Oklahoma City, July 14, 1923.

ROBINSON, CHRIS: Nov. 5, 1938, West Palm Beach, FL. LACC.

ROBINSON, JAY: NYC, Apr. 14, 1930.

ROBINSON, ROGER: Seattle, WA, May 2, 1941. USC.

ROCHEFORT, JEAN: Paris, 1930.

ROCK-SAVAGE, STEVEN: Melville, LA, Dec. 14, 1958. LSU.

ROGERS, CHARLES "BUDDY": Olathe, KS, Aug. 13, 1904. U. Kan.

ROGERS, GINGER (Virginia Katherine McMath): Independence, MO, July 16, 1911.

ROGERS, ROY (Leonard Slye): Cincinnati, Nov. 5, 1912.

ROGERS, WAYNE: Birmingham, AL, Apr. 7, 1933. Princeton.

ROLAND, GILBERT (Luis Antonio Damaso De Alonso): Juarez, Mex., Dec. 11, 1905.

ROLLINS, HOWARD E., JR.: 1951, Baltimore, MD.

ROMAN, RUTH: Boston, Dec. 23, 1922. Bishop Lee Dramatic School.

ROMANCE, VIVIANE (Pauline Ronacher Ortmanns): Vienna, Aust. 1912.

ROME, SIDNE: Akron, OH. Carnegie-Mellon.

ROMERO, CESAR: NYC, Feb. 15, 1907. Collegiate School.

RONSTADT, LINDA: Tucson, AZ, July 15, 1946.

ROONEY, MICKEY (Joe Yule, Jr.): Brooklyn, Sept. 23, 1920.

ROSE, REVA: Chicago, IL, July 30, 1940. Goodman.

ROSS, DIANA: Detroit, MI, Mar. 26, 1944.

ROSS, KATHARINE: Hollywood, Jan. 29, 1943. Santa Rosa Col.

ROSSELLINI, ISABELLA: Rome, June 18, 1952.

ROSSITER, LEONARD: Liverpool, Eng., Oct. 21, 1926.

ROUNDTREE, RICHARD: New Rochelle, NY, Sept. 7, 1942. Southern Ill.

ROURKE, MICKEY: Miami, FL, 1950.

ROWE, NICHOLAS: London, Nov. 22, 1966. Eton.

ROWLANDS, GENA: Cambria, WI, June 19, 1936.

RUBIN, ANDREW: New Bedford, MA, June 22, 1946. AADA.

RUDD, PAUL: Boston, MA, May 15, 1940.

RULE, JANICE: Cincinnati, OH, Aug. 15, 1931.

RUPERT, MICHAEL: Denver, CO, Oct. 23, 1951. Pasadena Playhouse.

RUSH, BARBARA: Denver, CO, Jan. 4, 1929. U. Calif.

RUSSELL, JANE: Bemidji, MI, June 21, 1921. Max Reinhardt School.

RUSSELL, JOHN: Los Angeles, Jan. 3, 1921. U. Calif.

RUSSELL, KURT: Springfield, MA, Mar. 17, 1951.

RUTHERFORD, ANN: Toronto, Can., Nov. 2, 1917.

RUYMEN, AYN: Brooklyn, July 18, 1947. HB Studio.

SACCHI, ROBERT: Bronx, NY, 1941. NYU.

SAINT, EVA MARIE: Newark, NJ, July 4, 1924. Bowling Green State U.

ST. JACQUES, RAYMOND (James Arthur Johnson):CT.

ST. JAMES, SUSAN (Suzie Jane Miller): Los Angeles, Aug. 14. Conn. Col.

ST. JOHN, BETTA: Hawthorne, CA, Nov. 26, 1929.

ST. JOHN, JILL (Jill Oppenheim): Los Angeles, Aug. 19, 1940.

SALDANA, THERESA: Brooklyn, NY, 1955.

SALINGER, MATT: New Hampshire, 1960. Princeton, Columbia.

SALMI, ALBERT: Coney Island, NY, 1925. Actors Studio.

SALT, JENNIFER: Los Angeles, Sept. 4, 1944. Sarah Lawrence Col.

SANDS, TOMMY: Chicago, Aug. 27, 1937.

SAN JUAN, OLGA: NYC, Mar. 16, 1927.

SARANDON, CHRIS: Beckley, WV, July 24, 1942. U. WVa., Catholic U.

SARANDON, SUSAN (Tomalin): NYC, Oct. 4, 1946. Catholic U.

SARGENT, RICHARD (Richard Cox): Carmel, CA, 1933. Stanford.

SARRAZIN, MICHAEL: Quebec City, Can., May 22, 1940.

SAVAGE, JOHN (Youngs): Long Island, NY, Aug. 25, 1949. AADA.

SAVALAS, TELLY (Aristotle): Garden City, NY, Jan. 21, 1925. Columbia.

SAVOY, TERESA ANN: London, July 18, 1955.

SAXON, JOHN (Carmen Orrico): Brooklyn, Aug. 5, 1935.

SCALIA, JACK: Brooklyn, NY, 1951.

SCARPELLI, GLEN: Staten Island, NY, July 1966.

SCARWID, DIANA: Savannah, GA. AADA, Pace U.

SCHEIDER, ROY: Orange, NJ, Nov. 10, 1935. Franklin-Marshall.

SCHELL, MARIA: Vienna, Jan. 15, 1926.

SCHELL, MAXIMILIAN: Vienna, Dec. 8, 1930.

SCHNEIDER, MARIA: Paris, Mar. 27, 1952.

SCHRODER, RICKY: Staten Island, NY, Apr. 13, 1970.

SCHWARZENEGGER, ARNOLD: Austria, 1947.

SCHYGULLA, HANNA: Katlowitz, Poland. 1943.

SCOFIELD, PAUL: Hurstpierpoint, Eng., Jan. 21, 1922. London Mask Theatre School.

SCOTT, DEBRALEE: Elizabeth, NJ, Apr. 2.

SCOTT, GEORGE C.: Wise, VA, Oct. 18, 1927. U. Mo.

SCOTT, GORDON (Gordon M. Werschkul): Portland, OR, Aug. 3, 1927. Oregon U.

SCOTT, LIZABETH (Emma Matso): Scranton, Pa., Sept. 29, 1922.

SCOTT, MARTHA: Jamesport, MO, Sept. 22, 1914. U. Mich.

SCOTT, RANDOLPH: Orange County, VA, Jan. 23, 1903. UNC.

SCOTT-TAYLOR, JONATHAN: Brazil, 1962.

SEAGULL, BARBARA HERSHEY (Herzstein): Hollywood, Feb. 5, 1948.

SEARS, HEATHER: London, 1935.

SECOMBE, HARRY: Swansea, Wales, Sept. 8, 1921.

SEGAL, GEORGE: NYC, Feb. 13, 1934. Columbia.

SELLARS, ELIZABETH: Glasgow, Scot., May 6, 1923.

SELLECK, TOM: Jan. 29, 1945.

SELWART, TONIO: Watenberg, Ger., June 9, 1906. Munich U.

SERNAS, JACQUES: Lithuania, July 30, 1925.

SETH, ROSHAN: New Delhi, India, 1942.

SEYLER, ATHENE (Athene Hannen): London, May 31, 1889.

SEYMOUR, ANNE: NYC, Sept. 11, 1909. American Laboratory Theatre.

SEYMOUR, JANE (Joyce Frankenberg): Hillingdon, Eng., Feb. 15, 1951.

SHARIF, OMAR (Michel Shalboub): Alexandria, Egypt, Apr. 10, 1932. Victoria Col.

SHARKEY, RAY: Brooklyn, NY, 1952. HB Studio.

SHATNER, WILLIAM: Montreal, Can., Mar. 22, 1931. McGill U.

SHAW, SEBASTIAN: Holt, Eng., May 29, 1905. Gresham School.

SHAW, STAN: Chicago, IL, 1952.

SHAWLEE, JOAN: Forest Hills, NY, Mar. 5, 1929.

SHAWN, DICK (Richard Shulefand): Buffalo, NY, Dec. 1, 1929. U. Miami.

SHEA, JOHN V.: North Conway, NH, Apr. 14, 1949. Bates, Yale.

SHEARER, MOIRA: Dunfermline, Scot., Jan. 17, 1926. London Theatre School.

SHEEDY, ALLY: NYC, June 13, 1962. USC.

SHEEN, CHARLIE: Los Angeles, Ca., 1966.

SHEEN, MARTIN (Ramon Estevez): Dayton, OH, Aug. 3, 1940.

SHEFFIELD, JOHN: Pasadena, CA, Apr. 11, 1931. UCLA.

SHEPARD, SAM (Rogers): Ft. Sheridan, IL, Nov. 5, 1943.

SHEPHERD, CYBILL: Memphis, TN, Feb. 18, 1950. Hunter, NYU.

SHIELDS, BROOKE: NYC, May 31, 1965.

SHIRE, TALIA: Lake Success, NY. Yale.

SHORE, DINAH (Frances Rose Shore): Winchester, TN, Mar. 1, 1917. Vanderbilt U.

SHOWALTER, MAX (formerly Casey Adams): Caldwell, KS, June 2, 1917. Pasadena Playhouse.

SIDNEY, SYLVIA: NYC, Aug. 8, 1910. Theatre Guild School.

SILVER, RON: NYC, July 2, 1946. SUNY.

SIMMONS, JEAN: London, Jan. 31, 1929. Aida Foster School.

SIMON, SIMONE: Marseilles, France, Apr. 23, 1910.

SIMPSON, O. J. (Orenthal James): San Francisco, CA, July 9, 1947. UCLA.

SINATRA, FRANK: Hoboken, NJ, Dec. 12, 1915.

SINCLAIR, JOHN (Gianluigi Loffredo): Rome, Italy, 1946.

SINDEN, DONALD: Plymouth, Eng., Oct. 9, 1923. Webber-Douglas.

SINGER, LORI: NYC, 1962, Juilliard.

SKALA, LILIA: Vienna. U. Dresden.

SKELTON, RED (Richard): Vincennes, IN, July 18, 1910.

SKERRITT, TOM: Detroit, MI, 1935. Wayne State U.

SLATER, HELEN: NYC, Dec. 14, 1963.

SMITH, ALEXIS: Penticton, Can., June 8, 1921. LACC.

SMITH, CHARLES MARTIN: Los Angeles, CA, 1954. CalState U.

SMITH, JACLYN: Houston, TX, Oct. 26, 1947.

SMITH, JOHN (Robert E. Van Orden): Los Angeles, Mar. 6, 1931. UCLA.

SMITH, LOIS: Topeka, KS, Nov. 3, 1930. U. Wash.

SMITH, MAGGIE: Ilford, Eng., Dec. 28, 1934.

SMITH, ROGER: South Gate, CA, Dec. 18, 1932. U. Ariz.

SMITHERS, WILLIAM: Richmond, VA, July 10, 1927. Catholic U.

SNODGRESS, CARRIE: Chicago, Oct. 27, 1946. UNI.

SOLOMON, BRUCE: NYC, 1944. U. Miami, Wayne State U.

SOMERS, SUZANNE (Mahoney): San Bruno, CA, Oct. 16, 1946. Lone Mt. Col.

SOMMER, ELKE (Schletz): Berlin, Nov. 5, 1940.

SORDI, ALBERTO: Rome, Italy, 1919.

SORVINO, PAUL: NYC, 1939. AMDA.

SOTHERN, ANN (Harriet Lake): Valley City, ND, Jan. 22, 1907. Washington U.

SOUL, DAVID: Aug. 28, 1943.

SPACEK, SISSY: Quitman, TX, Dec. 25, 1949. Actors Studio.

SPANO, VINCENT: Brooklyn, NY, Oct. 18, 1962.

SPENSER, JEREMY: Ceylon, 1937.

SPRINGER, GARY: NYC, July 29, 1954. Hunter Col.

SPRINGFIELD, RICK (Richard Springthorpe): Sydney, Aust. Aug. 23, 1949.

STACK, ROBERT: Los Angeles, Jan. 13, 1919. USC.

STADLEN, LEWIS J.: Brooklyn, Mar. 7, 1947. Neighborhood Playhouse.

STAFFORD, NANCY: Ft. Lauderdale, FL.

STALLONE, FRANK: NYC, July 30, 1950.

STALLONE, SYLVESTER: NYC, July 6, 1946. U. Miami.

STAMP, TERENCE: London, July 23, 1939.

STANDER, LIONEL: NYC, Jan. 11, 1908. UNC.

STANG, ARNOLD: Chelsea, MA, Sept. 28, 1925.

STANLEY, KIM (Patricia Reid): Tularosa, NM, Feb. 11, 1925. U. Tex.

STANWYCK, BARBARA (Ruby Stevens): Brooklyn, July 16, 1907.

STAPLETON, JEAN: NYC, Jan. 19, 1923.

STAPLETON, MAUREEN: Troy, NY, June 21, 1925.

STEEL, ANTHONY: London, May 21, 1920. Cambridge.

STEELE, TOMMY: London, Dec. 17, 1936.

STEENBURGEN, MARY: Newport, AR, 1953. Neighborhood Playhouse.

STEIGER, ROD: Westhampton, NY, Apr. 14, 1925.

STERLING, JAN (Jane Sterling Adriance): NYC, Apr. 3, 1923. Fay Compton School.

STERLING, ROBERT (William Sterling Hart): Newcastle, PA, Nov. 13, 1917. U. Pittsburgh.

STERN, DANIEL: Bethesda, MD, 1957.

STEVENS, ANDREW: Memphis, TN, June 10, 1955.

STEVENS, CONNIE (Concetta Ann Ingolia): Brooklyn, Aug. 8, 1938. Hollywood Professional School.

STEVENS, FISHER: Chicago, IL, Nov. 27, 1963. NYU.

STEVENS, KAYE (Catherine): Pittsburgh, July 21, 1933.

STEVENS, MARK (Richard): Cleveland, OH, Dec. 13, 1920.

STEVENS, STELLA (Estelle Eggleston): Hot Coffee, MS, Oct. 1, 1936.

STEVENSON, PARKER: CT, 1953.

STEWART, ALEXANDRIA: Montreal, Can., June 10, 1939. Louvre.

STEWART, ELAINE: Montclair, NJ, May 31, 1929.

STEWART, JAMES: Indiana, PA, May 20, 1908. Princeton.

STEWART, MARTHA (Martha Haworth): Bardwell, KY, Oct. 7, 1922.

STIMSON, SARA: Helotes, TX, 1973.

STING (Gordon Matthew Sumner): Wallsend, Eng., 1951.

STOCKWELL, DEAN: Hollywood, Mar. 5, 1935.

STOCKWELL, JOHN: Texas, 1961. Harvard.

STORM, GALE (Josephine Cottle): Bloomington, TX, Apr. 5, 1922.

STRAIGHT, BEATRICE: Old Westbury, NY, Aug. 2, 1916. Dartington Hall.

STRASBERG, SUSAN: NYC, May 22, 1938.

STRASSMAN, MARCIA: New Jersey, 1949.

STRAUSS, PETER: NY, 1947.

STREEP, MERYL (Mary Louise): Summit, NJ, June 22, 1949., Vassar, Yale.

STREISAND, BARBRA: Brooklyn, Apr. 24, 1942.

STRITCH, ELAINE: Detroit, MI, Feb. 2, 1925. Drama Workshop.

STRODE, WOODY: Los Angeles, 1914.

STROUD, DON: Hawaii, 1943.

STRUTHERS, SALLY: Portland, OR, July 28, 1948. Pasadena Playhouse.

SULLIVAN, BARRY (Patrick Barry): NYC, Aug. 29, 1912. NYU.

SUMMER, DONNA (LaDonna Gaines): Boston, MA, Dec. 31, 1948.

SUTHERLAND, DONALD: St. John, New Brunswick, Can., July 17, 1934. U. Toronto.

SVENSON, BO: Goteborg, Swed., Feb. 13, 1941. UCLA.

SWEET, BLANCHE: Chicago, June 18, 1896.

SWINBURNE, NORA: Bath, Eng., July 24, 1902. RADA.

SWIT, LORETTA: Passaic, NJ, Nov. 4. AADA.

SYLVESTER, WILLIAM: Oakland, CA, Jan. 31, 1922. RADA.

SYMS, SYLVIA: London, June 1, 1934. Convent School.

T, MR. (Lawrence Tero): Chicago, 1952.

TABORI, KRISTOFFER (Siegel): Los Angeles, Aug. 4, 1952.

TAKEI, GEORGE: Los Angeles, CA, Apr. 20. UCLA.

TALBOT, LYLE (Lysle Hollywood): Pittsburgh, Feb. 8, 1904.

TALBOT, NITA: NYC, Aug. 8, 1930. Irvine Studio School.

TAMBLYN, RUSS: Los Angeles, Dec. 30, 1934.

TANDY, JESSICA: London, June 7, 1909. Dame Owens' School.

Helen Slater	John Stockwell	Elizabeth Taylor	Philip Michael Thomas	Jo Van Fleet	James Victor

TAYLOR, DON: Freeport, PA, Dec. 13, 1920. Penn State U.

TAYLOR, ELIZABETH: London, Feb. 27, 1932. Byron House School.

TAYLOR, KENT (Louis Weiss): Nashua, IA, May 11, 1906.

TAYLOR, ROD (Robert): Sydney, Aust., Jan. 11, 1929.

TAYLOR-YOUNG, LEIGH: Wash., DC, Jan. 25, 1945. Northwestern.

TEAGUE, ANTHONY SKOOTER: Jacksboro, TX, Jan. 4, 1940.

TEAGUE, MARSHALL: Newport, Tn.

TEEFY, MAUREEN: Minneapolis, MN, 1954; Juilliard.

TEMPLE, SHIRLEY: Santa Monica, CA, Apr. 23, 1927.

TERRY-THOMAS (Thomas Terry Hoar Stevens): Finchley, London, July 14, 1911. Ardingly College.

TERZIEFF, LAURENT: Paris, June 25, 1935.

THACKER, RUSS: Washington, DC, June 23, 1946, Montgomery Col.

THAXTER, PHYLLIS: Portland, ME, Nov. 20, 1921. St. Genevieve.

THELEN, JODI: St. Cloud, MN., 1963.

THOMAS, DANNY (Amos Jacobs): Deerfield, MI, Jan. 6, 1914.

THOMAS, MARLO (Margaret): Detroit, Nov. 21, 1938. USC.

THOMAS, PHILIP MICHAEL: Columbus, OH, May 26, 1949. Oakwood Col.

THOMAS, RICHARD: NYC, June 13, 1951. Columbia.

THOMPSON, JACK (John Payne): Sydney, Aus., 1940. U. Brisbane.

THOMPSON, MARSHALL: Peoria, IL, Nov. 27, 1925. Occidental.

THOMPSON, REX: NYC, Dec. 14, 1942.

THOMPSON, SADA: Des Moines, IA, Sept. 27, 1929. Carnegie Tech.

THULIN, INGRID: Solleftea, Sweden, Jan. 27, 1929. Royal Drama Theatre.

TICOTIN, RACHEL: Bronx, NY, 1958.

TIERNEY, GENE: Brooklyn, Nov. 20, 1920. Miss Farmer's School.

TIERNEY, LAWRENCE: Brooklyn, Mar. 15, 1919. Manhattan College.

TIFFIN, PAMELA (Wonso): Oklahoma City, Oct. 13, 1942.

TILLY, MEG: Texada, Can., 1960.

TODD, ANN: Hartford, Eng., Jan. 24, 1909.

TODD, RICHARD: Dublin, Ire., June 11, 1919. Shrewsbury School.

TOLO, MARILU: Rome, Italy, 1944.

TOMLIN, LILY: Detroit, MI, Sept. 1, 1939. Wayne State U.

TOPOL (Chaim Topol): Tel-Aviv, Israel, Sept. 9, 1935.

TORN, RIP: Temple, TX, Feb. 6, 1931. U. Tex.

TORRES, LIZ: NYC, 1947. NYU.

TOTTER, AUDREY: Joliet, IL, Dec. 20, 1918.

TRAVERS, BILL: Newcastle-on-Tyne, Engl, Jan. 3, 1922.

TRAVIS, RICHARD (William Justice): Carlsbad, NM, Apr. 17, 1913.

TRAVOLTA, JOEY: Englewood, NJ, 1952.

TRAVOLTA, JOHN: Englewood, NJ, Feb. 18, 1954.

TREMAYNE, LES: London, Apr. 16, 1913. Northwestern, Columbia, UCLA.

TREVOR, CLAIRE (Wemlinger): NYC, March 8, 1909.

TRINTIGNANT, JEAN-LOUIS: Pont-St. Esprit, France, Dec. 11, 1930. Dullin-Balachova Drama School.

TRYON, TOM: Hartford, CT, Jan. 14, 1926. Yale.

TSOPEI, CORINNA: Athens, Greece, June 21, 1944.

TUCKER, FORREST: Plainfield, IN, Feb. 12, 1919. George Washington U.

TURNER, KATHLEEN: Springfield, MO, June 19, 1954. UMd.

TURNER, LANA (Julia Jean Mildred Frances Turner): Wallace, ID, Feb. 8, 1921.

TURNER, TINA: Georgia, 1939.

TUSHINGHAM, RITA: Liverpool, Eng., 1940.

TUTIN, DOROTHY: London, Apr. 8, 1930.

TWIGGY (Lesley Hornby): London, Sept. 19, 1949.

TYLER, BEVERLY (Beverly Jean Saul): Scranton, PA, July 5, 1928.

TYRRELL, SUSAN: San Francisco, 1946.

TYSON, CICELY: NYC, Dec. 19.

UGGAMS, LESLIE: NYC, May 25, 1943.

ULLMANN, LIV: Tokyo, Dec. 10, 1938. Webber-Douglas Acad.

USTINOV, PETER: London, Apr. 16, 1921. Westminster School.

VACCARO, BRENDA: Brooklyn, Nov. 18, 1939. Neighborhood Playhouse.

VALLEE, RUDY (Hubert): Island Pond, VT, July 28, 1901. Yale.

VALLI, ALIDA: Pola, Italy, May 31, 1921. Rome Academy of Drama.

VALLONE, RAF: Riogio, Italy, Feb. 17, 1916. Turin U.

VAN CLEEF, LEE: Somerville, NJ, Jan. 9, 1925.

VAN DE VEN, MONIQUE: Holland, 1957.

VAN DEVERE, TRISH (Patricia Dressel): Englewood Cliffs, NJ, Mar. 9, 1945. Ohio Wesleyan.

VAN DOREN, MAMIE (Joan Lucile Olander): Rowena, SD, Feb. 6, 1933.

VAN DYKE, DICK: West Plains, MO, Dec. 13, 1925.

VAN FLEET, JO: Oakland, CA, 1922.

VAN PATTEN, DICK: NYC, Dec. 9, 1928.

VAN PATTEN, JOYCE: NYC, Mar. 9, 1934.

VAUGHN, ROBERT: NYC, Nov. 22, 1932. USC.

VEGA, ISELA: Mexico, 1940.

VENNERA, CHICK: Herkimer, NY, Mar. 27, 1952. Pasadena Playhouse.

VENORA, DIANE: Hartford, Ct., 1952. Juilliard.

VENTURA, LINO: Parma, Italy, July 14, 1919.

VENUTA, BENAY: San Francisco, Jan. 27, 1911.

VERDON, GWEN: Culver City, CA, Jan. 13, 1925.

VEREEN, BEN: Miami, FL, Oct. 10, 1946.

VICTOR, JAMES (Lincoln Rafael Peralta Diaz): Santiago, D.R., July 27, 1939. Haaren HS/NYC.

VILLECHAIZE, HERVE: Paris, Apr. 23, 1943.

VINCENT, JAN-MICHAEL: Denver, CO, July 15, 1944. Ventura.

VIOLET, ULTRA (Isabelle Collin-Dufresne): Grenoble, France.

VITALE, MILLY: Rome, Italy, July 16, 1938. Lycee Chateaubriand.

VOHS, JOAN: St. Albans, NY, July 30, 1931.

VOIGHT, JON: Yonkers, NY, Dec. 29, 1938. Catholic U.

VOLONTE, GIAN MARIA: Milan, Italy, Apr. 9, 1933.

VON SYDOW, MAX: Lund, Swed., July 10, 1929. Royal Drama Theatre.

WAGNER, LINDSAY: Los Angeles, June 22, 1949.

WAGNER, ROBERT: Detroit, Feb. 10, 1930.

WAHL, KEN: Chicago, IL, 1957.

WAITE, GENEVIEVE: South Africa, 1949.

WALKEN, CHRISTOPHER: Astoria, NY, Mar. 31, 1943. Hofstra.

WALKER, CLINT: Hartfold, IL, May 30, 1927. USC.

WALKER, NANCY (Ann Myrtle Swoyer): Philadelphia, May 10, 1921.

WALLACH, ELI: Brooklyn, Dec. 7, 1915. CCNY, U. Tex.

WALLACH, ROBERTA: NYC, Aug. 2, 1955.

WALLIS, SHANI: London, Apr. 5, 1941.

WALSTON, RAY: New Orleans, Nov. 22, 1917. Cleveland Playhouse.

WALTER, JESSICA: Brooklyn, NY, Jan. 31, 1940. Neighborhood Playhouse.

WANAMAKER, SAM: Chicago, June 14, 1919. Drake.

WARD, BURT (Gervis): Los Angeles, July 6, 1945.

WARD, FRED: San Diego, Ca.

WARD, RACHEL: London, 1957.

WARD, SIMON: London, 1941.

WARDEN, JACK: Newark, NJ, Sept. 18, 1920.

WARNER, DAVID: Manchester, Eng., 1941. RADA.

WARREN, JENNIFER: NYC, Aug. 12, 1941. U. Wisc.

WARREN, LESLEY ANN: NYC, Aug. 16, 1946.

WARREN, MICHAEL: South Bend, IN, 1946. UCLA.

WARRICK, RUTH: St. Joseph, MO, June 29, 1915. U. Mo.

WASHBOURNE, MONA: Birmingham, Eng., Nov. 27, 1903.

WASHINGTON, DENZEL: Mt. Vernon, NY, Dec. 28, 1954. Fordham.

WASSON, CRAIG: Ontario, OR, Mar. 15, 1954. UOre.

WATERSTON, SAM: Cambridge, MA, Nov. 15, 1940. Yale.

WATLING, JACK: London, Jan. 13, 1923. Italia Conti School.

WATSON, DOUGLASS: Jackson, GA, Feb. 24, 1921. UNC.

WAYNE, DAVID (Wayne McKeehan): Travers City, MI, Jan. 30, 1914. Western Michigan State U.

WAYNE, PATRICK: Los Angeles, July 15, 1939. Loyola.

WEATHERS, CARL: New Orleans, LA, 1948. Long Beach CC.

WEAVER, DENNIS: Joplin, MO, June 4, 1924. U. Okla.

WEAVER, MARJORIE: Crossville, TN, Mar. 2, 1913. Indiana U.

WEAVER, SIGOURNEY (Susan): NYC, 1949. Stanford, Yale.

WEBBER, ROBERT: Santa Ana, CA, Sept. 14, 1925. Compton Jr. Col.

WEDGEWORTH, ANN: Abilene, TX, Jan. 21, 1935. U. Tex.

WELCH, RAQUEL (Tejada): Chicago, Sept. 5, 1940.

WELD, TUESDAY (Susan): NYC, Aug. 27, 1943. Hollywood Professional School.

WELDON, JOAN: San Francisco, Aug. 5, 1933. San Francisco Conservatory.

WELLER, PETER: Stevens Point, Ws., June 24, 1947. AmThWing.

WELLES, GWEN: NYC, Mar. 4.

WESTON, JACK (Morris Weinstein): Cleveland, OH, Aug. 21, 1915.

WHITAKER, JOHNNY: Van Nuys, CA, Dec. 13, 1959.

WHITE, CAROL: London, Apr. 1, 1944.

WHITE, CHARLES: Perth Amboy, NJ, Aug. 29, 1920. Rutgers U.

WHITE, JESSE: Buffalo, NY, Jan. 3, 1919.

WHITMAN, STUART: San Francisco, Feb. 1, 1929. CCLA

WHITMORE, JAMES: White Plains, NY, Oct. 1, 1921. Yale.

WHITNEY, GRACE LEE: Detroit, MI, Apr. 1, 1930.

WIDDOES, KATHLEEN: Wilmington, DE, Mar. 21, 1939.

WIDMARK, RICHARD: Sunrise, MN, Dec. 26, 1914. Lake Forest.

WILCOX, COLIN: Highlands, NC, Feb. 4, 1937. U. Tenn.

WILDE, CORNEL: NYC, Oct. 13, 1915. CCNY, Columbia.

WILDER, GENE (Jerome Silberman): Milwaukee, Ws., June 11, 1935. UIowa.

WILLIAMS, BILLY DEE: NYC, Apr. 6, 1937.

WILLIAMS, CINDY: Van Nuys, CA, Aug. 22, 1947. LACC.

WILLIAMS, DICK A.: Chicago, IL, Aug. 9, 1938.

WILLIAMS, EMLYN: Mostyn, Wales, Nov. 26, 1905. Oxford.

WILLIAMS, ESTHER: Los Angeles, Aug. 8, 1921.

WILLIAMS, JOBETH: Houston, Tx. BrownU.

WILLIAMS, ROBIN: Chicago, IL, July 21, 1952. Juilliard.

WILLIAMS, TREAT (Richard): Rowayton, CT. Jan. 1952.

WILLIAMSON, FRED: Gary, IN, Mar. 5, 1938. Northwestern.

WILLISON, WALTER: Monterey Park, CA., June 24, 1938. LACC.

WILSON, DEMOND: NYC, Oct. 13, 1946. Hunter Col.

WILSON, FLIP (Clerow Wilson): Jersey City, NJ, Dec. 8, 1933.

WILSON, LAMBERT: Paris, 1959.

WILSON, NANCY: Chillicothe, OH, Feb. 20, 1937.

WILSON, SCOTT: Atlanta, GA, 1942.

WINDE, BEATRICE: Chicago, Jan. 6.

WINDOM, WILLIAM: NYC, Sept. 28, 1923. Williams Col.

WINDSOR, MARIE (Emily Marie Bertelson): Marysvale, UT, Dec. 11, 1924. Brigham Young U.

WINFIELD, PAUL: Los Angeles, 1940. UCLA.

WINFREY, OPRAH: Kosciusko, Ms., 1953. TnStateU.

WINGER, DEBRA: Cleveland, OH, May 17, 1955. Cal State.

WINKLER, HENRY: NYC, Oct. 30, 1945. Yale.

WINN, KITTY: Wash., D.C., 1944. Boston U.

WINTERS, JONATHAN: Dayton, OH, Nov. 11, 1925. Kenyon Col.

WINTERS, ROLAND: Boston, Nov. 22, 1904.

WINTERS, SHELLEY (Shirley Schrift): St. Louis, Aug. 18, 1922. Wayne U.

WITHERS, GOOGIE: Karachi, India, Mar. 12, 1917. Italia Conti.

WITHERS, JANE: Atlanta, GA, Apr. 12, 1926.

WOODLAWN, HOLLY (Harold Ajzenberg): Juana Diaz, PR, 1947.

WOODS, JAMES: Vernal, UT, Apr. 18, 1947. MIT.

WOODWARD, JOANNE: Thomasville, GA, Feb. 27, 1930. Neighborhood Playhouse.

WOOLAND, NORMAN: Dusseldorf, Ger., Mar. 16, 1910. Edward VI School.

WOPAT, TOM: Lodi, WI, 1950.

WORONOV, MARY: Brooklyn, Dec. 8, 1946. Cornell.

WORTH, IRENE: (Hattie Abrams) June 23, 1916, Neb. UCLA.

WRAY, FAY: Alberta, Can., Sept. 15, 1907.

WRIGHT, TERESA: NYC, Oct. 27, 1918.

WYATT, JANE: Campgaw, NJ, Aug. 10, 1911. Barnard College.

WYMAN, JANE (Sarah Jane Fulks): St. Joseph, MO, Jan. 4, 1914.

WYMORE, PATRICE: Miltonvale, KS, Dec. 17, 1926.

WYNN, KEENAN: NYC, July 27, 1916. St. John's.

WYNN, MAY (Donna Lee Hickey): NYC, Jan. 8, 1930.

WYNTER, DANA (Dagmar): London, June 8, 1927. Rhodes U.

YORK, DICK: Fort Wayne, IN, Sept. 4, 1928. De Paul U.

YORK, MICHAEL: Fulmer, Eng., Mar. 27, 1942. Oxford.

YORK, SUSANNAH: London, Jan. 9, 1941. RADA.

YOUNG, ALAN (Angus): North Shield, Eng., Nov. 19, 1919.

YOUNG, LORETTA (Gretchen): Salt Lake City, Jan. 6, 1912. Immaculate Heart College.

YOUNG, ROBERT: Chicago, Feb. 22, 1907.

ZACHARIAS, ANN: Stockholm, Sw., 1956.

ZADORA, PIA: Forest Hills, NY. 1954.

ZETTERLING, MAI: Sweden, May 27, 1925. Ordtuery Theatre School.

ZIMBALIST, EFREM, JR.: NYC, Nov. 30, 1918. Yale.

Eli
Wallach

Lesley Ann
Warren

Billy Dee
Williams

Irene
Worth

Michael
York

Pia
Zadora

| Dawn
Addams | Edward
Andrews | Dorothy
Arnold | Anne
Baxter | Scott
Brady | Louise
Brooks |

1985 OBITUARIES

DAWN ADDAMS, 54, British-born film and stage actress, died of cancer May 7, 1985 in London. Her credits include such films as Night into Morning, Singin' in the Rain, Hour of 13, Plymouth Adventure, Young Bess, Unknown Man, The Moon Is Blue, The Robe, Riders to the Stars, Return to Treasure Island, Khybar Patrol, Mizar, The Bed, Treasure of Rommel, London Calling, North Pole, King in New York, Silent Enemy, Secret Professional, Long Distance, Two Faces of Dr. Jekyll, Follow That Man, Liars, Lessons in Love, Come Fly with Me, Black Tulip, Ballad in Blue, Vampire Lovers, Zeta One, Vault of Horror, Nikos and Judy. Surviving are her second husband, and a son by her first husband, Prince Vittorio Massimo of Italy.

EDWARD ANDREWS, 70, Georgia-born character actor on stage, screen and tv, died of a heart attack March 8, 1985 in Pacific Palisades, Ca. After a Broadway career, he appeared in over 50 films, including Birds Do It, The Thrill of It All, Advise and Consent, Young Doctors, Absent-Minded Professor, Young Savages, Elmer Gantry, Those Wilder Years, Tattered Dress, Tea and Sympathy, Phoenix City Story, Glass Bottom Boat, Charley and the Angels, Sixteen Candles, and Gremlins. He also appeared in several tv series. He is survived by his widow, two daughters and a son.

EVELYN ANKERS, 67, actress on stage, tv, and in 51 films, died of cancer Aug. 29, 1985 in her home in Haiku, Hi. Born of British parents in Valparaiso, Chile, she began her career in London as a child actress. Among her film credits are The Wolf Man, Hold That Ghost, Ghost of Frankenstein, Mad Ghoul, Son of Dracula, Captive Wild Woman, Weird Woman, Frozen Ghost, Invisible Man's Revenge, Sherlock Holmes and the Voice of Terror, Pearl of Death, Bachelor Daddy, Hit the Road, Burma Convoy, North to the Klondike, Pierre of the Plains, The Great Impersonation, Hers to Hold, All By Myself, His Butler's Sister, Ladies Courageous, Bowery to Broadway, French Key, Last of the Redmen, Lone Wolf in London, Black Beauty, Rembrandt, The Texan Meets Calamity Jane. Surviving are her husband of 43 years, actor Richard Denning, and a daughter.

DOROTHY ARNOLD, 66, retired film actress, died Nov. 13, 1984 in Palm Springs, Ca. After establishing herself as a nightclub singer, she went to Hollywood in 1938 and appeared in such films as The Storm, Secrets of a Nurse, Exposed, House of Fear, Unexpected Father, the serial The Phantom Creeps, Code of the Streets, Family Next Door, Hers for a Day, Pirates of the Sky, and Lizzie. She was married to and divorced from baseball's great Joe DiMaggio. A son, Joe, Jr., survives.

KENNY BAKER, 72, singer-comedian on stage, film, and radio, died of a heart attack Aug. 10, 1985 at his home in Solvang, Ca. He appeared on radio in the Jack Benny Show (1935–1939) and the Fred Allen Show (1940–1942). His film credits include King of Burlesque, A Day at the Races, The Harvey Girls, The Marx Brothers at the Circus, Calendar Girl and The Mikado. No survivors reported.

PATRICK BARR, 77, actor on stage, film and tv, died Aug. 29, 1985 in London. He was born in India and began his career on stage in London. He had appeared in scores of films, including Brain Machine, Duel in the Jungle, Dam Busters, It's Never Too Late, The Valiant, The Longest Day, Ring of Spies, Nora O'Neal, Billy Liar, Return of the Scarlet Pimpernel, Frightened Lady, The Blue Lagoon, Robin Hood, Singlehanded, Crest of the Wave, St. Joan, and The House of Whipcord. His widow and a daughter survive.

CHARITA BAUER, 62, NJ-born stage, radio, tv and screen actress, died Feb. 28, 1985 in NYC after a long bout with cancer. For more than 35 years she had appeared in tv soap series, including The Guiding Light in which she had acted since its radio days as the character Bertha (Bert) Bauer. She is survived by her father, and a son.

ANNE BAXTER, 62, Indiana-born stage, film and tv actress, died of a cerebral hemorrhage Dec. 4, 1985 after suffering a massive stroke on a sidewalk in New York City. After her Broadway debut, she made her first picture, Twenty Mule Team, in 1940. She received an Academy Award in 1946 for Best Supporting Actress in The Razor's Edge. Other film credits include The Great Profile, Charley's Aunt, Swamp Water, Crash Dive, Five Graves to Cairo, The Sullivans, The Eve of St. Mark, The Magnificent Ambersons, North Star, All About Eve (for which she was nominated for an Oscar), Follow the Sun, Outcasts of Poker Flat, O'Henry's Full House, My Wife's Best Friend, I Confess, Blue Gardenia, The Carnival Story, Bedeviled, One Desire, The Spoilers, The Come On, Three Violent People, Chase a Crooked Shadow, Summer of the 17th Doll, Cimarron, The Ten Commandments (1956), Guest in the House, Family Jewels, Jane Austen in Manhattan, The Busy Body. At the time of her death, she had been appearing in the tv serial "Hotel." She had married and divorced actor John Hodiak, and Australian rancher Randolph Galt. Her third husband, banker David Klee died in 1978. Surviving are three daughters.

SCOTT BRADY, 60, Brooklyn-born film and tv character actor, died of respiratory failure Apr. 16, 1985 in Woodland Hills, Ca. Among his many screen credits are Born to Fight, He Walked by Night, In This Corner, Port of New York, Undertow, Kansas Raiders, Undercover Girl, The Model and the Marriage Broker, Bronco Buster, Bloodhounds of Broadway, Perilous Journey, White Fire, Johnny Guitar, Gentlemen Marry Brunettes, The Vanishing American, Terror at Midnight, Maverick Queen, Blood Arrow, Operation Bikini, Black Spurs, Destination Inner Space, Journey to the Center of Time, Marooned, The Loners, China Syndrome, Gremlins. He is survived by his widow, two sons, Timothy and Terrence Tierney (his family name), and a brother, actor Lawrence Tierney.

BRIGGS, CHARLES, 53, actor and Screen Actors Guild activist, died Feb. 6, 1985 in Roswell, GA. He had appeared in such films as Home from the Hill, Captain Nesman, M.D., The Klansman, Norma Rae and The Executioner. On tv he appeared in Swamp Fox, Death Valley Days, Wagon Train, Gunsmoke, Maverick, Bonanza, The Virginian, Perry Mason, and The Mod Squad. Surviving are his widow and three children.

LOUISE BROOKS, 78, Kansas-born silent screen star, died of a heart attack Aug. 8, 1985 in her home in Rochester, NY, where she had lived since 1956. She appeared with the Martha Graham Dance Co. and on Broadway before making her film debut in 1925. Credits include The Street of Forgotten Men, American Venus, A Social Celebrity, It's the Old Army Game, The Show-Off, Love 'Em and Leave 'Em, Just Another Blonde, Evening Clothes, Rolled Stockings, City Gone Wild, Now We're in the Air, A Girl in Every Port, Beggars of Life, The Canary Murder Case, Pandora's Box, Diary of a Lost Girl, Prix de Beaute, Windy Riley Goes to Hollywood, It Pays to Advertise, The Public Enemy, Steel Highway, Empty Saddles, When You're in Love, King of Gamblers and Overland Stage Riders. She was married and divorced twice. Her memoirs, published in 1982, brought her back into public attention. No reported survivors.

YUL BRYNNER, 65, stage and screen actor, died of cancer Oct. 10, 1985 in New York City. He came to the U.S. from France in 1941 after supporting himself as an actor, singer and guitarist. After his Broadway debut he appeared in such films as Port of New York, The King and I which won him a 1956 Best Actor Academy Award, Ten Commandments, Anastasia, The Journey, Solomon and Sheba, Once More with Feeling, The Magnificent Seven, Taras Bulba, Escape to Zahrain, Kings of the Sun, Saboteur, Code Name Morituri, Invitation to a Gunfighter, Return of the Seven, Triple Cross, Double Man, The Long Duel, Battle of Neretva, Magic Christian, File of the Golden Goose, Madwoman of Chaillot, Romance of a Horsethief, Light at the Edge of the World, Fuzz, Westworld, Futureworld. Surviving are his fourth wife, actress-dancer Kathy Lee, a son and three daughters.

HUGH BURDEN, 72, playwright, stage, screen and tv actor, died May 17, 1985 of unreported cause in London. Born in Ceylon and educated in England, he made his stage debut in 1933. Among his film credits are Funeral in Berlin, The Way Ahead, Secret Partner, One of Our Aircraft Is Missing, No Love for Johnnie, Fame Is the Spur, The Ruling Class, One of Our Dinosaurs Is Missing, Blood from the Mummy's Tomb, House in Nightmare Park, Malta Story, and Dr. Fischer of Geneva. No reported survivors.

MARION BYRON, 73, Ohio-born comedienne, died after a long illness July 5, 1985 in Santa Monica, Ca. She made her film debut at 16 opposite Buster Keaton in Steamboat Bill, Jr. Subsequent films include Plastered in Paris, Broadway Babies of 1929, His Captive Woman, Song of the West, Playing Around, Golden Dawn, The Matrimonial, Girls Demand Excitement, Children of Dreams, The Heart of New York, Tenderfoot, Love Me Tonight, Gift of Gab, and her last (1938), Five of a Kind. She is survived by her husband of 53 years, screenwriter Lou Breslow and two sons.

RAFAEL CAMPOS, 49, stage, screen and tv actor, died of stomach cancer, July 9, 1985 in Woodland Hills, Ca. Born in the Dominican Republic, he came to the U.S. in 1949 and became involved in several theatrical productions, before being signed for the 1955 release "Blackboard Jungle." Subsequent credits include Trial, Dino, Sharkfighters, This Could Be the Night, The Light in the Forest, Tonka, Savage Sam, Lady in a Cage, Agent for H.A.R.M., Mr. Buddwing, The Appaloosa, The Doll Squad, Oklahoma Crude, Slumber Party '57, Where the Buffalo Roam, The Fever. He had appeared in numerous tv productions and series. He was twice married and divorced. Two daughters survive.

GEORGE CHANDLER, 87, Illinois-born vaudevillian, screen and tv actor, died of Alzheimer's disease June 10, 1985 in Hollywood, Ca. He had appeared in over 150 films, and had served as three-term president of Screen Actors Guild. He entered films in 1927 and had his first starring role two years later in Tenderfoot Thrillers. Subsequent credits include The Florodora Girl, In Gay Madrid, Only Saps Work, Lady Killer, Fog over Frisco, Murder Man, Stars over Broadway, Fury, Libeled Lady, Three Men on a Horse, Nothing Sacred, The Return of Frank James, Arizona, Tobacco Road, Roxie Hart, Ox-Bow Incident, Buffalo Bill, Since You Went Away, Without Love, Suspense, Dead Reckoning, Black Angel, Michigan Kid, Perfect Strangers, Hans Christian Anderson, Steel Cage, Apple Dumpling Gang Rides Again. Surviving are his widow, three sons and two stepsons.

INA CLAIRE, 92, nee Ina Fagan in Washington, one of the most celebrated stage comediennes, died following a stroke Feb. 21, 1985 in her home in San Francisco, Ca. She had appeared in only 9 films, Polly with a Past, The Awful Truth, The Royal Family of Broadway, Rebound, The Greeks Had a Word for Them, Ninotchka, Claudia, Hollywood Canteen, and The Two-Faced Woman. Her third husband, San Francisco lawyer and financier, died in 1975. She had been married previously to Chicago critic James Whittaker, and silent screen star John Gilbert. No immediate survivors.

JAMES CRAIG, 74, Tennessee-born stage and film actor, died of lung cancer June 28, 1985 in Santa Ana, Ca. After beginning his professional career in 1937, he changed his family name from Meader to Craig. Among his film credits are Arizona Ames, Born to the West, The Man They Could Not Hang, Taming of the West, Law and Order, Winners of the West serial, Kitty Foyle, All That Money Can buy, Unexpected Uncle, Valley of the Sun, Friendly Enemies, Northwest Rangers, Human Comedy, Lost Angel, Girls in Overalls, Swing Shift Maisie, Heavenly Body, Kismet, Gentle Annie, Marriage Is a Private Affair, She Went to the Races, Our Vines Have Tender Grapes, Dangerous Partners, Boys Ranch, Little Mr. Jim, Dark Delusion, Northwest Stampede, Side Street, Lady without Passport, Hurricane Smith, Fort Vengeance, Naked in the Sun, Manor Gun, Fort Utah, Hostile Guns, Bigfoot and Doomsday Machine. He was married to, and divorced from actresses Mary Jane Ray, Jill Jarman, Sumie Jassi. Surviving are two sons and a daughter.

JACKIE CURTIS, 38, playwright and actor, died of a drug overdose on May 15, 1985. His feature films were Flesh, Women in Revolt, WR: Mysteries of the Organism, Underground USA, Burroughs, and Big Badge. His father survives.

JORJA CURTRIGHT, age not reported, Texas-born actress on stage, screen and tv, died of a heart attack May 11, 1985 in Los Angeles, Ca. Her films include Hitler's Madmen, Whistle Stop, Heaven Only Knows, M, Love Is a Many Splendored Thing, and Revolt of Mamie Stover. Surviving are her husband, writer-producer-novelist Sidney Sheldon, and a daughter.

JOHNNY DESMOND, 65, Detroit-born Giovanni Alfredo de Simone, film and tv actor-singer, died of cancer Sept. 6, 1985 in Los Angeles, Ca. He had appeared in such movies as Calypso Heat Wave, Escape from San Quentin, Desert Hell, and China Doll. He survived by his widow and two daughters.

SELMA DIAMOND, 64, Canada-born comedy writer and actress on screen and tv, died of cancer May 13, 1985 in Los Angeles, Ca. After writing for many successful tv series, she appeared in such films as It's a Mad Mad World, My Favorite Year, Bang the Drum Slowly, The Twilight Zone and All of Me. No reported survivors.

FRANK FAYLEN, 79, St. Louis-born character actor of vaudeville, stage and screen, died of pneumonia Aug. 2, 1985 in Burbank, Ca. He was probably best known for Dobie's father in the tv series "Dobie Gillis." His film credits include Border Flight, Down the Stretch, King of Hockey, Address Unknown, Yanks Ahoy, Unknown Guest, And the Angels Sing, Bring on the Girls, The Lost Weekend, You Came Along, Perils of Pauline, Road to Rio, Copper Canyon, Francis, Passage West, Detective Story, Lusty Men, Hangman's Knot, Red Garters, It's a Wonderful Life, Funny Girl, Road to Rio and Grapes of Wrath. Surviving are his widow, actress Carol Hughes, two daughters.

STEPIN FETCHIT, 83, one of Hollywood's first black stars, died of heart failure and pneumonia Nov. 19, 1985 in Woodland Hills, Ca. He was born Lincoln Theodore Monroe Andrew Perry in Key West, Fl., but left home to join a carnival and subsequently to appear in vaudeville. He took the name Stepin Fetchit after winning money on a race horse by that name. His first film was In Old Kentucky in 1927, followed by Show Boat, Big Time, Fox Movietone Follies, Hearts in Dixie, Salute, The Kid's Clever, Cameo Kirby, The Ghost Talks, Swing High, Stand Up and Cheer, Carolina, Judge Priest, David Harum, Helldorado, Country Chairman, One More Spring, Charlie Chan in Egypt, Steamboat Round the Bend, Virginia Judge, Miracle in Harlem, Amazing Grace and Won Ton Ton the Dog Who Saved Hollywood (1976). He was married and divorced three times. A son survives.

JANE FRAZEE, 67, singer-actress in some 40 films, died Sept. 6, 1985 of pneumonia following a series of strokes in Newport Beach, Ca. Born in St. Paul as Mary Jane Frehse, she and her sister Ruth began careers singing and dancing in nightclubs until 1940 when Ruth married writer-producer Norman Krasna. Jane's first feature film was Moonlight and Melody followed by Hellzapoppin, Moonlight in Havana, When Johnny Comes Marching Home, Swing and Sway, Practically Yours, Rosie the Riveter, Kansas City Kitty, Swingin' on a Rainbow, Calendar Girl, A Guy Could Change, Ten Cents a Dance, and her last (in 1951) Rhythm Inn. In 1970 she became a real estate saleslady. She was married and divorced four times. A son and her sister survive.

RUTH GORDON, 88, actress and writer, died in her sleep of a stroke Aug. 28, 1985 in her summer home in Edgartown, Ma. She was born Ruth Gordon Jones in the Wollaston section of Quincy, Ma., and remained in touch with friends there until her death. After success in the theatre, she made her film debut in 1940 as Mary Todd in Abe Lincoln in Illinois, subsequently appearing in Two Faced Woman, Dr. Ehrlich's Magic Bullet, Action in the North Atlantic, Edge of Darkness, Inside Daisy Clover, Lord Love a Duck, Whatever Happened to Aunt Alice?, Rosemary's Baby (for which she received a 1968 Oscar for Best Supporting Actress), Where's Poppa?, Harold and Maude, The Big Bus, Every Which Way But Loose, Boardwalk, Scavenger Hunt, My Bodyguard, Any Which Way You Can, Jimmy the Kid, Maxie, Mugsy's Girls, Trouble at the Royal Rose, and Voyage of the Rock Aliens. She received a 1979 Emmy for her tv appearance in the Taxi series. With Garson Kanin (her husband for 43 years) she co-authored the screenplays for Pat and Mike, Adam's Rib, and A Double Life. She is survived by her son Jones Harris, and her husband.

Yul Brynner	**Rafael Campos**	**Stepin Fetchit**	**Ruth Gordon**	**Margaret Hamilton**	**Rock Hudson**

JETTA GOUDAL, 86, French-born actress on stage and screen, died Jan. 14, 1985 after a long illness in her Los Angeles, Ca., home. After appearing on stage in Europe, she came to the U.S. and after success on Broadway she made her film debut in 1923 in The Bright Shawl. Her credits include Forbidden Woman, Fighting Love, White Gold, Lady of the Pavements, The Green Goddess, Salome of the Tenements, Business and Pleasure, Her Man o' War, and Tarnished Youth, her last film before retiring in 1933. Surviving is her husband, film art director Harold Grieve.

KIRBY GRANT, 74, film and tv actor-singer, died in an auto accident Oct. 30, 1985 near Titusville, Fl., on his way to watch the launching of the space shuttle at Cape Canaveral. Born Kirby Grant Hoon in Butte, Mon., began his career with a dance band. He made his film debut in 1939 in Three Sons, and during the next 15 years appeared in over 40 movies, including Blondie Goes Latin, Hello Frisco Hello, Stranger from Pecos, Hi Good Lookin', Ghost Catchers, Penthouse Rhythm, The Spider Woman Strikes Back, The Lawless Breed, Trail of the Yukon, Call of the Klondike, Northwest Territory, Yukon Manhunt, Northern Patrol, Yukon Vengeance, and his last, The Court Martial of Billy Mitchell in 1955. He is probably best known for his tv series Sky King. His widow survives.

RICHARD GREENE, 66, British-born actor on stage screen and tv, died June 1, 1985 in his country home in Norfolk, Eng. A talent scout spotted him in an English touring company and signed him to a Hollywood contract. He made his debut in 1938 in Four Men and a Prayer, followed by some 40 pictures, including Hound of the Baskervilles, My Lucky Star, Stanley and Livingstone, Little Old New York, Flying Fortress, Kentucky, Now Barabbas, Desert Hawk, Black Castle, That Dangerous Age, Yellow Canary, Shadow of the Eagle, Captain Scarlet, Bandits of Corsica, Sword of Sherwood Forest, Blood of Fu Manchu, Kiss and Tell, Forever Amber, The Fan, and Lorna Doone. He was probably best known for the tv series The Adventures of Robin Hood that ran for 4 years. He was married and divorced twice. A daughter survives.

TOM GREENWAY, 75, stage and screen actor, died of a heart attack Feb. 8, 1985 in his home in Los Angeles, Ca. His career began at 15 on Broadway. His film credits include Westward the Women, High Noon, These Thousand Hills, Five Against the House, Jim Thorpe, Peyton Place, Love Me Tender, North by Northwest and How the West Was Won. He had appeared on tv in Bonanza, Maverick, West Point, Gunsmoke, Wells Fargo, The Medic, Wagon Train, Bat Masterson, Ben Casey, and The Untouchables. Surviving are his widow and a daughter.

MARGARET HAMILTON, 82, Ohio-born former teacher, stage, tv and film actress, died of a heart attack May 16, 1985 in Salisbury, Ct. When her Broadway hit, Another Language, was filmed, she went to Hollywood and made her screen debut in it in 1933. She subsequently appeared in character roles in over 70 pictures, including Driftwood, Bungalow 13, The Sun Comes Up, The Beautiful Blond from Bashful Bend, Riding High, Wabash Avenue, The Great Plane Robbery, Brewster McCloud, My Little Chickadee, George White's Scandals, State of the Union, and The Anderson Tapes, but was best known for the Wicked Witch of the West in The Wizard of Oz. A son survives.

HENRY HATHAWAY, 86, Sacramento-born director, and former actor, died of a heart attack on Feb. 11, 1985 in Los Angeles, Ca. He directed more than 60 films, including The Real Glory, Brigham Young Frontiersman, Kiss of Death, Heritage of the Desert, Wild Horse Mesa, The Lives of a Bengal Lancer, Home in Indiana, 13 Rue Madeleine, Call Northside 777, Down to the Sea in Ships, Fourteen Hours, 23 Paces to Baker Street, Sons of Katie Elder, Nevada Smith, and True Grit. Surviving are his widow and a son.

RICHARD HAYDN, 80, London-born actor on stage and screen, was found dead Apr. 25, 1985 in his home in Pacific Palisades, Ca. In 1939 he made his debut on Broadway and in 1941 on screen in Charley's Aunt, followed by Ball of Fire, Are Husbands Necessary?, Thunder Birds, Forever and a Day, No Time for Love, Henry Aldrich Boy Scout, Tonight and Every Night, Adventure, The Green Years, Cluny Brown, The Late George Apley, Foxes of Harrow, Singapore, Sitting Pretty, The Emperor Waltz, The Merry Widow, Never Let Me Go, Jupiter's Darling, Twilight for the Gods, Please Don't Eat the Daisies, Mutiny on the Bounty, Five Weeks in a Balloon, The Sound of Music, and Young Frankenstein. No reported survivors.

LOUIS HAYWARD, 75, stage, film and tv actor, died of lung cancer Feb. 21, 1985 in Palm Springs, Ca. Born Seafield Grant in Johannesburg, SA., he was educated in England where he began his career on stage. After his Broadway debut in 1934 he moved to Hollywood. His films include The Flame Within, A Feather in Her Hat, Anthony Adverse, The Luckiest Girl in the World, The Woman I Love, Midnight Intruder, The Rage of Paris, Duke of West Point, Condemned Women, The Saint in New York, Man in the Iron Mask, Son of Monte Cristo, Return of Monte Cristo, My Son My Son, Ladies in Retirement, And Then There Were None, Ruthless, Pirates of Capri, House by the River, The Young Widow, Repeat Performance, Saxon Charm, Walk a Crooked Mile, Fortunes of Captain Blood, Royal African Rifles, The Saint's Girl Friday, Duffy of San Quentin, The Christmas Kid, Chuka, The Phynx, and Terror in the Wax Museum (his last in 1973). His third wife and a son survive.

HAROLD HECHT, 77, New York-born producer and former dancer-choreographer, died of cancer May 25, 1985 in his Beverly Hills, Ca. home. He went to Hollywood as a dance director for Busby Berkeley. After serving in WW II, he formed a partnership with Burt Lancaster, and later with James Hill. His film "Marty" received 5 Academy Awards in 1955, including Best Picture. Other productions include The Flame and the Arrow, Ten Tall Men, Apache, The Kentuckian, Trapeze, Bachelor Party, Sweet Smell of Success, Separate Tables, Bird Man of Alcatraz, Taras Bulba, and Cat Ballou. Surviving are two daughters and three sons.

GEORGE HOLMES, 66, screen actor, died Feb. 19, 1985 in Los Angeles, Ca. His film career began in 1942 in It Happened in Flatbush. Other credits include The Man in the Trunk, Crash Dive, Roger Touhy—Gangster, The Falcon in San Francisco, Dark Alibi, Back Trail, Camelot, and Hello Dolly!. His widow survives.

ROCK HUDSON, 59, a romantic film idol on film and tv, died Oct. 2, 1985 after a long illness in his home in Beverly Hills, Ca. Born Roy Scherer, Jr. in Winnetka, Il, he later took his stepfather's name of Fitzgerald. He served in the Navy during WWII. In 1947 a talent scout changed his name to the one that became world famous from his many films and tv series. He had small roles in 28 pictures before being given billing and becoming the top money-making star from 1957–1965. Included among his credits are Magnificent Obsession, Bengal Brigade, Capt. Lightfoot, All That Heaven Allows, Giant, for which he received an Academy Award nomination, Written on the Wind, Farewell to Arms, Pillow Talk, Come September, Lover Come Back, A Gathering of Eagles, Send Me No Flowers, A Very Special Favor, The Undefeated, Tobruk, Darling Lili, Embryo, Avalanche, and The Ambassador. On tv he was seen in McMillan and Wife, Wheels, The Martian Chronicles, The Star Maker, World War III, and Dynasty. There were no immediate survivors. He was cremated and his ashes scattered in the Pacific Ocean.

ISABEL JEANS, 93, British actress on stage and screen for more than 60 years, died Sept. 4, 1985 in her native London. Her film credits include Tilly of Bloomsbury, The Rat, Easy Virtue, Down Hill, The Dictator, Tovarich, Garden of the Moon, Hard to Get, Secrets of an Actress, Fools for Scandal, Youth Takes a Fling, Man about Town, Good Girls Go to Paris, Suspicion, Colonel Blimp, Heavens Above, Gigi, It Happened in Rome, and A Breath of Scandal. No reported survivors.

LEATRICE JOY, 91, born Leatrice Joy Zeidler in New Orleans, silent screen star, died May 13, 1985 in Riverdale, NY. After her debut at 14, she made over 60 films from 1918 to 1951, including The Ten Commandments, Manslaughter, Triumph, Vanity, The Blue Danube, The Dressmaker from Paris, Pride of the Clan, Saturday Night, Air Hostess, Of Human Hearts, First Love, and Love Nest (her last in 1951). She retired to her home in Connecticut. She is survived by her daughter, Leatrice Gilbert Fountain, who wrote a recent biography of her father, actor and silent screen idol John Gilbert. She had been married and divorced three times.

HAL LeROY, 71, dancer-actor on Broadway and in films, died following cardiac surgery May 2, 1985 in Hackensack, NJ. Born John LeRoy Schotte in Cincinnati, Oh., he began dancing at an early age. At 16 he was in the Ziegfeld Follies, and appeared in the films Wonder Bar, Start Cheering, and Too Many Girls. He played the title role in the series of Harold Teen movies. There are no survivors.

JOHN LODGE, 82, former stage and screen actor who later served as governor of Connecticut, and as an ambassador, died of a heart attack while addressing the Women's National Republican Club in New York City. After his film debut in 1932 in The Woman Accused, he appeared in Murders in the Zoo, Under the Tonto Rim, Little Women, The Scarlet Empress, Menace, The Little Colonel, Koenigsmark, Ourselves Alone, The Tenth Man, Tonight at 11, Bank Holiday, Just Like a Woman, Queer Cargo, Premiere, Lightning Conductor, From Mayerling to Sarajevo (his last in 1940). He served in the Navy during WWII. Surviving are his widow and two daughters.

MARY MacLAREN, 85, Pittsburgh-born silent screen actress, died of respiratory problems Nov. 9, 1985 in Los Angeles, Ca. At 16 she was starred in "Shoes" and through 1924 appeared in such films as The Three Musketeers, The Wild Goose, Across the Continent, The Face in the Fog, Outcast, On the Banks of the Wabash, Under the Red Rose, Courageous Coward, The Dark Swan, and The Uninvited Guest. No reported survivors.

MARGO, 68, former dancer and actress on stage and screen, died from a brain tumor July 17, 1985 in her home in Pacific Palisades, Ca. Born in Mexico City, she began her career at 9 dancing with her uncle Xavier Cugat's band. At 15 she was signed for the movie "Crime without Passion," followed by Winterset, Lost Horizons, The Leopard Man, Viva Zapata!, and I'll Cry Tomorrow. She is survived by her husband of 40 years, actor Eddie Albert, a daughter, and a son, actor Edward Albert.

MARION MARTIN, 67, Philadelphia-born stage and screen actress, died of natural causes Aug. 13, 1985 in Santa Monica, Ca. After Broadway success, she was signed in 1938 for Universal's Sinners in Paradise, followed by Youth Takes a Fling, The Storm, Deadline for Murder, Suspense, Cinderella Jones, Queen of Burlesque, Angel on My Shoulder, That's My Girl, That Brennan Girl, Lighthouse, Thunder in the Pines, Come to the Stable, Key to the City, Boom Town, The Big Store, They Got Me Covered, Abbott and Costello in Hollywood, Mexican Spitfire's Baby, The Big Street, Girls of the Big House, Oh You Beautiful Doll, Tales of Manhattan, and her last Dakota Lil in 1950. Surviving are her husband and a brother.

MURRAY MATHESON, 73, Australian-born stage, screen and tv actor, died of heart failure Apr. 25, 1985 in Woodland Hills, Ca. After appearing on stage in Australia, England, Canada, and the U.S., he made his film debut in 1945 in The Ways to the Stars, followed by Hurricane Smith, Botany Bay, King of the Khyber Rifles, Love Is a Many-Splendored Thing, Wall of Noise, Signpost to Murder, Assault on a Queen, How to Succeed in Business without Really Trying, Twilight Zone—the Movie. Among his many tv credits are Banacek, McMillan and Wife, Charlie's Angels, Battlestar Galactica, McCloud, Vegas, Facts of Life, and the Bob Newhart Show. A sister survives.

PATTI McCARTY, 64, actress, died July 7, 1985 in Honolulu, Hi. Film credits include You'll Never Get Rich, Under Age, She Knew All the Answers, and several westerns with Buster Crabbe. A daughter survives.

MARVIN MILLER, 71, screen, radio and tv actor, died of a heart attack Feb. 8, 1985 in Santa Monica, Ca. He appeared in such films as Blood on the Sun, Johnny Angel, Deadline at Dawn, A Night in Paradise, Dead Reckoning, Intrigue, Smugglers Island, Peking Express, Hong Kong, Red Planet Mars, Forbidden, Off Limits, Story of Mankind, A Trip to Terror. He was best known as Michael Anthony, the bearer of checks in the tv series The Millionaire. He is survived by his widow, a son, and a daughter.

CLARENCE NASH, 80, who for over 50 years was the voice of Donald Duck in movies, died of leukemia Feb. 20, 1985 in Burbank, Ca. Although he had retired as a regular Disney employee, he was in constant demand for personal appearances. He also provided Donald's voice in all overseas releases, speaking phonetically in French, Spanish, Portugese, Japanese, Chinese and German. He was also the voices of Donald's nephews, Huey, Louie and Dewey, and his girl friend Daisy. When his parents moved from Oklahoma to California, he performed his entire repertoire of animal sounds for Walt Disney and was hired immediately. Surviving are his widow, and two daughters.

RICK NELSON, 45, the singing idol who grew up on tv in the series The Adventures of Ozzie and Harriet, died in a plane crash near DeKalb, Tx., Dec. 31, 1985. He and his band were on their way to fill an engagement in Dallas, Tx. While on the tv series from 1952 to 1966 he grew from an 11-year-old to a 25-year-old husband, father and singing star. He had also appeared in the films Here Come the Nelsons, Rio Bravo, The Wackiest Ship in the Army, Story of Three Loves, and Love and Kisses. He is survived by his four children, his mother Harriet Hilliard Nelson, and brother David.

DANDY NICHOLS, 78, British stage, screen and tv actress, died Feb. 6, 1985 in London. Among her many film credits are Help!, O Lucky Man, Georgy Girl, Nicholas Nickleby, Britannia Hospital, Plague Dogs, The Deep Blue Sea, Street Corner, Fallen Angel, The Winslow Boy, Blonde Sinner, The Birthday Party, and Hue and Cry. She was probably best known for the tv sitcom Till Death Do Us Part that became All in the Family in the U.S. No reported survivors.

JAMES F. NOLAN, 69, San Francisco stage, screen and tv actor, died of cancer July 29, 1985 in Woodland Hills, Ca. He had appeared in over 40 films, including Rogues Regiment, Little Miss Big, Girls on Probation, Miracle of the Bells, Guns of Hate, Fighting Father Dunne, Daughter of the Jungle, Alias the Champ, Mary Ryan Detective, The Big Caper, Portrait in Black, Dirty Harry, Airport, The Shootist, Charley Varick, All Night Long. No reported survivors.

LLOYD NOLAN, 83, San Francisco-born stage, screen and tv actor, died of lung cancer Sept. 27, 1985 in his home in Los Angeles, Ca. After appearing on Broadway, from 1934 to 1954 he had parts in over 70 films, including Atlantic Adventure, One Way Ticket, Devil's Squadron, Counterfeit, King of the Gamblers, Ebb Tide, Wells Fargo, Hunted Men, King of Alcatraz, St. Louis Blues, Magnificent Fraud, House across the Bay, Johnny Apollo, Mr. Dynamite, Guadalcanal Diary, Bataan, A Tree Grows in Brooklyn, Circumstantial Evidence, House on 92nd Street, Lady in the Lake, Bad Boy, Lemon Drop Kid, Crazylegs, Abandon Ship!, Hatful of Rain, Peyton Place, Portrait in Black, Never Too Late, Airport, Earthquake, Private Files of J. Edgar Hoover, Prince Jack, and (his last) Hannah and Her Sisters. On tv he appeared as Martin Kane Private Eye, and co-starred with Diahann Carroll in Julia. He is survived by his second wife and a daughter.

EDMOND O'BRIEN, 69, Brooklyn-born actor on stage and screen, died of Alzheimer's disease on May 8, 1985 in Inglewood, Ca. After appearing on Broadway, in 1939 he went to Hollywood for The Hunchback of Notre Dame, subsequently appearing in many films, including Winged Victory, The Killers, A Double Life, The Web, Fighter Squadron, Another Part of the Forest, An Act of Murder, White Heat, The Admiral Was a Lady, Two of a Kind, The Turning Point, Julius Caesar, Shanghai Story, The Barefoot Contessa (for which he received a 1955 Best Supporting Actor "Oscar"), Pete Kelly's Blues, 1984, The Bigamist, Last Voyage, The Great Impostor, Bird Man of Alcatraz, The Longest Day, 7 Days in May (Oscar nominated), Synanon, Fantastic Voyage, and The Wild Bunch. He was divorced from actresses Nancy Kelly and Olga San Juan. Two daughters and a son survive.

Marion
Martin

Rick
Nelson

Lloyd
Nolan

Edmond
O'Brien

Michael
Redgrave

Phil
Silvers

GEORGE O'BRIEN, 85, San Francisco-born star of silent and western films, died following a stroke Sept. 4, 1985 in Broken Arrow, Ok., where he had lived since 1979. He attained stardom in 1924's epic The Iron Horse, followed by over 70 others, including Three Bad Men, The Blue Eagle, Salute, Fig Leaves, Paid to Love, Sunrise, Is Zat So?, True Heaven, Noah's Ark, Masked Emotions, Seas Beneath, Riders of the Purple Sage, The Gay Caballero, Life in the Raw, When a Man's a Man, Cowboy Millionaire, Daniel Boone, Painted Desert, Fort Apache, She Wore a Yellow Ribbon, Gold Raiders, and (his last in 1964) Cheyenne Autumn. He had been married to actress Marguerite Churchill. A son and daughter survive.

HAROLD PEARY, 76, Portugese immigrant who became a stage, radio and film actor, died of a heart attack March 30, 1985 in Torrance, Ca. After starring on radio in The Great Gildersleeve, he went to Hollywood where he appeared in Comin' Round the Mountain, Country Fair, Look Who's Laughing, Here We Go Again, Seven Days Leave, The Great Gildersleeve, Gildersleeve's Bad Day, Gildersleeve's Ghost, Gildersleeve on Broadway, and Clambake. He was also seen in many tv shows. He is survived by a son.

WANDA PERRY, 67, actress, died Feb. 17, 1985 after a long illness in Hollywood, Ca. She was a child model in NYC before making her film debut at 16 in Murder at the Vanities, followed by such pictures as Kid Millions, Roberta, Rosalie, Born to Dance, The Great Ziegfeld, Crime Doctor's Man Hunt, Follow the Sun, and Mame. Surviving are a daughter and two sons.

SIR MICHAEL REDGRAVE, 77, distinguished British stage, screen and tv actor, and writer, died of Parkinson's disease March 2, 1985 after suffering from it for 12 years when it ended his career. Professionally, he started with the Liverpool Rep. in 1934, and became one of England's stellar actors. His over 50 film credits include Secret Agent, The Lady Vanishes, Stolen Life, The Remarkable Mr. Kipps, The Stars Look Down, Thunder Rock, Dead of Night, The Captive Heart, Fame Is the Spur, The Browning Version, The Importance of Being Earnest, 1984, Mourning Becomes Electra (Academy Award nomination), The Quiet American, Wreck of the Mary Deare, The Innocents, Young Cassidy, The 25th Hour, Behind the Mask, Goodbye Mr. Chips, Nicholas and Alexandra, and in 1971 his final feature The Go-Between. Surviving are his acting family, wife Rachel Kempson, daughters Vanessa and Lynn, and son Corin.

JIMMY RITZ, 81, one of the three zany Ritz Brothers comedy trio, died of heart failure Nov. 17, 1985 in Los Angeles, Ca. Brooklyn-born Jimmy Joachim, after graduating from high school, joined his brothers Al and Harry and in 1925 they began their joint careers in vaudeville. Their film appearances began in 1936 in Sing Baby Sing, followed by One in a Million, On the Avenue, Life Begins in College, You Can't Have Everything, Kentucky Moonshine, Straight Place and Show, Goldwyn Follies, The Three Musketeers, Argentine Nights, The Gorilla, Pack Up Your Troubles, Behind the 8 Ball, Never a Dull Moment, and Everything Happens to Us. They broke up when Al died in 1965. Survivors include his brother Harry, a sister, and a daughter.

HEINZ ERIC ROEMHELD, 83, Academy Award composer, died of pneumonia Feb. 11, 1985 in Huntington Beach, Ca. He scored, arranged or conducted for over 400 films before his retirement in 1964. He received an Oscar for the 1942 score of Yankee Doodle Dandy, and his most popular songs were Ruby, Valentino Tango, and Louise. Two daughters survive.

HELEN ROSE, 81, Chicago-born Academy Award costume designer, died Nov. 9, 1985 after a long illness in Palm Springs, Ca. She had designed for over 200 pictures, and was the recipient of two "Oscars" for The Bad and the Beautiful, and for I'll Cry Tomorrow. She was also nominated for The Great Caruso, The Merry Widow, Dream Wife, Executive Suite, Interrupted Melody, The Power and the Prize, The Gazebo, and Mister Buddwing. She also designed the wedding dress for Grace Kelly to Prince Rainier of Monaco. Surviving are her husband and a daughter.

ALEXANDER SCOURBY, 71, Brooklyn-born stage, screen and tv actor, died suddenly Feb. 22, 1985 in Boston, Ma. He was also known widely for his recordings of great works of literature for the blind. His films include With These Hands, Affair in Trinidad, Because of You, The Redhead from Wyoming, Glory Brigade, The Big Heat, The Silver Chalice, Sign of the Pagan, Giant, Ransom, Me and the Colonel, The Big Fisherman, Shaggy Dog, 7 Thieves, Man on the String, The Devil at 4 O'Clock. He was the narrator for Victory at Sea. He was the Metropolitan Opera's host for their "Live from the Met" broadcasts. He is survived by his widow, actress Lori March, and a daughter.

MICKEY SHAUGHNESSY, 64, NYC-born character actor and nightclub comedian, died of heart failure and lung cancer July 23, 1985 in Cape May, NJ. His film debut was 1952 in The Marrying Kind, followed by such pictures as Last of the Comanches, From Here to Eternity, Conquest of Space, Designing Woman, Slaughter on 10th Avenue, Don't Go Near the Water, The Burglar, Gunman's Walk, Don't Give Up the Ship, Edge of Eternity, Hangman, Adventures of Huckleberry Finn, College Confidential, Dondi, Pocketful of Miracles, How the West Was Won, A House Is Not a Home, Jailhouse Rock, and The Boatniks. Surviving are his widow, three sons and four daughters.

RANSOM SHERMAN, 87, Wisconsin-born writer, radio, film and tv actor, died Nov. 26, 1985 of undisclosed cause in Henderson, Nev. On film he had roles in Swing Your Partner, Yankee Fakir, The Bachelor and the Bobby-Soxer, Always Together, Gentleman's Agreement, Are You With It?, Winter Meeting, Countess of Monte Cristo, Whiplash, One Last Fling, Flaming Fury, Always Leave Them Laughing, and Pretty Baby. No reported survivors.

PHIL SILVERS, 73, Brooklyn-born comedian on stage, screen, tv and in vaudeville, burlesque and nightclubs, died in his sleep of natural causes Nov. 1, 1985 in his home in Los Angeles, Ca. After appearing in vaudeville, he made his Broadway debut in 1938, and the next year signed for his first movie, but he continued working in both media. His film credits include Hit Parade of 1941, Tom Dick and Harry, You're in the Army Now, Wild Man of Borneo, Lady Be Good, Roxie Hart, My Gal Sal, Footlight Serenade, All Through the Night, Coney Island, Cover Girl, Four Jills in a Jeep, Something for the Boys, Take It or Leave It, Diamond Horseshoe, A 1000 and One Nights, Top Banana, Lucky Me, It's a Mad Mad Mad World, The Oscar, A Funny Thing Happened on the Way to the Forum, Buona Sera Mrs. Campbell, and Guide for the Married Man. He was probably best known as Sgt. Bilko in the hit tv series The Phil Silvers Show. He leaves his widow and five daughters.

MICKEY SIMPSON, 72, character actor on screen and tv, died of a heart attack, Sept. 23, 1985 in Northridge, Ca. In 1935 he was a NYC heavyweight boxing champion before becoming Claudette Colbert's chauffeur, and getting small parts in films. Credits include Stagecoach, Song of Scheherazade, Tarzan and the Huntress, The Fighting Kentuckian, She Wore a Yellow Ribbon, When Willie Comes Marching Home, Wagonmaster, Surrender, A Lion Is in the Streets, New York Confidential, Giant, and The Greatest Story Ever Told. He acted in countless episodes of tv westerns. For 23 years he was honorary sheriff of Reseda, Ca. Surviving are his widow and three children.

| Simone Signoret | Gale Sondergaard | Dolph Sweet | Carol Wayne | Orson Welles | Grant Williams |

SIMONE SIGNORET, 64, born Simone Kaminker in Germany, she became one of France's most beloved stage, screen and tv actresses, writer, and political activist. She died of cancer Sept. 30, 1985 in her country home in Normandy. Her more than 40 films include Bolero, The Ideal Couple, Macadam, Fantomas, Sacrifice d'Honneur, The Living Corpse, Symphonie d'Amour, Back Streets of Paris, Dedee, Against the Wind, Four Days Leave, The Cheat, Casque d'Or, La Ronde, Diabolique, The Adultress, Witches of Salem, Room at the Top (for which she received a 1959 Oscar), Term of Trial, Naked Autumn, The Day and the Hour, Sweet and Sour, Love a la Carte, Ship of Fools (Academy award nomination), The Sleeping Car Murder, Is Paris Burning?, Deadly Affair, Games, The Sea Gull, Madame Rosa, and (her last) Guy de Maupassant. She is survived by her second husband, Yves Montand, and a daughter, actress Catherine Allegret, by her first husband, director Yves Allegret. Interment was in the Pere Lachaise cemetery in Paris.

KENT SMITH, 78, NYC-born stage, film and tv actor, died of congestive heart failure Apr. 23, 1985 in Woodland Hills, Ca. After his success on stage, he went to Hollywood for such films as The Garden Murder Case, The Cat People, Hitler's Children, Forever and a Day, This Land Is Mine, Curse of the Cat People, Youth Runs Wild, Spiral Staircase, Nora Prentiss, Magic Town, Voice of the Turtle, Jigsaw, The Fountainhead, My Foolish Heart, The Damned Don't Cry, Sayonara, The Earth Is Mine, The Balcony, A Distant Trumpet, Youngblood Hawke, The Trouble with Angels, Games, Death of a Gunfighter, Pete 'n' Tillie, Cops and Robbers. He was a regular on the tv series Peyton Place. Surviving are his second wife, actress Edith Atwater, and a daughter.

GALE SONDERGAARD, 86, Minnesota-born stage and film actress, died of cerebral vascular thrombosis Aug. 14, 1985 in Woodland Hills, Ca. Her film debut in 1936 in Anthony Adverse brought her an Academy Award for Best Supporting Actress. Subsequent films include Maid of Salem, Seventh Heaven, Life of Emile Zola, Lord Jeff, Juarez, The Cat and the Canary, The Mark of Zorro, The Letter, Black Cat, Paris Calling, My Favorite Blonde, A Night to Remember, Appointment in Berlin, The Strange Death of Adolf Hitler, Spider Woman, Christmas Holiday, Gypsy Wildcat, Enter Arsene Lupin, The Climax, Spider Woman Strikes Back, Anna and the King of Siam (Oscar nomination), The Time of their Lives, Pirates of Monterey, Road to Rio, East Side West Side, Pleasantville, Echoes, Hollywood Horror House, and Return of a Man Called Horse. A sister survives.

SAM SPIEGEL, 84, Austria-born Academy-Award-winning producer, died of natural causes Dec. 31, 1985 while vacationing on the Caribbean island of St. Martin. After fleeing Germany in 1933, he arrived in Hollywood in 1939 and used the name S. P. Eagle, producing such films as Tales of Manhattan, The Stranger, The Prowler, The African Queen, and Melba. After his success with On the Waterfront in 1954 he resumed using his real name, and produced The Strange One, Bridge on the River Kwai, Suddenly Last Summer, The Chase, Lawrence of Arabia, Nicholas and Alexandra, The Last Tycoon, and Betrayal. He received Best Picture "Oscars" for Waterfront, River Kwai, and Lawrence of Arabia. He is survived by his third wife, a son and a daughter.

CLAUDE STROUD, 78, character actor, and one of vaudeville's Stroud Twins, died of throat cancer, Oct. 16, 1985 in Santa Monica, Ca. After WWII he began his film career, appearing in such pictures as Gunfire, Border Rangers, All about Eve, Love Me or Leave Me, Cry-Baby Killer, The Rookie, Breakfast at Tiffany's, My Six Loves, Promises Promises, Man from Galveston, Ballad of Josie Coogan's Bluff, How to Save a Marriage and Ruin Your Life, Explosion, and Tick Tick Tick. His twin Clarence died in 1973. Surviving are his widow and two daughters.

DOLPH SWEET, 64, New York-born stage, screen and tv actor, died of cancer May 8, 1985 in Los Angeles, Ca. He appeared in over 30 films, including You're a Big Boy Now, The Swimmer, Heaven Can Wait, The New Centurians, Below the Belt, and Reds. His widow and a son survive.

TEX (EDWARD EARL) TERRY, 82, who appeared (usually as a villain) in over 300 western films, died May 18, 1985 in Coxville, Ind. In a career that began in 1922, among his credits are Apache Rose, Timberjack, The Badlanders, Oregon Trail, and Stars in My Crown. No reported survivors.

JOSEPH WALKER, 92, Colorado-born cinematographer and cameraman, died of undisclosed cause on Aug. 1, 1985 in Las Vegas, Nv. A 3-time Oscar nominee, he was given a special Academy Award in 1982 for "outstanding technical contributions for the advancement of the motion picture industry." Among his more than 160 credits are It Happened One Night, Mr. Deeds Goes to Town, Lost Horizon, Only Angels Have Wings, His Gal Friday, Mr. Smith Goes to Washington, Lady for a Day, You Can't Take It with You, Harriet Craig, Born Yesterday, and The Marrying Kind. He retired in 1952. Surviving are his widow and a son.

CAROL WAYNE, 42, Chicago-born actress, was drowned in Santiago Bay at the Pacific Coast resort of Manzanillo, Mexico. She could not swim, but was unafraid of the water. She was best known as the "Matinee Girl" on the Johnny Carson tv show, but had appeared in several films, including Viva Las Vegas, The Party, and The Heartbreaker. A son survives.

ORSON WELLES, 70, Wisconsin-born genius of stage, film, radio and tv, died of a heart attack Oct. 10, 1985 in the home of a friend in Hollywood. He lived in Las Vegas with his third wife, Italian actress Paola Mori (Countess di Girafalco). He was the "wonder boy" of Broadway and radio drama, before becoming an innovator in the film industry. In 1975 he received the Life-Time Achievement Award of the American Film Institute, and in 1984 the Directors Guild of America gave him its highest honor. He had been not only an actor, but a producer, director, and screenwriter for his films. In 1940, he and several actors from his Mercury Theatre group, went to Hollywood where his credits include Citizen Kane (for which his screenplay received an Academy Award, and his directing and acting were also nominated), The Magnificent Ambersons, Journey into Fear, Jane Eyre, Follow the Boys, Tomorrow Is Forever, The Stranger, Lady from Shanghai, Macbeth, Prince of Foxes, The Third Man, Black Rose, Napoleon, Three Cases of Murder, Othello, Confidential Report, Moby Dick, The Long Hot Summer, A Touch of Evil, Roots of Heaven, Compulsion, Crack in the Mirror, David and Goliath, Ferry to Hong Kong, Mr. Arkadin, The Trial, Lafayette, A Man for All Seasons, Is Paris Burning?, Falstaff, Casino Royale, Oedipus the King, Southern Star, An Immortal Story, House of Cards, Simon of the Desert, 13 Chairs, Waterloo, Julius Caesar, F for Fake, Catch-22, Ten Days Wonder, Treasure Island, Get to Know Your Rabbit, Voyage of the Damned, The Muppet Movie, Going for Broke, Butterfly, Where Is Parsifal?, and Is It You?. In addition to his widow, he is survived by three daughters, one by each of his wives.

GRANT WILLIAMS, 54, NYC-born tv and film actor, died of peritonitis and toxic poisoning July 28, 1985 in Los Angeles, Ca. After his film debut in Red Sundown (1956), he had roles in The Incredible Shrinking Man, Monolith Monsters, Lone Texan, 13 Fighting Men, The Leech Woman, Susan Slade, The Couch, PT-109, Away All Boats, Showdown at Abilene, Written on the Wind, Four Girls in Town. He was a regular on the tv series Hawaiian Eye. A brother survives.

TEX WILLIAMS, 68, country and western singer, and actor in over 25 western films, died of cancer Oct. 11, 1985 in Newhall, Ca. Surviving are his widow and a daughter.

INDEX

243

245

Hagerty, Julie, 109, 133, 138, 209
Hagerty, Mike, 18, 37
Haggard, H. Rider, 86
Haggerty, Captain, 114
Hagman, Larry, 226
Hahn, Archie, 37
Hahn, Don, 56
Hahn, Eric, 122
Hahn, Jordon, 80
Hahn, Steven, 131
Haig, Don, 205
Hail Mary, 217
Haim, Corey, 99, 120, 131, 226
Haines, Richard, 132, 134
Hairston, Damon, 126
Haitkin, Jacques, 110, 131
Hakim, Omar, 134
Halberstadt, Ira, 10
Halbreich, Gustavo, 176
Haldeman, Tim, 25
Hale, Barbara, 226
Hale, Birdie M., 73
Hale, Joe, 56
Hale, Steve, 56
Haley, Jack, 10, 120, 226
Haley, Mike, 106, 107
Halfpenny, John, 124
Hall, Albert, 104, 226
Hall, Allen, 120
Hall, Anthony Michael, 13, 125, 153, 226
Hall, Dolly, 133
Hall, Don, 34
Hall, James, 40
Hall, Janis, 106
Hall, Kenneth J., 123
Hall, Lois, 115
Hall, Mercedes, 13, 153
Hall, Ollie, 179
Hall, Patti, 107
Hall, Philip Baker, 120
Hall, Robert David, 117
Hall, Roger, 215
Hall, Sandra, 13
Hall, Tony, 90
Hall, William, 104
Hallahan, Charles, 47
Hallam, John, 22, 119, 134
Hallenbeck, E. Darrell, 110
Haller, Michael, 48
Hallhuber, Heino, 174
Hallier, Lori, 125
Halligan, Dick, 108
Halloran, J., 134
Hallyday, Johnny, 182
Halmi, Robert, 33
Halpern, Richard, 128
Halsted, Dana, 106
Hamamura, Jun, 201, 205
Hameed, Maqbool, 209
Hamil, Tom, 118
Hamill, Denis, 18
Hamill, John, 18
Hamill, Mark, 28, 226
Hamilton, Allen, 42
Hamilton, Arthur, 128
Hamilton, Frank, 120
Hamilton, George, 226
Hamilton, Guy, 77
Hamilton, Margaret, 239
Hamilton, Marilyn, 24
Hamilton, Murray, 107
Hamilton, Pat, 14, 208
Hamilton, Richard, 15, 47
Hamilton, Suzanna, 140, 152, 153, 180
Hamlin, George, 26
Hamlin, Harry, 226
Hamlin, Richard, 134
Hamlisch, Marvin, 92, 119
Hammer, Ben, 74
Hammer, John, 120
Hammer, Mark, 125
Hammil, John, 92
Hammill, Ellen, 110
Hammond, Dean, 84
Hammond, Ken, 164, 204
Hammond, Mark, 26
Hammond, Roger, 214
Hamon, Lucienne, 203
Hamori, Andras, 109
Hampshire, Susan, 226
Hampton, Adrienne, 18
Hampton, James, 65
Hampton, Janice, 136
Hampton, Mabel, 120
Hampton, Rebecca, 217
Hamra, Skip, 133
Hanada, Mitsushi, 208
Hancock, Scott, 81
Hand, Chip, 113
Handford, Peter, 140
Handler, Ken, 114
Handley, Colin, 117
Hanekata, Yoshimasa, 217
Haney, Carol, 10
Hanft, Helen, 26
Hanian, Sharon, 74
Hanin, Roger, 183
Hankins, Lindsay, 120
Hanks, Mark, 20
Hanks, Tom, 120, 121, 125, 226
Hanley, Daniel, 44
Hanlon, Julie, 132
Hanlon, Roy, 216
Hanlon, Tom, 18
Hanna, Ray, 121
Hannah, Barbara, 130
Hannah, Bob, 66
Hannah, Daryl, 226
Hannah, Page, 226
Hannan, Peter, 181, 212
Hannesson, John Thor, 173
Hannum, Tonda, 92
Hanover, Donna, 18
Hansen, Danna, 132
Hansen, Gary, 172
Hansen, Judith, 110
Hansen, Neil, 187
Hanson, Barry, 214
Hanson, Curtis, 46
Hanson, John, 116
Hanson, Judith, 126
Hanson, Paul, 54
Happy, Cliff, 47
Hapsas, Alex, 77
Hara, Kazutami, 212
Hara, Masato, 167, 184
Harada, Ernest, 125
Harada, Mieko, 184, 185
Harbrow, Nigel, 172
Hard Rock Zombies, 126
Hardie, James, 12
Hardie, Kate, 218
Hardin, Jerry, 12, 111, 125
Hardin, Ty, 120, 226
Harding, Jeff, 30, 136
Harding, Steve, 22
Hardison, Kadeem, 118
Hardman, Holly, 127
Hardwick, Derek, 122
Hardwicke, Edward, 110
Hardy, Robert, 170
Hardy, Valerie, 204
Hare, David, 69, 180
Hare, Will, 30, 54
Harewood, Dorian, 12, 226
Hargitay, Mariska, 106, 111
Hargrave, Doris, 20
Hargreaves, Craig, 34
Hargreaves, John, 164
Harlan, Robin, 107
Harmon, Allan, 128
Harmon, Mark, 226
Harnois, Elizabeth, 90
Harold, Theresa, 116
Harp, Steven, 208
Harper, David, 118
Harper, Don, 122
Harper, Jerry, 120
Harper, Tom, 106
Harper, Valerie, 226
Harrell, Edward, 130
Harrell, Georgia, 81
Harrington, Curtis, 126
Harrington, Derek, 212
Harrington, Geoff, 206
Harrington, Pat, 226
Harris, Amah, 90
Harris, Barbara, 131, 226
Harris, Bob, 43, 72
Harris, Brad, 125
Harris, Burtt, 119
Harris, Ed, 20, 43, 71, 78, 226
Harris, Enid, 72
Harris, Fred, 202
Harris, Gary, 87
Harris, J. Don, 116
Harris, Jonathan, 64, 132
Harris, Julie, 226
Harris, Kit, 105
Harris, Laura, 12
Harris, Mark, 112, 205
Harris, Martin, 204
Harris, Max, 215
Harris, Niki, 92
Harris, Philip, 122
Harris, Richard, 14, 118, 226
Harris, Rosemary, 226
Harris, Stuart, 180
Harris, Ted, 80
Harris, Timothy, 37
Harrison, Anna, 35
Harrison, Cynthia, 129
Harrison, Evangeline, 89
Harrison, George, 162, 203, 212
Harrison, Greg, 214, 226
Harrison, John, 122
Harrison, Jules, 202
Harrison, Ken, 35
Harrison, Linda, 44
Harrison, Lindsay, 108
Harrison, Martha, 29
Harrison, Nancy, 35
Harrison, Noel, 226
Harrison, Philip, 89
Harrison, Rex, 151, 226
Harrold, Kathryn, 109, 111, 226
Harrop, Ian, 172
Harryhausen, Ray, 136
Harshberger, Michael, 120
Hart, David, 131
Hart, Earnest, Jr., 130
Hart, Frank, 117
Hart, John R., 94
Hart, Roxanne, 207
Hart, Veronica, 114
Hart, Wendy, 107
Harte, Jerry, 134
Hartes, Eddie, 127
Hartigan, John, 17
Hartis, John, 126
Hartley, Gabrielle, 204
Hartley, James, 80
Hartley, Richard, 181, 207
Hartline, Gene, 13, 47, 53
Hartman, David, 226
Hartman, Elizabeth, 226
Hartman, Frank, 127
Hartman, Laura, 92
Hartman, Lauren, 121
Hartman, Phil, 64
Harton, Herb, 76, 131
Hartwell, Gloria, 217
Hartwick, Ray, 52
Hartzell, Duane, 30
Harvey, Erwin, 46
Harvey, Jason, 54
Harvey, Joan, 127
Harvey, Richard, 212
Harvey, Rodney, 114, 129
Harvey, Rupert, 126
Harvey, Stephen, 116
Harvey, Tania, 9
Harvey, Tom, 209
Harwood, Ronald, 215
Harwood, Shuna, 212
Hasegawa, Hajime, 117
Hasegawa, Kiyoshi, 205
Hashimoto, Kohji, 212
Hashimoto, Richard, 13, 153
Haskell, Kate, 120
Hasler, Bill, 204
Hassanein, Salah M., 61, 122
Hasse, Monika, 213
Hassen, Alaoui, 98
Hassett, Marilyn, 226
Hassett, Ray, 79
Hassinger, Nancy, 112
Hassle, Jan, 99
Hatfield, Hurd, 22
Hathaway, Henry, 239
Hatsui, Kotoe, 217
Hatten, Tom, 136
Hatten, Yankton, 113
Hattori, Akihiro, 167
Hauer, Rutger, 32, 128, 226, 227
Hauff, Reinhard, 156
Haufrect, Alan, 129
Haugen, David, 110
Haughton, David, 187
Haupt, Ulrich, 88
Hauraki, Kristofer, 172
Hausch, Greg, 43
Hause, Jeffrey, 132
Hausenberger, Mandy, 97
Hauser, Fay, 117
Hausserman, Mischa, 24
Haveland, Simon, 215
Havelka, Svatopluk, 207
Havens, Richie, 126, 127
Haver, June, 10, 227
Haviv, Eli, 129
Hawes, Susan, 31
Hawk, David, 128
Hawke, Ethan, 121
Hawkins, Alex, 29
Hawkins, Cory, 107
Hawkins, Millicent, 108
Hawkins, Richard, 120
Hawks, Howard, 152
Hawn, Goldie, 7, 152, 227
Haworth, Ted, 121
Hawthorne, Denys, 162
Hawthorne, Elizabeth, 216
Hawthorne, Nigel, 56
Hay, Harry, 120
Hayakawa, Sessue, 3
Hayashi, Fumiko, 197
Hayashi, Hikaru, 214
Hayashiya, Shinpei, 212
Hayden, Charlie, 99
Hayden, Dennis, 107
Hayden, Linda, 227
Haydn, Richard, 239
Hayek, Julie, 72
Hayes, Billie, 56
Hayes, Daryl, 13
Hayes, Helen, 150, 152, 227
Hayes, Jack, 108
Hayes, Melvyn, 134
Hayes, Ron, 73
Hayes, Siobhan, 128
Hayes, Terry, 179
Haygarth, Tony, 123, 162
Hayman, David, 216
Haynes, Jerry, 78
Haynie, Jim, 53
Hays, Robert, 31, 227
Hayt, Macine, 133
Hayward, Louis, 239
Hayward, Rachel, 207
Hayward, Susan, 151
Haywood, Chris, 175, 204, 214
Haywood, Mike, 169
Hayworth, Rita, 227
Haze, Meridith, 117
Head Office, 134, 135
Head, John, 135
Headley, Glenne, 26
Headly, Glenne, 82, 106
Healey, Barry, 90
Healy, David, 127
Heard, John, 15, 67, 102, 107, 227
Hearn, Chick, 118, 125
Hearne, Jennifer, 34
Heart, John X., 74
Heartbreakers, 111
Heath, D. Michael, 92
Heathcote, Thomas, 170
Heatherton, Joey, 227
Heaton, Tom, 75
Heaven Help Us, 15
Heavenly Bodies, 109
Heavenly Kid, The, 121
Hecht, Gina, 52
Hecht, Harold, 239
Hecht, Paul, 194
Heckart, Eileen, 150, 152, 227
Heckerling, Amy, 58, 109
Heckstall-Smith, Nick, 136
Hedahl, Mary, 26
Hedaya, Dan, 11, 72
Hedges, Clive, 166
Hedin, Serene, 135
Hedison, David, 201, 227
Hedley, Adrian, 119
Hee, Leila, 208
Heenan, Catherine, 122
Heer, Johanna, 196
Heffner, Kyle, 100, 125
Heflin, Van, 150
Hefner, Keith, 130
Hegyes, Robert, 227
Heim, Alan, 209
Heim, Carrie Kei, 134
Heimann, Betsy, 80
Heineman, Steve, 106
Heiner, Thomasine, 215
Heinsohn, Elisa, 110
Heise, Robert, 122
Heitzer, Don, 25, 133
Helf, Lauren, 120
Helfrich, Mark, 38
Helger, Anne Marie, 204
Helias, Pierre-Jakez, 200
Hell, Richard, 23
Heller, Jack, 108
Heller, Laurence, 202
Heller, Matthias, 196
Hellhole, 111
Hellman, Irving, 64
Helm, Levon, 87
Helm, Tiffany, 111, 120
Helman, Geoffrey, 215
Helmer, Heidi, 112
Helmond, Katherine, 91
Helpmann, Robert, 10
Hemingway, Chuck, 123
Hemingway, Mariel, 16, 126, 227
Hemming, Lindy, 180
Hemmings, David, 227
Henael, Richard, 201
Hench, Richard, 123
Henderson, Anthony, 132
Henderson, Bill, 118, 134
Henderson, Don, 91
Henderson, Duncan, 84
Henderson, Graham, 124
Henderson, Joseph, 130
Henderson, Marcia, 227
Henderson, Stephen, 76
Hendrickson, Gary, 75
Hendrie, Chris, 59
Hendry, Gloria, 227
Henke, Daniel, 134
Henner, Marilu, 41, 48, 227
Hennessy, Don, 109
Hennessy, Noreen, 64, 114
Hennig, Winfried, 156
Henreid, Paul, 227
Henrie, Madeleine, 70
Henriksen, Lance, 74
Henriquez, Ron, 42
Henry IV, 210
Henry, Bob, 48
Henry, Buck, 227
Henry, Carol, 172
Henry, Chris, 111
Henry, Christopher, 115
Henry, Justin, 14, 227
Henry, Laura, 109
Henry, Pam, 109
Hensick, Tamara, 17
Hensler, Paul G., 116
Hensley, Sonya, 92
Henson, Betty Lou, 12
Henson, Brian, 49
Henson, Frank, 97
Henson, Heather, 136
Henson, Jim, 109, 124, 215
Henson, John, 169
Henwood, Ray, 216
Henze, Jurgen, 213
Hepburn, Audrey, 150, 227
Hepburn, Katharine, 36, 117, 150, 152, 227
Hepton, Bernard, 186
Herald, Peter V., 34
Herbener, Rachel, 214
Herbert, Dawn, 92
Herbert, James, 46, 66
Herbert, Martin, 152
Herbert, Rachel, 215
Hercules II, 128, 129
Herd, Richard, 124
Here Come the Littles, 117
Herlihy, Ed, 25, 64
Herlihy, Joyce, 212
Herlin, Jacques, 58
Herman, Miki, 28
Herman, Paul, 26
Herman, Pee-Wee, 7, 64
Hern, Art, 110
Hernandez, Andres, 218
Hernandez, Andy "Sugarcoated", 129
Hernandez, Eddy, 106
Hernandez, Humberto, 206
Hernandez, Naldy, 216
Hernandez, Oneida, 218
Hernandez, Robert, 106
Hero, 99
Herod, Thomas, Jr., 134
Herouet, Marc, 209, 210
Heroux, Denis, 154
Heroux, Justine, 217
Herranz, Miguel Angel, 165
Herrier, Mark, 112
Herrin, Kym, 115
Herring, Martin, 215
Herring, Pembroke, 58, 140
Herrmann, Edward, 26, 61, 120, 227
Hersch, Kerry, 120
Hershey, Barbara, 227
Hersholt, Jean, 150
Hervey, Jason, 25, 64
Herz, Michael, 122, 123, 131, 132, 134
Herzberg, Paul, 212
Herzer, Julio, 84
Herzhaft, Beth, 48
Herzner, Norbert, 217
Herzog, Mitch, 129
Herzog, Werner, 159, 208
Heslov, Grant, 75, 128
Hess, David, 204
Hess, Linda, 92
Hesseman, Howard, 25
Hessler, Gordon, 130
Hester, Mark, 56
Hester, Paul, 175
Heston, Charlton, 151, 227
Hewitt, Martin, 118, 119, 227
Heyman, John, 119
Heyward, Andy, 117, 132
Heywood, Anne, 227
Hgour, Boujema, 201
Hibbard, Don, 120
Hice, Fred, 12
Hickey, William, 50, 51, 77, 128
Hickinbotham, Ian, 199
Hickman, Darryl, 227
Hickman, Dwayne, 227
Hicks, Barbara, 91, 214
Hicks, Catherine, 130
Hicks, Grant, 152
Hicks, Richard, 218
Hicks, Scott, 204
Hidaka, Shinya, 205
Hidalgo, Isabel, 207
Hidalgo, Luis E., 133
Hierrezuelo, Gabriel, 200
Hieu, Joseph, 24
Higgenbotham, John, 99
Higginbotham, Ian, 58
Higgins, Anthony, 123, 199
Higgins, Colin, 109
Higgins, Michael, 35, 57, 114
Higgins, Robert A., 119
High Voltage, 63
Highbie, John, 17
Highfield, Ron, 216
Hilarion, Georges, 206
Hildebrand, Frank E., 132, 213
Hildreth, Gary, 119, 135
Hileman, Gary, 9
Hill, Amy, 62
Hill, Arthur, 90, 227
Hill, Carla, 117
Hill, Charles, 131
Hill, Clayton, 9, 118
Hill, Dana, 58
Hill, Debra, 134
Hill, Dennis M., 80
Hill, Frankie, 107, 201
Hill, George Roy, 152
Hill, Lon, 96
Hill, Michael J., 44
Hill, Steven, 227
Hill, Terence, 227
Hill, Walter, 37, 41
Hillaire, Dorothy (Smilie), 120
Hillbeck, Fernando, 128
Hillebrandt, Stanley, 208
Hiller, Wendy, 151, 227
Hilliard, Harriet, 227
Hilliard, Ray, 120
Hillman, Hand, 113
Hillman, William, 113
Hills Have Eyes II, The, 122, 123
Hillstead, Mary, 121
Hilterman, Joost, 128
Hilton-Jacobs, Lawrence, 106
Himatsuri, 216, 217
Himeda, Shinsaku, 210
Hinchcliffe, Barbara, 120
Hinchley, Pippa, 169
Hindman, Bill, 112
Hindman, Earl, 53
Hinds, Richard, 10
Hine, Michele, 49
Hine, Rupert, 128
Hines, David, 132
Hines, Gregory, 89
Hines, Robert, 180
Hingle, Pat, 12, 37, 227
Hinkly, Simon, 166
Hintlian, Matt, 127
Hinton, S. E., 134
Hinz, Michael, 204
Hipwell, Elizabeth, 112
Hira, Mikijiro, 208
Hirao, Masaaki, 205
Hirdler, Howard, 24, 64
Hirsch, David, 107
Hirsch, Judd, 227
Hirsch, Steve, 126
Hirsch, Tina, 121

254

261

263

266